# What's on the CD?

The CD included with the *MCSE: NT Server 4 in the Enterprise Study Guide* contains several valuable tools to help you prepare for your MCSE exams. The contents of the folders you'll find on the CD, and the steps for installing the various programs are described below. Please consult the README file located in the root directory of the CD for further product information.

## The Edge Tests: *Windows NT Server 4.0 in the Enterprise* Exam Preparation Software

This Edge Test demo provides sample test questions similar to those you'll encounter when you take the NT Server 4.0 in the Enterprise exam. Two versions of the test are provided, one for Windows 3.1 and 3.11 systems, and one for Windows 95 and NT systems. To install the *Windows NT Server 4 Enterprise* exam prep software for Windows 3.1, 3.11, or 95, run the SETUP.EXE file located in the folder that coincides with your operating system (EDGETEST\WIN3_1 or EDGETEST\WIN95_NT). For Windows NT 4.0, you must first copy the contents of the Win95_NT folder into a subdirectory on your hard drive and run the DELIVERY.EXE file from there.

## Microsoft *Train_Cert Offline* Web Site and *Internet Explorer 3.0*

Look to Microsoft's *Train_Cert Offline* Web site, a quarterly snapshot of Microsoft's Education and Certification Web site for all of the information you need to plot your course for MCSE certification. You'll need to run *Internet Explorer* 3.0 to access all of the features of the *Train_Cert Offline* Web site, so we've included a free copy on the CD. To install *Internet Explorer 3.0*, run the SETUP.EXE file located in the MICROSFT\IE3\CD folder. To install the *Train_Cert Offline* Web site to your system, run the SETUP file located in the MICROSFT\OFFLINE folder.

## Transcender Corporation's *NT-EnterpriseCert 4.0* Demo & Certification Sampler

Transcender's *NT Server 4.0 Enterprise* exam prep software provides you with a selection of sample test questions similar to those you'll encounter in the MCSE: NT Server 4.0 in the Enterprise exam. To install the NT-EnterpriseCert 4.0 demo, run the SETUP.EXE file located in the TRANSCND\NT4ENT folder. The Transcender *Certification Sampler* lets you preview samples of all of Transcender's Microsoft exam simulations. To install the Transcender demos, simply run the SETUP.EXE file located in the TRANSCND\SAMPLER folder.

## Microsoft *TechNet Technical Information Network*

This evaluation copy of Microsoft's *TechNet Technical Information Network* gives you access to a vast database of information related to Microsoft products and technologies. It includes more than 100,000 pages of articles, technical notes, service packs, and Knowledge Bases. To install the *TechNet Technical Information Network* program to your computer, run the SETUP.EXE file located in the TECHNET folder. For further installation instructions or to review the user license for this product, please read the MANSETUP text file located in the TECHNET folder.

# MCSE:
# NT® Server 4
# in the Enterprise
# Study Guide

**Lisa Donald**

with **James Chellis**

NETWORK PRESS ®
SYBEX

San Francisco ■ Paris ■ Düsseldorf ■ Soest

Associate Publisher: Guy Hart-Davis
Acquisitions Manager: Kristine Plachy
Acquisitions and Developmental Editor: Neil Edde
Editor: Alison Moncrieff
Technical Editor: Pamela C. Lee
Book Design Director: Catalin Dulfu
Book Designer: Seventeenth Street Studio
Graphic Illustrator: Patrick Dintino
Electronic Publishing Specialist: Bill Gibson
Production Coordinator: Grey B. Magauran
Indexer: Matthew Spence
Cover Designer: Archer Design

Screen reproductions produced with Collage Complete.
Collage Complete is a trademark of Inner Media Inc.

SYBEX is a registered trademark of SYBEX Inc.
Network Press and the Network Press logo are trademarks of SYBEX Inc.

TRADEMARKS: SYBEX has attempted throughout this book to distinguish proprietary trademarks from descriptive terms by following the capitalization style used by the manufacturer.

The authors and publisher have used their best efforts to prepare this book and the content is based upon final release software whenever possible. Portions of the manuscript may be based upon pre-release versions supplied by software manufacturer(s). The authors and the publisher make no representation or warranties of any kind with regard to the completeness or accuracy of the contents herein and accept no liability of any kind including but not limited to performance, merchantability, fitness for any particular purpose, or any losses or damages of any kind caused or alleged to be caused directly or indirectly from this book.

SYBEX is an independent entity from Microsoft Corporation, and not affiliated with Microsoft Corporation in any manner. This publication may be used in assisting students to prepare for a Microsoft Certified Professional Exam. Neither Microsoft Corporation, its designated review company, nor SYBEX warrants that use of this publication will ensure passing the relevant Exam. Microsoft is either a registered trademark or trademark of Microsoft Corporation in the United States and/or other countries.

Library of Congress Card Number: 96-72282
ISBN: 0-7821-1970-0

Manufactured in the United States of America

10 9 8 7 6

October 9, 1996

Dear SYBEX Inc. Customer:

Microsoft is pleased to inform you SYBEX Inc. is a participant in the Microsoft®
Independent Courseware Vendor (ICV) program. Microsoft ICVs design,
develop, and market self-paced courseware, books, and other products that
support Microsoft software and the Microsoft Certified Professional (MCP)
program.

To be accepted into the Microsoft ICV program, an ICV must meet set criteria. In
addition, Microsoft reviews and approves each ICV training product before
permission is granted to use the Microsoft Certified Professional Approved Study
Guide logo on that product. This logo assures the consumer that the product has
passed the following Microsoft standards:

- The course contains accurate product information.
- The course includes  labs and activities during which the student can
  apply knowledge and skills learned from the course.
- The course teaches skills that help prepare the student to take
  corresponding MCP exams.

Microsoft ICVs continually develop and release new MCP Approved Study
Guides. To prepare for a particular Microsoft certification exam, a student may
choose one or more single, self-paced training courses or a series of training
courses.

You will be pleased with the quality and effectiveness of the MCP Approved
Study Guides available from SYBEX Inc..

Sincerely,

Holly Heath
ICV/OCV Account Manager
Microsoft Channel Programs, Education & Certification

**MICROSOFT INDEPENDENT COURSEWARE VENDOR PROGRAM**

## Software License Agreement: Terms and Conditions

The media and/or any online materials accompanying this book that are available now or in the future contain programs and/or text files (the "Software") to be used in connection with the book. SYBEX hereby grants to you a license to use the Software, subject to the terms that follow. Your purchase, acceptance, or use of the Software will constitute your acceptance of such terms.

The Software compilation is the property of SYBEX unless otherwise indicated and is protected by copyright to SYBEX or other copyright owner(s) as indicated in the media files (the "Owner(s)"). You are hereby granted a single-user license to use the Software for your personal, noncommercial use only. You may not reproduce, sell, distribute, publish, circulate, or commercially exploit the Software, or any portion thereof, without the written consent of SYBEX and the specific copyright owner(s) of any component software included on this media.

In the event that the Software or components include specific license requirements or end-user agreements, statements of condition, disclaimers, limitations or warranties ("End-User License"), those End-User Licenses supersede the terms and conditions herein as to that particular Software component. Your purchase, acceptance, or use of the Software will constitute your acceptance of such End-User Licenses.

By purchase, use or acceptance of the Software you further agree to comply with all export laws and regulations of the United States as such laws and regulations may exist from time to time.

**SOFTWARE SUPPORT.** Components of the supplemental Software and any offers associated with them may be supported by the specific Owner(s) of that material but they are not supported by SYBEX. Information regarding any available support may be obtained from the Owner(s) using the information provided in the appropriate read.me files or listed elsewhere on the media.

Should the manufacturer(s) or other Owner(s) cease to offer support or decline to honor any offer, SYBEX bears no responsibility. This notice concerning support for the Software is provided for your information only. SYBEX is not the agent or principal of the Owner(s), and SYBEX is in no way responsible for providing any support for the Software, nor is it liable or responsible for any support provided, or not provided, by the Owner(s).

**WARRANTY.** SYBEX warrants the enclosed media to be free of physical defects for a period of ninety (90) days after purchase. The Software is not available from SYBEX in any other form or media than that enclosed herein or posted to

www.sybex.com. If you discover a defect in the media during this warranty period, you may obtain a replacement of identical format at no charge by sending the defective media, postage prepaid, with proof of purchase to:

SYBEX Inc.
Customer Service Department
1151 Marina Village Parkway
Alameda, CA 94501
(510) 523-8233
Fax: (510) 523-2373
e-mail: info@sybex.com
WEB: HTTP//:WWW.SYBEX.COM

After the 90-day period, you can obtain replacement media of identical format by sending us the defective disk, proof of purchase, and a check or money order for $10, payable to SYBEX.

**DISCLAIMER.** SYBEX makes no warranty or representation, either expressed or implied, with respect to the Software or its contents, quality, performance, merchantability, or fitness for a particular purpose. In no event will SYBEX, its distributors, or dealers be liable to you or any other party for direct, indirect, special, incidental, consequential, or other damages arising out of the use of or inability to use the Software or its contents even if advised of the possibility of such damage. In the event that the Software includes an online update feature, SYBEX further disclaims any obligation to provide this feature for any specific duration other than the initial posting.

The exclusion of implied warranties is not permitted by some states. Therefore, the above exclusion may not apply to you. This warranty provides you with specific legal rights; there may be other rights that you may have that vary from state to state. The pricing of the book with the Software by SYBEX reflects the allocation of risk and limitations on liability contained in this agreement of Terms and Conditions.

**SHAREWARE DISTRIBUTION.** This Software may contain various programs that are distributed as shareware. Copyright laws apply to both shareware and ordinary commercial software, and the copyright Owner(s) retains all rights. If you try a shareware program and continue using it, you are expected to register it. Individual programs differ on details of trial periods, registration, and payment. Please observe the requirements stated in appropriate files.

**COPY PROTECTION.** The Software in whole or in part may or may not be copy-protected or encrypted. However, in all cases, reselling or redistributing these files without authorization is expressly forbidden except as specifically provided for by the Owner(s) therein.

*For Rick, Kevin and Katie*

# Acknowledgments

Writing this book has truly been an educational experience. I went into the writing thinking it was going to be a piece of cake, and it was actually hard work. Luckily I had help.

First, I want to thank Neil Edde and Alison Moncrieff at Sybex for all of their guidance, help, hard work, and patience. They were both a pleasure to work with.

I also want to thank Pamela Lee, the technical editor, who also contributed the chapter on troubleshooting. Thanks to Cathy Moya for her help on the TCP/IP and the Internet Routing chapter. These two were great pinch hitters.

Thanks to James Chellis for giving me the chance to write the book, and for having faith in me to get it done. Thanks also to Matt Strebe and Charles Perkins for helping me fill in some blanks.

The Sybex production team—Electronic Publishing Specialist Bill Gibson, Production Coordinator Grey Magauran and Graphic Illustrator Patrick Dintino—also did a great job. Thanks to everyone for their hard work.

Finally thanks to my family and friends for their support.

# Contents at a Glance

# Table of Contents

# Table of Exercises

# Introduction

COMPUTERS AND COMPUTER networks require increasingly well-trained network professionals to install and maintain them. As the computer network industry grows in both size and complexity, the need for proven ability is becoming more important. To address this need, certification programs for administrators have been designed to ensure that the people who manage and support computer networks are qualified to do so.

The first large-scale certification program to be recognized by the computing industry was Novell's Certified NetWare Engineer (CNE) program. When I got my CNE in 1989, I was immediately able to switch jobs and receive a 50% increase in my salary. CNEs were at a premium due to supply and demand. Novell was a market leader in the networking field through the late 1980s and early 1990s.

In 1993 Microsoft came out with the Windows NT operating system. Windows NT came in two flavors, NT Workstation and NT Server. NT Workstation was designed to be a powerful desktop operating system, and NT Server was designed to support large heterogeneous networks. After a few versions were released, the NT craze began. Novell's reign of the network operating system began to decline as Microsoft NT began to take over the market. This has led to a need for qualified individuals who know how to manage NT networks. Right now there are not enough certified Microsoft professionals to fulfill the market demands; this is what makes Microsoft certification a hot ticket to higher pay.

Microsoft has four certification programs to ensure that computer professionals are qualified to support NT. The Microsoft Certified Professional program includes:

- Microsoft Certified Product Specialist (MCPS)

- Microsoft Certified Systems Engineer (MCSE)

- Microsoft Certified Solution Developer (MCSD)

- Microsoft Certified Trainer (MCT)

Each of these programs addresses different needs in the computer industry. The MCPS designates proficiency in a specific Microsoft product. The MCSE designates that you are a professional proficient in the core components of Microsoft's networking strategies, including several products in the BackOffice suite. The MCSD is for programmers, while the MCT is for individuals who teach others about Microsoft technologies. This book covers a core requirement for the MCSE certification.

## Is This Book for You?

This book is written for those who want to be certified as an MCPS or an MCSE. To achieve these certifications all you need to do is pass Microsoft's certification exams. Sound easy? Well, it's not that easy. In order to pass the exam, you need to prepare. You can prepare by attending a class or through self-study. Attending a class can be cost prohibitive—classes run around $2,000 a week. I'm an MCT so, of course, I believe in the value of classroom training, but I recognize that it's not an option for everyone. I've also noticed that the official Microsoft classes don't sufficiently cover everything you need to know to pass the related exam.

Self study is much more cost effective (even if you factor in the equipment you will need to purchase). However, it requires a great deal of discipline to read through and practice the hands-on exercises that are included in this book. It's nice to know, though, that you will be rewarded for your hard work. Getting my Microsoft certification meant a 40% increase in my consulting fees the first year.

One of the hardest aspects of the certification exams is the large amount and variety of subject material you are tested on. Even people that have worked with the product can have a hard time passing the exams because, while they are familiar with most aspects of NT, they may have what I call "Swiss-cheese" knowledge in other areas.

My familiarity with this exam has led me to focus on the key areas that you will be tested on. It's interesting to note that while this exam is Windows NT Server 4 in the Enterprise, it doesn't get into enterprise topics like bridges, routers, and wide area networking that are normally associated with enterprise environments. It does cover topics like trust relationships and managing groups in a multi-domain environment. The test reflects Microsoft's spin on how NT is set up in an enterprise environment.

My main goal in writing this book has been to cover all the areas you will be tested on. The idea is that you read the book, practice the exercises, answer the review questions, and pass the exam. Hopefully you also learn something that makes you a valuable asset in the networking world, because that is the point of the certification programs.

# What Does This Book Cover?

This book covers everything you need to know in order to pass the NT Server 4 in the Enterprise exam, and provides a solid introduction to NT in multi-domain environments. It covers:

- Features and components of directory services

- NT Server directory services in the enterprise

- Planning a domain model in the enterprise environment

- Internetwork connectivity

- System analysis and capacity planning

- Trust relationships

- Troubleshooting and repair

- and more...

All of the information is designed to give you practical training that provides both real world skills and the knowledge you need to pass your NT Server in the Enterprise exam.

# How Do You Become an MCSE?

Attaining Microsoft Certified Systems Engineer (MCSE) status is a serious challenge. The exams cover a wide range of topics and require dedicated study and expertise. This is, however, why the MCSE certificate is so valuable. If achieving MCSE status were easy, the market would be flooded quickly by MCSEs and the certification would quickly become meaningless. Microsoft, keenly aware of this fact, has taken steps to ensure that the certification means its holder is truly knowledgeable and skilled.

To become an MCSE, you must pass four core requirements and two electives. Most people select the following exam combination for the MCSE core requirements for the 4.0 track (the most current track):

### NETWORKING REQUIREMENT

70-58: Networking Essentials

### CLIENT REQUIREMENT

70-73: Implementing and Supporting Windows NT Workstation 4.0

### WINDOWS NT SERVER 4.0 REQUIREMENT

**70-67:** Implementing and Supporting Windows NT Server 4.0

### WINDOWS NT SERVER 4.0 IN THE ENTERPRISE REQUIREMENT

**70-68:** Implementing and Supporting Windows NT Server 4.0 in the Enterprise

For the electives, you have about ten choices. The two most popular electives at present are:

**70-53:** Internetworking Microsoft TCP/IP on Microsoft Windows NT 3.51 (4.0 will be available soon.)

**70-75:** Implementing and Supporting Microsoft Exchange Server 4.0

*For a complete description of all the MCSE options, see the Microsoft Roadmap to Education and Certification on the CD that comes with this book.*

*This book is a part of a series of Network Press MCSE study guides, published by Sybex, that covers four core requirements and two electives, the entire MCSE track.*

### Where Do You Take the Exams?

You may take the exams at any of more than 800 Authorized Prometric Testing Centers (APTCs) around the world. For the location of an APTC near you, call (800) 755-EXAM (755-3926). Outside the United States and Canada, contact your local Sylvan Prometric Registration Center.

To register for a Microsoft Certified Professional exam:

1. Determine the number of the exam you want to take.

2. Register with the Sylvan Prometric Registration Center that is nearest to you. At this point you will be asked for advance payment for the exam. At this writing, the exams are $100 each. Exams must be taken within one year of payment. You can schedule exams up to six weeks in advance or as late as one working day prior to the date of the exam. You can cancel or reschedule your exam if you contact Sylvan Prometric at least two working days prior to the exam. Same-day registration is available in some locations, although this is subject to space availability. Where same-day registration is available, you must register a minimum of two hours before test time.

3. After you receive a registration and payment confirmation letter from Sylvan Prometric, call a nearby APTC to schedule your exam.

When you schedule the exam, you'll be provided with instructions regarding appointment and cancellation procedures, ID requirements, and information about the testing center location.

### Tips for Taking the Exam

Here are some general tips for taking the exams successfully:

- Arrive early at the exam center so you can relax and take one last review of your study materials, particularly tables and lists of exam-related information.

- Read the questions carefully. Don't be tempted to jump to an early conclusion. Make sure you know *exactly* what the question is asking.

- Don't leave any unanswered questions; they count against you.

- When answering multiple-choice questions you're not sure about, use a process of elimination to get rid of the obviously incorrect questions first; this will improve your odds if you need to make an educated guess.

- Because the hard questions will eat up the most time, save them for last. You can move forward and back through the exam.

## How to Use This Book

This book can provide a solid foundation for the serious effort of preparing for the Windows NT Server 4.0 in the Enterprise exam. To best benefit from this book, you might want to use the following study method:

1. Study a chapter carefully, making sure you fully understand the information.

2. Complete all hands-on exercises in the chapter, referring to the chapter so that you understand each step you take.

3. Answer the review questions related to that chapter. (You will find the answers to these questions in Appendix A.)

4. Note which questions you did not understand, and study the sections in the book that apply to those questions again.

**5.** Study each chapter in the same manner.

**6.** Before taking the exam, try the practice questions included on the CD that comes with this book. They will give you a good idea of what you can expect to see on the real test.

*If you prefer to use this book in conjunction with other types of training, you have many options. Both classroom and online training are widely available. Cyberstate University, for example, offers an online MCSE training program that centers around this book and the other books in this series. Cyberstate can be reached at (888) 438-3382. Many companies offer local classroom training. Free network training referral services, such as EdgeTek, at (800) 800-1638, can help you locate available resources.*

To learn all the material covered in this book, you will need to study regularly and with discipline. Try to set aside the same time every day to study, and select a comfortable and quiet place in which to do it. If you work hard, you will be surprised at how quickly you learn this material. Good luck.

## What's on the CD?

The CD contains several valuable tools to help you study for your MCSE exams:

- The Edge Test for NT Server 4.0 in the Enterprise demo provides an excellent supplement for reviewing the materials in this book.

- Transcender Corporation's NT-EnterpriseCert 4.0 demo also provides an excellent supplement for reviewing the materials in this book.

- Evaluation Copy of Microsoft's TechNet Database is a wealth of useful articles on Microsoft products and technologies, and valuable network utilities and service packs.

- Microsoft's Train_Cert Offline provides information about Microsoft Education, as well as the MCSE program.

- Microsoft's Internet Explorer 3.0 is a popular Web browser which you can use to view Train_Cert Offline and to surf the Internet.

# Planning a Domain Model in the Enterprise Environment

THIS CHAPTER INTRODUCES the Microsoft Windows NT domain model. You will learn what a domain model is and compare it to two other networking models—the workgroup model and the client-server model. You will also learn to identify the three server roles from which you can choose during the NT Server installation. You will see how domains can be implemented through the four NT domain models. You will learn how multiple domains are interconnected in an enterprise environment through an administrative link called a trust. Finally, this chapter reviews the terminology Microsoft uses to describe how the domains communicate with each other through NT Directory Services.

# Introduction to the Enterprise Environment

NT SERVER CAN be installed in a simple computing environment, or a more complex enterprise environment. A simple computing environment typically consists of one or more servers in a single domain and a single location. An enterprise environment typically contains multiple servers in multiple domains and locations.

Microsoft has made the distinction between NT Server and NT Server in an enterprise for the purpose of their certification program. Though NT Server and NT Server in an enterprise are very similar, they differ simply in that an *enterprise* is a network that encompasses more than one domain. The enterprise environment encompasses everything that NT Server does and then adds information appropriate to a complex multi-domain environment, including material on trust relationships and group strategies across domains.

In order to understand how to manage an enterprise environment, you have to be able to manage a single-domain environment. This book will address single-domain issues first, and then focus on issues unique to the enterprise environment.

# Networking Models

I N A NETWORK, computers can communicate with each other in some way. The main goal of networking is to allow users to share resources; this is typically done through a user *logon*. After a user logs on, they can access certain resources based on the permissions they have been given.

There are different ways to structure a network. Three commonly used networking models are the workgroup model, the client-server model, and the NT domain model. By contrasting the NT domain model to workgroup and client-server models, you will be able to see the advantage of the domain model in an enterprise network.

## The Workgroup Model

The *workgroup model* (sometimes referred to as peer-to-peer) is a decentralized networking model, which means that all account administration is local to each machine and that each machine maintains its own account database. This produces a great deal of extra administrative work. For example, let's assume we have a three-node (three-user) workgroup. Each user needs to access resources on all three machines. This means that each user has to maintain an accounts database that defines the other two users in their workgroup.

Ideally each user would keep the same user account name and password on all three accounts databases. However, in the workgroup model, they may have different user account names and password restrictions; this could be confusing for users and administrators. Figure 1.1 illustrates the workgroup model.

**FIGURE 1.1**

The workgroup model

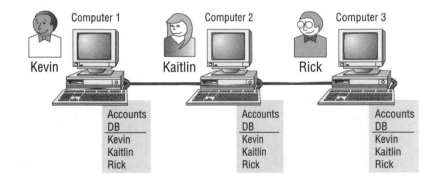

*This model can be appropriate for fairly small networks, but as the network grows, the administration becomes very intensive.*

NT Workstation can be configured to use the workgroup model.

## The Client-Server Model

The *client-server model* is a centralized model, unlike the workgroup model; this means that all administration is centralized at the server. Clients can log on to a server via the server's account database and access resources associated with that server. And each user has been added only once to the FS1 accounts database. Figure 1.2 shows a client-server model in which any of the three users are able to access resources on FS1.

**FIGURE 1.2**

The client-server model with a single server

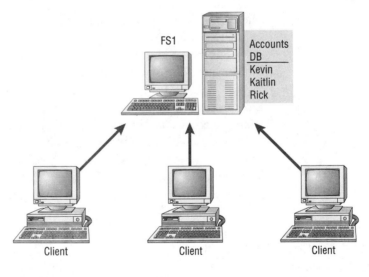

The client-server model's drawback is that, in an enterprise environment, users are likely to need access to resources on more than one server. In order for the users to access more than one server, the administrator must give users a new account for each additional server they need to access. This model creates more work for administrators and confuses users. Administrators must add the users to each file server's accounts database and users may have to remember different account names and passwords because they could have different names and passwords on each server. Figure 1.3 shows a single user who needs to access resources on FS1, FS2, and FS3.

**FIGURE 1.3**

The client-server model
with multiple servers

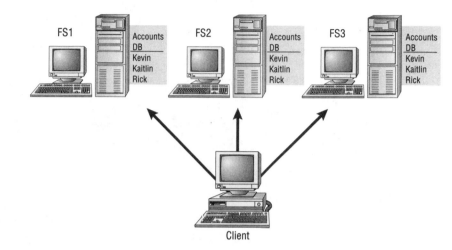

## The Domain Model

The NT *domain model* is an integral part of the NT enterprise environment. The use of the domain model allows administrators to group users, groups, and resources logically. It is critical to plan domains carefully; well planned domains ensure that the time an administrator spends managing the network is spent efficiently.

The NT domain model is scalable to small or large organizations. In small networks, a single domain is preferable. In larger, more complex networks, multiple domains may be necessary.

In the domain model all administration is centralized to an NT Server that has been designated as the *primary domain controller* (PDC). So, instead of logging on to a server, you log on to a domain. Based on your privileges, you can then access any resources from within that domain. Some of the computers that can be within the NT domain include NT Servers, NT Workstations, Windows 95 clients, Windows for Workgroups clients, LanManager clients, and DOS clients (if they have installed the MS redirector). Figure 1.4 illustrates the domain model.

**FIGURE I.4**

The domain model

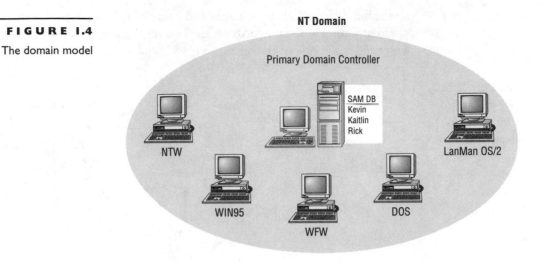

The accounts database that resides on the PDC is called the *Security Accounts Manager* (SAM) database. The SAM database is copied to servers that have been designated as *Backup Domain Controllers* (BDCs). There are two advantages of using BDCs. The first is that it allows users to log on and authenticate to either the PDC or a BDC (*load balancing*). The second is that BDCs are also used for fault tolerance. In the event that the PDC becomes unavailable, a BDC can be "promoted" to a PDC. PDCs and BDCs will be covered in more detail in the next section, "NT Server Roles."

In the enterprise environment, it is possible and likely to have more than one domain. In order to avoid the extra administrative work inherent in the client-server model, NT uses a link called a *trust* to join two or more domains into a single administrative unit. This allows each user to have a single logon account regardless of the number of domains they need to access.

The trust relationship will be covered in the "Trust Relationships" section later in this chapter. The next section will cover the NT Server roles in more detail.

# NT Server Roles

BEFORE YOU BEGIN to install NT Servers in your domain, you will need to decide what role your server will play. NT Server can be assigned one of three roles: Primary Domain Controller (PDC), Backup Domain Controller (BDC), or *member server*. The PDC and BDCs for your domain will hold the SAM database that keeps track of all of your account management. Member servers are able to act as file, print, and application servers without the overhead of account administration.

*The term member server is new with the arrival of NT 4.0. In NT 3.51 and earlier, a non-domain controller was simply referred to as an NT server. Because this was sometimes confusing, NT 4.0 uses the designation member server to identify a server installed as a non-domain controller.*

It is critical that you plan your server roles prior to installation. Once a server has been installed as a domain controller it cannot be changed to a member server (or vice-versa) without being reinstalled; this is because domain controllers and member servers do not have the same *Registry* structure.

*The Registry is a database structure that resides on all NT machines; it describes the configuration of the computer. Each machine has a unique Registry, and the Registry structures of NT Workstation, NT member servers, and NT domain controllers are all organized differently.*

Also, it is important to place domain controllers in the domain where they will reside. Once a domain controller is associated with a domain, it cannot be moved. During a domain controller's installation it is assigned a domain security ID. This ID cannot be modified without reinstallation.

*Once a PDC or BDC has been associated with a domain, it cannot move to another domain without reinstalling the server. Once a server has been installed as a member server, it cannot become a domain controller without reinstalling the server.*

The following subsections will cover the PDC, BDC, and member servers in more detail.

## Primary Domain Controller

The *primary domain controller* (PDC) holds the directory database (or SAM database) for the entire domain and is the only server that can make changes to the database. It is the first NT server to be installed into the domain and is assigned a domain security ID (SID) that is used to define the domain. The PDC contains the domain's master SAM database.

The PDC's SAM database is read-write, the BDC's databases are read-only. All administration for the domain takes place through the PDC. This is sometimes confusing because, as an administrator sitting at a BDC using administrative utilities, you might assume that you are administering the SAM on the BDC. In fact, you are using a front end application at the BDC to administer the SAM database on the PDC.

Once changes are made at the PDC, the changes are then "pushed" out, or copied, to the BDCs. By default the changes to the SAM database are sent out every five minutes. After the synchronization is complete, BDCs have an exact duplicate on the PDC's SAM database. In Chapter 7, I will cover BDC synchronization in more detail.

In Figure 1.5 you can see how the account changes are pushed from the PDC to the domain BDCs during domain synchronization.

**FIGURE 1.5**

SAM updates

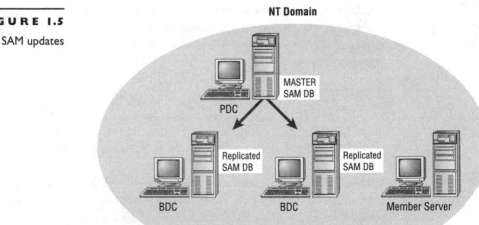

*You should also note that you can change the domain name. The domain name is simply an entry in the domain SID. However, you can only change the domain name at the PDC, and the PDC sends the name change to the BDCs during domain synchronization.*

*It is not a good idea to change your domain name because you will have to edit all references to it manually through Administrative Tools. You will also have to reestablish your trust relationships. The best thing to do is plan your domain name carefully prior to installation.*

# Backup Domain Controllers

*Backup domain controllers* (BDCs) are NT servers that have been configured as a domain controller server and receive copies of the PDC's SAM database. In this section you will learn what the benefits of a BDC are, issues that arise during a BDC's installation, how BDCs are synchronized, and how to plan the number of BDCs your network will need.

### Benefits of Backup Domain Controllers

Backup domain controllers serve two main functions. They are used for offloading logon authentication from the PDC and they are used for fault tolerance.

One reason that you would want to offload the logon authentication process is due to the number of users an NT domain can support. A domain can have several thousand users. For example, assume your domain has 20,000 users. You do not want one PDC to have to authenticate 20,000 user logon requests. This would cause major network traffic and response would be slow during peak logon hours (for example, first thing in the morning and after lunch).

If your domain spans a *wide area network* (WAN) link, you might also want to put a BDC on remote sides of the WAN link. This has two advantages. The first advantage is speed. If you can authenticate to a local BDC as opposed to a PDC across a WAN link, you will get better performance. The second advantage is fault tolerance. If the WAN link goes down, at least the users will still be able to log on through the BDC and access resources on their side of the WAN link.

Even if your domain does not span a WAN link, it is still advisable to have at least one BDC for fault tolerance purposes. If a PDC becomes unavailable due to maintenance or failure, a BDC can easily be promoted to a PDC. If your network only had one PDC and no BDCs, and your PDC became unavailable, you would be in big trouble because no network logon service or network access would be available. Promoting a BDC to a PDC will be covered in more detail in Chapter 7.

### Installation Issues Regarding Backup Domain Controllers

When you install BDCs, the PDC must be up and running. During the installation process, if you've chosen to make your server a domain controller, you will be prompted for the role your server will play, PDC or BDC. If you choose BDC, you will be prompted for the domain name, an administrative account name, and the administrative password. At this point the installation will go out and contact the PDC. If the PDC is not available, the installation will not complete.

The PDC will then respond with the domain SID. All domain controllers within a domain share the same domain SID. In order to change domains, you would have to change domain SIDs by reinstalling the server; this is why planning your server role and the domain in which it will reside is so critical.

### Synchronizing Primary Domain Controllers and Backup Domain Controllers

As previously mentioned, the SAM database is read-write on a PDC and read-only on BDCs. This means that the PDC must send updates to the BDCs on a regular basis in order for the SAM databases to be synchronized. This is a major area of confusion for users and administrators. If you are sitting at a BDC making changes to the SAM database it is easy to assume that you are editing the SAM database on the BDC. In fact, you are editing the SAM database on the PDC and your changes are being propagated to the BDC.

It is easy to prove this fact by shutting down your PDC by choosing the Shut Down option. After your PDC is shut down try to change a password or modify a user on the BDC, you will get an error message stating that the PDC is unavailable. Also, if the PDC is on the other side of a WAN link and the WAN link goes down, no administration is possible.

By default the PDC will update the BDCs with any changes to the SAM database every five minutes. It is possible, however, to change the frequency with which the BDC's SAM database is synchronized through the Registry at the PDC. I will cover this in greater detail in Chapter 7. If the updates have not yet been sent it can cause confusion to the users. For example, if the administrator changes a user's password, the user cannot use the new password immediately if they are being authenticated by a BDC. At this point the user can wait until the PDC updates the BDC or the administrator can force the update through the Server Manager Utility.

### Planning Your Backup Domain Controllers

You should have at least one BDC per domain for fault tolerance. Depending on whether your domain spans a WAN link and on the number of users you are supporting, you might need more BDCs.

If your domain spans a WAN link you should consider placing BDCs on each remote WAN link. This allows users to authenticate locally, and it provides fault tolerance if the WAN link goes down. Factors to consider while deciding if you need BDCs on remote WAN links are:

- the number of users on the remote WAN link

- the speed of your WAN link

- the cost

Consider the number of users that need logon authentication. The rule of thumb is that you need a BDC for each 2,000 users. This rule assumes that you are using a 486/66 machine with 32MB of RAM. It also assumes that the BDC will only be used to service logon requests.

The cost consideration has two aspects. What would it cost to add a BDC to the remote WAN link? What would it cost in terms of productivity if the WAN link went down and users were not able to access the network? If you are already planning to put a member server at the remote WAN link, you should consider installing it as a BDC so you can utilize your existing investment without having to dedicate a machine just to function as a BDC.

## Member Servers

A *member server* is an NT server that does not contain the domain SAM database (instead it contains a local SAM database). The server is able to act as a file, print, and application server without the overhead of accounts administration. An example of a member server would be an NT Server running a BackOffice application like SQL Server or SMS Server. This situation would allow the server to run its specialized applications without the overhead of authenticating logon requests and SAM database synchronization.

Member servers have their own machine SID. Because they do not have a domain SID like PDCs and BDCs, they can move from one domain to another without requiring reinstallation.

Now that you understand the roles a server can play, you will learn about how to manage a multiple domain environment through trust relationships.

# Trust Relationships

N AN ENTERPRISE environment, a *trust* is an administrative link that combines two or more domains. A trust allows a user in one domain to access a resource in another domain without having a user account in each domain. The domain where the user is located is the *trusted* or *account* domain, and the domain where the resource is located is called the *trusting* or *resource* domain.

The greatest confusion in understanding trust relationships lies in their usual depiction. When a user wants to access a resource, most people will think of an arrow pointing from the user to the resource, which implies that the resource is trusted by the user; this is not correct. Figure 1.6 shows the incorrect way of envisioning the trust relationship.

**FIGURE 1.6**

The incorrect way of seeing trust relationships

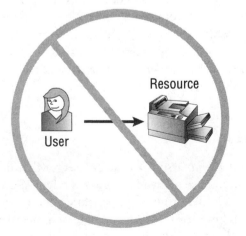

The correct way of envisioning trust relationships is with the arrow pointing to the user from the resource, meaning that the user is trusted by the resource.

Once you can get past this understandable confusion, you are halfway to understanding trust relationships. Figure 1.7 illustrates the correct way to envision the trust relationship.

**FIGURE 1.7**

The correct way of seeing trust relationships

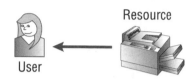

Resource

User

*A mnemonic for remembering the way trust relationships work is "Trust Ed" or trusted. When diagramming trust relationships, I draw a model representing two domains. One domain will have a user named Ed who wants to access a resource in another domain. I point the arrow to him. Ed is the user the resource trusts, the trusted domain, or "TrustEd" domain. In Figure 1.8 the arrow is pointing toward user Ed.*

**FIGURE 1.8**

The trust relationship arrow

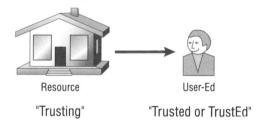

Resource          User-Ed

"Trusting"     "Trusted or TrustEd"

In the following example, you have two domains, NORTH and SOUTH. Users in the NORTH domain need to access resources in the SOUTH domain. In order for the trust relationship to be setup correctly, the NORTH domain would be defined as the trusted domain and the SOUTH domain would be the trusting domain. The arrowhead would be pointing from the SOUTH to the NORTH domain. Figure 1.9 shows the correct trust relationship between the NORTH and SOUTH domains.

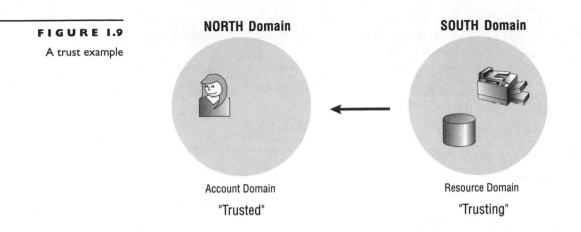

If you had users and resources in both domains and wanted bi-directional access, you would implement a two-way trust. For example, you have two domains, EAST and WEST. The users in EAST want to access resources in WEST and the users in WEST want to access resources in EAST. A two-way trust would make this access possible. The two-way trust relationship is shown in Figure 1.10. I will cover the actual implementation of the trust relationship in Chapter 2, "Installing and Maintaining NT Server 4.0."

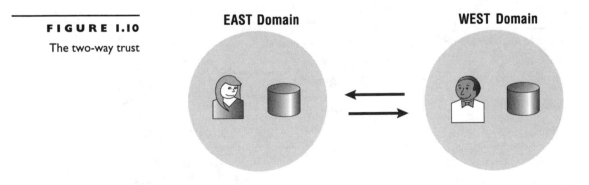

In the next section you will learn about the four NT domain models. The domain model you choose will impact the number of trust relationships you will need to manage.

# The Four NT Domain Models

ICROSOFT DEFINES FOUR domain models:

- The Single Domain Model

- The Single Master Domain Model

- The Multiple Master Domain Model

- The Complete Trust Domain Model

One thing to consider in choosing a domain model is the number of accounts your domain will need to support. An account can be a user, computer, or group. NT limits the size of the SAM database for practical purposes. A Windows NT domain can support up to 40,000 accounts.

It is important to understand the domain models you will choose from. During the planning stages, you want to choose a domain model that will be appropriate to your environment. The main criteria you will evaluate when choosing your domain model are:

- The number of accounts in your domain (The practical limit of accounts per domain is 40,000.)

- The geographic scope of your domain

- How users and resources will be defined within the domain

Choose carefully. A poorly planned domain model can lead to complex trust relationships and additional administrative work.

## The Single Domain Model

As the name implies, the *single domain* model consists of a single domain. For small networks, the single domain model is the easiest to manage. The advantage of the single domain model is that there are no trust relationships to manage. The single domain model also provides the most centralized administration of the four domain models.

The disadvantage to using the single-domain model is that you might have poor performance on your domain controllers when supporting a large SAM database. For example, when supporting 40,000 accounts in a single domain, you would need domain controllers running on Pentium class machines with 128MB of RAM. Browsing can also be slow with a large number of servers. Figure 1.11 illustrates the single domain model.

**FIGURE 1.11**

The single domain model

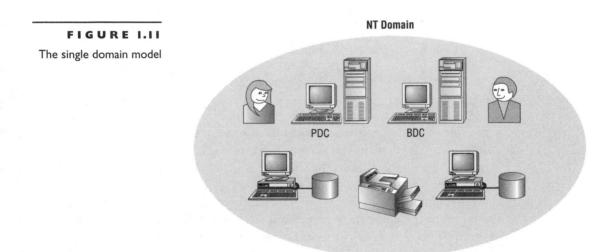

**NT Domain**

PDC    BDC

## The Master Domain Model

In the *master domain model* all user accounts are centralized in a master accounts domain. All resources are located at resource domains. The master domain model allows you to centralize all of your account administration to a master or user accounts domain. In this model, your resources are decentralized because administrators in the resource domain have control over their resources.

You can see in Figure 1.12 that the master domain, ABCCORP, contains all of the user accounts for the organization, while SALES, MARKETING, and SUPPORT are the resource domains. This allows each department to have full control over their resources.

Trusts in the master domain model are one-way because all user accounts are centralized to the master or accounts domain. The domain where the users are located becomes the trusted domain. The domains where the resources are located become the trusting domains.

**FIGURE 1.12**

The master domain model

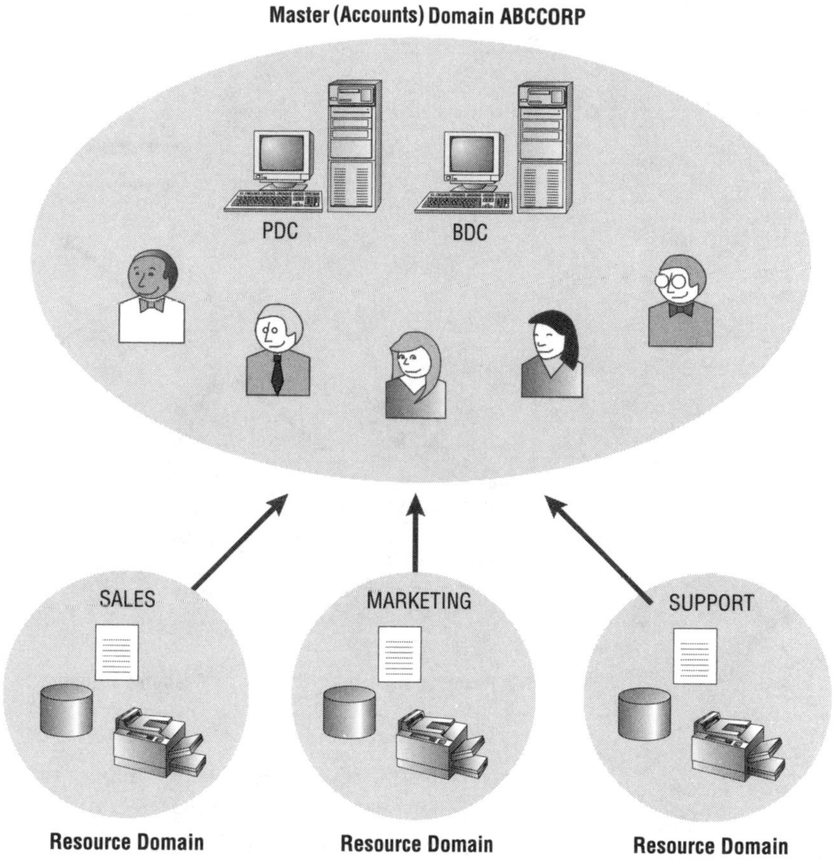

**Master (Accounts) Domain ABCCORP**

PDC          BDC

SALES                    MARKETING                    SUPPORT

Resource Domain          Resource Domain          Resource Domain

## The Multiple Master Domain Model

The master domain model is not appropriate for very large companies because the master domain can only support 40,000 accounts in its SAM database. To overcome this limitation, the *multiple master domain* model makes the NT enterprise scalable by allowing multiple master domains. This domain model is especially useful in environments where there are more than 40,000 users or the network is spread over a large geographic area.

Figure 1.13 illustrates the multiple master domain model. In this figure, the network is broken down into domains by division, in this case ABCCORP and ABCPROD for the Corporate and Production divisions of ABC Corp. This could easily be broken down by large geographic areas, for example NAMERICA and SAMERICA for the North America and South America divisions of the ABC Corp.

**FIGURE 1.13**

A multiple master
domain model

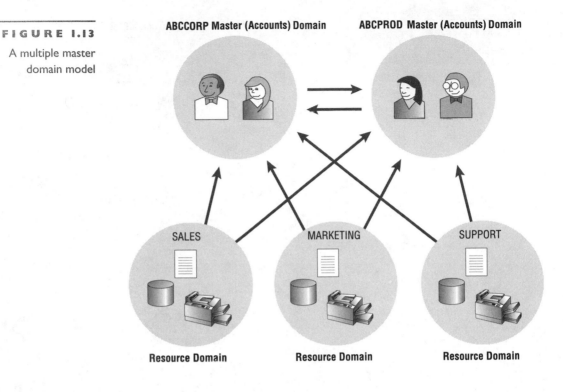

ABCCORP Master (Accounts) Domain    ABCPROD Master (Accounts) Domain

SALES    MARKETING    SUPPORT

Resource Domain    Resource Domain    Resource Domain

Trust relationships in the multiple master domain model are complex. Each of the resource domains must trust each of the master domains. In addition you need a two-way trust between each of the master domains. The formula for determining the number of trusts you will need is as follows:

$$M(M-1)+(R \times M)=n$$

In this formula M represents the number of master or accounts domains and R represents the number of resource domains. Assuming we have a model based on Figure 1.13 we would have 2 master domains and 3 resource domains.

$$2(2-1)+(2 \times 3)=8$$

In this example we would need to define eight trust relationships. It is important to consider the number of trust relationships you will need when planning domain models, as the number of trust relationships will affect the amount of administrative overhead in domain management.

# The Complete Trust Domain Model

The complete trust domain model assumes that accounts and resources are located in each domain. This model is useful in environments where local administrators want to control account management and resource management.

This model allows decentralized account management. It also allows departments to implement account policies specific to their domains. For example, in a single-domain environment you can only have one account policy per domain. This would mean that if you had one department, Payroll for example, that wanted to use ten-character passwords, but the rest of the domain only require five-character passwords, you would have to choose a fixed number of characters for use by both departments. In the complete trust model, Payroll has its own domain and can have ten-character passwords while the other domains can choose to have five-character passwords or tailor other account policies to suit their needs. I will cover account policies in more detail in Chapter 3.

As you can see in Figure 1.14, trust relationships can become very complex. This is the greatest drawback of using the complete trust domain model in an enterprise environment.

The formula for calculating trust relationships within a complete trust domain model is as follows (where N represents the number of domains):

$$N(N-1)=n$$

Based on the four domains in Figure 1.14, the formula for our trust relationships would be:

$$4(4-1)=12$$

There are a total of 12 trust relationships to manage. In an enterprise environment, this is the least desirable domain model. This domain model is typically seen in environments where NT has been installed at the departmental level without any central Management Information System (MIS) planning.

| SUMMARY OF DOMAIN MODELS | NUMBER OF USERS | ACCOUNTS | RESOURCES |
|---|---|---|---|
| Single Domain | <40,000 | Centralized | Centralized |
| Master Domain | <40,000 | Centralized | Decentralized |
| Multiple Master Domain | Any number | Centralized among Master Domains | Decentralized |
| Complete Trust | Any number | Decentralized | Decentralized |

**FIGURE 1.14**

The complete trust
domain model

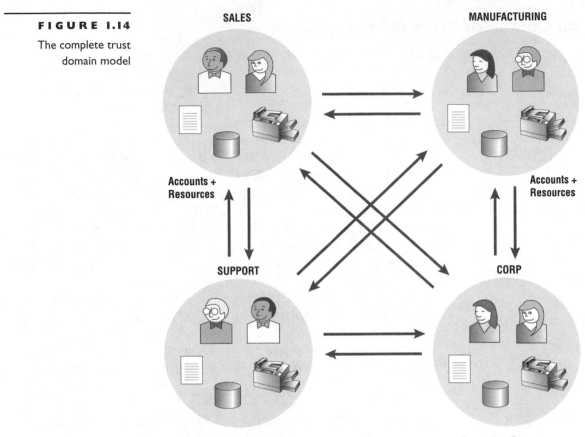

# NT Directory Services

Now THAT YOU understand what a domain model is and how trust relationships work, we'll turn our attention to NT Directory Services. NT Directory Services is the directory database or SAM database that resides on each domain's PDC; it is also the system by which that SAM database is distributed to the domains' BDCs. Directory Services addresses two main administrative tasks.

1. Providing a synchronized database between the PDC and BDCs within a domain.

2. Providing administrative links through the trust relationship when a network is composed of multiple domains.

One of the major goals of NT is to provide a networking architecture that works well in an enterprise environment. To meet the needs of the enterprise network, NT does the following:

- allows users to have a single logon regardless of the number of domains to which they need access

- allows administrators to manage accounts and resources from a central location

- supports user accounts, passwords, and services in diverse environments

- uses network services to automatically update network and account information

Windows NT Directory Services meets all of the above design criteria. By implementing the Windows NT domain model, users are able to take advantage of a flexible, yet powerful way of organizing and using network resources.

# Chapter Summary

THE WINDOWS NT domain model is a powerful and flexible model for maintaining network accounts and resources. The role the NT server model will play in the domain is determined by the configuration defined when the server is installed. NT Server can be assigned one of three roles:

- Primary Domain Controller (PDC)

- Backup Domain Controller (BDC)

- Member Server

It is important to plan your server roles carefully, because domain controllers cannot migrate to other domains and member servers cannot become domain controllers without reinstallation.

A trust links domains together. Trust relationships can be one-way trusts or two-way trusts. The number of trust relationships necessary is typically determined by the domain model chosen. Windows NT defines four domain models:

- Single domain model

- Master domain model

- Multiple master domain model

- Complete trust domain model

The enterprise environment is defined by having multiple domains in multiple locations. NT provides the framework to support this complex network environment through Directory Services. Directory Services supports synchronization of the SAM database within a domain as well as linking domains together through trust relationships.

# Review Questions

1. You have two domains, Domain A and Domain B. Kevin is a user in Domain A and he wants to be able to access a resource in Domain B. What is the minimal trust relationship you need to establish for Kevin to access resources in Domain B?

   **A.** Configure Domain A to trust Domain B.

   **B.** Configure Domain B to trust Domain A.

   **C.** Configure a two-way trust between Domain A and Domain B.

**2.** Your company has two offices, one in San Francisco and one in Los Angeles. Your company has decided to place a high speed WAN link between the two locations and use a single domain model. They have also decided to put a PDC at the San Francisco location and a BDC at the Los Angeles location. You are the manager of the Los Angeles location and have decided to install the BDC even though the WAN link has not yet been installed. You receive an error message during the installation telling you that the domain controller for this domain cannot be located. What do you do?

   **A.** Choose bypass error message. The BDC will complete the installation, and when the PDC becomes available it will automatically synchronize.

   **B.** Install the BDC as a member server and upgrade it to BDC when the WAN link is installed.

   **C.** Install the BDC as a PDC in it's own domain. After the WAN link becomes available you can merge the two domains together.

   **D.** Wait until the WAN link becomes available before installing the BDC.

**3.** You have been experiencing very heavy traffic to your PDC during the morning hours and when users are returning from lunch. You decide to add another machine to help offload the logon authentication from the PDC. Which is the best solution?

   **A.** Add a BDC to your existing domain and manually migrate the SAM database.

   **B.** Add a member server to your existing domain, copy the SAM database, and start the Netlogon service.

   **C.** Add a BDC to your existing domain and specify an administrative account and password during installation.

   **D.** Add a BDC to your existing domain and stop the Netlogon service on your PDC.

4. Your company has two main divisions, East and West. Each division implemented Windows NT without any coordination from MIS. Now they want to be able to share network resources between the EAST and WEST domains. What is the easiest way to configure the domains?

   **A.** Configure EAST to trust WEST.

   **B.** Configure WEST to trust EAST.

   **C.** Setup a two-way trust between EAST and WEST.

   **D.** Start from scratch and implement a master domain model.

5. You installed an NT server for the Sales department. The server was supposed to be installed into the SALES domain, but the WAN link to SALES was down during the installation. You installed the server as a member server in the MIS domain. What do you do now?

   **A.** When the WAN link comes up, change the configuration of the server so it is now part of the SALES domain.

   **B.** Upgrade the server to a BDC so it can be moved to the SALES domain.

   **C.** Wait until the WAN link comes up and reinstall the server so it can be associated with the proper domain.

6. Your network has four domains, NORTH, EAST, WEST, and SOUTH. All domains contain users and resources. The NORTH domain contains all the corporate resources that users in all domains need to access. The resources in WEST, EAST and SOUTH are all local resources and do not require access to users outside their domains. What are the minimum trust relationships that need to be established?

   **A.** Establish one-way trust relationships in which EAST, WEST, and SOUTH trust NORTH.

   **B.** Establish one-way trust relationships in which NORTH trusts EAST, WEST, and SOUTH.

   **C.** Establish a two-way trust between NORTH and SOUTH, NORTH and WEST, and NORTH and EAST.

   **D.** Establish two-way trusts between all four domains.

**7.** Your company is in a single location. You have six NT servers and 200 users. Your company wants to centralize management and wants users to be able to access resources from other departments. Which of the following options is the best solution?

**A.** Create a single domain and install one server as a PDC and another server as a BDC, then setup the remaining servers as part of the domain.

**B.** Use the master domain model. In the master domain install one server as PDC and another server as a BDC. Put each department in its own resource domain and install their department server as PDC.

**C.** Create a single domain that has a PDC and a BDC, and install the departmental servers as member servers in their own workgroup.

**D.** Set up each department in its own domain. Use the Complete Trust domain model to ensure that users can access resources in other domains.

**8.** Your domain currently has a PDC that is a Pentium with 32MB of RAM. You want to install a new server that is an Alpha with 64MB of RAM. You prefer that the new machine be the PDC. What do you do?

**A.** When installing the new machine specify the machine as PDC, this will automatically make the old machine a BDC.

**B.** When installing the new machine configure it as a BDC, then after the installation, you can promote it to a PDC.

**C.** Install the new machine as a member server, copy the SAM from the PDC, configure the old machine as a BDC, and promote the new machine to PDC.

**D.** Install the new machine as the PDC, then copy the SAM from the original PDC, then demote the original PDC to BDC.

**9.** Your PAYROLL domain contains resources that users in other domains will never need to access. Your SALES and MARKETING domains frequently need to share resources across the SALES and MARKETING domains. Occasionally users in PAYROLL also need to access resources in the SALES and MARKETING domains. What do you need to do to setup the trust relationships?

**A.** Configure a one-way trust from SALES and MARKETING to trust PAYROLL, then configure a two-way trust between SALES and MARKETING.

**B.** Configure a one-way trust from PAYROLL to trust SALES and MARKETING, then configure a two-way trust between SALES and MARKETING.

**C.** Set up a two-way trust between SALES and MARKETING, create duplicate user accounts in the domains for PAYROLL users who need to access resources in domains other than PAYROLL.

**D.** Setup two-way trust relationships between PAYROLL, SALES, and MARKETING.

# Installing and Maintaining NT Server 4

HE LAST CHAPTER defined the Windows NT domain model. In this chapter you will implement the concepts covered in Chapter 1 by installing NT Server 4.0 in its own domain. You will also create an enterprise environment by installing a second server into a second domain. Then you will install NT Workstation and learn how it can be added to a domain. Finally you will learn how to implement a trust relationship between the two domains you have created. This chapter will cover the following specific areas:

- Windows NT Server Planning

- Overview of the Windows NT Server Installation

- Installation of NT Server

- Joining a Domain

- Implementing a Trust Relationship

# Windows NT Server Planning Issues

EFORE YOU ARE ready to install Windows NT Server, you must determine the following:

- Minimum hardware requirements for NT Server

- The partitioning scheme your server will use

- The file system type your server will use

- Licensing for your server

# Minimum Hardware Requirements

In order to install NT Server, you must meet minimum hardware requirements. Before beginning installation, check that your hardware is on the Windows NT *Hardware Compatibility List* (HCL). The hardware on this list has been tested and verified as compatible with Windows NT Server. Microsoft will only support hardware that is on the HCL. If you are not sure if your hardware is on the HCL, you can contact the hardware vendor, or check on the Internet at:

```
http://microsoft.com/ntserver/hcl /hclintro.htm
```

or

```
http://microsoft.com/isapi/hwtest/hsearchn4.idc
```

In addition to being on the HCL, system requirements for installation are listed in Table 2.1.

| | COMPONENT | NT SERVER REQUIREMENT |
|---|---|---|
| **TABLE 2.1**<br>The minimum system requirements for NT Server | Processor | Intel 486/33 or higher<br>MIPS® R4x00-based processor<br>PReP-compliant PowerPC-based processor<br>Digital Alpha AXP™-based processor |
| | Memory | Intel and RISC-based computers require 16MB of RAM (this is the minimum for the OS, most servers will require additional RAM depending on their specific configuration) |
| | Free hard disk space | Intel platform requires 125MB<br>RISC platform requires 160MB<br>(please note using 32K clusters could increase this requirement to 200MB) |
| | Display | The video adapter must be VGA resolution or better |
| | Other drivers | Intel platforms require a 3.5 floppy drive, installation can be CD- or network-based<br>RISC platforms require a SCSI CD device for installation |

| TABLE 2.1 | COMPONENT | NT SERVER REQUIREMENT |
|---|---|---|
| The minimum system requirements for NT Server (continued) | Optional components | The NT courseware describes network interface cards and their associated cabling as optional. Typically, NT Server is installed into a network, which would then define this component as required. The mouse or pointing device is also described as optional, but due to the graphical nature of Windows NT, a mouse is highly desirable. |

## Server Partitions

A *server partition* is a logical subdivision of a server hard disk. You can define one logical partition or multiple partitions on a single physical hard drive. Each partition is assigned its own drive letter, and you are able to logically organize your folders and files based on your partitions.

NT Server requires a *system partition* and a *boot partition* for storing operating system files and the files needed to boot NT. The system partition is the active partition on an Intel-based computer. On a RISC-based computer the active partition is determined by firmware. The boot partition is the partition that contains the NT system files. During the installation process, you will be prompted for the location and name of the directory where the NT system files will be copied. By default the directory where the operating system files are stored is called WINNT.

*It is possible to place the system and boot partition on the same partition.*

Figure 2.1 illustrates how a drive might be partitioned.

| FIGURE 2.1 |
|---|
| NT disk partitions |

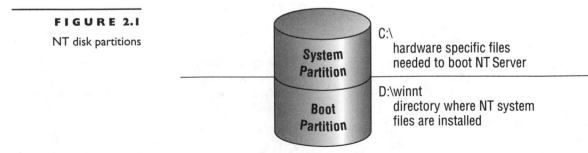

This is one area of NT in which the terminology is somewhat counter intuitive. The NT boot files are on the system partition and the NT system files are on the boot partition.

*It is interesting to note that in NT 3.51, the default directory the boot partition used was called* WINNT35. *For systems that upgrade to NT 4.0, NT 4.0 will install into the* WINNT35 *directory. It can seem strange for NT Server 4.0 to be installed into a directory called* WINNT35, *so now they use a more generic directory name,* WINNT.

## Selecting a File System

Windows NT supports two file systems: *File Allocation Table* (FAT) and *New Technology File System* (NTFS). Table 2.2 lists the distinctions between the two.

| **TABLE 2.2** FAT v. NTFS | **FAT** | **NTFS** |
|---|---|---|
| | Supported by DOS, OS/2, Windows 95, and Windows NT (Should be used if you need to dual-boot and access the partition from another OS) | Only supported under the NT OS |
| | No local security available | Local security is available |
| | Does not support Macintosh files | Supports Macintosh files |
| | Does not support NetWare file and directory permissions during NetWare migration | Supports NetWare file and directory permissions during migration |
| | Does not support NT file compression | Supports NT file compression |
| | Can be converted to NTFS at any time | NTFS can never be converted to FAT. The only way to go from NTFS to FAT is to backup the data, reformat the partition as FAT, and then restore the data to the new FAT partition |
| | Maximum partition size of 4GB | Maximum partition size of 16EB |

*If you are wondering what an EB is, it is an exabyte (over a trillion MB!). While current disk technology is nowhere near the exabyte range, technically NTFS can support it.*

One option to consider when partitioning your disk and planning your file system is to make a small disk partition that will contain your system partition. There is a configuration file called BOOT.INI that resides in your system partition. You are often required, in order to ensure successful NT Server booting, to edit BOOT.INI when using the Disk Administrator utility to create logical partitions because the BOOT.INI file is responsible for pointing to where the NT system files are. If BOOT.INI is not edited correctly and it is on a FAT partition, you can boot to DOS and edit the BOOT.INI file with a DOS text editor; this allows you to get back into NT Server. If BOOT.INI is not edited correctly and it is on an NTFS partition, you will run into problems because NT loader will not be able to find the NT system files.

The boot partition can then be stored on an NTFS partition if you are concerned with local security. During installation of NT, you are able to specify whether you want to use FAT or NTFS as your partition type. I will cover the BOOT.INI file in greater detail in Chapter 18, "Troubleshooting."

*NT 3.51 supported the HPFS file system associated with OS/2. This file system is no longer supported in NT 4.0. You should also note that the Windows 95 FAT32 file system is not supported by Windows NT.*

## Licensing Mode

During the installation of NT Server you will be prompted to select a licensing mode. NT Server supports two modes: *per-server licensing* and *per-seat licensing*.

### Per-Server Licensing

The per-server mode is the traditional method for licensing. In this mode the server must be licensed for each concurrent connection. For example, let's assume you have five users and three servers, as shown in Figure 2.2. All five users need to access each of the three servers. Each of the three servers must be licensed per server, supporting five connections.

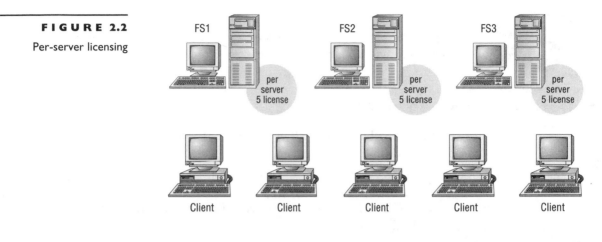

**FIGURE 2.2**

Per-server licensing

In an enterprise environment, where users will need to access resources on multiple servers, per-server licensing can become very expensive. However, per-server licensing becomes practical when NT Server is used as an Internet Server because you may not know if the remote clients connecting to your server are already licensed or not.

### Per-Seat Licensing

The per-seat licensing mode is more practical for the enterprise environment. By purchasing a Client Access License (CAL) for each seat, each client is licensed at the client side and can access as many servers as needed.

When using the per-seat licensing method, you use the License Manager to record the CALs. In Figure 2.3, note that the servers are licensed only for the server software, and the right to access the server is licensed at the client.

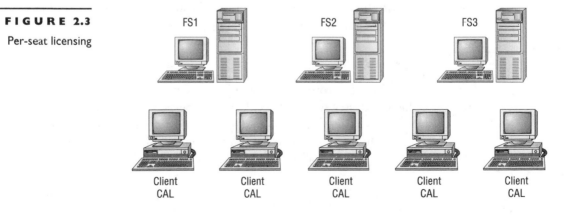

**FIGURE 2.3**

Per-seat licensing

*If you choose per-server licensing you can always convert to per-seat licensing, but you cannot convert from per-seat to per-server.*

## Selecting Network Protocols

During installation you will be asked to provide information regarding your NT Server's protocol selection. The listed protocols you can choose from are:

- NetBEUI

- NWLink IPX/SPX (Internetwork Packet Exchange/ Sequenced Packet Exchange)

- TCP/IP (Transmission Control Protocol/ Internet Protocol)

### NetBEUI

*NetBEUI* is the most efficient of the three protocol choices. It has very little overhead and works very well in small LANs. The drawback of NetBEUI is that it is a non-routable protocol and does not work in WAN environments. NetBEUI is not selected by default during the NT Server installation.

### NWLink IPX/SPX

*NWLink IPX/SPX* is Microsoft's implementation of Novell's IPX/SPX protocol and is selected by default in the NT Server installation. It is widely used in networks which require NetWare connectivity. NWLink IPX/SPX differs from Novell's IPX/SPX protocol by providing NetBIOS support within NWLink. NetBIOS support is required for NT browsing services. I cover the NWLink IPX/SPX protocol in greater detail in Chapter 9, "NetWare Connectivity."

### TCP/IP

The *TCP/IP* protocol is the most widely used of the three protocols. It is a de facto industry standard. TCP/IP is the best choice for supporting large heterogeneous networks. It also requires the most configuration of the three protocols. The TCP/IP protocol is selected by default during the installation of NT Server. If you choose to use TCP/IP, you must either be a DHCP client to a

DHCP server (see Chapter 11, "TCP/IP Support), or you must supply an IP address, a subnet mask, and a default gateway. I will cover the TCP/IP protocol in more detail in Chapter 11.

### Other Protocols Supported by NT Server

While you won't see the *DLC protocol* from the main screen during installation, NT Server also supports it. The DLC protocol is used when connecting to IBM mainframes, or by direct-connect printers.

The *AppleTalk protocol* is not displayed during the installation of NT Server either. The AppleTalk protocol is installed during the installation of Services for Macintosh; I will cover this in more detail in Chapter 10, "Macintosh Connectivity."

*It's interesting to note that NT 3.5 defaulted to NWLink IPX/SPX protocol and NT 3.51 defaulted to the TCP/IP protocol. Now NT 4.0 Server defaults to both of these protocols and NT 4.0 Workstation defaults to TCP/IP only.*

# Overview of Windows NT Server Installation

NT SERVER 4.0 installs in four phases. The installation phases are:

- Phase 0: Preparation for NT Server installation

- Phase 1: Gathering information about your computer

- Phase 2: Windows NT networking

- Phase 3: Finishing setup

## Phase 0: Preparation for NT Server Installation

Phase 0 begins the NT installation. In this phase NT copies enough files so that it is able to run a limited version of NT Server. Once this limited version of NT Server is running, the installation is able to complete more quickly because of NT's multitasking capabilities.

During phase 0, the installation program tries to detect which hardware your computer is using. Specifically, NT will try and detect your video adapter and any mass storage devices. Once it finds this information, the installation program will ask the installer on which partition NT should be installed, which file system should be used, and in which directory the NT system files should be stored.

## Phase 1: Gathering Information about Your Computer

Phase 1 of the NT installation gathers information about your computer. During this phase, you will be prompted for the following information:

- **Name and Organization:** Give your name and organization. This information is used for licensing purposes only. A username is required, but the organization is optional.

- **Licensing Mode:** Select which licensing mode you will implement—per server or per seat.

- **Computer Name:** Choose a computer name. It is critical that the computer name be unique to all other computer names on the network. This name is used for browsing purposes. I will cover browsing in greater detail in Chapter 7, "NT Domain Management."

- **Type of server:** Primary Domain Controller (PDC), Backup Domain Controller (BDC), or member server. You should have already planned which type of server to install.

- **Administrator Password:** Choose an administrator password. The password can be up to 14 characters in length.

- **Emergency Repair Disk (ERD):** Create an emergency repair disk. It is a good idea to do this because it could be useful in fixing system problems later on. ERDs are machine-specific and you should create one for each NT machine.

- **Optional Components:** Select optional components. Optional components include Accessibility Options, Accessories, Communications, Games, Microsoft Exchange, and Multimedia.

# Phase 2: Windows NT Networking

Phase 2 of the installation prompts you to supply the following information regarding your network configuration:

- **Direct or Dial-In Connection to Network:** Tell whether you are connected to the network or are dialing in to the network. For installing NT Server, you will most likely be connected to the network.

- **Optional Install of Internet Information Server (IIS):** Choose whether or not you want to install IIS.

- **Adapter and Protocols:** Select the network adapter and protocols you are using. Based on your selection, Phase 2 will load any appropriate drivers and complete bindings of protocols to your network adapters driver.

- **Additional Network Services:** Choose from such services as Services for Macintosh, or Gateway Services for NetWare.

- **Domain:** Specify the domain your computer should belong to.

# Phase 3: Finishing Setup

In the last phase of installation, NT requires the following information in order to complete configuration:

- **Date/Time and Time Zone:** NT will pick up the date and time from your computer by default. NT will default to Greenwich Mean Time, so you will probably need to edit this.

- **Video Driver:** Further customize your video settings. After you select your video settings, you are asked to test the settings before they are saved. This is to prevent you from selecting a video setting that does not function.

# Simulating an NT Enterprise Environment

I N ORDER TO prepare for this exam, you should have as much hands-on experience with NT as possible. Throughout the book, you will be asked to complete hands-on exercises. You will install two NT Servers in separate domains to simulate an enterprise environment and complete the exercises within that environment. Ideally, you will have the equipment to complete these exercises.

## Equipment Necessary for Book Exercises

In order to complete the exercises in this book, you will need to have the equipment listed in Table 2.3.

| TABLE 2.3 | EQUIPMENT | COMMENTS |
|---|---|---|
| Equipment necessary for book exercises | Two 486/33 or higher Processor computers with at least 16MB of RAM | These should preferably be on the hardware compatibility list. If your computer is not on the list, try installing NT Server anyway; it might work. In a test environment we do not have to follow requirements as strictly as you would want to in a production environment. |
| | Each computer should have at least a 500MB hard drive. | You will set up two partitions on each computer: a 300MB partition for NT Server and a 175MB partition. Leave 25MB of free space. |
| | NT Server 4.0 software | Used to install your two PDCs. |
| | NT Workstation 4.0 software | Used to complete exercises. |
| | Two network interface cards and appropriate cabling and hardware | The least expensive way to connect your two computers will be to buy two Ethernet cards with BNC connectors. Then you will only need an RG-58 AU coaxial cable, two T-connectors (these should come with the card), and two 50 ohm terminators. The cable should be around $5.00 and the terminators should be between $3.00-$5.00 each. This is much cheaper than using Token Ring or Ethernet with RJ-45 connectors and a concentrator. |

| **TABLE 2.3** | **EQUIPMENT** | **COMMENTS** |
|---|---|---|
| Equipment necessary for book exercises (continued) | CD-ROM drive on at least one computer | If your second computer does not have a CD-ROM drive, don't worry. After we install the first computer, you will be able to share the CD-ROM on your first computer and do network installations. |
| | Backup of your current hard drives | These installations will overwrite your existing hard drives. If there is anything you want to save, you should back up and test your backup before continuing. |
| | 4 Scratch high density floppies | These floppies will be used to create installation startup diskettes and the emergency repair diskette (ERD). |

Figure 2.4 illustrates how your two computers will be configured at the end of this chapter. You will use COMPUTER2 in a dual-boot mode; this way you will be able to maximize use of your equipment to do the approaching exercises. Completing the exercises in this book will give you the hands-on practice necessary to pass the exam.

| **FIGURE 2.4** |
|---|
| Configuration of practice machines |

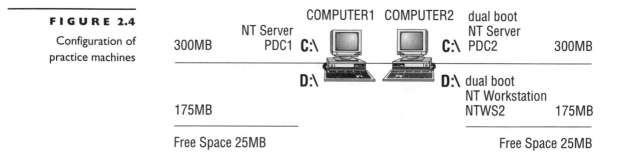

## Hard Drive Preparation

Note that COMPUTER2 in Figure 2.4 will support two operating systems. In order to support two operating systems your hard drives should be configured as follows, prior to installation:

| PARTITION | MINIMUM SIZE | FILE SYSTEM |
|---|---|---|
| C:\ | 300MB | FAT |
| D:\ | 175MB | FAT |
| free space | 25MB | |

If you have additional hard-disk space you can modify these numbers; you just want to make sure that you meet the minimum numbers listed. To partition your disks, use the DOS FDISK utility. Use the DOS FORMAT command to format your partitions. Remember to use the /S switch with FORMAT on the C: partition to copy the DOS system files. You will also need to install the drivers for your CD-ROM to access the NT Server installation CD. If you have any questions, please refer to your DOS manual or your CD-ROM documentation.

Note that you can partition and format your drives through NT, but partition both your computer's drives as you were just directed; it will be simpler for you. This partitioning scheme will be used to support the dual roles that your computers will use throughout the book.

## Gathering Information for Your Configuration

During the NT installation, you will be prompted for information specific to your configuration. In order to be prepared, have the following information available.

- **Name:** Your name (for licensing)

- **Organization:** Optional (for licensing)

- **CD-Key:** Provided with NT Server software

- **Computer Name:** NetBIOS name, can be up to 15 characters, must be unique to network (Example: PDC1)

- **Network Adapter Card and Settings:** To determine settings run setup program provided with your card. Refer to product documentation

- **Domain Name:** Name of your domain, must be unique to all other domain names (Example: DOMAIN1)

## Installation of NT Servers for the Enterprise Environment

Now you are ready to install NT Server. Exercise 2.1 details the steps you will go through as you install NT Server as a PDC.

---

**EXERCISE 2.1**

## Installing NT Server

**1.** Boot your computer to DOS.

**2.** From the DOS prompt, enter **x:\i386>WINNT** (where *x* is the CD-ROM's drive letter). The Windows NT Setup screen will appear and will ask you where the Windows NT files are located. By default this will show the directory from where you ran WINNT. Press Enter to continue.

**3.** Next, the WINNT program will create the three NT boot floppies (use three of the high density blank diskettes for this step). They will be used to start the installation and provide the storage device drivers for your computer. Please note the order in which the diskettes will be created: Windows NT Server Setup Disk #3, Windows NT Server Setup Disk #2, and Windows NT Server Setup Boot Disk #1.

**4.** After the floppies have been created, the NT Server Setup Boot Disk is already in the floppy drive, and all you need to do is press Enter to reboot. The computer will boot to the Windows NT Setup screen. It may take a few minutes to load the necessary setup files.

**5.** When prompted, insert Windows NT Server Setup Disk #2 and press Enter. At this point more files will be copied and the Windows NT kernel will load.

**6.** The Welcome to Setup screen will appear. To continue setting up Windows NT Server, press Enter.

**7.** NT will now attempt to detect your mass storage devices. Press Enter to continue.

**8.** When prompted, insert Windows NT Server Setup Disk #3 and press Enter.

**9.** You will then see a list of any storage devices the setup program has recognized in your computer. If this list is correct press Enter. If this list is not correct, choose S and provide the driver for your mass storage device. (If you have a SCSI drive, then you will only see your SCSI controller.) At this point the installation program will install the drivers for the NT-supported file systems, FAT and NTFS, and the appropriate device drivers for your computer.

**10.** The license agreement screen will now appear. This is a new screen to NT 4.0. Page down until you have read the entire agreement, and press F8 to accept the license agreement.

**11.** The next screen will display what hardware and software components have been detected on your computer. The list should look something like this:

- **Computer**: Standard PC

- **Display**: Auto Detect

- **Keyboard**: XT, AT, or Enhanced Keyboard

- **Keyboard Layout**: US

- **Pointing Device**: Microsoft Serial Mouse

- **No Changes**: The above list matches my computer.

If this information is correct press Enter.

**12.** The Setup program will now ask you on which drive you want the NT system files installed. Choose the C: partition and press Enter.

**13.** The next screen will ask you how to partition your drive. Select "leave the current file system intact (no changes)" and press Enter.

**14.** The location where you install NT Server is \WINNT. Press Enter to continue.

**15.** The NT Server Setup screen will now display a notice that the setup program will examine your hard disk(s) for corruption. Press Enter to continue. (The NT Server Setup program will now copy some files. This may take a few minutes.)

**16.** After the filecopy is complete you will be prompted to restart your computer. Remove any floppies and press Enter. Your computer will restart and NT Server will load. While NT is loading, the CHKDSK utility will automatically check your partitions.

**17.** The Windows NT Setup screen will appear next. To begin Phase 1 of the installation, "Gathering information about your computer," click Next.

**18.** You will be prompted to personalize the installation. Type in your name and organization. Click Next.

**19.** Next you will be prompted to type in the registration CD-KEY. After you type in the CD-KEY, click Next.

**20.** The licensing mode screen now appears. Choose Per Server, select 10 concurrent connections, and click Next.

**21.** Now type in your computer name. Choose whatever name you want; however, it will be referred to as **PDC1** throughout the exercises. Click Next to continue.

**22.** The Server Type screen will prompt you to select your server type. Click Primary Domain Controller and then click Next.

**23.** Now specify an administrator account password. This password must be 14 characters or less. You will need to type the password and re-type it in the confirm password box. You might want to leave this blank because this is only a practice machine. Click Next.

**24.** When prompted to create an Emergency Repair Disk, choose Yes and supply a blank, high density floppy.

**25.** The select components screen appears; accept the default choices and click Next.

**26.** Phase 2 of the installation "Installing NT Networking" is now ready to begin. Click Next to continue.

**27.** The NT Server Setup screen will ask you how your computer should participate on the network. Select "wired to the network" and click Next .

**28.** The Microsoft Windows NT Server Setup will now ask you whether you want to install the Microsoft Internet Information Server (IIS). Deselect this choice by unchecking the box. You will install IIS in Chapter 12, "Internet Information Server." Click Next to continue.

**29.** NT setup will now search for your network adapter. Click Start Search to begin the search. After your adapter is found, click Next.

**30.** The Network Protocols screen will appear. Leave the default selections of TCP/IP and NWLink IPX/SPX Compatible Transport and click Next.

**31.** The Network Services screen will appear. Keep the default services, RPC configuration, NetBIOS interface, Workstation, and Server. Click Next.

**32.** Click Next again to install your network components.

**33.** The network card setup screen will appear. You will be prompted to verify the hardware configuration for your card. If this information is correct, click Continue. If this information is not correct, modify the options as required and then click Continue.

**34.** Because we chose to install TCP/IP you will now be prompted to configure TCP/IP. You will get the following message: "If there is a DHCP server, TCP/IP can be configured dynamically to provide an IP address. If you are not sure, ask your system administrator. Do you wish to use DHCP?" Choose No. The setup program will now copy files related to the networking components you have chosen.

**35.** The IP address configuration screen will appear. Click the "Specify an IP address" option. Choose:

- **IP Address**: 131.200.2.1

- **Subnet Mask**: 255.255.255.0

- **Default Gateway**: leave blank

Click OK.

**36.** The Network Bindings screen will appear. Keep all the default settings and click Next.

**37.** You will now be prompted to click Next to start the network.

**38.** Now, you will supply your computer's name and domain name. You can name your domain whatever you wish. However, during the exercises, I will refer to it as DOMAIN1. Click Next. Don't be concerned if your system takes a few minutes to check for duplicate domain names.

**39.** The third and final phase of setup begins now, and you will see the Finishing Setup screen. Click Finish, and the setup program will complete some configuration information based on the options you have chosen.

**40.** The next installation screen will prompt you for Date/Time properties. NT picks up the date and time from your computer's CMOS information. The time zone will default to Greenwich Mean Time, so select the correct setting for your time zone. Click Close.

**EXERCISE 2.1 (CONTINUED FROM PREVIOUS PAGE)**

**41.** Next, NT will detect your video adapter. If the correct video driver appears, choose Okay. If the correct video driver does not appear, you can customize it after NT is installed. You accomplish this with Control Panel ≻ Display.

**42.** Select the Test button to test your display. Click OK to set and test your video driver; this will take five seconds. NT will ask, "Did you see the test bitmap properly?" If the display is correct, select Yes. Select OK to save your settings. Click OK again to close the Display Settings window.

**43.** NT will now complete copying the NT system files. When the file copy is complete, you will be prompted to insert a floppy; this will become your Emergency Repair Disk. Insert a floppy and click OK. Finally, remove any floppies, and reboot your computer. NT Server should now be installed.

In Exercise 2.2 you will install your second machine as an NT Server in it's own domain in order to simulate the enterprise environment.

**EXERCISE 2.2**

### Installing a Second NT Server

For this exercise, complete all the steps listed in Exercise 2.1, but substitute the following numbers for their Exercise 2.1 correspondents:

**20.** Now type in your computer name. Choose whatever name you want, however it will be referred to as **PDC2** throughout the exercises. Click Next to continue.

**34.** The IP address configuration screen will appear. Click the "Specify an IP address" option. Choose:

- **IP Address**: 131.200.2.2

- **Subnet Mask**: 255.255.255.0

- **Default Gateway**: leave blank

Click OK.

**37.** Here again you will supply your computer's name and domain name. You can name your domain whatever you wish. However, during the exercises, it will be referred to as **DOMAIN2**. After supplying this information, click Next. Don't be concerned if it takes NT a few minutes to check for duplicate domain names.

## Installing NT Workstation

To add a computer to a domain, you must first install NT Workstation 4.0 on your PDC2, as directed in Exercise 2.3. Figure 2.5 illustrates the partitioning and operating systems that will be installed on your computers. Your computers will dual-boot to different operating systems; this way you can use a minimum of equipment and still simulate an enterprise environment. NT Server will be installed on the C: partition and NT Workstation will be on the D: partition. After you complete Exercise 2.3 you will boot PDC2 as NT Workstation and add it to DOMAIN1.

**FIGURE 2.5**

COMPUTER2's
Configuration

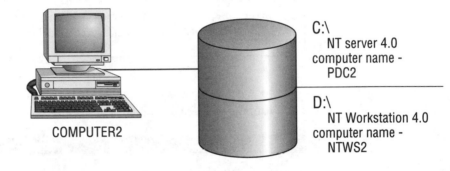

COMPUTER2

C:\
NT server 4.0
computer name -
PDC2

D:\
NT Workstation 4.0
computer name -
NTWS2

---

**EXERCISE 2.3**

### Installing NT Workstation

**1.** Boot your computer to DOS.

**2.** From the DOS prompt, enter **x:\i386>WINNT** (where *x* is the CD-ROM's drive letter). The Windows NT Setup screen will appear and will ask you where the Windows NT files are located. By default the files are in the directory from where you ran WINNT. Press Enter to continue.

**3.** Next, the WINNT program will create the three NT boot floppies (use three of the high density blank diskettes for this step). They will be used to start the installation and provide the storage device drivers for your computer. Please note the order in which the diskettes will be created: Windows NT Workstation Setup Disk #3, Windows NT Workstation Setup Disk #2, and Windows NT Workstation Setup Boot Disk #1. After the floppies are created, the NT Workstation Setup Boot Disk is already in the floppy drive, and all you need to do is press Enter to reboot. The computer will boot to the Windows NT Setup screen. It may take a few minutes to load the necessary setup files.

**4.** When prompted, insert Windows NT Workstation Setup Disk #2 and press Enter. At this point more files will be copied and the Windows NT kernel will load.

**5.** The Welcome to Setup screen will appear. To continue setting up Windows NT Workstation, press Enter.

**6.** NT will now attempt to detect your mass storage devices. Press Enter to continue.

**7.** When prompted, insert Windows NT Workstation Setup Disk #3 and press Enter.

**8.** You will see any storage devices that the setup program has recognized on your computer. If this list is correct press Enter. If this list is not correct, choose S and provide the driver for your mass storage device. (If you have a SCSI drive, then you will only see your SCSI controller.) At this point the installation program will also install the drivers for the file systems that NT supports, FAT and NTFS. The appropriate device drivers for your computer will also be installed.

**9.** The license agreement screen will now appear. This is a new screen with NT 4.0. Page down until you have read the entire agreement and press F8 to accept it.

**10.** The next screen will display the hardware and software components that have been detected on your computer. The list should look something like this:

- **Computer**: Standard PC

- **Display**: Auto Detect

- **Keyboard**: XT, AT, or Enhanced Keyboard

- **Keyboard Layout**: US

- **Pointing Device**: Microsoft Serial Mouse

- **No Changes**: The above list matches my computer.

If this information is correct press Enter.

**11.** The Setup program will now ask on which drive you want the NT system files installed. Choose the D: partition and press Enter. It is important that you choose D:, so that you don't accidentally overwrite the NT Server's files. The next screen will ask you how to partition your drive. Select "leave the current file system intact (no changes)" and press Enter.

**12.** Install NT Workstation in \WINNT.WKS. Press Enter to continue.

**13.** The NT Workstation Setup screen informs you that the setup program will examine your hard disk(s) for corruption. Press Enter to continue.

**14.** The NT Workstation Setup program will now copy the NT system files. This may take a few minutes.

**15.** After the file copy is complete you will be prompted to restart your computer. Remove any floppies and press Enter.

**16.** Your computer will restart and NT Workstation will load.

**17.** The Windows NT Setup screen will appear. To begin Phase 1 of the installation, "Gathering information about your computer," click Next.

**18.** The Setup Options screen will appear, and you will be prompted for the type of setup you prefer. Choose Typical and click Next.

**19.** You will now be prompted to personalize the installation. Type your name and organization.

**20.** Next you will be prompted to type in the registration CD-KEY. After you type in the CD-KEY, click Next.

**21.** Type in your computer name. Choose whatever name you want, however it will be referred to as **NTWS2** throughout the exercises. Click Next to continue.

**22.** Now specify an administrator account password. This must be 14 characters or less. You will need to type the password and re-type it in the confirm password box. You might want to leave this blank because this is only a practice machine. Click Next.

**23.** When prompted to create an Emergency Repair Disk, choose Yes and click Next.

**24.** The Windows NT Components screen appears, choose "install the most common components" and click Next.

**25.** Phase 2 of the installation "Installing NT Networking" is now ready to begin. Click Next to continue.

**26.** The NT Workstation Setup screen will now ask you how your computer should participate on the network. Select "this computer will participate on a network" then select "wired to the network" and click Next.

**27.** NT setup will now search for your network adapter. Click Start Search, and setup will try to detect your network adapter. After setup finds your adapter, click Next.

**28.** The network protocols screen will appear. Keep the default selection of TCP/IP and click Next.

**29.** Click Next to install your network components.

**30.** The network card setup screen will appear. You will be prompted to verify the hardware configuration for your card. If the information on the card setup screen is correct, click Continue. If this information is not correct, modify the options as required and click Continue.

**31.** Because we chose to install TCP/IP you will now be prompted to configure TCP/IP. You will get the following message: "If there is a DHCP server, TCP/IP can be configured dynamically to provide an IP address. If you are not sure, ask your system administrator. Do you wish to use DHCP?" Choose No.

**32.** The setup program will now copy files related to the networking components you have chosen.

**33.** The IP address configuration screen will appear. Click the "Specify an IP address" option. Choose:

- **IP Address:** 131.200.2.3

- **Subnet Mask:** 255.255.255.0

- **Default Gateway:** leave blank

Click OK.

**34.** You will now be prompted to click Next in order to start the network.

**35.** Now, you will supply your computer's name and the networking model to which the computer will be installed. Confirm your computer name and select WORK-GROUP under "make this computer a member of." Use the default workgroup name of WORKGROUP and click Next.

**36.** Now the third and final phase of setup begins, and you will see the Finishing Setup screen. Click Finish, and the setup program will complete some configuration information.

---

**37.** The next installation screen will prompt you for Date/Time properties. NT will pick up the date and time from your computer's CMOS information. The time zone will default to Greenwich Mean Time, so select the correct setting for your time zone. After you provide this information, click Close.

**38.** Next, NT will detect your video adapter. If the correct video driver appears, choose OK. If the correct video driver does not appear, you can customize it at this point.

**39.** Select the Test button to test your display. Click OK to set and test your video driver; this will take five seconds. NT will ask, "Did you see the test bitmap properly?" If the display is correct, select Yes. Select OK to save your settings. Click OK again to close the Display Settings window.

**40.** NT will now complete copying the NT system files. When the file copy is complete, you will be prompted to insert a floppy to become the Emergency Repair Disk. Insert a floppy and click OK. Finally, remove any floppies, and reboot your computer. NT Workstation should now be installed.

# Joining a Domain

N CHAPTER 1, "Planning a Domain Model in the Enterprise Environment," I defined the workgroup model and the domain model. Windows NT Workstation can be installed into a workgroup or a domain. If you install NT Workstation into a workgroup, you can always move it to a domain, and doing so provides more centralized administration.

In order for a computer to join a domain, you must create the computer's account. You can create a computer account in two ways—from the domain controller or from NT Workstation. I will cover both options in more detail in the following subsections.

Once a computer joins a domain, the drop-down list in the Logon Information dialog box will display two choices, workgroup and domain. Here the user decides to which they will log on.

## Creating a Computer Account from a Domain Controller

To install a computer from a domain controller, you must be logged on as a user who is a member of the ADMINISTRATORS group, or as a user who has the "add workstations to the domain" system right. System rights will be covered in more detail in Chapter 3, "User and Group Management." At the domain controller, you will use the Server Manager Utility to add the computer account to the domain. I think of this as the pre-authorization method. Now when the user goes to join the domain from NT Workstations Control Panel ➤ Network box, all they have to do is specify the domain and they are in.

In Exercise 2.4, you will create a computer account, in order to join a domain. For successful completion of this exercise, your computers should be set up as shown in Figure 2.6.

**FIGURE 2.6**

The Exercise 2.4 computer setup

← Your 2nd computer should now be booted to NT Workstation

**EXERCISE 2.4**

### Creating a Computer Account from a Domain Controller

The following steps should be completed from PDC1.

**1.** Click the Start menu ➤ Programs ➤ Administrative Tools (common) ➤ Server Manager.

**2.** Select Computer ➤ Add to Domain.

**3.** Click NT Workstation or Server and type **NTWS2** in the computer name dialog box.

**4.** Click Close in the Add Computer to Domain dialog box. Your computer should now be displayed through Server Manager.

The following steps should be completed from NTWS2.

**5.** Click Start menu ➣ Settings ➣ Control Panel ➣ Network.

**6.** From the identification tab, click Change.

**7.** Under the "member of" section click DOMAIN, and type in your domain name (example, **DOMAIN1**). Click OK.

**8.** A dialog box will now appear and state "welcome to the DOMAIN1 domain." Click OK.

**9.** You will now be prompted to shut down and restart your computer so that the settings will take effect. Click Yes to restart your computer.

## Creating a Computer Account from NT Workstation

You can also create a computer account from NT Workstation. This method skips the "pre-authorization" used in creating a computer account from a domain controller. Because, in this method, the computer account is not created through Server Manager, you need to know an administrative account and password when joining the domain through Control Panel ➣ Network.

This method of joining a domain is less desirable because you do not want to give your users administrative names and passwords (for security reasons).

In Exercise 2.5, you will remove your computer from the domain, so that in Exercise 2.6 you can create a computer account from NT Workstation.

EXERCISE 2.5

### Removing a Computer from a Domain

**1.** Click the Start menu ➣ Programs ➣ Administrative Tools (common) ➣ Server Manager.

**2.** Highlight NTWS2 ➣ Select Computer ➣ Remove from Domain.

**3.** You will see a message stating "Removing NTWS2 from the domain will render it incapable of authenticating domain logons until it is added to another domain," and asking, "Are you sure you want to remove NTWS2 from the DOMAIN1 domain?" Click Yes.

**4.** You will receive a confirmation dialog box stating that NTWS2 was successfully removed from the domain.

The following steps should be completed from NTWS2.

**5.** Click the Start menu ➤ Settings ➤ Control Panel ➤ Network.

**6.** From the identification tab, click Change.

**7.** Under the "member of" section click WORKGROUP, and type in your workgroup name as **WORKGROUP**. Click OK.

**8.** A dialog box will now appear and state "Warning, removing this computer from DOMAIN1 domain will result in the loss of access by domain user accounts. Are you sure you want to remove this computer from this domain?" Click Yes.

**9.** You will see a Welcome to the WORKGROUP workgroup dialog box. Click OK. Click Close.

**10.** You will be prompted to shut down and restart your computer so that the settings will take effect. Click Yes to restart your computer.

## Creating a Computer Account from an NT Workstation

Complete the following steps from NTWS2.

**1.** Click the Start menu ➤ Settings ➤ Control Panel ➤ Network.

**2.** From the identification tab, click Change.

**3.** Under the "member of" section click DOMAIN, and type in your domain name (example, **DOMAIN1**). Select the Create a Computer Account in the Domain box. Under the administrator heading type in the administrator name and password. Click OK.

**4.** A dialog box will appear stating, "Welcome to the DOMAIN1 domain." Click OK. Then click Close.

**5.** You will now be prompted to shut down and restart your computer so that the settings will take effect. Click Yes to restart your computer.

# Implementing Trust Relationships

N CHAPTER 1 you learned what a trust was and how (in theory) a trust works. In this section you will learn how to implement a trust. You will start out by implementing a one-way trust, then by implementing a two-way trust.

In Figure 2.7, you will see user ED in DOMAIN1 who wants to access a resource in DOMAIN2; this makes DOMAIN1 "trusted" and DOMAIN2 "trusting."

**FIGURE 2.7**

Implementing a one-way trust

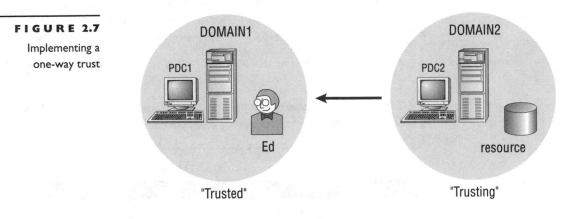

In Exercise 2.7 you will implement this trust relationship. Exercise 2.7 assumes that both of your computers have been booted to NT Server.

---

**EXERCISE 2.7**

### Implementing a One-Way Trust

Complete the following steps from PDC1.

**1.** Click the Start menu ➤ Programs ➤ Administrative Tools (common) ➤ User Manager for Domains.

**2.** Select Policies ➤ Trust Relationships.

---

**EXERCISE 2.7 (CONTINUED FROM PREVIOUS PAGE)**

**3.** The Trust Relationship dialog box will appear. In the Trusting domains box, click Add. The Trusting Domains dialog box will appear. For Trusting Domain, type in **DOMAIN2**. Type in a password of **XYZ** and re-type the password to confirm it. Click OK.

Complete the following steps from PDC2.

**4.** Click the Start menu ➢ Programs ➢ Administrative Tools (common) ➢ User Manager for Domains.

**5.** Select Policies ➢ Trust Relationships.

**6.** The Trust Relationship dialog box will appear. In the Trusted domains box, click ADD. The Add Trusted Domains dialog box will appear. For Trusted Domain, type in **DOMAIN1**. Type in a password of **XYZ**. Click OK.

**7.** A confirmation dialog box will appear stating, "Trust relationship with DOMAIN1 successfully established." The one-way trust is now complete. Click OK.

---

To establish a two-way trust, you go through the same steps, but you reverse the "trusted" and the "trusting" domains. Figure 2.8 shows the two-way trust relationship.

**FIGURE 2.8**

Two-way trust implementation

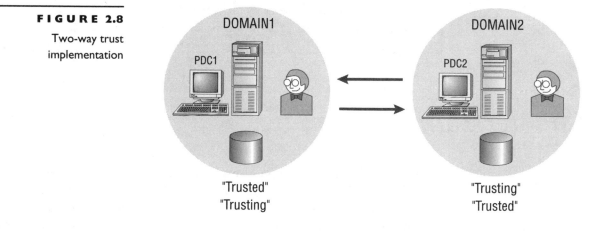

In Exercise 2.8 you will complete a two-way trust.

---

**EXERCISE 2.8**

### Implementing a Two-Way Trust

Complete the following steps from PDC2.

**1.** Click the Start menu ➤ Programs ➤ Administrative Tools (common) ➤ User Manager for Domains.

**2.** Select Policies ➤ Trust Relationships.

**3.** The Trust Relationship dialog box will appear. In the Trusting domains box, click Add. The Trusting Domains dialog box will appear. For Trusting Domain, type in **DOMAIN1**. Type in a password of **XYZ** and re-type the password to confirm it. Click OK.

Complete the following steps from PDC1.

**4.** Click the Start menu ➤ Programs ➤ Administrative Tools (common) ➤ User Manager for Domains.

**5.** Select Policies ➤ Trust Relationships.

**6.** The Trust Relationship dialog box will appear. In the Trusted domains box, click Add. The Add Trusted Domains dialog box will appear. For Trusted Domain, type in **DOMAIN2**. Type in a password of **XYZ**. Click OK.

**7.** A confirmation dialog box will appear stating "Trust relationship with DOMAIN2 successfully established." The two-way trust is now complete. Click OK.

---

# Chapter Summary

N CHAPTER 2 you learned pre-planning issues to address prior to installing Windows NT Server. You also learned that the NT Server installation occurs in four phases: Phase 0 prepares NT Server for installation; Phase 1 gathers information about your computer; Phase 2 sets up NT networking; and

Phase 3 finishes setup. Chapter 2 also prepared you to complete the exercises in this book and showed you how to install NT Server and NT Workstation. You also learned the two methods for joining a domain. Finally, you learned how to implement one-way and two-way trust relationships.

# Review Questions

1. To create a computer account at a domain controller, which utility do you use?

   **A.** Server Manager

   **B.** Control Panel ➤ Network

   **C.** User Manager for Domains

   **D.** Computer Account Manager

   **E.** License Manager

2. Which utility is used to implement a trust relationship?

   **A.** Server Manager

   **B.** Control Panel ➤ Network

   **C.** User Manager for Domains

   **D.** Computer Account Manager

3. To install NT Server, the minimum requirement for your processor is:

   **A.** 386/16

   **B.** 486/25

   **C.** 486/33

   **D.** 486/100

   **E.** Pentium Processor

**4.** To install NT Server, the minimum requirement for your RAM is:

**A.** 12MB

**B.** 16MB

**C.** 32MB

**D.** 64MB

**5.** The NT 4.0 partitions that can be created during the WINNT installation process are (choose all that apply):

**A.** FAT

**B.** HPFS

**C.** NTFS

**D.** CDFS

**6.** If you were concerned about local security, which file system would be your best choice?

**A.** FAT

**B.** HPFS

**C.** NTFS

**D.** CDFS

**7.** If you wanted to dual-boot to NT Server and Windows 95, which file system(s) would be supported on both platforms? Choose all that apply.

**A.** FAT

**B.** HPFS

**C.** NTFS

**8.** The two licensing modes NT Server can use are:

**a.** _____

**b.** _____

**9.** The protocols you can select during NT installation are:

    **a.** _____

    **b.** _____

    **c.** _____

**10.** The two methods of joining a domain are:

    **a.** _____

    **b.** _____

# User and Group Management

CHAPTER

3

N CHAPTER 2, "Installing and Maintaining NT 4.0," you learned how to install NT Server in a domain. In this chapter you will learn how to manage the users and groups in your domain through the User Manager for Domains, a utility through the Administrative Tools group which is automatically installed on NT Server domain controllers. You can also manage your domain's security policies. In this chapter you will learn about the following:

- Creating, copying, renaming, and deleting user accounts

- Managing user properties

- Creating and deleting local and global groups

- Managing local and global groups

- Security policy management

# User Account Management

O NE OF THE fundamental tasks in network management is creating user accounts. Each user who requires network access should have their own account. The user account is the combination of a user account name and a password. Each user has permissions to access certain network resources. These permissions are based on the user's account and the groups with which the user is associated.

In this section you will learn how to create and manage a user account and to manage the properties of a user account.

# Creating a New User Account

Creating user accounts is a fundamental task in any network environment, and in NT you use the User Manager for Domains utility to accomplish it.

*In order to create a user account, you must be a member of the DOMAIN ADMINS group or a member of the ACCOUNT OPERATORS group. I will cover these groups in more detail later in this chapter.*

When creating a user account, the one required step is to provide a logon name. The other options you encounter when creating a new user account concern specific controls over your user account's logon environment. For example, you might want your users to log on during the work week, but not on weekends. I will cover these account management options in detail in this section.

*When you create a user account, you are actually creating an account security ID (SID). The username is a property of the SID. For ease-of-use, you see the user name as opposed to the SID. For example, it is easier to administer BUD than it is to administer S-1-5-21-1639788-1291022950-1609722162-500, which is Bud's SID.*

---

### Choosing a Network Naming Convention

Before you begin to create your user accounts, choose a naming convention. A naming convention is a consistent naming format. Naming conventions allow you to manage your network consistently. For example, you don't want to have users KATIE and JSMITH on the same domain because these names utilize two different naming conventions, first name and first initial-last name. Instead, you want DONALDK and SMITHJ. The following are some examples of naming conventions:

- Last name and first initial: SMITHJ

- First initial, middle initial, and last name: JMSMITH

- Employee ID: 1970

While this chapter focuses on user account management, you might also want to establish naming conventions for other resources such as printers and file servers. Consistent naming conventions make it easier for users to access resources and for administrators to manage resources.

Normally, in a production environment you will not use first names as logon account names. This is especially true in an enterprise environment where you might have 100 Johns. But because we are in a simple test environment, we will use first names.

Exercise 3.1 presents the basic steps for creating new user accounts. These accounts will be required for the other exercises in this chapter.

*Perform the exercises in this Chapter from PDC1 while logged on as ADMINISTRATOR.*

---

**EXERCISE 3.1**

### Creating a New User Account

**1.** Click Start ➢ Programs ➢ Administrative Tools (common) ➢ User Manager for Domains.

**2.** Click the User Menu ➢ New User. The New User dialog box appears, as shown below.

| New User | | |
|---|---|---|
| Username: | | Add |
| Full Name: | | Cancel |
| Description: | | Help |
| Password: | | |
| Confirm Password: | | |
| ☑ User Must Change Password at Next Logon | | |
| ☐ User Cannot Change Password | | |
| ☐ Password Never Expires | | |
| ☐ Account Disabled | | |

Groups  Profile  Hours  Logon To  Account  Dialin

**3.** Type in the Username, **KEVIN**.

**4.** Uncheck the User Must Change Password at Next Logon checkbox.

**5.** Click Add.

**6.** Add the users KAITLIN, RICK, and BUD by repeating steps 2-5.

*In an enterprise environment, you might have to create hundreds of user accounts at a time. Instead of using User Manager for Domains, consider using the* NET USER *command line utility within a batch file. Refer to Windows NT Help for specific usage of the* NET USER *command.*

As you saw in Exercise 3.1, there are several additional user configuration options available in the New User dialog box. All of the configuration options are explained in Table 3.1.

| **TABLE 3.1**<br>New User dialog<br>box options | OPTION | OPTION DEFINED |
|---|---|---|
| | Username | This is the only required field within this box. Choose names that are consistent with your naming conventions. Example: JSMITH |
| | Full Name | Used to provide more information. Example: John Smith |
| | Description | Used to provide optional information, which might include title, department, or location. Example: Sales |
| | Password and Confirm Password | Initial password to be assigned to user. For security purposes, it is not a good idea to use readily available information, such as logon ID. Instead, consider using random passwords that are supplied to the user prior to their first logon. |
| | User Must Change Password at Next Logon | Checked by default. The first time a user logs on, this option forces them to change their password. |
| | User Cannot Change Password | This option prevents a user from changing their password. It is useful for accounts like GUEST or accounts that are shared by more than one user. If this option is checked, a member of the ADMINISTRATORS group must change the user's password. |

| | OPTION | OPTION DEFINED |
|---|---|---|
| **TABLE 3.1** New User dialog box options (continued) | Password Never Expires | This option is useful for service accounts, the passwords of which you do not need to change. |
| | Account Disabled | Disables an account, making it unaccessible. This is useful for template accounts or accounts that are not currently being used. |
| | Account Locked Out | This box is grayed out (so that it is not visible in Exercise 3.1) unless the account has been locked. Account lockout will be covered later in this chapter. |

*User names can be up to 20 characters. It is easiest to use alphanumeric characters, but you can include other characters. You cannot, however, include the following characters: " / \ [ ] : ; | , + * ? < >*

*After you have created the user account, you will notice that the Password and Confirm Password text boxes in the New User dialog box are filled in with 14 asterisks. This makes the password more secure. By looking at this screen, there is no way to tell how long a user account password is.*

## Disabling and Deleting User Accounts

If a user account is no longer needed, you can and should disable or delete it. User accounts that are not being used pose a potential security threat because an intruder could break into your network through the inactive account. For example, after inheriting a network, I was doing some routine maintenance and noticed a user account that was part of the DOMAIN ADMINS group. The user had left the company months before, but the account was still active. We were lucky no one had broken into our network. I deleted the account.

The difference between a disabled account and a deleted account is that a disabled account can be reactivated at a later date. A deleted account is permanently erased. It is important to be sure you will never need an account again before you delete it. As noted earlier in this chapter, each user account has an associated security ID (SID). When you delete a user, you delete the associated SID and it's gone forever. Therefore, if you think you might need the account in the future, you should disable it as opposed to deleting it.

### Disabling an Account

When an account is disabled, it cannot be accessed. You would disable an account if it was not going to be used for a period of time or if it was being used as a template account. I will cover template accounts in more detail in the "Copying a User Account" section.

Here's another reason you might want to disable an account. Let's say you have an accounting manager, Penny, who's leaving the company. Your first reaction might be to delete her user account. When a replacement is found, you would then add that user's account and add them to the groups to which the accounting manager needs to belong. It's easier to just disable Penny's account, and when the replacement is found, rename the user account and assign a new password. Penny's account would already be configured properly for the newcomer, saving you some work.

### Deleting an Account

If you are sure that a user account will never be needed again, you can delete it. The only accounts that cannot be deleted are the built-in accounts, ADMINISTRATOR and GUEST. (However, these accounts can be renamed.)

In Exercise 3.2, you will disable one of the users created in Exercise 3.1, and then in Exercise 3.3, you will delete that same user account.

---

**EXERCISE 3.2**

### Disabling a User Account

You will start this exercise by disabling BUD's user account.

**1.** Click Start ➢ Programs ➢ Administrative Tools (common) ➢ User Manager for Domains.

**2.** Double click User BUD.

**3.** In the User dialog box check the Account Disabled option.

**4.** Bud's account is now disabled.

---

---

**EXERCISE 3.3**

### Deleting a User Account

Next, you will delete BUD's account.

**1.** Select Start ➣ Programs ➣ Administrative Tools (common) ➣ User Manager for Domains.

**2.** Click User BUD.

**3.** Click the User Menu ➣ Delete.

**4.** You will receive a warning message letting you know that once you delete this user account, it will be gone forever, click OK.

**5.** One last chance to change your mind! Click Yes to delete BUD.

---

## Renaming User Accounts

Once an account has been created, you can rename it at anytime. Renaming a user allows the user to retain all associations from the previous name. The name is actually just a property of the SID. There are several reasons why you might need to rename an account.

- The user has changed their name, for example through marriage

- The username was spelled incorrectly

- The user has left and a new user has taken their place

In Exercise 3.4, you will assume that KAITLIN now wants her logon ID to be KATIE.

*Renaming a user account does not change any "hard-coded" names, such as home directories. Those changes will have to be implemented manually.*

---

**EXERCISE 3.4**

### Renaming a User

**1.** Select Start ➤ Programs ➤ Administrative Tools (common) ➤ User Manager for Domains.

**2.** Click User KAITLIN.

**3.** Click the User Menu ➤ Rename.

**4.** The dialog box will prompt you with Change To:. Type **KATIE** and click OK.

---

## Managing User Properties

You can manage the following properties through the User Manager for Domains:

- Groups associated with the user

- Users profile information

- Logon hours

- Logon workstations

- Account information

- Dial-in information

To manage a user account's properties, you can either double-click on the user, or select User Menu ➤ Properties. The User dialog box will appear.

### Groups Associated with the User

In NT, you normally manage groups as opposed to users because it is much more efficient. One of the properties associated with a user account is their group memberships. You can associate a user with a group through the group button in the New User dialog box. Later in this chapter you will learn that you can also add members to a group by managing a group's properties. For now, Exercise 3.5 will show you how to associate a user with a group.

---

**EXERCISE 3.5**

### Associating a User with a Group

First, you will create a group.

**1.** Select Start ➢ Programs ➢ Administrative Tools (common) ➢ User Manager for Domains.

**2.** Click the User Menu ➢ New Global Group.

**3.** In the Group Name dialog box, type **SALES** and click OK.

Now you will associate Kevin with the SALES group.

**4.** In the User Manager for Domains window, double-click KEVIN to open his User Properties.

**5.** Click the Groups box and in the Not Member of box select SALES and click Add.

**6.** Click OK to save the change and exit the Groups box. Click OK to exit the User Properties dialog box.

Kevin is now a member of the SALES global group.

---

### User Profile Information

The user environment profile option allows you to customize a user's environment. Through the user profile you can set the following:

- User profile path
- Logon script name
- Home directory

Figure 3.1 shows the User Environment Profile dialog box. Each of the options available through this box are defined in the following subsections.

**USER PROFILES** User Profiles contain information regarding the NT environment. Profiles can be used by an individual or shared between users. Examples of profile settings include the desktop appearance, program groups, and screen colors. Profiles are fairly complex, and Chapter 5, "Policies and Profiles," is dedicated to this topic.

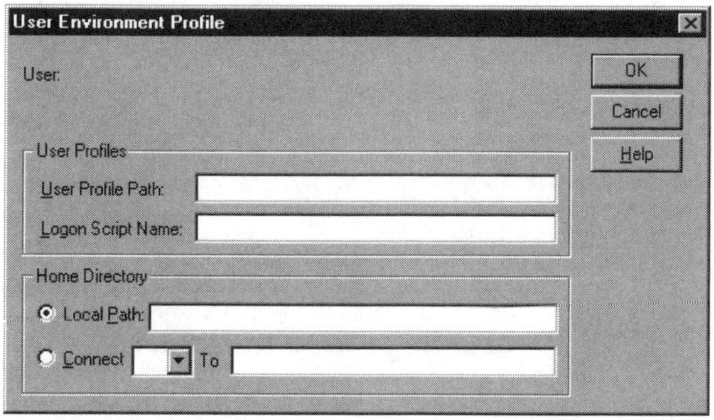

FIGURE 3.1

The User Environment
Profile dialog box

```
User Environment Profile                                    [X]
 User:                                          ┌──────────┐
                                                │    OK    │
                                                └──────────┘
 ┌─User Profiles─────────────────────────────┐  ┌──────────┐
 │ User Profile Path:  [                    ] │  │  Cancel  │
 │                                            │  └──────────┘
 │ Logon Script Name:  [                    ] │  ┌──────────┐
 └────────────────────────────────────────────  │   Help   │
 ┌─Home Directory────────────────────────────┐  └──────────┘
 │ ⦿ Local Path: [                          ] │
 │ ○ Connect  [  ▼] To [                    ] │
 └────────────────────────────────────────────┘
```

**LOGON SCRIPTS** Logon scripts are files that will run every time the user logs on to the network. They are usually batch files, but can also be executable files. You might use logon scripts for compatibility with non-NT clients. For example, if you have DOS clients, you could use logon scripts to define the clients' network connections every time they log on. Logon scripts can be customized to a single user or can be shared by many users. In the User Environment Profile dialog box, you assign a logon script by typing in the logon script's file name.

The authenticating server will look for the logon script in the NETLOGON directory of the authenticating server. The NETLOGON directory is usually on the \WINNT\SYSTEM32\REPL\IMPORT\SCRIPTS directory. Because a PDC or a BDC can authenticate a user, they require logon scripts. One way to manage logon scripts is to place them on the PDC and then replicate them to the BDC; this ensures that the logon script will be on the server that authenticates the user. I will cover directory replication in greater detail in Chapter 7, "NT Domain Management."

**HOME DIRECTORIES** Users can store their personal files in special directories called *home directories*. You can create home directories on the user's local drive or on a shared network directory. When creating a home directory, use the variable %USERNAME% in the directory path. By using this variable the system will substitute the user's logon name for the %USERNAME% variable. One advantage to using variables is that you only have to specify the variable once, making system administration easier because you don't have to type each user's logon name.

*If you use logon names of greater than eight characters, MS-DOS clients will not be able to access their home directories; this is a limitation of the FAT file system.*

In Exercise 3.6 you will create a home directory that user RICK will access from a network share.

---

**EXERCISE 3.6**

### Creating Home Directories

The first thing you must do before creating home directories is create a network share where the home directories will reside.

**1.** Select Start ➢ Programs ➢ Windows NT Explorer.

**2.** Click the C: drive. Select File ➢ New ➢ Folder.

**3.** In the New Folder box type **HOME.**

**4.** Select File ➢ Sharing ➢ Shared As and confirm the share name as HOME. Click OK.

Next you will set up the home directory.

**1.** Select Start ➢ Programs ➢ Administrative Tools (common) ➢ User Manager for Domains.

**2.** Double-click RICK.

**3.** Click Profile.

**4.** Under Home Directory click Connect. Choose drive letter Z:. In the To box type **\\PDC1\HOME\%USERNAME%.**

**5.** Click OK.

**6.** Click Profile again. You will notice that the %USERNAME% variable has been replaced by RICK.

**7.** Close the User Manager for Domains.

Finally, you will confirm that the home directory was created.

**1.** Select Start ➢ Programs ➢ Windows NT Explorer.

**2.** Click the HOME directory under C: and verify that you created the home directory for Rick.

### Logon Hours

Logon hours specify when a user is able to log on to the domain and access domain servers. Users are allowed to log on 24 hours a day by default, but you may limit this. You might want to limit your logon hours for security purposes or so that users do not log on during backup hours.

In Exercise 3.7, you will configure KATIE so that she is not able to log on between 12:00AM and 2:00AM Monday through Friday.

---

**EXERCISE 3.7**

### Limiting Logon Hours

**1.** Click Start ➤ Programs ➤ Administrative Tools (common) ➤ User Manager for Domains.

**2.** Double-click KATIE to open the Logon Hours dialog box, as shown below.

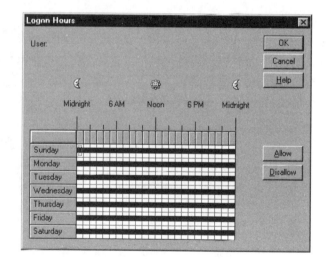

**3.** Click Hours.

**4.** Position the cursor on Monday Midnight. Each box represents one hour, so while holding your primary mouse button, drag the cursor one position to the right and down to Friday. Click Disallow, and the boxes should be cleared. Click OK. Click OK again.

---

**Logon Workstations**

The Logon Workstations dialog box allows you to specify workstation(s) from where a user can log on. This dialog box can be accessed by clicking Logon To in the New User dialog box. You have two options to choose from in the Logon Workstations dialog box:

- User May Log On To All Workstations

- User May Log On To These Workstations

By default a user can log on to all workstations.

When you choose the User May Log On To These Workstations option, you are able to specify the computer name from which the user is allowed to log on. Figure 3.2 shows a Logon Workstations dialog box in which user RICK has been restricted so that he is only able to log on from the PDC1 machine.

**FIGURE 3.2**

The Logon Workstations dialog box

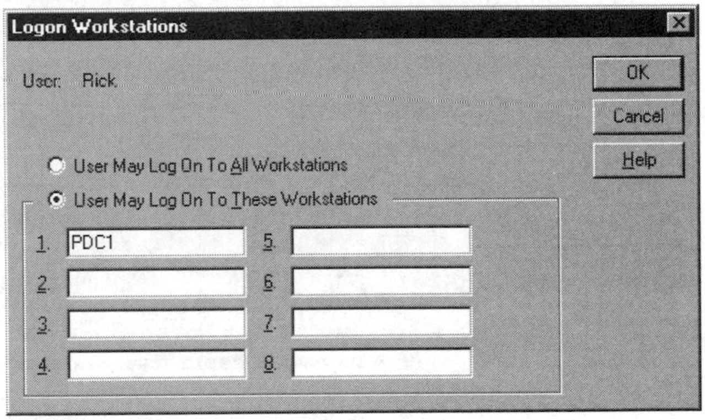

In Exercise 3.8, you will use Logon Workstation restrictions to allow Rick to only log on from PDC1.

---

**EXERCISE 3.8**

### Setting Logon Workstation Restrictions

**1.** Select Start ➤ Programs ➤ Administrative Tools (common) ➤ User Manager for Domains.

**2.** Double-click RICK.

**3.** Click Logon To.

**4.** Click User May Log On To These Workstations.

**5.** In box 1., type **PDC1**. Click OK

**6.** In the User Properties dialog box, click OK.

---

### Account Information

The Account Information dialog box, shown in Figure 3.3, allows you to specify the account type and when it will expire. Access this box by clicking Account in the User Properties dialog box.

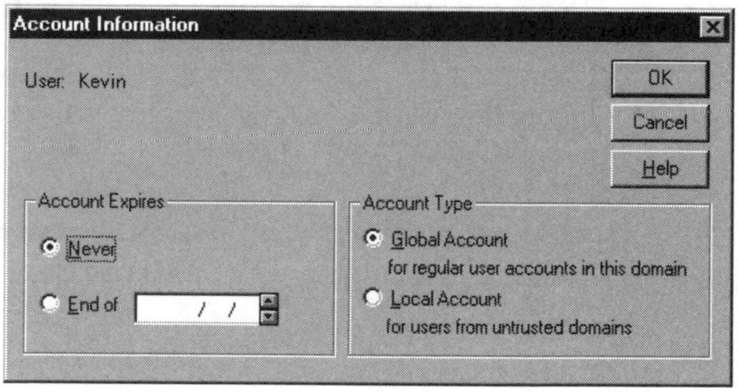

**FIGURE 3.3**

The Account Information dialog box

There are two options for account expiration: never (the default option) or a specified end date. By choosing the latter option, you can specify a date when an account will be deactivated. You might use this option if you were in an educational environment and you wanted the students' accounts to expire on the last day of class. You might also use this option if you had contract workers with fixed contract dates and you wanted their accounts to expire on their last day of work.

There are two options for account type as well: global and local. The global account is a regular user account within a domain; this is the default account that is created when you add a new user. The local account is in the local database as opposed to a domain user in the domain database.

You should rarely, if ever, need to create local accounts. The following example highlights why you might want to use local accounts. Let's say you are a user in Domain A and you need to access resources in Domain B. Domain A and Domain B have no trust relationship. In order to access resources in Domain B you can create a local account with the same name and password as your account in Domain A. Creating local accounts leads to the problems inherent in the workgroup network model covered in Chapter 1, "Planning a Domain Model."

### Dialin Information

The Dialin Information dialog box is used to grant users permissions pertaining to dial-up networking. Access this box by clicking Dialin in the New User Properties dialog box. Dial-up networking is a complex topic, and I will cover it in greater detail in Chapter 14, "Remote Access Service."

## Managing User Properties for Multiple User Accounts

So far we have looked at managing individual user properties. You might want to modify multiple users at once. In Exercise 3.9, you will create three new users, LARRY, MOE, and CURLY, and you will manage all three of them.

*When modifying multiple users, use the Shift key to select multiple contiguous users. Use the Control key to select multiple users who are not contiguous.*

## Using Templates to Copy User Accounts

It can be useful to have template accounts established so that when a user is added you only need to copy the user account from the template account instead of creating a new one from scratch. In Exercise 3.10, you will create a template user account. In Exercise 3.11, you will create new users by copying the template user account.

**EXERCISE 3.9**

## Managing Properties of Multiple Users

**1.** Select Start ➤ Programs ➤ Administrative Tools (common) ➤ User Manager for Domains.

**2.** Click User ➤ New User.

**3.** Type in the user's name—in this exercise, **LARRY**.

**4.** Uncheck the User Must Change Password at Next Logon option.

**5.** Click Add.

**6.** Add the users **MOE** and **CURLY** by repeating steps 2-5. After all three users are created, click Close.

**7.** Click CURLY, and while holding down the Control key, click LARRY and MOE.

**8.** Now that you've selected the three users you want to manage, press Enter.

**9.** The User Properties dialog box appears and you see CURLY, LARRY, and MOE in the Users box.

**10.** Click the Groups box in the New User dialog box, and in the Not Members of box select SALES and click Add. Click OK.

**11.** Click the Profile box, and under Home Directory click the Local Path radio button. For path specify `C:\USERS\%USERNAME%`. Click OK.

**12.** Click Hours. Deselect all hours for Sunday and Saturday. Click OK.

**13.** Click Account, and under Account Expires, select End of. For End of date, pick one month from today and click OK.

**14.** From the User Properties dialog box, click OK.

All three users' properties have now been edited.

*Consider placing a # sign in front of your template names. This will force the template accounts to be placed on the top of the user list in User Manager for Domains. It also will help you easily identify which accounts are template accounts.*

**EXERCISE 3.10**

## Creating a Template User Account

**1.** Click Start ➤ Programs ➤ Administrative Tools (common) ➤ User Manager for Domains.

**2.** Click User ➤ New User.

**3.** Type in the template user's name, **#SALES_TEMPLATE**.

**4.** Under Description, type **SALES USER**.

**5.** Check the Password Never Expires option and uncheck the User Must Change Password at Next Logon option.

**6.** Click the Groups box and in the Not Member of box click SALES, and then click Add. Click OK.

**7.** Click the Profile box and click the Local Path radio button. For the path type **c:\users\%USERNAME%**. Click OK.

**8.** Click OK again to create #SALES_TEMPLATE and return to the User Manager for Domains main window.

**EXERCISE 3.11**

## Copying a Template to Create a New User Account

**1.** Click #SALES_TEMPLATE user. Go to User ➤ Copy.

**2.** In the Username box, type in **SALESUSER1**. Uncheck User Must Change Password at Next Logon and Password Never Expires. Click Add. Click Close.

**3.** Now double-click SALESUSER1 to open the User Properties dialog box.

**4.** Click the Groups box and you will see that SALESUSER1 copied the group membership from #SALES_TEMPLATE. Click OK.

**5.** Click the Profile box and notice the home directory has been set to connect drive S: to \\PDC1\HOME\SALESUSER1. Click Add, then click Close.

Now that you have learned to manage user accounts, you will focus in the next section on group management. You will learn the differences between local and global groups and how local and global groups interact with each other.

# Group Management

Agroup is a special account type that includes multiple user accounts. Using group accounts makes NT system administration easier because instead of managing users individually, you can manage the group. For example, if you have 10 salespeople who have the same security requirements, you could create a group called SALES and manage SALES as opposed to managing 10 individual users.

As with user accounts, the Windows NT domain environment uses two kinds of groups: local and global. In this section you will learn what local and global groups are. You will also learn how local and global groups interact with each other in a single domain and in an enterprise environment. The default local and global groups will be defined, and you will learn how to create your own local and global groups.

*Local and global group interaction receives considerable attention in the NT Server in the Enterprise exam. You want to be an expert at this!*

## Local and Global Groups

The concept of local and global groups is often confusing. Local groups reside in a computer's local accounts database, and global groups reside in the domain accounts database. You might be wondering why you need two different types of groups; it's a question I've asked myself. The assumption is that an NT network can have NT Workstations, NT member servers and NT domain controllers. NT Workstations and NT member servers cannot use global groups. In order to manage resources on NT Workstations and NT member servers, you have to use local groups.

**NT Groups and the Security Account Manager**

To understand the difference between local and global groups, you need to understand how the Security Account Manager (SAM) is defined on different NT machines.

As mentioned in Chapter 1, all NT machines have their own SAM. The SAM can be local to a machine or it can be a domain SAM which is shared by all domain controllers. If you use the User Manager for Domains utility, you are managing the domain SAM. If you use the User Manager utility found on NT Workstations and NT member servers you are managing a SAM local to the machine on which you are using User Manager. Table 3.2 lists where SAMs reside and the utilities used to manage them.

| | | | |
|---|---|---|---|
| **TABLE 3.2**<br>SAM locations | **MACHINE TYPE** | **SAM** | **UTILITY TO MANAGE ACCOUNTS** |
| | NT Workstation | local SAM | User Manager |
| | NT member server | local SAM | User Manager |
| | NT PDC | Domain SAM | User Manager for Domains |
| | NT BDC | Domain SAM | User Manager for Domains |

Figure 3.4 shows the type and location of SAM databases that exist within a domain. Notice that the PDC and BDC share the domain SAM and that the member servers and NT Workstations have their own local SAM.

Local groups can be created on NT Workstations and NT Servers configured as member servers or domain controllers. Global groups can only be created on NT domain controllers.

**Local Group Defined**

The following are characteristic of local groups:

- You create local groups in order to grant users permissions to resources or to allow users to perform specific tasks.

- You can create local groups on NT Workstations, NT member servers, or NT domain controllers.

**FIGURE 3.4**

SAM database management

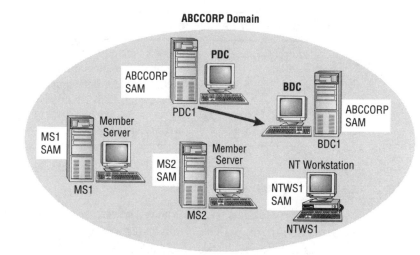

- Local groups can contain users from within their local database, users from within their domain, or global groups from their domain or a trusted domain.

- Local groups remain local to the computer's local SAM database.

### Global Group Defined

The following are characteristic of global groups:

- Global groups logically group together users with similar rights requirements.

- Global groups can only be created on NT Server domain controllers.

- Global groups can only contain users from within their domain.

### Memberships within Local and Global Groups

The question you're probably asking is what groups can contain. Table 3.3 summarizes group memberships within a domain.

| TABLE 3.3 | GROUP TYPE | CAN CONTAIN |
|---|---|---|
| Group memberships within a domain | Local Group | user accounts from the local machine's SAM accounts from the domain's SAM global groups from the domain's SAM global groups from any trusted domains' SAMs |
| | Global Group | user accounts from the domain's SAM |

# Default Local and Global Groups

Microsoft has tried to make it easier for us by pre-defining several local and global groups. The idea is that there are elements common to all networks—for example, backups and administrators. The BACKUP and ADMINISTRATORS groups are pre-defined with all the necessary rights to accomplish backup and administration. All you need to do is plug in the appropriate users to these default groups.

### Default Local Groups

The default local groups that are defined on NT domain controllers are listed in Table 3.4.

| TABLE 3.4 | LOCAL GROUP | DESCRIPTION | INITIAL MEMBERS |
|---|---|---|---|
| Default local groups | ACCOUNT OPERATORS | Members can administer domain users and groups, as well as create, delete, and manage users, local groups, and global groups. | Blank |
| | ADMINISTRATORS | Members have full control to administer all computer and domain operations. Examples include installing OS system and programs, all account management, sharing directories and printers, and managing directories and printers. | ADMINISTRATOR and DOMAIN ADMINS global group |
| | BACKUP OPERATORS | Members have all permissions necessary to back up and restore servers regardless of file and directory permissions. | Blank |

| TABLE 3.4 Default local groups (continued) | LOCAL GROUP | DESCRIPTION | INITIAL MEMBERS |
|---|---|---|---|
| | GUESTS | Contains users who should have guest access to the domain. | DOMAIN GUESTS global group |
| | PRINT OPERATORS | Members can manage the printers within the domain and share and stop sharing printers. | Blank |
| | REPLICATOR | Used for directory replication. | Blank |
| | SERVER OPERATORS | Members can manage the domain servers by sharing and stop sharing resources, formatting server hard disks, logging on locally at servers, backing up and restoring servers, and shutting down servers. | Blank |
| | USERS | Regular domain users | DOMAIN USERS global group |

*NT Workstation does not contain ACCOUNT OPERATORS, PRINT OPERATORS, or SERVER OPERATORS. It does contain a group called POWER USERS, which is not present on NT domain controllers.*

### Default Global Groups

The global groups that are present on NT domain controllers are listed in Table 3.5.

| TABLE 3.5 Default global groups | GLOBAL GROUP | DESCRIPTION | INITIAL MEMBERS |
|---|---|---|---|
| | DOMAIN ADMINS | Members can administer the domain. | ADMINISTRATOR |
| | DOMAIN GUESTS | Members have limited guest access. | GUEST |
| | DOMAIN USERS | Contains ordinary users | All users within domain with exception of GUEST |

*Because NT Workstation does not support global groups, these are all unique to NT Server domain controllers.*

## Special Groups

NT Server also uses special groups, which are not managed like local or global groups. Rather, they are managed by the system. You become a member of special groups by default, or by the type of network activity you engage in. The special groups are defined in table 3.6.

**TABLE 3.6**
Special groups

| SPECIAL GROUP | DESCRIPTION |
|---|---|
| CREATOR OWNER | The user account that created or took ownership of a resource |
| EVERYONE | Includes anyone who can access the computer |
| INTERACTIVE | Members are local to the computer that they are accessing, meaning that they are physically at the computer. |
| NETWORK | A member can be anyone who is accessing the computer from a connected network computer. |

## How Local and Global Groups Work Together

Local and global groups work together. The idea is that you can create a local group on the machine that has a resource you want to access and assign access permissions to the local group. Then you create a global group that allows you to group user accounts with similar needs together. Then you add the global group to the local group.

### A Shortcoming of Using Local Groups Exclusively

To help you understand the need for local and global groups, let's look at the following example. You have a group consisting of three users—Marcia, Jan, and Cindy. You want the group to be responsible for backing up all the machines in your domain. You have already learned that NT Workstation and NT Server configured as a member server can only have local groups. One way to manage the backups is to create a local group called BACKUP on each machine (see Figure 3.5).

FIGURE 3.5

Exclusive use of local groups

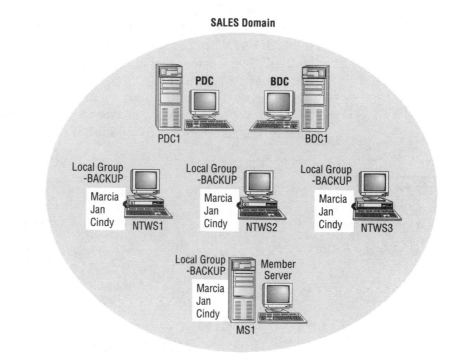

**SALES Domain**

You could then assign the permissions necessary to perform backups to the local group and make Marcia, Jan, and Cindy members of the BACKUP local group. This would accomplish the goal of allowing these three users to back up your workstations. The problem with using local groups exclusively is that, as you add workstations, you need to add Marcia, Jan, and Cindy to the BACKUP local group on each workstation. You would also have administrative overhead if you fired Marcia and replaced her with Greg. At that point, you would have to delete Marcia from each machine's local group and replace her with Greg.

## Global Groups as a Management Tool

The previous example has two shortcomings. Every time you add a new workstation, you will have to add three users to your BACKUP local group. You would also have a problem if you fired Marcia and replaced her with Greg or if you simply added another staff member, Peter. Each local group would have to be modified to show the new group memberships. This could be administration-intensive if you have a large number of workstations.

Using global groups as a management tool allows you to manage workstations more efficiently. In Figure 3.6, you can see that by creating a global group at your PDC, you can add your backup users to a global group called GLOBAL BACKUP. You can then add Marcia, Jan, and Cindy to GLOBAL BACKUP. You would still need a local group at each workstation with the permissions assigned to it to perform backups. The trick is that instead of adding users to the local groups, you add the global group GLOBAL BACKUP. Now you can make membership changes to GLOBAL BACKUP, and they will automatically be reflected at the workstations.

**FIGURE 3.6**

Global groups used as management tools

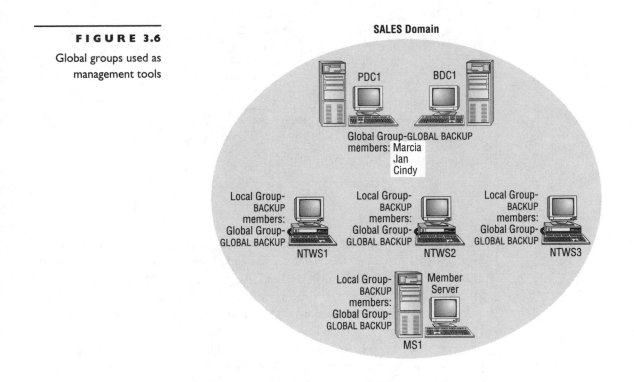

**Using Groups the Microsoft Way**

Microsoft recommends that you use groups as follows:

    **1.** At the resource, create a local group and assign the permissions the local group will need to access the resource.

**2.** At the domain controller, create a global group and add the users who need access to the resource to the global group.

**3.** Add the global group to the local group.

*You will want to chant these steps over and over to yourself. Many of the test questions deal with group management.*

Now that you know how local and global groups work, the next section will teach you how to create local and global groups.

## Creating Local Groups

You can create local groups with the User Manager for Domains utility. You can name your local group anything you want as long as the name is unique in your accounts database. Choose your local group's name carefully, because groups cannot be renamed.

Local groups are represented by a group icon with a computer behind it. Exercise 3.12 provides the steps for creating a local group.

---

**EXERCISE 3.12**

**Creating a Local Group**

**1.** Select Start ➣ Programs ➣ Administrative Tools (common) ➣ User Manager for Domains.

**2.** Click User ➣ New Local Group.

**3.** Type in the group name, **LOCAL SALES**.

**4.** Under description, type **Practice Local Group**.

**5.** For members, click Add (notice you only see global groups and users, local groups aren't listed because you can't add a local group to a local group).

**6.** Select CURLY, LARRY, AND MOE and click Add. Click OK.

**7.** In the New Local Group dialog box, click OK to create the new group.

---

*You can add multiple users to your group at once by holding down the Control key as you select your group's users.*

## Creating Global Groups

As with local groups, global groups are created through User Manager for Domains. As noted earlier, a global group can only be created on a PDC and can only contain user accounts from within its domain database unless you install the client software with the applications to manage the domain from another computer. You can name the global group anything you like, as long as the name is unique. Once the global group is created, it cannot be renamed.

Global groups are represented by a group icon with a globe behind it. Exercise 3.13 provides the steps for creating a global group.

---

**EXERCISE 3.13**

**Creating a Global Group**

1. Select Start ➤ Programs ➤ Administrative Tools (common) ➤ User Manager for Domains.

2. Click User ➤ New Global Group.

3. Type in the group name, **GLOBAL SALES**.

4. Under description, type **Practice Global Group**.

5. Select CURLY, LARRY, AND MOE and click Add. Click OK (notice you only see users from your domain, because a global group can't contain users from other domains or local or global groups).

You have created your new global group.

---

## Deleting Local and Global Groups

To delete a local or global group, all you need to do is select the group from the User Manager for Domains main window and press Delete. You will receive a warning that deleting the group is an irreversible action. You will then have one last chance to confirm the deletion of the group before it's deleted forever.

*You may have noticed this section did not cover renaming a group. It is not possible to rename a group in Windows NT.*

## Managing Groups across Domains

In Chapter 1 you learned that two or more domains can be linked through a trust. Once the trust relationship has been established, you can manage groups and resources across domains in an enterprise environment. In Figure 3.7, you see that the SALESDOM domain contains users who need to access a resource, the APPS server in the CORPDOM.

**FIGURE 3.7**

Group interaction across domains

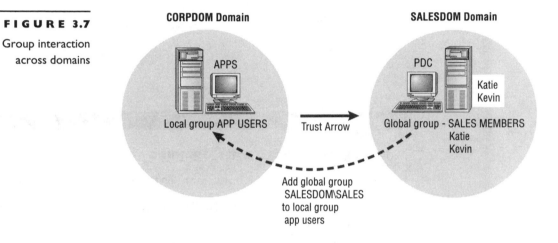

In Figure 3.7, the group interaction across domains would be implemented as follows:

**1.** Users in the SALESDOM domain need to access resources in the CORPDOM domain. Create a trust relationship where CORPDOM trusts SALESDOM.

**2.** At the APPS server in the CORPDOM domain, create a local group and call it APP USERS. Grant the access rights the users will need to access the APPS server's resources. (I cover access rights in detail in Chapter 4.)

**3.** In the SALESDOM domain, create a global group called SALES, and add the users who need to access the APPS server's resources.

**4.** Add the global group SALES to the local group APP USERS on the APPS server.

In Exercise 3.14 you will manage groups across domains. Figure 3.8 displays what Exercise 3.14 will accomplish. You have users Kevin and Katie in DOMAIN1 who want to access a file resource, a network share called DATA in DOMAIN2 on the machine PDC2.

**FIGURE 3.8**

Setup for Exercise 3.14

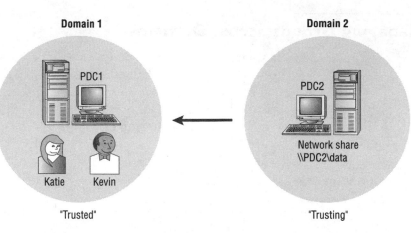

**Domain 1**

PDC1

Katie    Kevin

"Trusted"

**Domain 2**

PDC2

Network share
\\PDC2\data

"Trusting"

---

**EXERCISE 3.14**

## Managing Groups across Domains

For this exercise, both of your machines should be running as NT domain controllers.

**1.** Establish a trust relationship so that the DOMAIN2 domain trusts the DOMAIN1 domain (this should already be completed from Exercise 2.7).

**2.** From PDC2 in DOMAIN2, create a local group called DATAUSERS. Next, assign the necessary permissions the DATAUSERS local group needs to access the file resource. We will skip this step because I won't cover the concept of creating, sharing, and assigning permissions to resources until Chapter 4.

**3.** From PDC1 in DOMAIN1, create a global group called GLOBALDATA, and add Kevin and Katie to the GLOBALDATA global group.

**4.** From PDC2, double-click the DATAUSERS local group. Click Add. At the top of the dialog box, you will see a List Names From box. Choose DOMAIN1 from the list. In the names box click GlobalData and click Add. Click OK. In the Local Group Properties dialog box, click OK again. The global group GLOBALDATA has now been added to the local group DATAUSERS.

# Security Policy Management

THE SECURITY POLICIES used by your domain reflect how the logon/ password requirements will be set, what rights users have to perform system actions, and how you can track selected account-related activities through auditing. The management of these policies is an accounts management issue, not a resource management issue. I will cover resource management in Chapter 4.

Security policy management covers:

- Account Policies

- User Right Policies

- Auditing

The account policies determine password and logon requirements. The user right policies determine the rights that users and groups have when trying to accomplish network tasks. The auditing policy is used to track accounts management. I will cover each of these policies in greater detail in the sections to follow.

## Managing the Account Policy

The account policy controls password policies and determines how to handle unsuccessful logon attempts. The default account policy allows users to have blank passwords. Figure 3.9 shows the default account policies that are used by NT Server in a domain environment. Because the logon name/password is the first level in NT security, you should always require passwords.

Depending on the security requirements of your domain, you can set the account policies as appropriate for your environment. For example, if your environment has average security needs, you might set minimum password length at five characters and force password changes every 60 days. If you are in an environment that requires a higher level of security, you might set minimum password length at 10 characters and force changes every 30 days.

**FIGURE 3.9**

The Account Policy
dialog box

It is important to realize that account policies are set for the domain. This means that if one group only required five-character passwords and another group required 10-character passwords, you would have to choose a number that both groups could use.

Through the account lockout option in the Account Policy dialog box you are able to control, based on unsuccessful logon attempts, when a user account gets locked out. This prevents unauthorized users from logging on illegally by guessing a password after several attempts.

*You cannot customize account policies for individuals or groups. The account policies affect the entire domain.*

There are two main settings in the account policies window:

- Password restrictions
- Account lockout

### Password Restrictions

Password restrictions govern minimum and maximum password age, password length, and password uniqueness. Table 3.7 defines each password restriction.

| **TABLE 3.7**<br>Password restrictions | PASSWORD<br>RESTRICTION | DEFINITION |
|---|---|---|
| | Maximum Password Age | How many days the password is valid. You can choose Password Never Expires or you can choose a set number of days. The range for maximum password age is 1-999 days. |
| | Minimum Password Age | How many days a user must keep a password before it can be changed. You can choose Allow Changes Immediately or you can choose a set number of days. The range for minimum password age is 1-999 days. |
| | Minimum Password Length | The minimum number of characters a password can contain. You can choose Permit Blank Password (not recommended) or you can specify a number between 1-14. |
| | Password Uniqueness | This restriction forces a user to pick new passwords when changing passwords. You can select Do Not Keep Password History or you can have the system keep track of the last 1-24 passwords used. If you selected 10, a user would have to have 10 unique passwords before they could go back to their original password. |

### Account Lockout

Use account lockout to specify how many invalid logon attempts should be tolerated. The account lockout concept is the same as that applied by your bank with regard to your ATM card. If somebody were to steal your ATM card, they wouldn't be able to keep guessing your access code until they got it right. Typically, if you use the card trying three unsuccessful access codes in a row, the ATM machine will keep it, and you have to ask the bank for your card back.

Account lockout works the same way. You can configure account lockout so that after $x$ number of unsuccessful logon attempts within $y$ number of minutes, the account will be locked until the administrator unlocks it or for $z$ number of minutes. The administrator determines the $x$, $y$, and $z$ variables. Table 3.8 defines the account lockout option.

| TABLE 3.8<br>Account lockout options | ACCOUNT<br>LOCKOUT OPTION | DEFINITION |
|---|---|---|
| | No Account Lockout | Default setting, does not use account lockout. |
| | Account Lockout | Enables account lockout. Default values set lockout at 5 bad attempts within 30 minutes. Account remains locked for 30 minutes. |
| | Lockout After | Determines the number of bad logon attempts that can be made before the account locks. Setting can be from 1-999. |
| | Reset Count After | Determines number of minutes between two failed logon attempts. Settings can be from 1-99,999 minutes. |
| | Lockout Duration | Can choose forever, which forces someone from the administrators group to unlock the account, or duration, which allows you to pre-determine the number of minutes the account will be locked. Settings can be from 1-99,999 minutes. |

In Exercise 3.15, you will set account lockout options and have a user exceed the lockout threshold. Then you will learn to unlock an account.

**EXERCISE 3.15**

**Managing Account Lockouts**

**1.** Select Start ➣ Programs ➣ Administrative Tools (common) ➣ User Manager for Domains.

**2.** Click Policies ➣ Account.

**3.** In the bottom half of the screen click the Account lockout button.

**4.** Specify lockout after 3 bad logon attempts.

**5.** Specify reset count after 3 minutes.

**6.** Click the forever button under lockout duration, and click OK.

**7.** Press Ctrl+Alt+Del and select Logoff. Click OK. This will end your Windows NT session.

**8.** Press Ctrl+Alt+Del and log on as user KATIE with a password of XYZ.

**9.** You will receive an error message stating that the system can't log you on. Click OK.

**10.** Repeat steps 8 and 9 three more times; you should get a message stating "Unable to log you on because your account has been locked out, please contact your administrator." Click OK.

**11.** Log on as ADMINISTRATOR.

**12.** Select Start ➢ Programs ➢ Administrative Tools (common) ➢ User Manager for Domains.

**13.** Double-click KATIE to see her user properties. Notice the Account Locked Out box is checked. Uncheck this box and click OK. You have unlocked KATIE's account.

## Managing the User Rights Policy

The User Rights policies determines what rights a user or group has on the network. User rights apply to the system and are different from permissions, which apply to a specific object. An example of user rights is the Back up Files and Directories right. This right allows users and groups to back up files and directories no matter what permissions have already been assigned to the file system. The other user rights are similar in function, in that they deal with accessing the system. There are two types of user rights—basic rights or advanced rights. Basic rights display automatically when accessing the User Rights Policy dialog box. Advanced user rights require that you check the Show Advanced User Rights box in the User Rights Policy dialog box. To access the User Rights Policy dialog box, choose Policies ➢ User Rights from the User Manager for Domains utility. Figure 3.10 shows the User Rights Policy dialog box.

## User Rights

Table 3.9 lists user rights, what each right does, and what user or group is assigned each right by default.

**TABLE 3.9**

User rights

| RIGHT | DESCRIPTION | GRANTED TO BY DEFAULT |
|---|---|---|
| Access this computer from network | Allows a user to connect to the computer from the network | ADMINISTRATORS, EVERYONE |
| Add workstations to domain | Allows a user to add workstations to a domain (join a domain). While the Grant To box appears blank, the ADMINISTRATORS and ACCOUNT OPERATORS groups are able to add workstations to a domain. | Blank |
| Backup files and directories | Allows a user to backup all files and directories, regardless of how the file and directory permissions have been set | ADMINISTRATORS, BACKUP OPERATORS, SERVER OPERATORS |
| Change the system time | Allows a user to change the internal time of the computer | ADMINISTRATORS, SERVER OPERATORS |

| **TABLE 3.9**<br>User rights (continued) | **RIGHT** | **DESCRIPTION** | **GRANTED TO BY DEFAULT** |
|---|---|---|---|
| | Force shutdown from a remote system | This option is vaporware and has been reserved for future implementations of NT. (Note: there's a utility in the resource kit that will do this.) | ADMINISTRATORS, SERVER OPERATORS |
| | Load and unload device drivers | Allows a user to dynamically unload and load device drivers | ADMINISTRATORS |
| | Log on locally | Allows a user to log on at the computer where the user account has been defined | ACCOUNT OPERATORS, ADMINISTRATORS, BACKUP OPERATORS, PRINT OPERATORS, SERVER OPERATORS |
| | Manage auditing and security log | Allows a user to manage the security log that is generated when auditing has been enabled. This right does not allow configuration of the audit policy. | ADMINISTRATORS |
| | Restore files and directories | Allows a user to restore files and directories regardless of file and directories permissions | ADMINISTRATORS, BACKUP OPERATORS, SERVER OPERATORS |
| | Shut down the system | Allows a user to shut down NT | ACCOUNT OPERATORS, ADMINISTRATORS, BACKUP OPERATORS, PRINT OPERATORS, SERVER OPERATORS |
| | Take ownership of files or other objects | Allows a user to take ownership of files and directories | ADMINISTRATORS |

*Making certain changes to the User Rights policy can cause major problems with the operating system. Do not change any User Rights unless you understand the effect the change will have.*

One of the common problems users experience relates to the Log On Locally option. When a regular user logs on at a workstation the logon is successful. When a regular user logs on at a domain controller, they receive an error message and the logon is unsuccessful. Table 3.8 listed that only ACCOUNT OPERATORS, ADMINISTRATORS, BACKUP OPERATORS, and PRINT OPERATORS can log on locally. In Figure 3.11, you see that Katie may want to log on at the PDC or from her workstation.

**FIGURE 3.11**

Local user versus network user

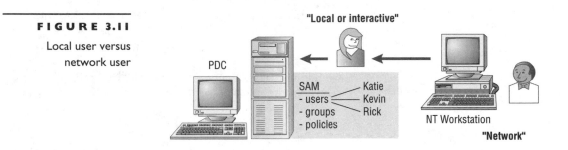

If Katie is at the PDC she is considered a local or interactive user. Because Katie is not a member of a group that has Log On Locally privileges, she should not be able to log on. She will have no problem logging on from NT Workstation because then she is considered a network user and the group EVERYONE has the Access to This Computer from the Network right. In Exercise 3.16, you will duplicate this problem and see how it can be corrected by applying user rights.

**EXERCISE 3.16**

**Assigning User Rights**

**1.** Log off your current session. Press Ctrl+Alt+Del and select Logoff. Click OK.

**2.** Press Ctrl+Alt+Del to begin logon.

---

**EXERCISE 3.16 (CONTINUED FROM PREVIOUS PAGE)**

**3.** Log on as user KATIE with no password. The following error message will display: "The local policy of this system does not permit you to log on interactively." Click OK.

**4.** Now log on as ADMINISTRATOR.

**5.** Select Start ➢ Programs ➢ Administrative Tools (common) ➢ User Manager for Domains.

**6.** Go to User Policy ➢ User Rights.

**7.** In the Right box, click the drop-down list to see the user rights available. Select Log On Locally and click Add, select Domain Users and click Add. Click OK.

**8.** Click OK to exit the User Rights Policy dialog box.

Now you will log off as ADMINISTRATOR and log on as KATIE.

**9.** Press Ctrl+Alt+Del and click Logoff. Click OK.

**10.** Press Ctrl+Alt+Del to begin logon, type **KATIE** in the User name box, and click OK. You should now be successfully logged on as KATIE.

**11.** Log off as KATIE and log back on as ADMINISTRATOR.

---

### Advanced User Rights

Advanced user rights are typically rights that are used by programmers writing applications for NT. They are documented in the Win32 Software Developers Kit (SDK). Table 3.10 defines the three advanced rights that might be more commonly used.

| **TABLE 3.10** Advanced user rights | **ADVANCED RIGHT** | **DESCRIPTION** | **GRANTED TO BY DEFAULT** |
|---|---|---|---|
| | Bypass traverse checking | Allows a user to move through the directory trees of a computer, even if the user does not have any permissions to the traversed directories | EVERYONE |

| TABLE 3.10 Advanced user rights (continued) | ADVANCED RIGHT | DESCRIPTION | GRANTED TO BY DEFAULT |
|---|---|---|---|
| | Create a pagefile | Allows a user to create a pagefile | ADMINISTRATORS |
| | Log on as a service | Allows a process to register with the system as a service; this is used with processes like directory replication | Blank |

## Managing the Audit Policy

You can audit activities that pertain to user management through the audit policy. Depending on what you choose to audit, you can create audit logs that track different management tasks such as the monitoring of successful or unsuccessful logon attempts. In the Audit Policy dialog box, shown in Figure 3.14, you can select the specific event you want to audit and whether to audit success, failure, or both, of selected events.

Table 3.11 describes what each audit event tracks.

| TABLE 3.11 Audit events defined | AUDIT EVENTS | DESCRIPTION |
|---|---|---|
| | Logon and logoff | Tracks when a user logs on, logs off, or makes a network connection |
| | File and object access | Used with file and directory access or print access |
| | Use of user rights | Used when a user exercises a user right, with the exception of logon and logoff |
| | User and group management | Tracks creation, deletion, and management of users and groups |
| | Security policy changes | Tracks changes to user rights, audit, or trust relationship policies |
| | Restart, shutdown, and system | Tracks shutdowns and restarts of the computer. Also used to track events that affect system security or the security log |
| | Process tracking | Tracks events such as program activation, object access, and process exit |

In Exercise 3.17, you will create an audit policy for auditing successful or unsuccessful logon attempts.

---

**EXERCISE 3.17**

## Creating an Audit Policy

**1.** Select Start ➢ Programs ➢ Administrative Tools (common) ➢ User Manager for Domains.

**2.** Select Policies ➢ Audit to call up the Audit Policy dialog box, shown below.

**3.** Select Audit These Events.

**4.** Check Logon and Logoff Success and Failure. Click OK.

**5.** Now you will log off your current session. Press Ctrl+Alt+Del and select Logoff. Click OK.

**6.** Press Ctrl+Alt+Del to begin logon and log on as ADMINISTRATOR.

**7.** Click Start ➢ Programs ➢ Administrative Tools (common) ➢ Event Viewer.

**8.** Select Log ➢ Security.

**9.** Click any of the audited events to see a description.

---

# Chapter Summary

N THIS CHAPTER you learned how to manage users, groups, and security policies. You learned that you use the User Manager for Domains utility to manage your users and groups. User management consists of creating, deleting, renaming, or managing user properties.

In group management you learned the difference between a local group and a global group and how the two kinds of groups interact with each other. The keys to managing local and global groups lie in the following points:

- Local groups are created on the local machine where a group of users needs to access a resource.

- Global groups are created at the PDC, and you add users to the global group.

- Global groups can be added to local groups.

You learned how local and global groups interact in an enterprise environment and how to create and delete local and global groups.

You learned the definition of security policy management, account policies, user rights policies, and audit policies. Managing account policies allows you to determine how logon will be handled based on your security needs. User rights policies determine how a user can access the system. Audit policies allow you to audit successful or unsuccessful events relating to managing your accounts.

# Review Questions

1. You have decided to put all of your home directories on a shared directory on the CORP server in the MASTER domain. The shared directory is called USERS. You want to create the home directories for the users as the users are created. You use the User Environment Profile dialog box in User Manager for Domains. Which option do you choose?

    **A.** Click the connect radio button and type in a drive letter. In the path specify \\MASTER\USERS\%LOGONNAME%.

    **B.** Click the local path radio button and type in the shared path of \\MASTER\CORP\USERS\%USERNAME%.

    **C.** Click the connect radio button and type in a drive letter. In the path specify \\CORP\USERS\%USERNAME%.

    **D.** Click the connect radio button and type in a drive letter. In the path specify \\CORP\USERS\%LOGONID%.

**2.** Local groups can reside on (choose all that apply):

    **A.** Windows 95 Workstations

    **B.** NT Workstations

    **C.** NT member servers

    **D.** NT domain controllers (PDC and BDCs)

**3.** Global groups can reside on (choose all that apply):

    **A.** Windows 95 Workstations

    **B.** NT Workstations

    **C.** NT member servers

    **D.** NT domain controllers (PDC and BDCs)

**4.** You have a user named Katie who needs to manage user and group accounts. What are the minimum rights you can give her so she will be able to manage users and groups?

    **A.** Add her to the ADMINISTRATORS local group.

    **B.** Add her to the DOMAIN ADMIN global group.

    **C.** Add her to the SERVER OPERATORS local group.

    **D.** Add her to the ACCOUNT OPERATORS local group.

    **E.** Add her to the ACCOUNT OPERATORS global group.

5. Your company has been using the NT Workgroup model. You have now decided that you want your users to participate in a domain model. You install NT Server as a PDC in Domain CORP. Now one of your junior technicians needs to go to each NT Workstation and add it to the domain. What are the minimum rights you can give him to accomplish his task?

   **A.** Add him to the ADMINISTRATORS local group.

   **B.** Add him to the DOMAIN ADMIN global group.

   **C.** Add him to the SERVER OPERATORS local group.

   **D.** Add him to the ACCOUNT OPERATORS local group.

   **E.** Assign him the Add Workstations to Domain user right.

6. Your company is using the master domain model. All of your user accounts are in the CORP domain. Your CORP domain has a PDC and two BDCs. Your resource domains are EAST and WEST and they each have one PDC and one BDC. Your users are forced to change passwords every 30 days, but some users are using the same password every time their old password expires. What can you do to fix this problem?

   **A.** Configure the account policy on the CORP domain's PDC to set password uniqueness to 5.

   **B.** Configure the account policy on the PDC and the two BDCs in the CORP domain to set minimum password age to 30.

   **C.** Configure the account policy on the PDC and the two BDCs in the CORP domain to set password uniqueness to 5.

   **D.** Click the require unique passwords button in the account policy box on the PDC in the CORP domain.

7. The home directory variable used to substitute a logon name for the home directory is:

   **A.** %LOGONNAME%

   **B.** %USERNAME%

   **C.** %USER%

   **D.** %LOGONID%

8. Your company uses a master domain model. The user accounts are in the CORP domain, which has one PDC and two BDCs. The resources are in the resource domains of EAST and WEST. EAST and WEST each have one PDC and one BDC. Everyday you back up the network servers between 2:00AM and 5:00AM. You don't want your users to log on during the backup period. What do you do?

   A. Configure each account's user properties so the users cannot log on between 2:00AM and 5:00AM.

   B. Configure CORP's domain policy to not allow any domain user to log on between 2:00AM and 5:00AM.

   C. Configure the accounts policy on each domain controller in the CORP domain to disallow logon between 2:00AM and 5:00AM.

   D. Configure the accounts policy on each domain controller in the CORP, EAST and WEST domains to disallow logon between 2:00AM and 5:00AM.

9. You use the master domain model. All user accounts are in the ABC domain and all resources are in the SALES and ACCT domain. You hire a user named Terry and you want her to be able to manage all of the printers in the resource domains, and also be able to create new users and groups in the accounts domain. What are the minimum assignments you can make so that Terry can perform these actions?

   A. Make Terry a member of the DOMAIN ADMIN global group on the ABC domain and make her a member of the global group PRINT OPERATORS on the SALES and ACCT domains.

   B. Make Terry a member of the ACCOUNT OPERATORS global group on the PDC in the ABC domain and make her a member of the global group PRINT OPERATORS on the SALES and ACCT domain.

   C. Make Terry a member of the ACCOUNT OPERATORS local group on the PDC in the ABC domain and make her a member of the local group PRINT OPERATORS on the SALES and ACCT domain.

   D. Make Terry a member of the ADMINISTRATORS local group on the ABC domain and make her a member of the PRINT OPERA-TORS global group on the SALES and ACCT domains.

10. Your company has been using the NT domain model. You have just hired a new MIS employee. You want the new employee to be able to share and stop share resources as well as back up and restore the server. You also want her to be able to down the server if needed. You do not want her to be able to do any account management. What do you do?

    A. Add her to the ADMINISTRATORS local group.

    B. Add her to the DOMAIN ADMIN global group.

    C. Add her to the SERVER OPERATORS local group.

    D. Add her to the ACCOUNT OPERATORS local group.

    E. Assign her the Manage Server user right.

11. Your company uses the master domain model. You have a master domain, CORP, and three resource domains, MIS, SALES, and ACCT. The MIS, SALES, and ACCT domains trust the CORP domain. The MIS domain has an e-mail application on the APP server. All users need to access this application. What do you do?

    A. Create a local group on the APP server called EMAIL USERS and assign the permissions that the e-mail users will need, then add the global group DOMAIN USERS from the CORP domain to the local group EMAIL USERS.

    B. Add trust relationships, so that CORP trusts MIS, SALES, and ACCT. Create a global group called EMAIL USERS on the MIS domain and add users. Assign the necessary rights to access the e-mail application to EMAIL USERS.

    C. Add a trust relationship so that MIS trusts SALES and ACCT. Create a global group on MIS called EMAIL USERS and add users. Assign the necessary rights to the EMAIL USERS group.

    D. Create a global group on the APP server called EMAIL USERS and assign the permissions that the EMAIL USERS group will need, then add the global group DOMAIN USERS from the CORP domain to the global group EMAIL USERS.

**12.** Your boss read an article on how programs could be written to break into your domain. The program worked by generating random passwords until it was able to log on. What option should be set in account policies to prevent this from happening?

   **A.** Set minimum password age to 5.

   **B.** Set password uniqueness to 7.

   **C.** Set minimum password length to 15.

   **D.** Configure account lockout.

**13.** You have just hired Rick to take care of your backups. You want him to be able to back up files and directories, but you don't want him to be able to restore the backup. What do you do?

   **A.** Add him to the DOMAIN ADMIN global group.

   **B.** Add him to the BACKUP OPERATORS local group.

   **C.** Assign him the Backup file and directories user right.

   **D.** Make him a member of the SERVER OPERATORS local group.

# Resource Management

CHAPTER

4

I N THE LAST chapter you learned how to manage users and groups. In this chapter you will learn how to manage resources. A resource is any part of a computer system or network. Through resource management you will make resources available for network access and control how resources can be accessed by assigning network security. Examples of resources include disk drives (files and folders) and printers.

A resource can be local or shared over a network. For example, on my workstation, I store data. No other users need to access my data so it is local, not shared. On the other hand, the network could have an applications server that would store the common applications all users need to access. These resources would be shared and network security applied. In this chapter you will focus on managing disk resources, such as folder and file resources. Specifically, this chapter will cover:

- NT Permissions and Security

- Creating and Sharing Resources

- Auditing File Resources

# NT Security and Permissions

N T SECURITY IS a way to control what resources user and group accounts are able to access and what level of access they are allowed. One of the features of Windows NT is a required logon. After logging on, based on their user ID, the user is then able to access the resources to which they have been given permission. Permissions can be granted through the user account or through group memberships.

Permissions determine what resources users can access and how they actually go about accessing them. For example, if your network has an applications server, you would normally want your users to be able to access common applications like a word processor or spreadsheet application. You do not want regular users to change your application files; they should just be able to use them. In this case, you would give your users Read rights. However, you want your administrators to be able to change the application files if needed, so they could have Full Control rights. NT security allows you to customize what users can access based on their logon names.

NT has two different types of security—local security and network security. Local security governs a local user. A local user or *interactive* user is a user who is sitting at the machine where the resource is located. Network security controls how users can access the resource over a network *share*, an arrangement in which network users access the resource via the network.

It is important to note that most access will occur through network shares. Normally most of your resources will reside on network servers. Typically, users do not physically log on at the server, but rather at their workstations. Most environments keep the servers in a secure location—for example, a locked room. So even if users wanted to log on locally, they would not be able to.

In the following sections, you will first learn how to implement local and network security.

# Managing Local Resources

MANAGING A LOCAL resource allows you to specify what access a user account has to a local resource. A local resource is a resource that is physically associated with the machine on which you are working. Local security only governs a user that is logged on at the machine where the resource is located. For file system resources, you will typically use the FAT or NTFS file system (see Chapter 2, "Installing and Maintaining NT 4.0"). In order to support local security, you must be using the NTFS file system, as the FAT file system does not offer any local security.

Let's assume that you have two users who share the same workstation. These users are considered local users because they are sitting at the resource machine. Katie is the manager of the sales department and keeps sensitive information regarding her employees. Kevin is her assistant and should not be able to access these files. If the workstation used FAT partitions, there would be no way to limit what Kevin could access. He would be on his honor not to look. NTFS allows for more control by allowing access based on what NTFS permissions have been assigned. Permissions can be applied separately for Katie and Kevin through their logon names and passwords.

# NTFS Security

You can apply NTFS permissions to a folder or to a file. It is most common to use folder permissions. All of the files within the folder will use the permissions assigned to the folder. It's fairly easy to manage permissions at the folder level. It is labor intensive to manage permissions on every single file.

Assume for a moment that you have a word processor application to which you want the EVERYONE group to have Read rights. All the files that comprise the word processor application should allow Read rights. By default, all files within the applications folder have the same permissions as the folder. So by applying rights at the folder you are done.

Or consider a case where you are also using a word processor application, but this application has a metering file associated with it to track who is accessing the application. You still want the EVERYONE group to have Read rights to the application, but you want the EVERYONE group to have Change rights on the metering file. The users want Change rights so that, as they access the application, they can edit the metering file.

Table 4.1 defines the type of access rights that can be assigned to NTFS folders.

| **TABLE 4.1**<br>NTFS folder permissions | **ACCESS RIGHT** | **DEFINITION** |
| --- | --- | --- |
| | No Access | No Access means that the user has no rights to the folder. No access is an overriding right. That means that even if the user has other permissions through group memberships, No Access will override the other rights that have been assigned and the user will have No Access. |
| | List | List allows a file or subdirectory name to be viewed. You can also change to a directory's subdirectory with the List right. |

| TABLE 4.1 NTFS folder permissions (continued) | ACCESS RIGHT | DEFINITION |
|---|---|---|
| | Read | Read is similar to List. Read allows you to view a file or subdirectory. With Read you can also change to a directories subdirectory. The difference between List and Read is that Read allows you to view data files and run applications. |
| | Add | Add allows you to add files and subdirectories to the directory. |
| | Add & Read | Add & Read combines the rights associated with the add and read permissions. |
| | Change | Change allows you to list, add, and read. In addition you can change data within a file or delete files and subdirectories. |
| | Full Control | Full Control allows you to list, read, add, and change. In addition you can change permissions on subdirectories and files. You can also take ownership of subdirectories and files. |
| | Special Directory Access | Special Directory Access allows you to customize what rights you want to be assigned. Special Directory Access options include Read, Write, Execute, Delete, Change Permissions, and Take Ownership. |
| | Special File Access | Special File Access allows you to customize what rights you want to be assigned. Special File Access options include Read, Write, Execute, Delete, Change Permissions, and Take Ownership. |

Table 4.2 defines the NTFS rights that can be assigned to a file. You will notice that they are fairly similar.

| TABLE 4.2 NTFS file permissions | ACCESS RIGHT | DEFINITION |
|---|---|---|
| | No Access | No Access means that the user has no rights to the file. No Access is an overriding right. That means that even if the user has other permissions through group memberships, No Access will override the other rights and the user will have no access. |
| | Read | Read allows you to view a file. If the file is a program file, Read allows you to execute the file. |

| TABLE 4.2 | ACCESS RIGHT | DEFINITION |
|---|---|---|
| NTFS file permissions (continued) | Change | Change includes the privileges associated with the Read right. Change also allows you to change the data within a file or to delete a file. |
| | Full Control | Full Control implies the rights Read and Change. In addition, with the Full Control right, you can change permissions on a file or take ownership of a file. |
| | Special Access | Special Access allows you to customize what rights you want to be assigned. Special Access options include Read, Write, Execute, Delete, Change Permissions, and Take Ownership. |

*You may notice the terms* folder *and* directory *being used interchangeably. They refer to the same thing.*

## Implementing Local Security

You can assign local file resource permissions through the My Computer Utility, through Windows NT Explorer, or by running the Winfile command line utility. In Exercise 4.1, you will begin by converting a FAT partition to NTFS. After you convert the partition you will assign local permissions and then log on as various different accounts with different access rights in order to test how permissions are used.

## Other Options in the Directory Permissions Dialog Box

The Directory Permissions dialog box provides information such as the directory name and owner. In this box you can specify how permissions should be applied to the directory and the subdirectories. You can also specify what users and groups have permissions to the directory and subdirectories.

**EXERCISE 4.1**

## Assigning Local Permissions

This exercise should be completed from PDC1. In the first part of this exercise, you will convert a FAT partition to NTFS.

**1.** Select Start ➢ Programs ➢ Windows NT Explorer.

**2.** Click the D: drive and selct File ➢ Properties.

Notice that you have tabs for General, Tools, and Sharing, but not for Security. You cannot apply local security to a FAT partition. Remember, you can convert from FAT to NTFS, but you can't convert from NTFS to FAT.

**3.** To convert the FAT partition to NTFS, select Start ➢ Programs ➢ Command prompt.

**4.** At the prompt type **CONVERT D: /FS:NTFS** and press Return. You will get a message asking if you want to schedule the conversion for the next time the system restarts. Type **Y** for yes and press Return.

**5.** At the command prompt type **EXIT** to leave the command prompt.

**6.** Select Start ➢ Shut Down. Select Restart the computer and click Yes. As the system restarts you will notice that your D: drive has been converted from FAT to NTFS.

Converting a partition allows you to preserve all existing data whereas another format would erase any existing data. Now that the partition is NTFS you can apply local permissions.

**7.** After the computer restarts, log on as ADMINISTRATOR.

**8.** Select Start ➢ Programs ➢ Windows NT Explorer.

**9.** Click the D: drive and select File ➢ Properties. Notice that now you get a Security tab. Click Cancel.

Next you will create a directory structure to which you can apply permissions.

**10.** Using the graphic below as a reference diagram, create the DATA, WP DOCS, and SS DOCS directories. To do this click the D: drive. Select File ➢ New ➢ Folder, and type **DATA**.

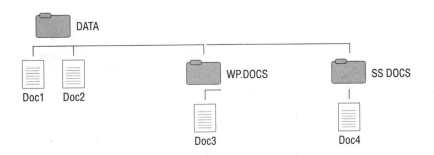

**11.** Double-click Data under Contents. Then Click DATA, select File ➢ New ➢ Folder, and type **WP DOCS.**

**12.** Repeat Step 11, but type **SS DOCS**.

**13.** Select File ➢ New ➢ Text Document to create a file in the DATA directory. Name the file **DOC1**.

**14.** Double-click WP Docs under contents. Then click WP DOCS and select File ➢ New ➢ Text Document to create a file in the WP DOCS subdirectory. Name the file **DOC3**. After you create DOC3 double-click DOC3 to open the document. Type anything you like, save the changes, and exit NotePad.

Now create users for testing the local permissions. Create users PEONDUDE and SUPERDUDE.

**15.** Select Start ➢ Programs ➢ Administrative Tools (common) ➢ User Manager for Domains.

**16.** Go to the User menu ➢ New User. Type in **PEONDUDE** and uncheck the User Must Change Password at Next Logon box. Click Add.

**17.** Repeat Step 16, but type in **SUPERDUDE** to create the second user. Then click Close.

You are now ready to apply local permissions to your users. In the first instance you will grant PEONDUDE the Read right for the DATA directory. You will intentionally not check Replace Permissions on Subdirectories so you can see what happens.

**18.** Go back to Windows NT Explorer. Single-click the D : \DATA directory. Click your secondary mouse button and choose Properties.

**19.** In the Properties dialog box, click the Security tab. Click Permissions to open the Directory Permissions dialog box, shown below.

**Directory Permissions**

Directory:     E:\data
Owner: Administrators
☐ Replace Permissions on Subdirectories
☑ Replace Permissions on Existing Files
Name:

| | |
|---|---|
| 🌐 Everyone | Full Control (All) (All) |

Type of Access: | Full Control |

| OK | Cancel | Add... | Remove | Help |

**20.** From the Directory Permissions dialog box, you will first remove the EVERYONE group permissions. While Everyone is highlighted, click Remove.

**21.** Click Add and click Show Users.

**22.** Select PEONDUDE from the list and click Add. The default access is Read, so click OK.

**23.** Add the DOMAIN ADMINS group with Full Control permission. In the Directory Permissions dialog box, click OK again.

**24.** Press Ctrl+Alt+Del to log off as ADMINISTRATOR and log on as PEONDUDE. (If you get a message stating that this computer's local policy does not allow you to log on locally, see Exercise 3.16.)

**25.** Select Start ➤ Programs ➤ Windows NT Explorer.

**26.** Select the D:\DATA directory and open the DOC1 file. Because PEONDUDE has the Read right you should be able to open this file. Now try to edit and save the file. You should not be able to save this file. Exit without saving by selecting File ➤ Exit. Do not save changes.

**27.** Now select D:\DATA\WP DOCS and open DOC3. Try to edit and save DOC3. The file should be saved because you did not check Replace Permissions on Sub-directories in Step 20. This means the EVERYONE group still has full control on subdirectories and PEONDUDE is part of the EVERYONE group.

Now let's see what could happen if you leave the EVERYONE group with Full Control Access.

**28.** You should still be logged on as PEONDUDE and be in Windows NT Explorer. Click D:\DATA\WP DOCS. Click your secondary mouse button and choose Properties. Click the Security tab and click Permissions to open the Directory Permissions dialog box.

**29.** In the Directory Permissions dialog box, remove EVERYONE and Add PEON-DUDE with Full Control access rights. Click Cancel. You do not want to complete this operation.

*Beware! PEONDUDE could have taken access away from all users except himself. In the real world you will want to avoid this scenario. (Although as a member of DOMAIN ADMINS, you could always take ownership if necessary.)*

**30.** Log off and log back on as ADMINISTRATOR.

### Resource Owner

The top of the Directory Permissions dialog box shows the current directory and the directory's *owner*. In Windows NT, every file and directory has an associated owner. The owner controls how permissions are assigned. By default, the user who creates the resource is the owner. If the user is not a member of the ADMINISTRATORS group, their logon ID will be displayed as the owner. If the user is a member of the ADMINISTRATORS group, the owner is the ADMINISTRATORS group.

In NT you can also take ownership. To take ownership of a file or directory, you must be a member of the ADMINISTRATORS group, have full control, or have special access with the Take Ownership right. Taking ownership is a one-way process. A user can take ownership, but cannot give it back.

Let's assume Penny is the manager of the payroll department. She is the owner of the PAYROLL folder. The permissions on the folder do not allow anyone but Penny to access PAYROLL. Penny gets sick and is not able to come in and process payroll checks on payday. To avoid a riot you need to get into the PAYROLL folder. As a member of the ADMINISTRATORS group you can take ownership to access PAYROLL.

Now let's assume that you are up to no good. You just want to be sneaky and see what everyone else is earning. You again take ownership of PAYROLL. The only problem you run into is that once you take ownership you can't give it back, and now Penny knows you've been up to no good. You can also track files that have been accessed through the Take Ownership right through file auditing, which I will cover in more detail later in this chapter.

## Default Permissions

The default permissions for NTFS local security grant Full Access to everyone. To set permissions, you actually remove everyone and then add the groups that should have permission.

## Default Permission Replacement on Files and Directories

When you assign directory permissions the default options are:

- permissions are not replaced on subdirectories

- permissions are replaced on files

What does this mean? Assume that you have the directory structure shown in Exercise 4.1, Step 10.

Now assume that you have decided that you want the SALES global group to have the Read right to the DATA directory. If you delete the EVERYONE group from the access list and add the SALES global group with the Read right, the default rights replacement would be that the SALES global group would have Read rights to DATA and the two files under DATA, DOC1 and DOC2.

The WP DOCS directory and SS DOCS directory would retain their original rights where the EVERYONE group has Full Control.

*If you want your subdirectory structure to have the same rights as the directory, make sure you check the Replace Permissions on Subdirectories box. This is not the default.*

# Managing Network Resources

ONE OF THE main benefits of having a network is the ability to share resources. By sharing file resources, you can take advantage of centralized management. This means that users can share application and data files from a central location, rather than storing all application and data files on their local hard drives. Sharing reduces disk space requirements and administrative overhead.

Creating a resource is as simple as creating a folder. In this section you will learn how to create and share a resource, what the network permissions are, what default network permissions are, how to apply network permissions, and how to access a network share.

## Creating and Sharing Resources

Creating a directory or folder is easy. Sharing a folder is equally easy. You just need to be logged in as a user with the ability to create a network share. A folder can be shared in many ways. The following utilities can be used to share a resource:

- My Computer
- Windows NT Explorer
- Server Manager
- WINFILE command line utility

In order to share a folder, a user must be a member of the ADMINISTRA-TORS or SERVER OPERATORS group. Table 4.3 defines the options for sharing a folder.

| **TABLE 4.3** Sharing options defined | SHARING OPTIONS | DESCRIPTION |
|---|---|---|
| | Not Shared | Resource is only available locally. |
| | Shared As | Resource can be used locally or over the network. |
| | Comment | Allows an optional comment. In some utilities this comment displays through the browse list. |
| | User Limit | Allows you to specify the number of concurrent connections for the share. This could be useful on an applications directory where you only have 10 licenses. |

In Exercise 4.2, you will create a folder through the Windows NT Explorer utility, and then you will share the folder.

**EXERCISE 4.2**

**Creating and Sharing a Resource**

Completed this exercise from PDC1 while logged on as ADMINISTRATOR.

**1.** Select Start ➤ Programs ➤ Windows NT Explorer.

**2.** Click the C: drive and select File ➤ New ➤ Folder.

**3.** Type in **SHARED** as the folder's name.

**4.** Click your secondary mouse button and click the Sharing tab page, as shown below.

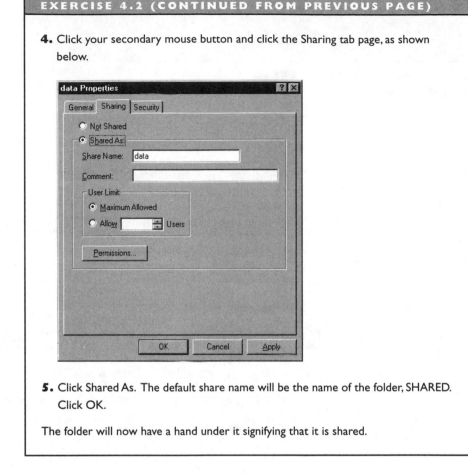

**5.** Click Shared As. The default share name will be the name of the folder, SHARED. Click OK.

The folder will now have a hand under it signifying that it is shared.

## Setting Permissions on Network Shares

Setting permissions on network shares is similar to setting permissions on local resources. The difference is that you can apply network permissions to any local file system, for example FAT, NTFS, or CDFS (CDFS is the CD file system). On a network share you can only apply permissions at the folder level, not the file level. Network permissions are also less complicated. Table 4.4 defines the network share permissions.

**TABLE 4.4**

Network share
permissions defined

| SHARE PERMISSION | DESCRIPTION |
|---|---|
| No Access | Prevents any access to a shared directory or its files. No access overrides any other rights a user may have through their logon account or group memberships. |
| Read | Allows you to view files and subdirectories, change a directory to a subdirectory, or view data and run applications. |
| Change | Change allows the permissions associated with the Read right, and also allows you to add files and subdirectories, change a file's data, or delete files and directories. |
| Full Control | Full Control allows the permissions associated with the Read and Change rights. Also, a user with Full Control can change permissions or take ownership on an NTFS partition. |

### Default Network Permissions

When a network share is created, the EVERYONE group gets the Full Control network permissions by default; this is something that you want to watch out for if you are used to other network operating systems. Most operating systems give No Access permission to network users by default. In Windows NT the opposite is true.

### Implementing Network Permissions

Network permissions can be implemented through the same utilities you used to create a network share earlier in this chapter.

In Exercise 4.3, you will assign network permissions to the SHARED directory that you created in Exercise 4.2. The DOMAIN USERS group will have Read permission to the network share and the DOMAIN USERS group will have Full Control.

**EXERCISE 4.3**

## Assigning Network Permissions

Complete this exercise from PDC1 while logged on as ADMINISTRATOR.

**1.** Select Start ➤ Programs ➤ Windows NT Explorer.

**2.** Click the C : drive, single-click the SHARED folder.

**3.** Select File ➤ Properties.

**4.** Click the Sharing tab page.

**5.** Click the Permissions button in the Access Through Share Permissions dialog box, shown here.

**6.** The EVERYONE group should be highlighted. Click Remove to delete this assignment.

**7.** Click Add to call up the Add Users and Groups dialog box.

**8.** Click DOMAIN USERS and click Add. DOMAIN USERS will get Read access by default. Click OK.

**9.** Click Add again. Select DOMAIN ADMINS. From the Type of Access box, choose Full Control. Click OK. Click OK again twice at the next two prompts.

## Accessing Network Resources

Once a resource has been shared, users with the appropriate permissions can access it. In Exercise 4.4 you will log on to DOMAIN1 from NTWS1. You will then access the share you created in Exercise 4.3.

---

**EXERCISE 4.4**

### Accessing a Network Resource

For this exercise you will use your first machine as PDC1 in DOMAIN1. Your second machine, NTWS2, should be booted as NT Workstation. The following steps should be completed from NTWS2.

**1.** Press Ctrl+Alt+Del to access the Logon dialog box. Log on as user KEVIN from DOMAIN1.

**2.** Double-click Network Neighborhood.

**3.** Click PDC1 and you will see SHARED.

**4.** Click SHARED and you have accessed a network resource.

---

In Exercise 4.5 you will map a network drive to SHARED; this will be a persistent connection. That means that each time you log on as KEVIN you will have a drive mapping to the SHARED resource.

---

**EXERCISE 4.5**

### Creating a Persistent Network Drive

For this exercise you will use your first machine as PDC1 in DOMAIN1. Your second machine, NTWS2, should be booted as NT Workstation. The following steps should be completed from NTWS2 while logged on as KEVIN.

**1.** Select Start ➤ Programs ➤ Windows NT Explorer.

**2.** Select Tools ➤ Map Network Drive.

**3.** From the Drive menu, choose F:.

**4.** In the Path box select \\PDC1\SHARED. You can type the path or you can select it from the Shared Directories box by expanding PDC1 and clicking Shared. Click OK.

Kevin will now have drive F: mapped to \\PDC1\SHARED each time he logs on.

---

## Flow of Resource Access

It is important to understand how a resource is accessed. By understanding this process, you will be able to troubleshoot access problems more easily.

A user account must have appropriate permissions to access a resource. Resource access is determined through the following steps:

1. At logon an access token is created for the logon account.

2. When a resource is accessed, NT checks the access control list (ACL) to see if the user should be granted access.

3. If the user is on the list, the ACL checks the access control entries (ACE) to see what type of access the user should be given.

I will cover these steps in more detail in the following subsections.

### Access Token Creation

Each time a user account logs on an access token is created. The access token contains the SID of the currently logged on user. It also contains the SIDs for any groups the user is associated with. Once an access token is created, it is not updated until the next logon.

Let's assume that Kevin needs to access the sales database and that SALESDB is the name of the shared database. Kevin logs on, but is not able to access the database. You do some detective work and find that Kevin has not been added the SALES global group and that to have proper access to SALESDB he needs to be a member of SALES global group. You add KEVIN to SALES global group and call him up to let him know everything is working. KEVIN tries to access the sales database, and is still unable to do so. KEVIN logs out and logs back on, and now he can access the database.

In the previous example, KEVIN's access token identifying him as a member of the SALES global group was not updated to reflect his new group membership until he logged off and logged back on. At that point a new access token was created identifying KEVIN as a member of the SALES global group.

*Access tokens are only updated during the logon sequence. They are not updated on the fly. That means if you add a user to a group, they need to log off and log on for their access token to be updated.*

### Access Control List

Each object in NT has an associated ACL. An object is defined as a set of data that can be used by the system, or a set of actions which can be used to manipulate system data. Examples of objects include, directories, files, network shares, and printers. The ACL is a list of user accounts and groups that are allowed to access the resource. Figure 4.1 shows how ACLs are associated with each object. For each ACL there is an access control entry that defines what a user or a group can actually do at the resource.

**FIGURE 4.1**

Access control lists

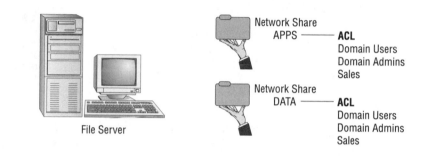

Network Share
APPS ——— **ACL**
Domain Users
Domain Admins
Sales

Network Share
DATA ——— **ACL**
Domain Users
Domain Admins
Sales

File Server

### Access Control Entry

Each ACL has an associated ACE. The purpose of the ACE is to list what permissions are associated with the users and groups on the ACL. The No Access right is always listed first in the ACE. If the No Access right is present, it will override any other rights that a user has been given, and no access will be granted. In Figure 4.2, you see the ACEs that have been associated with the ACLs.

**FIGURE 4.2**

Access control entries

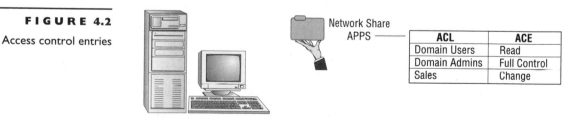

Network Share
APPS ———

| ACL | ACE |
|---|---|
| Domain Users | Read |
| Domain Admins | Full Control |
| Sales | Change |

File Server

### Resource Access Examples

Let's look at how resource access is accomplished in the following examples.

BOGIE is a member of the SALES and MANAGERS groups. He wants to access the SALESDB share. The SALESDB object has the ACL and ACEs shown in Figure 4.3.

**FIGURE 4.3**

Example 1 of resource access

User Account Bogie

Access Token for Bogie
- Bogie
- Sales
- Managers

Object SALESDB

| ACL | ACE |
|------|------|
| Sales | Change |
| Managers | Full Control |
| Accountants | Read |
| Marketing | Read |

Because BOGIE is a member of the SALES and MANAGERS groups and those groups have been granted access to SALESDB, BOGIE can access SALESDB. The ACE for SALES allows the group the Change right. The ACE for MANAGER allows the Full Control right. Thus, BOGIE has full control over the SALESDB share.

Now consider a situation where RUDY is a member of the DOMAIN GUESTS and RESEARCHERS groups. He wants to access the NEWRESEARCH share. The NEWRESEARCH object has the ACL and ACEs shown in Figure 4.4.

**FIGURE 4.4**

Example 2 of resource access

User Account Rudy

Access Token for Rudy
- Rudy
- Domain Guests
- Researchers

Object NEWRESEARCH

| ACL | ACE |
|------|------|
| Researchers | Change |
| Domain Admins | Full Control |
| Managers | Full Control |
| Domain Guests | No Access |

Because RUDY is a member of DOMAIN GUESTS and DOMAIN GUESTS have the No Access right, it does not matter what rights RUDY may have from other group associations; he has no access.

## Interaction between Local and Network Security

Local and network security work together. The most restrictive access will determine what a user can do. For example, if the local directory is NTFS and the default permissions have not been changed, the EVERYONE group would have the Full Control right. If that local directory was shared as SHARE and the permissions were set so that only the SALES group had Read rights, then only the SALES group could access that share.

Conversely, if the local NTFS permissions only allowed the MANAGERS group to read a local directory, and that directory had been shared with default permissions allowing the EVERYONE group Full Control rights, only the MANAGERS group would be able to access the directory with Read permissions because Read is the more restrictive permission.

# *Auditing File Resources*

F ILE RESOURCES CAN be audited on NTFS partitions, allowing you to see how resources are being accessed. By default, auditing is not enabled. Some reasons you would use auditing follow:

- You are trying to determine how many people are accessing your word processor so you will know how many licenses to purchase.

- You have a directory with sensitive data and you want to see who is accessing it.

- You have a data file that keeps changing and you want to track who is making the changes.

Through auditing you are able to track the success or failure of the following file events.

- Read
- Write
- Execute

- Delete

- Change Permissions

- Take Ownership

You can configure auditing to audit specific users or groups, or you can configure auditing to audit anyone who accesses a specific resource.

*One way to think of auditing is to compare it to IRS auditing. The IRS does not have the resources to track every item that goes on our tax returns. So what they do is to set up a system to detect certain red-flag conditions; when a flag goes up, the IRS examines the tax return in question more thoroughly. As taxpayers, we are not necessarily aware of what will trigger a red flag.*

In auditing file resources, an administrator can determine what file events should be audited. If the auditing detects any abnormalities, the administrator can set up more extensive auditing to determine if a security violation is taking place.

Once the audit has occurred, the administrator or a user with the Manage Auditing and Security Log right can view the audit logs through the Event Viewer. In Exercise 4.6, you will setup auditing and view the audit log.

---

**EXERCISE 4.6**

### Auditing File Resources

Complete this exercise from PDC1 while logged on as ADMINISTRATOR. This exercise assumes you have completed Exercise 4.1 to complete the file structure used and that the partition is NTFS. First, you will need to enable file auditing.

**1.** Select Start ➢ Programs ➢ Administrative Tools (common) ➢ User Manager for Domains.

**2.** Select Policies ➢ Audit.

**3.** Click Audit These Events and check the File and Object Access Success and Failure boxes to open the Audit Policy dialog box, shown below. Click OK.

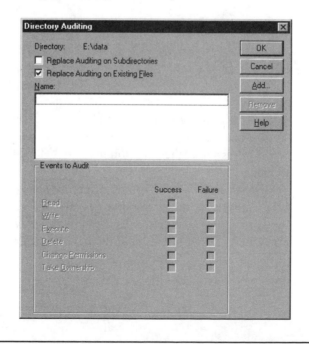

Now you will set up File auditing on an NTFS folder.

**4.** Select Start ➢ Programs ➢ Windows NT Explorer.

**5.** At the D: drive click the DATA folder and select File ➢ Properties.

**6.** Click the Security tab and click Auditing to open the Directory Auditing dialog box, shown below.

**7.** Check the Replace Auditing on Subdirectories box.

**8.** Click Add to specify which users you want to audit. Choose Everyone and click Add. Click OK.

**9.** The Events to Audit section has now become active. Click Success and Failure for Read, Write, Execute, and Delete. Click OK. Close the Directory Auditing dialog box.

Finally, you will trigger an audit.

**10.** From the D:\DATA folder, double-click DOC1 to open it. While the file is open make some changes. Then save and close the file.

Now you can view the audit log.

**11.** Select Start ➤ Programs ➤ Administrative Tools (common)➤ Event Viewer.

**12.** Select Log ➤ Security.

**13.** Your audited events will be stamped with the date and time, so you will be able to determine the events that triggered an audit. You'll notice that auditing generates a very high overhead.

# Chapter Summary

N THIS CHAPTER you learned about resource management and that you can manage both local resources and network resources. To manage a local resource, the partition must be NTFS, but any network share can be managed.

Local security allows you to set permissions on a local NTFS partition. If a user is physically at the resource's location, (i.e. not using the resource as a network resource) then local security is the only security the user will be governed by. If a user is accessing the resource over the network, then the resource can have network security as well. If a resource has both local and network security applied to it, a user will work under the more restrictive of the two sets of permissions.

You also learned how to audit file resources, which allows you to keep track of file events. By using file auditing you can see how a particular resource is being accessed; this can be very useful in high security environments.

# Review Questions

1. TERRY is a member of the SALES and MIS groups, the APPS share has the following rights assigned:

   | USER/GROUP | ASSIGNMENT |
   | --- | --- |
   | EVERYONE | No Access |
   | MIS | Full Control |
   | TERRY | Change |

   What are TERRY's rights at APPS?

   **A.** Full Control

   **B.** Change

   **C.** Change and Full Control

   **D.** No Access

2. You have just created a share on the DATA folder. You have not assigned any permissions. What can PEONUSER do at the DATA folder?

   **A.** Nothing, no rights have been assigned

   **B.** Read

   **C.** List

   **D.** Full Control

3. LARS is a member of the MIS group and is working at the APPS server. The APPS folder is on a FAT partition on the APPS server. The MIS group has Change permissions to a share called APPS in the APPS folder. The EVERYONE group has Read permission. What is(are) LARS' permission(s)?

   A. Change

   B. Read

   C. Read and Change

   D. Full Control

4. You want to create a network share for your DATA folder. Which of the following groups are able to create a network share? Choose all that apply.

   A. Any user can create a share.

   B. ADMINISTRATORS

   C. SERVER OPERATORS

   D. ACCOUNT OPERATORS

5. Auditing file resources allows you to determine which file resources are being accessed. Which of the following conditions must be met to enable auditing? Choose all that apply.

   A. You must be logged on as a user who is part of the ADMINISTRA-TORS group.

   B. Under the Policies menu of User Manager for Domains, you must go to the audit menu and select audit File and Object Access.

   C. The auditing service must be started.

   D. The partition you want to audit has to be NTFS.

   E. The partition you want to audit has to be shared.

   F. The partition type must be FAT or NTFS.

**6.** What rights are needed to view the audit logs generated by file auditing? Choose all that apply.

    **A.** You must be logged on as a user who is part of the ADMINISTRA-TORS group.

    **B.** You must be logged on as a user who originally enabled the auditing.

    **C.** You must be logged on as a user who has the Manage Auditing and Security Log right.

    **D.** You must be logged on as a user who has the Manage Auditing right.

**7.** What utility is used to view the audit logs generated by file auditing?

    **A.** Server Manager

    **B.** Event Viewer

    **C.** Audit Manager

    **D.** User Manager for Domains

**8.** Which utilities can be used to create a network share? Choose all that apply.

    **A.** Server Manager

    **B.** My Computer

    **C.** Windows NT Explorer

    **D.** User Manager for Domains

**9.** If you wanted to assign local permissions so that a user could add, delete, or read a file, what would be the minimum assignment you could make?

    **A.** Write

    **B.** Read and Delete

    **C.** Change

    **D.** Full Control

# User Profiles, System Policies, and Hardware Profiles

CHAPTER

5

I N THIS CHAPTER you will learn about managing the configuration of an NT Server computer through user profiles, system policies, and hardware profiles. *User profiles* are used to save each user account's desktop configuration. *System policies* are used to control user environments and computer configurations. *Hardware profiles* are used to manage portable computers which may have different configurations based on their location.

User profiles are necessary to preserve a user's desktop environment from one logon to the next. Imagine how frustrated you would be if you had customized your desktop with all your favorite configurations. Then you logged out, and the next time you logged on everything was gone. You probably wouldn't be very happy.

NT Server creates a profile folder for your user account the first time you log on, and it stores your configuration preferences. Each time you log off, your folder is updated with changes you have made, so that the next time you log on, everything is the way you left it.

In this chapter you will learn how to create local user profiles, how to create and manage *roaming profiles* (profiles that are available over the network), and how to create *mandatory profiles* (profiles that Administrators can manage, but users cannot change).

System policies allow administrators to have a great deal of control over how users access their desktops and how each computer is configured. System policies work by updating the Registry parameters that relate to the logged-on user and the local computer. System policies that relate to users can be assigned to all users, a group, or an individual user. Through system policies, administrators have greater control over the users' work environments than they do through user profiles.

Hardware profiles offer flexibility in a mobile computing environment where a computer may have different configurations based on its current location. If multiple hardware profiles exist, the user can specify which hardware profile should be used at computer startup.

# How NT Server Stores Configuration Information

N T SERVER STORES all configuration information in a database called the *Registry*. The Registry is a hierarchical database that controls all of the configuration information related to the NT operating system. When you modify a user's profile or implement a system policy, you are actually editing the Registry. The Registry keys that are related to user profiles and system policies are the HKEY_CURRENT_USER subtree key and the HKEY_LOCAL_MACHINE subtree key. The HKEY_CURRENT_USER key contains all configuration information for the user who is logged on, including the user's folders, screen colors, and Control Panel settings. HKEY_LOCAL_ MACHINE contains the configuration information that relates to the computer, such as hardware, the SAM, security, software, and system information.

The HKEY_CURRENT_USER subtree is based on the current user's security ID and is unique for each user. This means that if the user account KEVIN logs on, HKEY_CURRENT_USER would consist of customized configurations for the user account KEVIN. If the user account KATIE logs on, HKEY_CURRENT_ USER consists of KATIE's customized configurations. This allows multiple user accounts to share the same computer, yet retain customized desktop preferences.

The HKEY_LOCAL_MACHINE portion of the Registry is used to configure the local computer. Options that are set within the HKEY_LOCAL_MACHINE subtree are common for all users, meaning whoever logs on to the local computer has the same configuration.

Through user profiles, you can only control information in the HKEY_ CURRENT_USER subtree. Through system policies, you are able to control information in the HKEY_CURRENT_USER subtree and the HKEY_LOCAL_ MACHINE subtree.

# User Profiles

USER PROFILES DETERMINE each user's desktop configuration. The user profile can be used to save each user's desktop arrangement, program items, personal program groups, network and printer connections, screen colors, mouse settings, and more. By default, user profiles are created locally on the machine that the user account logs onto, but you can create roaming profiles so they can be accessible on the network.

By default, users are able to change their profiles, but administrators can create read-only profiles using mandatory user profiles.

In this section you will learn about the benefits of user profiles and what can be stored in user profiles. You will also learn about local user profiles, roaming user profiles, and mandatory user profiles.

## Benefits of User Profiles

User profiles provide the following benefits:

- They allow users to save and retain their desktop settings by updating their local profile folder each time they log off.

- They can be configured for network use so that a user gets their profile from any NT Server computer that they log on to.

- User profiles can be used by a single user or can be assigned to a group of users. If assigning a profile to a group of users, you must assign one at a time after first making a copy of the profile for each user.

- They allow multiple users to share the same computer, yet still retain individual desktop settings.

- The Administrator can configure profiles to be edited by the owner of the profile, or they can save profiles as *mandatory* read-only files so that users cannot change their profiles.

## Configuration Information Stored in User Profiles

User profiles store many configuration options in NT. For example, if the user account KATIE changed her desktop appearance, created a shortcut, or added items to her Startup folder, her user profile would keep track of her changes. The next time she logged on, her desktop would be saved from her last session. Most of the desktop settings related to personal preference and work requirements within NT can be saved in a user profile. Table 5.1 lists many of the settings that are saved by user profiles.

| **TABLE 5.1**<br>User-defined settings saved by user profiles | **NT SETTING** | **SOME EXAMPLES** |
|---|---|---|
| | Windows NT Explorer | View of NT Explorer, mapped network drives, types of files that are displayed |
| | Control Panel | Screen appearance, accessibility properties, mouse and keyboard settings |
| | Printer Settings | Network printer connections |
| | Taskbar | All taskbar settings including program items and their properties |
| | Accessories | Preference settings for Clock, Calculator, and NotePad |
| | Online Help Bookmarks | Any bookmarks the user has defined in the NT Help program |
| | Windows NT-based Applications | If the NT-based application supports user configuration settings, these can be saved in the user profile |

## Local User Profiles

Each time you log on to an NT computer, the system checks to see if you have a local user profile in a folder called PROFILES that lives under the root directory where NT Server was installed (most likely, C:\WINNT). In the PROFILES folder, the system checks for a sub-folder that matches the user's logon name. If the user has never logged in at the local computer, no profile folder will exist for them, and the system will create a folder that matches the logon name and copy into it the contents of the DEFAULT USER profile. This way, all users initially start out with the same profile, but as they modify the default profile, their changes are saved in their custom profile folder. The custom profile folder contains a file called NTUSER.DAT and directory links to desktop items.

The drawback of local user profiles is that they are only available on the computer where they were created. For example, if RICK logged on at COMPUTER1 and changed his desktop, his user profile would be saved on COMPUTER1. If he logged on at COMPUTER2, he would receive the default profile, or the profile he last used at COMPUTER2.

In Exercise 5.1, you will create a new user and view the profile folder that is created. You will also prove that user profiles are local to the computer where they are created.

---

**EXERCISE 5.1**

### Creating Local User Profiles

For this exercise, you should have NT Server running on PDC1 and your second computer booted as NT Workstation, NTWS2. Both computers should be logged onto DOMAIN1 as ADMINISTRATOR.

Complete the following steps from PDC1.

1. In User Manager for Domains, create a new user named TESTER. Make sure you uncheck the User Must Change Password at Next Logon option.

2. Select Start ➢ Programs ➢ Windows NT Explorer.

3. Open the C:\WINNT\PROFILES folder. Notice that TESTER does not have a folder because he has never logged on.

4. Log off of the ADMINISTRATOR account and log on as TESTER.

5. Select Start ➢ Settings ➢ Control Panel ➢ Display.

6. Click the Appearance tab of the Display Properties dialog box.

7. In the Scheme box, choose Rainy Day and click OK.

8. Select Start ➢ Programs ➢ Windows NT Explorer.

9. Open the C:\WINNT\PROFILES folder. Notice that TESTER now has a folder because he has logged on.

10. Log off as TESTER and log back on as TESTER. Notice that the Rainy Day color scheme is now a part of TESTER's saved profile.

The next part of the exercise should be completed from NTWS2.

11. Log on to the DOMAIN1 domain as TESTER. Notice that you receive the default profile and not the profile that was created on PDC1. Local profiles are only available on the computer on which they were created.

In order for a profile to be accessible to any computer on the network, it must be a *roaming* profile. Roaming profiles are covered in the next subsection.

## Roaming User Profiles

A roaming profile is stored on the server and allows a user to access their profile, regardless of which computer they log on to. This is nice for users who want to have a consistent look and feel to their desktop no matter which computer they access.

In the last section, the user account TESTER had a local user profile that was only available at PDC1. In Exercise 5.2, you will make a roaming profile for TESTER that can be accessed from PDC1 or NTWS2.

---

**EXERCISE 5.2**

### Creating a Roaming Profile

This exercise should be completed from PDC1 while logged on as ADMINISTRATOR.

**1.** Select Start ➤ Programs ➤ Windows NT Explorer.

**2.** Create a share on the C:\WINNT\PROFILES folder called PROFILES and then close the Windows NT Explorer.

**3.** Select Start ➤ Programs ➤ Administrative Tools (common) ➤ User Manager for Domains.

**4.** Double-click TESTER to open the User Properties dialog box.

**5.** Click Profile to open the User Environment Profile dialog box.

**6.** In the User Profile Path box type, **\\PDC1\PROFILES\TESTER** and click OK. Close User Manager for Domains.

The next step should be completed from NTWS2.

**7.** Log on to DOMAIN1 as TESTER. Notice that the user profile that you created in Exercise 5.1 is now available to TESTER regardless of the location they are logging in from.

## Mandatory User Profiles

A mandatory profile can't be modified by anyone except an Administrator.

It's possible that you may not want a user to be able to change their profile. For example, you may have a user who knows just enough about configuring their computer that they can really make a mess of the configuration, but they don't know enough to fix it once it's messed up. You might also have a group of users who share a profile and you don't want one user to be able to modify the profile for the entire group.

By creating a mandatory profile, the user can still make changes to the desktop, but those changes cannot be saved, and the next time the user logs on, they receive the mandatory profile.

By default the user profiles are named NTUSER.DAT. The .DAT extension indicates that the profile is a regular profile and it can be updated by the user. Mandatory profiles are created by going into the profile folder and changing the extension on the NTUSER.DAT file from .DAT to .MAN. In essence you are creating a read-only profile.

*If the user has been assigned a mandatory profile, and the profile is not available, the logon will not be successful. If you choose to use mandatory profiles, you should consider directory replication which is covered in Chapter 7, "NT Domain Management."*

# System Policies

S YSTEM POLICIES ARE new to NT Server in version 4.0, although you might be familiar with them from Windows 95. These policies are used to control the computers' system configuration and the users' work environment; they work by editing the Registry of NT computers to reflect the system configurations. System policies are edited through the System Policy Editor, a tool within the Administrative Tools group. It is much easier to edit through the System Policy Editor, which is a GUI interface, than editing the text-based Registry.

System policies can be set for specific users, computers, groups, or all users. By default, no system policies are used unless they are created by an administrator through the System Policy Editor found in the Administrative Tools.

The system policies can be applied to a user, group, or computer. By applying a system policy to a user or group, you manage the HKEY_CURRENT_ USER portion of the Registry. If you apply a system policy to a computer, you manage the HKEY_LOCAL_MACHINE portion of the Registry. The system policy works by overwriting any existing Registry configurations.

Through the System Policy Editor, you can configure system policies for the following:

- **Default computer:** specifies default settings for any NT computer within the domain, and writes to the HKEY_LOCAL_MACHINE portion of the Registry.

- **Default user:** sets defaults for any user that logs on from an NT computer, and writes to the HKEY_CURRENT_USER portion of the Registry.

- **User:** allows you to create a customized system policy for a specific user, and affects the HKEY_CURRENT_USER portion of the Registry.

- **Group:** similar to user, but through group, you can apply system policies to a group of users.

- **Computer:** allows you to customize computer settings that apply to the HKEY_LOCAL_MACHINE portion of the Registry to a specific computer.

In the next subsections, you will learn which properties can be managed through user or group policies, and which properties can be managed through computer policies.

## User and Group System Policies

User and group system policies can be applied to DEFAULT USER, to a specific user or to a group. Through the user and group system policies, you are able to specify the configuration options shown in Table 5.2.

| | |
|---|---|
| **TABLE 5.2** User and group system policy options | |

| POLICY | OPTIONS |
|---|---|
| Control Panel | Allows you to specify display settings such as hiding Screen Saver and Appearance tabs. |
| Desktop | Used to configure Wallpaper and Color scheme. |
| Shell | Can be used to configure restrictions such as Hide Network Neighborhood and Don't Save Settings on Exit. |

| TABLE 5.2 | POLICY | OPTIONS |
|---|---|---|
| User and group system policy options (continued) | System | Allows you to set restrictions such as Disable Registry editing tools and Run only allowed Windows applications. |
| | Windows NT Shell | Allows you to configure NT custom folders and specify restrictions relating to the NT shell. |
| | Windows NT System | Used to specify whether or not to Parse AUTOEXEC.BAT and whether or not to Run logon scripts synchronously. |

By default, the system looks for system policies on the PDC in the NET-LOGON share in a file called NTCONFIG.POL. The NETLOGON share points to the following folder:

%WINNTROOT%\SYSTEM32\REPL\IMPORT\SCRIPTS

If you want your system policy to be enforced system wide you should note this file name and location.

The following conditions determine which system policy will be used if the user has multiple system policies assigned through user and group memberships:

- If the user has a user system policy set, their system policies are the HKEY_CURRENT_USER portion of the Registry. This allows specific user policies to take precedence over default user or group system policies that may have been assigned.

- If the user is a member of any groups that have system policies defined and does not have a user policy defined, then the group system policies will be merged into the HKEY_CURRENT_USER portion of the Registry by priority.

- If the User does not have a user policy assigned or does not have any group policies, they will have the HKEY_CURRENT_USER portion of the Registry updated with any changes that have been made to the DEFAULT USER system policy.

*If a user profile and a system policy are both present, and they specify common options, the system policy configuration options will overwrite the user profiles configuration within the Registry.*

In the following example, we will assume that user LARS is a member of HR and MANAGERS. He has a user system policy set for LARS, and system policies set for HR and MANAGERS. The group system policy for MANAGERS has a higher priority than the group system policy for HR. The options have been configured as shown in Table 5.3.

| **TABLE 5.3** | **OPTION** | **HR** | **MANAGERS** | **LARS** |
|---|---|---|---|---|
| User system policies example | Color Scheme | Evergreen 256 | Rose 256 | Blue and Black |
| | Hide Screen Saver Tab in Control Panel, Display | not set | not set | hide |
| | Hide Appearance Tab in Control Panel, Display | not set | not set | hide |
| | Shell Restrictions, Hide Network Neighborhood | not set | hide | not set |
| | Shell Restrictions, Save Settings on Exit | not set | hide | not set |

Based on the system policies defined in Table 5.3, the system policies Lars would be governed by are shown in Table 5.4.

| **TABLE 5.4** | **OPTION** | **LARS' COMBINED POLICY** |
|---|---|---|
| Example of effective user system policies | Color Scheme | Blue and Black (from LARS' settings) |
| | Hide Screen Saver Tab in Control Panel, Display | hide (from LARS' settings) |
| | Hide Appearance Tab in Control Panel, Display | hide (from LARS' settings) |
| | Shell Restrictions, Hide Network Neighborhood | not set (group system policy not used if user system policy exists) |
| | Shell Restrictions, Save Settings on Exit | not set (group system policy not used if user system policy exists) |

In Exercise 5.3 you will create a system policy for a user.

---

**EXERCISE 5.3**

## Creating a System Policy for a User

This exercise should be completed from PDC1 while logged on as ADMINISTRATOR.

**1.** Use User Manager for Domains to create user LARS. Make sure that you uncheck the User Must Change Password at Next Logon box.

**2.** Select Start ➢ Programs ➢ Administrative Tools (common) ➢ System Policy Editor. You will see the System Policy Editor dialog box, shown here.

**3.** Click File ➢ New Policy. Notice that you now see Default Computer and Default User within the System Policy Editor dialog box.

**4.** Click Edit ➢ Add User. Click Browse, and click LARS, then click Add. Click OK and LARS will appear in the System Policy Editor dialog box.

---

**5.** Double-click LARS to bring up the Policies tab page of the lars Properties dialog box, shown here.

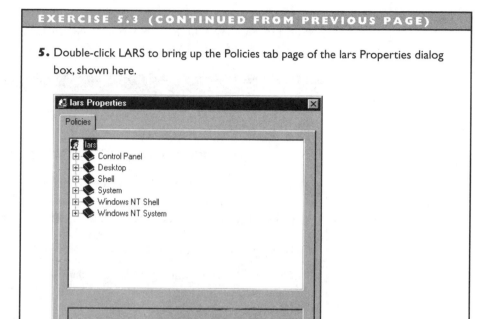

**6.** Click Control Panel ➤ Display, and check the Restrict Display box; notice that the bottom of the dialog box becomes active. Check the Hide Screen Saver tab box and the Hide Appearance tab box.

**7.** Click Desktop and check the Color Scheme box. In the Scheme name drop down box, choose Blue and Black and click OK.

**8.** Click File ➤ Save, and the Save As dialog box will appear. Choose C:\WINNT \SYSTEM32\REPL\IMPORT\SCRIPTS and save the file as NTCONFIG.

**9.** Log off and log on as LARS. Notice that your color scheme has changed.

**10.** Select Start ➤ Settings ➤ Control Panel ➤ Display. Notice that the Display Properties dialog box is now missing the Screen Saver and Appearance tabs.

**11.** Log off and log back on as ADMINISTRATOR.

In Exercise 5.4, you will create a user that will be a member of two different groups, HR and MANAGERS. You will then create system policies for both groups, and assign the MANAGERS group a higher system profile priority.

### Creating a System Policy for Groups and Assigning Priorities

This exercise should be completed from PDC1 while logged on as ADMINISTRATOR.

**1.** Use User Manager for Domains to create the global groups HR and MANAGERS. Create a user named PAM and make sure that you uncheck the User Must Change Password at Next Logon box. Add PAM to the HR and MANAGERS groups.

**2.** Click Start ➣ Programs ➣ Administrative Tools (common) ➣ System Policy Editor.

**3.** Click File. At the bottom of the File menu choose
`C:\WINNT\SYSTEM32\REPL\IMPORT\SCRIPTS\NTCONFIG.POL`.

**4.** Click Edit ➣ Add Group. Enter HR and click OK.

**5.** Double-click HR to open the HR policies.

**6.** Click Shell ➣ Restrictions and check the Hide Network Neighborhood box and the Don't Save Settings on Exit box.

**7.** Click Desktop and check the Color Scheme box. In the Scheme Name drop-down box, choose Evergreen 256 and click OK.

**8.** Select File ➣ Save. Exit the System Policy Editor.

**9.** Log off and log on as PAM.

**10.** Notice the color scheme PAM is now using, and that the Network Neighborhood item is missing.

**11.** Log off and log back on as ADMINISTRATOR.

**12.** Click Start ➣ Programs ➣ Administrative Tools (common) ➣ System Policy Editor.

**13.** Click File and choose
`C:\WINNT\SYSTEM32\REPL\IMPORT\SCRIPTS\NTCONFIG.POL`.

**EXERCISE 5.4 (CONTINUED FROM PREVIOUS PAGE)**

**14.** Click Edit ➢ Add Group. Enter MANAGERS and click OK.

**15.** Double-click MANAGERS to open the MANAGERS policies.

**16.** Click Desktop and check the Color Scheme box. In the Scheme Name drop-down box, choose Rose 256 and click OK.

**17.** In this step, you will assign the MANAGERS group higher priority than the HR group. Choose Options ➢ Group Priority, and the Group Priority dialog box, shown here, will appear.

**18.** Click MANAGERS and click the Move Up box. Click OK.

**19.** Select File Menu ➢ Save. Exit the System Policy Editor.

**20.** Log off and log on as PAM. Notice that PAM is now using the Rose 256 color scheme because MANAGERS has a higher priority. Because the MANAGERS group did not specify Hide Network Neighborhood or Don't Save Settings on Exit, those options were picked up from PAM's HR group membership.

**21.** Log off and log on as ADMINISTRATOR.

**22.** Use User Manager for Domains to add LARS to the HR and MANAGERS groups.

**23.** Log off and log on as LARS. Notice that he still uses the LARS effective system policy based on the examples shown in Table 5.3 and Table 5.4.

**24.** Log off and log on as ADMINISTRATOR.

## Computer System Policies

System policies can also be set for the Default Computer or a specific NT computer using the computer's NetBIOS name. Setting a computer system policy allows you to edit the HKEY_LOCAL_MACHINE portion of the computer's Registry. The options that can be configured through computer system policies are listed in Table 5.5.

| | POLICY | OPTIONS |
|---|---|---|
| **TABLE 5.5**<br>Computer system policies | Network | Allows you to specify whether the computer should be able to receive remote updates, and whether the updates should be manual or automatic. |
| | System | Used to set SNMP configuration information and whether any programs should be run at startup. |
| | Windows NT Network | Specifies whether you can create hidden drive shares on NT Server or NT Workstation. |
| | Windows NT Printer | Can be used to configure whether to disable the browse thread on the computer, set scheduler priority, and whether to beep for error enabled. |
| | Windows NT Remote Access | Used to configure RAS options such as wait interval for callback and auto disconnect. |
| | Windows NT Shell | Allows you to configure custom shared program folders, custom shared desktop icons, custom shared Start menu, and custom shared Startup folder. |
| | Windows NT System | Used to specify logon and file system information. Logon policies include options like displaying a logon banner and not displaying the name of the last user who logged on. File system policies include not allowing creation of 8.3 files with long file names and not updating last access time. |
| | Windows NT User Profiles | Can specify whether to automatically detect slow connections and whether to time-out on dialog boxes. |

If the Default Computer and a custom computer system policy have been created, the custom computer policy takes precedence. In Exercise 5.5, you will create a custom computer system policy.

---

**EXERCISE 5.5**

### Creating a Computer System Policy

This exercise should be completed from PDC1 while logged on as ADMINISTRATOR.

**1.** Click Start ➢ Programs ➢ Administrative Tools (common) ➢ System Policy Editor.

**2.** Click File ➢
`C:\WINNT\SYSTEM32\REPL\IMPORT\SCRIPTS\NTCONFIG.POL`.

**3.** Click Edit ➢ Add Computer. Enter PDC1 and click OK.

**4.** Double-click PDC1 to open the PDC1 system policies.

**5.** Click Windows NT System ➢ Logon.

**6.** Check the Logon Banner box. In the Caption box, type **HELLO**. In the Text box type, **WELCOME ALL AUTHORIZED USERS TO PDC1**.

**7.** Check the Do Not Display Last Logged On User Name box. Click OK.

**8.** Select File ➢ Save, and then exit System Policy Editor.

**9.** Log off and log back on as ADMINISTRATOR. Notice that you did not get the text messages. The Registry was just updated and you will need to log off and log back on to notice the changes. Log off and log back on as ADMINISTRATOR; now you should notice the logon banner and that the last user to log on is no longer displayed in the User Name box.

---

# Hardware Profiles

Hardware profiles are used to specify different hardware configurations for a single computer. For example, assume that you have a laptop computer that can be placed in a docking station or used independently. When the computer is in the docking station, it is part of the network, and when it is used independently it does not participate on the network.

If a computer has had a hardware profile specified, the user is able to choose which hardware profile should be loaded during system startup. In Exercise 5.6, you will create a hardware profile for your computer, so that it can have the networking components installed. Or through an alternate profile, it can choose not to install the networking components.

---

**EXERCISE 5.6**

### Creating a Hardware Profile

This exercise should be completed from PDC1 while logged on as ADMINISTRATOR.

**1.** Click Start ➤ Settings ➤ Control Panel ➤ System.

**2.** Click the Hardware Profile tab.

**3.** Click Copy and the To box, name the new profile UNDOCKED COMPUTER and click OK.

**4.** Highlight the UNDOCKED COMPUTER profile, and click Properties. Click the Network tab, and check the Network-disabled hardware profile. Click OK.

**5.** From the System Properties dialog box, click OK.

**6.** Shut down and restart your computer. As the system reboots, notice that you have an option to choose the hardware profile you want to load. Choose UNDOCKED COMPUTER.

**7.** Log on as ADMINISTRATOR. Notice that if you try to access the network, you are unsuccessful because no networking components are installed.

**8.** Shut down and restart your computer. When you see the hardware profile list, choose Original Configuration. Log on as ADMINISTRATOR.

# Chapter Summary

I N THIS CHAPTER you learned about user profiles, system policies, and hardware profiles. Each of these topics deals with the configuration of your computer. User profiles govern the desktop appearance. System policies govern some of the desktop appearance, but they mainly control what you do at the desktop. Hardware profiles are used to create different hardware configurations for portable computers.

The main benefit of user profiles is that they allow a user to save their desktop from one session to the next. By default user profiles are stored and made available on the computer where the user profile was created. If a user wants to access the profile from any networked NT Server computer, the profile must be roaming. Roaming profiles are created by creating a network share on the profile folder and then pointing to the shared profile path through User Manager for Domains. Users can also modify their own profiles by default. By renaming the NTUSER.DAT file to NTUSER.MAN, the administrator can create a read-only mandatory profile that the user cannot modify.

System policies allow administrators to control what users can do within the desktop and how the networked NT computers will be configured. System policies can be applied to all NT users in the entire system, a group of users, a specific user, all computers, or specific computers. System policies work by editing the HKEY_CURRENT_USER and HKEY_LOCAL_COMPUTER portions of the Registry.

Hardware profiles are used to maintain multiple hardware profiles for machines which might have different configurations, such as a portable computer that uses a docking station.

# Review Questions

**1.** Where are user profiles stored by default?

**A.** %WINNTROOT%\PROFILES

**B.** %WINNTROOT%\POLICIES

**C.** %WINNTROOT%\SYSTEM32\REPL\IMPORT\SCRIPTS

**D.** %WINNTROOT%\SYSTEM32\REPL\EXPORT\SCRIPTS

**2.** Which folder does the system check by default when looking for system policies?

**A.** %WINNTROOT%\PROFILES

**B.** %WINNTROOT%\POLICIES

**C.** %WINNTROOT%\SYSTEM32\REPL\IMPORT\SCRIPTS

**D.** %WINNTROOT%\SYSTEM32\REPL\EXPORT\SCRIPTS

**3.** What is the name of the system policy file that NT Server looks for by default?

**A.** CONFIG.POL

**B.** NTCONFIG.POL

**C.** NTUSER.DAT

**D.** USER.DAT

**4.** What is the name of the file used to store user profiles?

**A.** CONFIG.POL

**B.** NTCONFIG.POL

**C.** NTUSER.DAT

**D.** USER.DAT

**5.** KATIE is a member of the SALES group and the MANAGERS group. The system policy defines that DEFAULT USER uses the Blue and Black color scheme. The SALES system policy defines the Blues 256 color scheme. The MANAGERS system policy defines the Celery 256 color scheme. KATIE's system policy defines the Rose 256 color scheme. What will KATIE's color scheme be when she logs on?

**A.** Blue and Black

**B.** Blues 256

**C.** Celery 256

**D.** Rose 256

**6.** Which of the following configuration options can be specified through a user profile? Choose all that apply.

**A.** Network printer connections

**B.** Taskbar settings

**C.** Whether display settings should be restricted

**D.** Desktop color scheme

**E.** Whether to disable the Registry editor

**7.** Which of the following configuration options can be specified through a user system policy? Choose all that apply.

**A.** Network printer connections

**B.** Taskbar settings

**C.** Whether display settings should be restricted

**D.** Desktop color scheme

**E.** Whether to disable the Registry editor

8. Which Registry keys are updated through system policies? Choose all that apply.

   **A.** HKEY_CURRENT_USER

   **B.** HKEY_CURRENT_CONFIG

   **C.** HKEY_CLASSES_ROOT

   **D.** HKEY_USERS

   **E.** HKEY_LOCAL_MACHINE

9. If KEVIN is a member of the SALES group and the MANAGERS group, and both groups have system policies defined, how does the system know which policy to apply?

   **A.** It's based on KEVIN's primary group as defined in User Manager for Domains.

   **B.** You can specify group priority in System Policy Editor.

   **C.** You can specify group priority in User Manager for Domains.

   **D.** Group priority is based on the group names' alphabetical order.

10. What utility is used to create and manage system policies?

    **A.** User Manager for Domains

    **B.** System Policy Editor

    **C.** System Policy Manager

    **D.** Server Manager

11. How are mandatory profiles specified?

    **A.** By clicking the Mandatory check box in User Manager Editor

    **B.** By renaming the NTUSER.DAT file to NTUSER.MAN

    **C.** By checking the User Mandatory Profiles box in User Manager for Domains

    **D.** By renaming the NTUSER.DAT file to NTUSER.MDT

# NT Client
# Administration

N THIS CHAPTER you will learn about NT client administration using the Network Client Administrator utility. Using this utility you are able to:

- Make network installation startup disks

- Make installation disk sets

- Copy client-based network administration tools

- View remoteboot client information

Network installation startup disks are used to install NT Server, NT Workstation, Windows 95, Windows for Workgroups, or the Network Client for MS-DOS over the network. This assumes that the OS software you want to install has been copied to a network share. Through the Network Client Administrator, you copy to a floppy disk the software necessary to make the connection to the network share point and begin OS installation.

The Make Installation Disk Sets option of the Network Client Administrator is used to create installation disk sets for Microsoft Network Client for MS-DOS, LAN Manager for MS-DOS, LAN Manager for OS/2, RAS for MS-DOS, and TCP/IP-32 for Windows for Workgroups. The installation disk sets are then used to manually copy the software to connect the NT network to the appropriate client type.

If you use the Copy Client-based Network Administration Tools option of the Network Client Administrator, you can create a network share to NT Administrative Tools which allows you to administer the NT domain from NT member servers, NT Workstations, or Windows 95 clients.

Through View Remoteboot Client information, you can view information about the *remoteboot* service. The remoteboot service is used to start diskless computers over the network. Through Network Client Administrator, you are able to view, but not configure the remoteboot service.

*The remoteboot service is not covered on the exam and it's not even covered in the NT Server documentation. If you plan on using the remoteboot service, it's worth buying the NT Server Resource Kit version 4.0, which covers this topic.*

*Due to equipment and software requirements, there are no exercises in this chapter. Instead, I will present the steps you need to follow to complete tasks covered in this chapter.*

# Making Network Installation Startup Disks

THROUGH THE NETWORK Client Administrator, you can automate network installations of the operating systems listed in Table 6.1.

| MICROSOFT OPERATING SYSTEM SUPPORTED | VERSION(S) |
|---|---|
| Network Client for MS-DOS | version 3.0 |
| Windows for Workgroups | version 3.11 |
| Windows 95 | N/A |
| NT Workstation | versions 3.5, 3.51, and 4.0 |
| NT Server | versions 3.5, 3.51, and 4.0 |

**TABLE 6.1**

Operating systems supported through startup disks

Automating network software installations is easier and faster than installing from a floppy or CD. Assume that you have just received 100 new computers that need to have Windows 95 installed. You could install each computer from a CD or you could install each computer from the network. Network installation is especially useful if your computers do not have CD-ROM players.

## Preparing Distribution Files for Network Installation

In order to install network software, you first have to choose a server that has enough disk space to accommodate the distribution files for the OS you want to install. In our example, you will be installing Windows 95 and you want to use PDC1 as the server with the share point (network connection). You would complete the following steps:

1. On PDC1, choose the drive where you want to place the Windows 95 distribution files.

2. Create a directory structure for the distribution files and copy the files from a floppy or CD.

3. Create a network share on the directory that contains the distribution files.

Now that a share point has been set for the distribution files, you need to connect your new computer to the share so that you can install Windows 95. Because your new computer probably does not have software installed on it to connect to the network, the Make Network Installation Startup Disk option of the Network Client Administrator comes in handy. This option allows you to create a floppy diskette that has enough software on it to get you to the network and start the network installation of your chosen OS.

*The NT Server 3.51 CD contains the distribution files for Windows for Workgroups. The NT Server 4.0 CD contains the Windows 95 distribution files. You still need a license for each computer onto which you install these operating system.*

## Creating Network Installation Startup Disks

After a network share has been created for the OS you want to install over the network, the next step is to create a network installation startup disk. To create the network installation startup disk, use the Network Client Administrator found within the Administrative Tools group. When you open the Network Client Administrator, you see the dialog box shown in Figure 6.1.

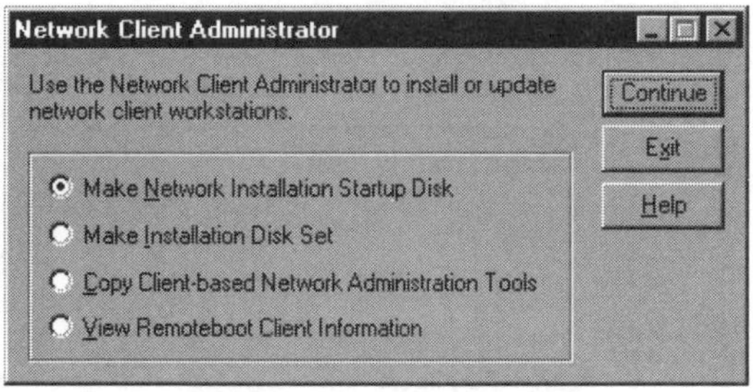

**FIGURE 6.1**

The Network Client
Administrator dialog box

To create a network installation startup disk, you will need a high density floppy diskette that has been formatted and is bootable to DOS. Once you have prepared the diskette, click the Make Network Installation Startup Disk button and click Continue. At this point, you will see the Share Network Client Installation Files dialog box, shown in Figure 6.2.

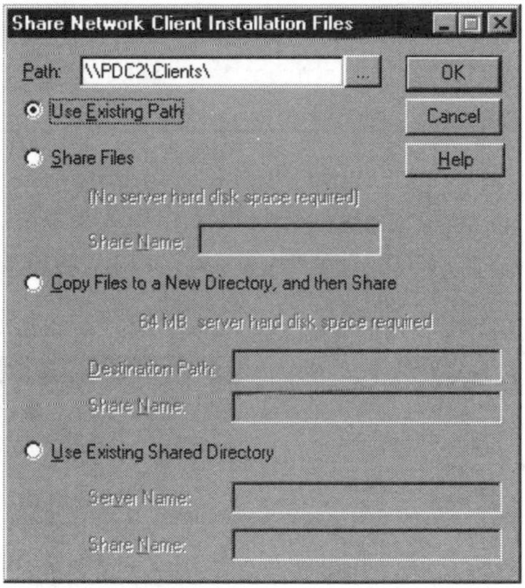

**FIGURE 6.2**

The Share Network Client
Installation Files dialog box

Through the Share Network Client Installation Files dialog box, you can specify the network location of the OS distribution files you will be using during the network installations. Your four choices are listed in Table 6.2.

| TABLE 6.2 Options for sharing network client files | SHARE NETWORK CLIENT FILES OPTION | DESCRIPTION |
|---|---|---|
| | Use Existing Path | Use this option if you have already used the Network Client Administrator to create a network installation disk, and you want to use an existing path that was previously used. |
| | Share Files | Allows you to create a new share on a distribution CD. You should note that accessing a CD will be slower than accessing a share from the hard drive. The benefit of this option is that it does not take up any disk space. |
| | Copy Files to a New Directory, and then Share | This option is used to copy files from the source media to the specified destination, and then to create a network share. |
| | Use Existing Shared Directory | This option assumes that you have already copied the distribution files and created a network share, and allows you to point to the existing share. |

After you have specified the location of the network distribution files, you are ready to begin configuration of your network client disk. The Target Workstation Configuration dialog box, shown in Figure 6.3, will appear.

**FIGURE 6.3**

The Target Workstation Configuration dialog box

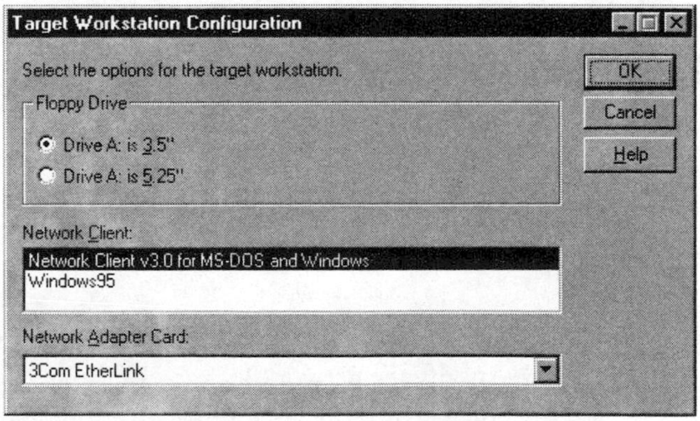

Within the Target Workstation Configuration dialog box, you are able to specify the following configuration information regarding your target workstation:

- Floppy drive type

- Network Client

- Network Adapter Card

The floppy drive type can be 3.5" or 5.25". The network clients that appear by default are the Network Client v3.0 for MS-DOS and Windows or Windows 95. This software will be used to connect to the network. The last option on this screen allows you to select the network adapter card your target computer is using. The drop-down list provides a list of choices. Hopefully your network card is on this list.

*One of the weaknesses of the Network Client Administrator is that if your card is not on this list, there is no other choice that would allow you to provide your own driver. If you fall into this category, its easier to use the Make Installation Disk Set (that will be covered in the next section) to make your network connection.*

After you have completed the information in the Target Workstation Configuration dialog box, you will see the Network Startup Disk Configuration box, shown in Figure 6.4.

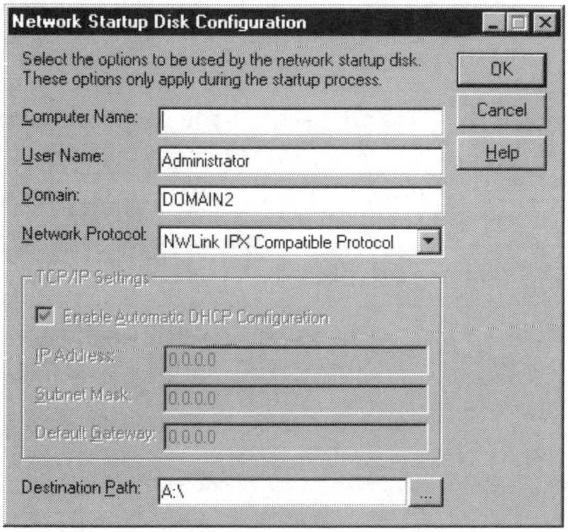

**FIGURE 6.4**

The Network Startup Disk Configuration dialog box

**Network Startup Disk Configuration**

Select the options to be used by the network startup disk. These options only apply during the startup process.

Computer Name: 

User Name: Administrator

Domain: DOMAIN2

Network Protocol: NWLink IPX Compatible Protocol

TCP/IP Settings

☑ Enable Automatic DHCP Configuration

IP Address: 0.0.0.0

Subnet Mask: 0.0.0.0

Default Gateway: 0.0.0.0

Destination Path: A:\

OK | Cancel | Help

In the Network Startup Disk Configuration dialog box, you can specify the following configuration information:

- Computer name
- User name
- Domain
- Network protocol
- Destination path

This information is used to automate the network connection to the distribution files you have already specified.

*If you use the same network installation disk for multiple computers, you will encounter problems due to duplicate computer names. To use the same disk, you will need to edit the SYSTEM.INI file to specify a unique computer name; this assumes that all other configuration information is identical.*

# Making Installation Disk Sets

TO MAKE INSTALLATION disk sets, copy software to floppy disks manually. The software can then be copied manually to computers so that they are able to connect to the NT network. Installation disk sets are useful if you can't connect to the network to download software. Table 6.3 lists the network client disks that can be created and the number of disks each set requires.

| | CLIENT DISK SET | NUMBER OF DISKS REQUIRED |
|---|---|---|
| **TABLE 6.3**<br>Installation disk sets | Network Client v3.0 for MS-DOS and Windows | 2 |
| | Remote Access v1.1a for MS-DOS | 1 |
| | TCP/IP 32 for Windows for Workgroups 3.11 | 1 |

| TABLE 6.3 | CLIENT DISK SET | NUMBER OF DISKS REQUIRED |
|---|---|---|
| Installation disk sets (continued) | LAN Manager v2.2c for MS-DOS | 4 |
| | LAN Manager v2.2c for OS/2 | 4 |

# Copying Client-Based Network Administration Tools

B Y DEFAULT, YOU are only able to manage NT domains from NT Server domain controllers (PDC or BDCs). By using the Copy the Client-based Network Administration Tools option of the Network Client Administrator, you are able to create a network share to the client-based administration tools on the NT Server CD or you can copy the client-based administration tools to a hard disk and create a network share.

Once the files are shared you can connect to the share and install the administrative tools onto the appropriate client. This allows you to manage NT domains from NT member servers, NT Workstation, and Windows 95 computers.

Table 6.4 shows the utilities that are supported on the NT and the Windows 95 platforms.

| TABLE 6.4 | ADMINISTRATIVE TOOL | NT MEMBER SERVER OR NT WORKSTATION | WINDOWS 95 |
|---|---|---|---|
| Platform support for client-based administration tools | User Manager for Domains | ✓ | ✓ |
| | Server Manager | ✓ | ✓ |
| | Event Viewer | ✓ | ✓ |
| | DHCP Manager | ✓ | |
| | WINS Manager | ✓ | |
| | User Profile Editor | ✓ | |

| TABLE 6.4 | ADMINISTRATIVE TOOL | NT MEMBER SERVER OR NT WORKSTATION | WINDOWS 95 |
|---|---|:---:|:---:|
| Platform support for client-based administration tools (continued) | Services for Macintosh Manager | ✓ | |
| | Remote Access Administrator | ✓ | |
| | Remoteboot Manager | ✓ | |

# Chapter Summary

THROUGH THE NETWORK Client Administrator, you are able to:

- Create network installation startup disks
- Make installation disk sets
- Copy client-based network administration tools
- View remoteboot client information

Use the Create Network Installation Startup Disks option to copy the necessary software to a startup disk which is used to make a network connection to a network share point that contains distribution software. This allows software to be installed over the network, as opposed to using CDs or floppy diskettes. The advantages of using network installations are that they are usually faster and more convenient.

If you use the Make Installation Disk Sets option of Network Client Administrator, you are able to copy network client or service files to floppy disks. Then you can manually update your computers via the installation disk set.

The Copy Client-based Network Administration Tools option of Network Client Administrator allows you to create a share to the Network client utilities, or it allows you to copy the administrative tools to shared hard-disk space. Once a share has been created for the administration tools, members of the ADMINISTRATORS group can connect to the shared folder and install the administrative tools to a Windows NT member server, NT Workstation, or a Windows 95 computer.

# Review Questions

1. Which of the following options is not available through the Network Client Administrator?

   **A.** Creating installation disk sets

   **B.** Creating NT boot diskettes

   **C.** Making NT network installation startup disks

   **D.** Viewing remoteboot client information

2. Which of the following operating systems can be installed through network installation startup disks? Choose all that apply.

   **A.** Network Client for MS-DOS

   **B.** Windows for Workgroups

   **C.** Windows 95

   **D.** NT Workstation

   **E.** NT Server

   **F.** LAN Manager for MS-DOS

   **G.** LAN Manager for OS/2

3. Which of the following operating systems can have installation disk sets created? Choose all that apply.

   **A.** Network Client for MS-DOS

   **B.** TCP/IP 32 for Windows for Workgroups

   **C.** Windows 95

   **D.** NT Workstation

   **E.** RAS for MS-DOS

   **F.** LAN Manager for MS-DOS

   **G.** LAN Manager for OS/2

**4.** Which of the following configuration options must be specified for a network startup disk? Choose all that apply.

**A.** Computer name

**B.** User name

**C.** Address of network interface card

**D.** Domain name

**5.** Which of the following administrative tools are available on a Windows 95 client? Choose all that apply.

**A.** Server Manager

**B.** User Profile Editor

**C.** User Manager for Domains

**D.** Event Viewer

**E.** DHCP Manager

**6.** Which of the following administrative tools are available on an NT Workstation? Choose all that apply.

**A.** Server Manager

**B.** User Profile Editor

**C.** User Manager for Domains

**D.** Event Viewer

**E.** DHCP Manager

**7.** Which platforms can the administrative tools be copied to based on what's provided on the NT Server 4.0 CD? Choose all that apply.

**A.** Network Client for MS-DOS

**B.** Windows for Workgroups

**C.** Windows 95

**D.** NT Workstation

**E.** NT member server

**F.** LAN Manager for MS-DOS

**G.** LAN Manager for OS/2

# NT Domain
# Management

I N THIS CHAPTER you will learn about NT domain management, the features of which include the Server Manager utility, SAM synchronization for PDC and BDCs, and computer browser services. Server Manager is a powerful administrative utility that you can use to manage a domain and the computers within a domain. Through Server Manager you can also view and manage the properties of a local computer or remote computers.

SAM synchronization is the process of copying a master SAM database and all of its updates from the PDC to the BDCs. By default, SAM synchronization occurs every five minutes, but you will learn how to control SAM synchronization through manual updates using Server Manager, and automatic updates by editing the PDC's Registry values.

The browser service allows you to view the available network resources by managing which domains, servers, and computers are currently active on your network. You will learn how the browser service works, the roles browser computers can play, and how computer failures affect browser services.

# Server Manager

T HE SERVER MANAGER is a utility within the Administrative Tools group. It is used to manage NT domains and the computers within the domains. Using the Server Manager you can do the following as they relate to a local or a remote computer:

- View and configure properties
- Manage shared directories
- Manage services

In addition to helping you manage specific computers, Server Manager helps you out with domain functions, such as:

- Managing domain controllers

- Adding or deleting computers from a domain

- Selecting the domain you want to manage (assuming you have rights to manage a remote domain)

In this section you will learn how to use Server Manager to manage computers and domain functions.

## Using Server Manager to Manage Computers

You can use the Server Manager utility to manage the computers within a domain. The main advantage of Server Manager is that it can be used to manage the local computer or remote computers.

When the Server Manager Utility is opened it displays all computers that are part of the domain. From the Server Manager dialog box, shown in Figure 7.1, you can tell which machines are part of the domain, the computers' NetBIOS names, and the roles the computers play within the domain. The Server Manager dialog box is accessed by opening Server Manager within the Administrative Tools group.

Notice that the top of the Server Manager dialog box specifies that you are looking at the DOMAIN1 domain. The three machines that are part of the DOMAIN1 domain are BDC1, NTWS2, and PDC1. For each computer there is an icon to the left of the computer name that represents the computer's role within the domain. It's easier just to look at the type field which gives a description of each computer's role. In the type field you can tell that BDC1 is a Backup Domain Controller, NTWS2 is an NT Workstation, and PDC1 is a Primary Domain Controller. If a computer is currently active in the domain, it is displayed in boldface. If a computer is not currently active within the domain (for example, it's not currently turned on), it is grayed out. If you have a hard time seeing the bold/dimmed feature, you are not alone; there's not very much contrast.

To manage a specific computer, highlight it. If the computer is active and you have the appropriate permissions, you can manage that machine.

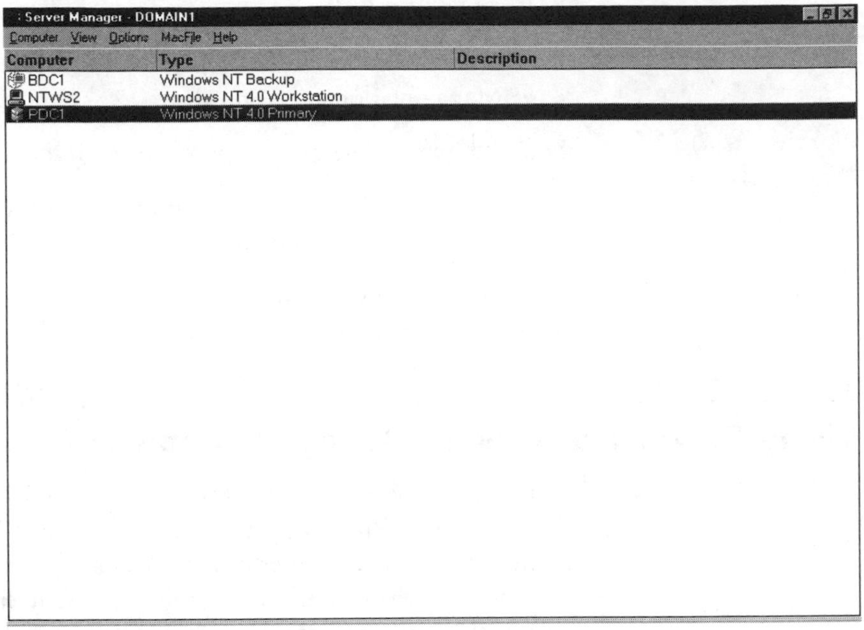

**FIGURE 7.1**

The Server Manager
dialog box

In order to manage a computer, you need to be a member of the DOMAIN ADMINS global group, the ADMINISTRATORS local group, or the SERVER OPERATORS local group on the domain controller for the domain you want to manage. The ACCOUNT OPERATORS group can also use Server Manager, but only to add computers to the domain.

Suppose you have the appropriate rights to use Server Manager, and you choose to manage PDC1 (highlighted). If the machine is not active and you try to manage it, you will get the error message shown in Figure 7.2.

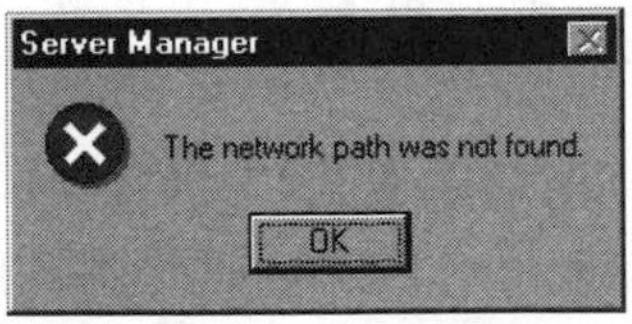

**FIGURE 7.2**

Error accessing
inactive computer

### Managing a Computer's Properties

Once you have selected a computer to manage, you are able to view and manage the following properties of the computer:

- Active user sessions

- Shared resources

- Opened resources

- Directory replication

- Alerts

I cover all these topics in detail in the following subsections.

**PROPERTIES DIALOG BOX** Once you have chosen a computer to manage you can double-click on the computer name in the Server Manager dialog box to display the Properties dialog box. The Properties dialog box shows usage statistics summarizing the connections and resources currently being used on the selected computer. The usage summary displays the number of sessions, open files, file locks, and open named pipes there are on the computer. Table 7.1 defines these statistics.

| **TABLE 7.1**<br>Usage summary statistics | **SUMMARY OPTION** | **DESCRIPTION** |
|---|---|---|
| | Sessions | Shows the number of remote users that are accessing the computer. |
| | Open Files | Shows the total of all files currently opened by remote users. |
| | File Locks | Shows the number of files currently locked by remote users. A file lock prevents a file or subdirectory from being accessed. |
| | Named Pipes | Shows how many named pipes are currently open. A named pipe is used for interprocess communications with other local or remote processes. |

In Exercise 7.1, you will use Server Manager to view the properties of PDC1 before and after it has accessed the network.

---

**EXERCISE 7.1**

## Viewing Computer Properties through Server Manager

You must have completed the exercises from Chapter 2 in order to do this excercise. In order to complete the exercises in this chapter, you should have your machines booted as NT Server PDC1, and NT Workstation NTWS2. You should be logged on to DOMAIN1 on both computers as ADMINISTRATOR.

Complete the following steps from PDC1.

**1.** Select Start ➢ Programs ➢ Administrative Tools (common) ➢ Server Manager.

**2.** Double-click PDC1 to open the Properties dialog box, shown here.

**3.** Note the number of:

Sessions_____

Open Files_____

File Locks_____

Open Named Pipes_____

Complete the following steps from NTWS2:

**4.** Click the Network Neighborhood icon.

**5.** Double-click PDC1 to display the folders that have been shared on PDC1. Click the DATA folder you shared in Exercise 4.1. Open the DOC1 document and leave it open. Open the DOC3 document from within the WP DOCS folder and leave it open.

---

**EXERCISE 7.1 (CONTINUED FROM PREVIOUS PAGE)**

Complete the following steps from PDC1:

**6.** Now that you have opened some files from NTWS2, record the Usage summary information again. (You might need to close the dialog box and reopen it to refresh.)

Note the number of:

Sessions_____

Open Files_____

File Locks_____

Open Named Pipes_____

---

It is interesting to note in Exercise 7.1 that as you accessed network resources, the Server Manager reflected the network usage changes in its statistics summary. If you want to see more specific information regarding the network connections, look at the User Sessions dialog box which I cover in the next subsection.

**USER SESSIONS DIALOG BOX** Within the Properties dialog box of Server Manager there is a Users button which calls up the User Sessions dialog box. The User Sessions dialog box displays all users and the resources that each user is currently connected to on the specified computer.

In the User Sessions dialog box, you also disconnect specific users or all users from the specified computer. Your users will be able to reconnect if they try to access the resource again; disconnect does not log them off.

The User Sessions dialog box provides detailed information on the current user connections. You can see who is accessing the computer, as well as the name of the computer where they are logged on. You can also see the number of resources they have open, the amount of time each resource has been open and the amount of time each resource has remained idle. It is also possible to determine whether the resource is being accessed via Guest access.

This information could be useful in situations where you want to monitor a resource for usage statistics, security purposes, or troubleshooting.

Let's assume that you chose the per-server licensing method that was described in Chapter 2. If you were close to exceeding your server license connections, you could use the User Sessions dialog box to determine which connections had been idle the longest. Based on this information, you could disconnect inactive connections to make it possible for other users to access the computer. If you suspected a security violation, you could also use this utility to monitor real-time access to a specified computer.

Figure 7.3 shows the Shared Resources User Sessions dialog box.

**FIGURE 7.3**

The User Sessions dialog box

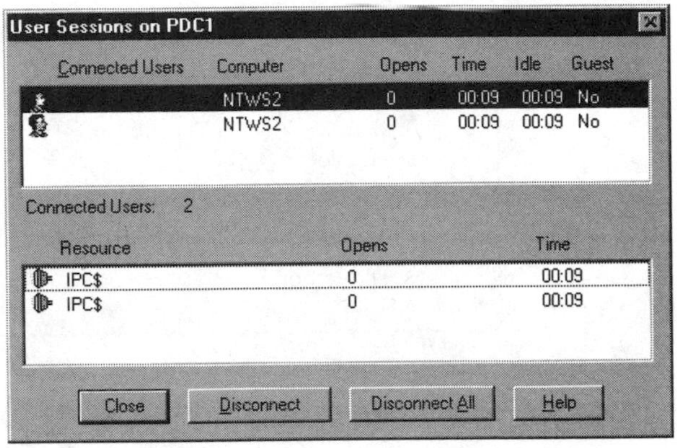

Notice that the User Sessions dialog box has two subscreens. The top subscreen provides a list of all currently connected users and statistics regarding their connections. The bottom subscreen shows which resources the highlighted user from the top subscreen currently has opened. The entries for the User Sessions dialog box are all defined in Table 7.2.

**TABLE 7.2**

User Sessions entries

| USER SESSION ENTRY | DEFINITION |
|---|---|
| Connected User | Displays all users who are currently accessing the computer from the network. |
| Computer | Displays the local computer's NetBIOS name from where the network user is connecting. |
| Opens (for connected user) | Displays the total number of resources the network user has open. |
| Time (for connected user) | Displays in hours and minutes the total time the user has been connected to the computer. |
| Idle | Displays in hours and minutes the amount of time that has passed since the user last initiated any activity. |

| TABLE 7.2 | USER SESSION ENTRY | DEFINITION |
|---|---|---|
| User Sessions entries (continued) | Guest | Indicates (yes or no) whether the user logged in with a regular user account or through Guest access. |
| | Number of connected users | Displays the total number of users that are connected to the computer. |
| | Resource | Displays the resources a specified user is accessing. |
| | Opens (for resource) | Displays the number of opens the specified user has on the open resource. |
| | Time (for resource) | Displays in hours and minutes the time a specified user has been accessing the resource. |
| | Disconnect | Allows you to selectively disconnect users who are accessing the specified computer. |
| | Disconnect All | Allows you to disconnect all users who are currently accessing the computer over the network. |

*The User Sessions dialog box shows the resources that each user has open. Five different resource types are defined. They are shared directories, named pipes, shared printers, communication device queues (only with LAN Manager Servers), and unknown resource types.*

All of the information within the User Sessions dialog box is read-only. You are able to view information regarding user sessions, but you cannot modify anything. The exception to this is the Disconnect and Disconnect All buttons. These buttons are for administrative purposes only. You would use these buttons if you needed to clear connections for maintenance purposes or to free up licensed connections.

*You should warn users before disconnecting them so that they can save any open data. Failure to do this may result in loss of data and very irate users. You can send messages through Server Manager or the NET SEND command line utility.*

**SHARED RESOURCES DIALOG BOX** The Shares button in Server Manager opens the Shared Resources dialog box. This box shows a list of all the resources that have been shared on the computer. Shared resources consist of user-created shares and special system-created shares. A system-created share should not be deleted unless you are sure of the effect deleting the share will have on the system. For each shared resource there is an icon. Note that even hidden shares are shown in the list. If you recall, hidden shares end with a dollar sign. Therefore anyone able to use Server Manager will be able to see all of your shares including the hidden ones. Shares can consist of:

- Shared directories

- Shared printers

- Named pipes

- Communication-queue devices (on LanManager Servers)

- Unknown types

Notice that the Shared Resources dialog box, shown in Figure 7.4, is showing shared folders and shared printers for the computer PDC1.

**FIGURE 7.4**

The Shared Resources dialog box

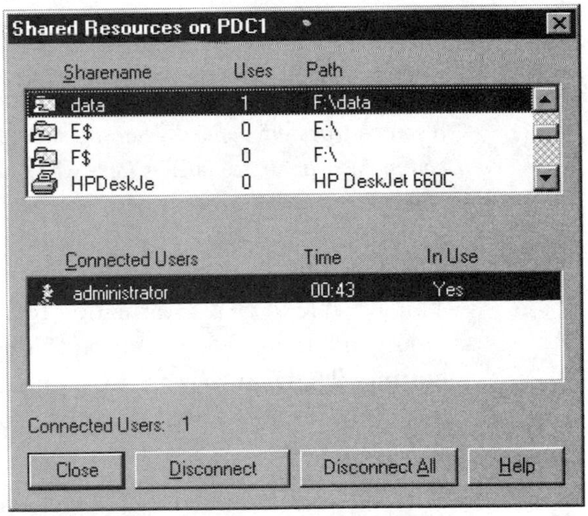

The benefit of the Shared Resources dialog box is that it shows all of the shares that are currently associated with the specified computer. Without this utility, you would have to check different utilities to see the different active shares. For example, you would use File Manager for viewing shared folders and Print Manager for viewing shared printers. Shared Resources is also useful for looking at the shared resources of remote computers. If you were to use File Manager or Print Manager, you would only be able to view shared resources on the local computer.

Through the Shared Resources dialog box you can see how many users are accessing resources on a specified computer. Assume that you are monitoring an Applications server. Through the Shared Resources dialog box you could see which users are accessing the different shared applications. Specifically, you could monitor usage to the WP share, the DB share, the EMAIL share for shared folders and the LASER share for the attached laser printer. Table 7.3 defines the Shared Resource entries.

| **TABLE 7.3**<br>Shared Resource entries | **SHARED<br>RESOURCE ENTRY** | **DESCRIPTION** |
|---|---|---|
| | Sharename | Lists all the resources that have been shared on the computer. |
| | Uses | Defines the total number of connections currently open on the specified resource. |
| | Path | Specifies the path of the selected resource. |
| | Connected Users | Displays the total number of network users that are currently connected to the highlighted resource. |
| | Time | Displays the number of hours and minutes that specified users have been connected to the highlighted resource. |
| | In Use | Allows you to determine whether the specified resource is currently being accessed by the user. |
| | Number of connected users | Displays a summary of the total number of users connected to the specified resource. |
| | Disconnect | Allows you to disconnect a selected user from a selected resource. |
| | Disconnect all | Allows you to disconnect all users from a specified resource. |

You should note that the Shared Resources dialog box shows all of the shares that are defined on a computer whether or not they are currently being accessed on the computer. In the next subsection you will be able to see the resources currently being accessed.

**OPEN RESOURCES DIALOG BOX** The In Use button within the Properties dialog box of Server Manager displays the Open Resources dialog box, shown in Figure 7.5, which lists all open resources of the specified computer. This box differs from the Shared Resources box in that it only lists active resources instead of all resources that have been shared, active or not. If you were going to down a computer for administrative purposes, looking at the Open Resources dialog box would be an easy way to see which resources were currently opened and needed to be closed out prior to downing the computer.

Through the Open Resources dialog box you can see which resources are open, which user (or computer) opened the resource, the permissions the user has on the opened resource, any locks on the open resource, and the path of the open resource.

**FIGURE 7.5**

The Open Resources dialog box

```
Open Resources on PDC1                                    [X]

Open Resources:     2
File Locks:         0

        Opened by       For      Locks    Path
   📄 administrator     Read     0        F:\data
   📄 administrator     Read     0        F:\data\wp docs


   [ Close ]  [ Refresh ]  [ Close Resource ]  [ Close All Resources ]  [ Help ]
```

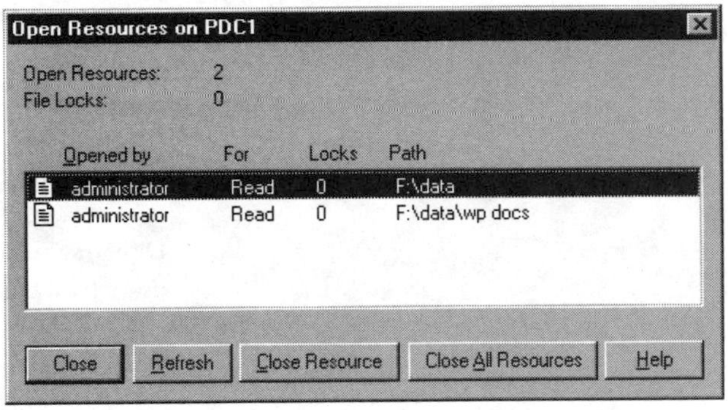

Table 7.4 defines the Open Resources dialog box elements.

**TABLE 7.4**

Open Resource elements defined

| OPEN RESOURCE ELEMENT | DESCRIPTION |
| --- | --- |
| Open Resources | Displays a summary of all open resources on the computer. |
| File Locks | Displays a summary of all file locks on the computer. |
| Opened by | Displays the name of the user or computer who has the resource open. |

| | OPEN RESOURCE ELEMENT | DESCRIPTION |
|---|---|---|
| **TABLE 7.4**<br>Open Resource<br>elements defined | For | Displays the permissions granted at the time the resource was opened. |
| | Locks | Displays the number of locks on the specified resource. |
| | Path | Displays the path of the open resource. |
| | Refresh | Updates the information on the screen. |
| | Close Resource | Allows you to close a specific resource on the specified computer. |
| | Close All Resources | Allows you to close all resources associated with the specified computer. |

**DIRECTORY REPLICATION DIALOG BOX** The Replication button within the Properties dialog box of Server Manager allows you to configure and monitor directory replication. Directory replication is the process of taking a master directory structure from one computer (called an *export computer*) and copying it to another computer (called an *import computer*).

Directory replication is a *push service*, which means that it pushes the data from the export computer to the import computer(s). If data is changed on the export computer it will be pushed or exported to the import computer(s). If data is changed on the import computer it will be lost the next time replication occurs because replication maintains a mirror copy of the export computer's directory structure and replaces that on the import computer. Because it is a push service, directory replication is useful for maintaining mirrored copies of read-only data structures.

Directory replication is most commonly used for logon scripts and read-only data. By default, logon scripts are read from the `%WINNTROOT%\SYSTEM32\REPL\IMPORT\SCRIPTS` directory of the domain controller that authenticates the user. If your users can potentially authenticate to the PDC or BDCs, you can use directory replication to manage logon scripts centrally on the PDC and then copy them to the BDCs automatically. By default, the `%WINNTROOT%\SYSTEM32\REPL\EXPORT` directory on the export computer is copied to the `%WINNTROOT%\SYSTEM32\REPL\IMPORT` directory on the import computer(s). Figure 7.6 illustrates directory replication from a PDC to two BDCs.

**FIGURE 7.6**

Directory replication

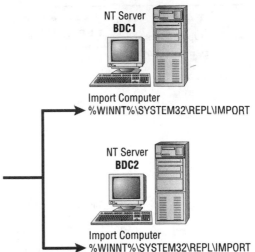

NT Server
**PDC1**

Export Computer
%WINNT%\SYSTEM32\REPL\EXPORT

NT Server
**BDC1**

Import Computer
%WINNT%\SYSTEM32\REPL\IMPORT

NT Server
**BDC2**

Import Computer
%WINNT%\SYSTEM32\REPL\IMPORT

Only NT Servers can be used as export computers. NT Servers or NT Workstations can be used as import computers. It is possible to export from one computer to a single import computer or to multiple import computers. Export and import computers can exist within the same domain or they can span domains.

In order for directory replication to be enabled, there are several configuration steps that must be completed; they are listed here.

Steps for the export computer:

1. Create a user account that will be used by the Directory Replicator service. This user must be a member of the REPLICATOR local group and the BACKUP OPERATORS local group, and should also have the Logon as a Service user right.

2. Configure the Directory Replicator service.

3. Configure directory replication through Server Manager for the export computer.

Steps for the import computer:

1. If you are within the same domain or a trusted domain, use the user account that was created to manage directory replication on the export computer, otherwise create a user to be used for replication that is a

member of the REPLICATOR local group. The user must also have the Logon as a Service user right.

**2.** Configure the directory replicator service.

**3.** Configure directory replication through Server Manager for the import computer.

In Exercise 7.2, you will complete the steps to enable directory replication using both of your machines as NT Server. PDC1 will be your export computer and PDC2 will be your import computer.

---

**EXERCISE 7.2**

## Configuring Directory Replication

This exercise requires that both of your computers be running as NT Server and that you are logged on to both computers as ADMINISTRATOR.

Complete the following steps from PDC1:

**1.** Select Start ➢ Programs ➢ Administrative Tools (common) ➢ User Manager for Domains.

**2.** Create a new user called REPLICATE. Make sure you uncheck the User Must Change Password at Next Logon option. Add REPLICATE to the REPLICATOR local group and BACKUP OPERATORS local group.

**3.** Click Policies ➢ User Rights. Click the Show advanced user rights box. From the drop-down rights list select Logon as a Service and click Add. You will now be in the Add Users and Groups dialog box. Click Show Users and select REPLICATE. Click Add and click OK. Click OK once more to close the User Rights dialog box.

**4.** Select Start ➢ Programs ➢ Administrative Tools (common) ➢ Server Manager.

**5.** Highlight PDC1 and choose Computer ➢ Services.

**6.** Click the Directory Replicator service and click Start. The directory replicator service should start. In the next step you will configure directory replication to restart automatically every time you reboot NT Server.

**7.** Double-click the Directory Replicator service to open the Service on PDC1 dialog box, shown here.

**8.** The Directory replicator service should be configured for Startup type Automatic. Under Log on as, select This Account and type **REPLICATE**. Click OK. (If you receive an error stating that the account is invalid, try configuring it again, but clear the asterisks on the password and clear password. This appears to be a glitch on some systems when a password is not used.) Or try clicking the ellipsis (...) button and choose your user from the list. Click Close.

**9.** Go back to the main menu of Server Manager. Double-click PDC1 and click replication. You'll see the Directory Replication dialog box, shown here.

**10.** Click Export Directories. Click Add to add PDC1 to the To List and click OK.

---

Before you configure the import directory, the next step is to place a text file in your export directory: `C:\WINNT\SYSTEM32\REPL\EXPORT\SCRIPTS`. If directory replication is successful, you will be able to see that this file has been copied at the end of this exercise.

**11.** Open My Computer ➤ `C:\WINNT\SYSTEM32\REPL\EXPORT\SCRIPTS`.

**12.** Click File ➤ New ➤ Text Document. Create a file called `TEST`.

The next steps should be completed on PDC2.

**13.** Select Start ➤ Programs ➤ Administrative Tools (common) ➤ Server Manager.

**14.** Highlight PDC2 and choose Computer ➤ Services.

**15.** Click the Directory Replicator service and click Start. The directory replicator service should start. In the next step you will configure directory replication to automatically restart every time you reboot NT Server.

**16.** Double-click the Directory Replicator service.

**17.** The Directory Replicator service should be configured for Startup type Automatic. Under Log on as, select This Account and click the ellipsis (...) button. In the List Names From box select DOMAIN1 and choose REPLICATE. Click Add and then Click OK. If necessary, clear the Password and Confirm Password boxes. Click OK. Notice that the user automatically is assigned the Logon as a Service right for PDC2. Click OK and then click Close to close the Services dialog box.

**18.** Go back to the main menu of Server Manager. Double-click PDC2 and click Replication.

**19.** Click Import Directories and the From List, add PDC2 and click OK. Click OK in the Directory Replication dialog box.

Now verify that the `TEST` file that you created shows up in the `C:\WINNT\SYSTEM32\REPL\IMPORT\SCRIPTS` directory. Beware that the file can take up to five minutes to show up, so this might be a good time to take a break.

---

**ALERTS DIALOG BOX** The Alerts option of the Properties dialog box allows you to specify which user or computer should be contacted in the event that an alert is generated. By default, an alert is only displayed on the computer that generates the alert. For example, PDC1 is running out of space on drive c:. When the disk is almost full an alert will be generated on PDC1 letting you know that you're almost out of space and that you need to delete some files on c:. If PDC1 is in a locked room, you would not see this message until the next time you went into the computer room and looked at PDC1's monitor (or your users called you to complain that c: was out of space).

The Alerts option allows you to forward duplicate alerts to a specific user or a specific computer. In the case of PDC1, you might want to send the alert to the ADMINISTRATOR user account, or to your specific workstation using the computer's NetBIOS name. Then if an alert occurs, the message would pop up on the specified target letting you know the event that generated the alert and the machine from which the alert was generated.

*The machine that generates the alert will document the alert in the Event Viewer. The machine that receives the forwarded alert will only receive a pop-up message, no entry will be logged in the remote computer's Event Viewer.*

In Exercise 7.3, you will send alerts generated on PDC1 to user ADMINIS-TRATOR regardless of what machine they are logged on to. You will also send alerts to NT Workstation, NTWS2.

---

**EXERCISE 7.3**

### Configuring Alert Notification

Complete this exercise from PDC1.

**1.** From Server Manager double-click PDC1.

**2.** Click Alerts in the Properties dialog box to display the Alerts dialog box, shown here.

**3.** In the New Computer or Username box type **ADMINISTRATOR** and click Add. Then type **NTWS2** and click Add. Click OK. Alerts will now be sent to the specified user and computer.

## Managing Shared Directories

As previously mentioned, one of the advantages of Server Manager is that you can manage remote computers. Specifically, you can manage shared directories on the local computer or on a remote computer. In Chapter 4 you learned how to create shared directories on a local computer through the My Computer utility. The My Computer utility allows you to manage shares on a local computer, but not on a remote computer.

To manage shared directories with Server Manager, you highlight the computer you want to manage, and select Shared Directories from the menu, as shown in Figure 7.7.

**FIGURE 7.7**

Accessing shared
directories through
Server Manager

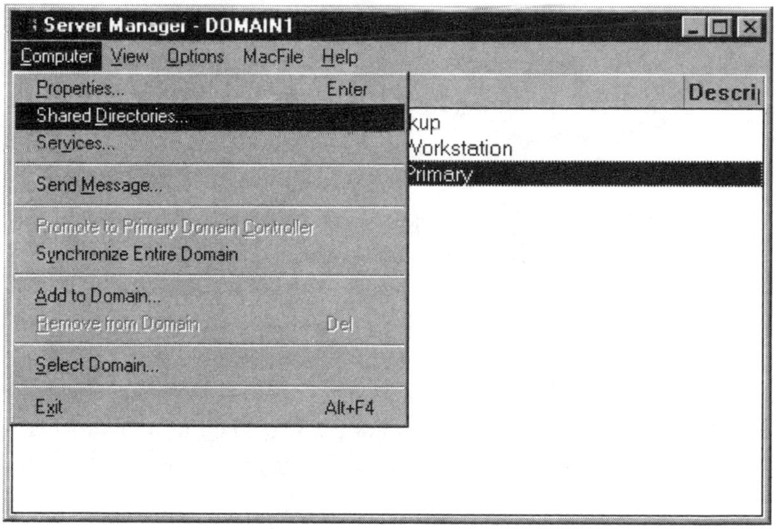

The Shared Directories dialog box allows you to manage shares on remote computers. You can create a share, stop a share, and manage a share.

To manage a shared directory you follow the same steps that were covered in Chapter 4 in the "Creating and Sharing Resources" section. In Exercise 7.4, you will create a shared directory on a remote computer using Server Manager.

---

**EXERCISE 7.4**

### Creating a Remote Share through Server Manager

This exercise requires that you are running PDC1 and NTWS2. You should be logged on to both computers as ADMINISTRATOR.

Complete the following steps from PDC1.

**1.** From Server Manager, highlight NTWS2.

**2.** Select Computer ➤ Shared Directories. Click New Share.

**3.** Specify TEMP as the Share Name and type in **C:\TEMP** for the Path. Click OK.

---

### Managing Services of a Computer

You are able to manage the services on computers within a domain through Server Manager's Services option. Services are processes used to perform system functions or to provide an application programming interface (API) that other processes can use. The Services option allows you to start, stop, and pause services.

The options you can configure through Services in Server Manager are identical to the services that you can configure through Control Panel ➤ Services. The advantage of the Server Manager Services option is that you can manage services on a local computer or on a remote computer. Through Control Panel's Service option, you can only manage the services of the local computer.

The Services dialog box allows you to control how services are used on each computer. Table 7.5 defines the configuration options you can choose through the Services dialog box.

| **TABLE 7.5** Services dialog box configuration options | **SERVICES OPTION** | **DEFINITION** |
| --- | --- | --- |
| | Service | Displays all of the services installed on the computer. |
| | Status | Displays the status of the service as started or paused. If this field is blank the service is stopped. |

| TABLE 7.5<br>Services dialog box<br>configuration options<br>(continued) | SERVICES<br>OPTION | DEFINITION |
|---|---|---|
| | Startup | Displays different ways to start the service. You can configure the service to start automatically on system startup, or to start manually by a user or another service. You can also disable the service. |
| | Start | Starts the selected service manually. |
| | Stop | Stops the selected service manually. |
| | Pause | Pauses the selected service manually. |
| | Continue | Restarts a paused service. |
| | Startup button | Allows you to configure the startup parameters for a service, including the user account the service will use. |
| | HW Profiles | If you have chosen to use hardware profiles (covered in Chapter 5), you can configure different services to be enabled or disabled based on the hardware profile you are using. |
| | Startup Parameters | Allows you to specify which parameters should be associated when starting a specific service. |

## Sending Messages

The Send Message option within Server Manager allows you to send a message to all users currently connected to the specified computer. Normally if you are going to down a machine or disconnect users, you would send a message as a courtesy. The connected users would then have an opportunity to save their data before they were disconnected. You should note that the message will only be sent to connected PC users running the Messenger service. To send a message to Mac users, you would use the MacFile option covered in Chapter 10, "Macintosh Support."

*If you want to send a message to a specific user, use the NET SEND command line utility. For help type* **NET SEND /?**.

# Using Server Manager to Manage Domains

Server Manager can be used for domain management as well as computer management. It can be used to promote a BDC to a PDC. Server Manager can also be used to synchronize the SAM database on your domain controllers. You can also add computers to a domain through Server Manager, and select the domain that you want to manage.

### Promoting a BDC to PDC

You can promote a BDC to a PDC through Server Manager. You would promote a BDC for the following reasons:

- The PDC has failed and it will not be restored immediately

- You are planning to down the PDC for scheduled maintenance

You can promote a BDC to PDC in two ways. The promotion method you use will be based on whether or not the original PDC is running when the promotion takes place. In the first example we'll assume the PDC is running. In the second example we'll assume the PDC has failed unexpectedly and is not running.

**PROMOTING A BDC WHILE THE PDC IS AVAILABLE** To promote a BDC to PDC when the original PDC is still running, you would:

1. Select the BDC through Server Manager.

2. From the Computer menu select Promote to Primary Domain Controller.

After you have done these two things, the BDC is promoted and the PDC demoted. This option is the easier of the two.

**PROMOTING A BDC WHEN THE PDC IS UNAVAILABLE** If the PDC has failed, you would complete the following steps:

1. From Server Manager, select the BDC, and from Computer, choose Promote to Primary Domain Controller.

2. When the original PDC comes back online, use Server Manager, select the original PDC, and choose Demote Primary Domain Controller from the Computer menu (this is the only instance in which you have this option).

### Domain SAM Synchronization

As mentioned in Chapter 1, "Planning a Domain Model," SAM synchronization occurs every five minutes by default. It is also possible to force SAM synchronization manually using Server Manager. You would synchronize the SAM database manually if you had made a large number of user administrative changes and you didn't want to wait five minutes for those changes to be replicated. There are two ways to force domain SAM database synchronization. You can synchronize a single BDC to the PDC, or you can synchronize the entire domain.

In Figure 7.8, a single BDC requests immediate synchronization.

**FIGURE 7.8**

BDC initiated synchronization

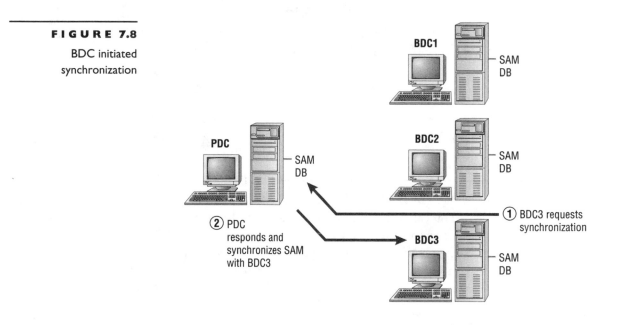

If the BDC initiates the synchronization, it will be the only BDC that is manually synchronized. This initiation would be appropriate if you had many BDCs on different WAN links, but you only needed to update a specific BDC.

To synchronize a specific BDC to the PDC, you highlight the BDC you want to synchronize (manually), and choose Computer ➤ Synchronize with Primary Domain Controller.

To synchronize an entire domain, as shown in Figure 7.9, you would highlight the PDC in Server Manager and choose Computer ➢ Synchronize Entire Domain.

**FIGURE 7.9**

PDC initiated
synchronization

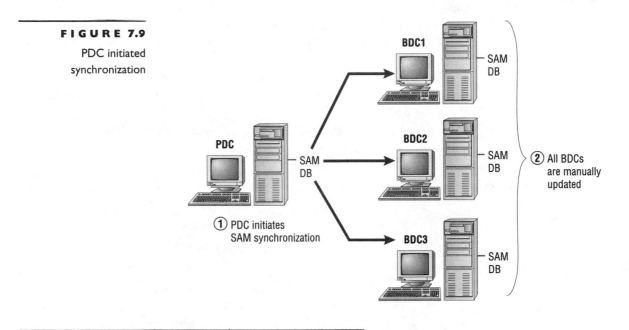

### Adding Computers to a Domain

You can add a computer to a domain through Server Manager. This addition allows a computer account to become part of the NT domain. The user can then configure their computer to participate in the domain through the installation process or through Control Panel ➢ Network. Joining a domain was covered in detail in Chapter 2, "Installing and Maintaining NT 4.0."

### Domain Selection

Use the Domain Selection option to select the NT domain or NT Workgroup that you want to manage through Server Manager. By default the dialog box will only show the domain to which the computer belongs and any trusted domains. You can type the name of another domain or workgroup if no trust relationship exists.

# PDC/BDC SAM Synchronization

A NYTIME CHANGES ARE made to the SAM database, those changes need to be broadcast to the BDCs so that they can remain synchronized. The synchronization process works in the following manner:

1. When changes have been made to the PDC database, the PDC database sends out an announcement letting the BDCs know that a change has occurred.

2. The BDC sends a packet to the PDC requesting that the SAM database changes be sent.

3. The PDC responds by sending the updates to the BDC.

By default, the synchronization occurs every five minutes. This can be configured through the Registry on the PDC, through the REGEDT32 Registry Editor. The Registry key that controls PDC to BDC SAM synchronization is:

```
\HKEY_Local_Machine\System\CurrentControlSet\
     Services\Netlogon\Parameters
```

*Editing the Registry incorrectly can cause system failure. Use this utility with great caution and at your own risk.*

You can also control BDC synchronization over WAN links by specifying a ReplicationGovernor value on the remote BDCs. The ReplicationGovernor is used to specify how often a BDC responds to a PDC's synchronization announcement and how large the data buffer that transfers the domain synchronization information can be.

# Browser Services

T HE NT *BROWSER SERVICE* is used to display the NT domains, servers, and resources available on an NT domain. The NT browser service then displays the network resources through browse lists. Browse lists are viewed through the Network Neighborhood utility, the Windows NT Explorer, and File Manager.

For example, assume Lynne wants to see what resources are available on her domain. She would use the Windows NT Explorer or Network Neighborhood utility to view the network resources. The information she sees through these utilities is a result of contacting a browser computer and the browser computer returning a list of available resources.

In this section you will learn the roles a browser computer can play, how browser computers work together, how browser computers are chosen, and how browsing works in an enterprise environment.

## Roles Browser Computers Can Play

In each NT domain, the computers within the domain are assigned different browser roles. These computers work together to compile a list of all network resources and make that list available to computers within the domain. The computers that provide browsing services are, as a group, called the NT Browser system.

The following machines are considered potential browser computers:

- NT Server 3.5 or higher

- NT Advanced Server 3.1

- NT Workstation 3.1 or higher

- Windows 95

- Windows for Workgroups 3.11

The five roles that a computer can play within the browser system are:

- Domain master browser

- Master browser

- Backup browser

- Potential browser

- Non-browser

Each of the browser roles is defined in the following subsections.

### Master Browsers and Domain Master Browsers

Each *master browser* is responsible for maintaining the *master browse list* for the domain. By default the domain master browser is always the PDC. The browse list consists of all domains within the network and all computers on the network that can share network resources. The computers are added to the browse list by sending a server announcement packet to the master browser. The server announcement packet is basically a "here I am" message. When the master browser receives the packet, it adds the sending computer to the browse list. Any computer that is running NT Server, NT Workstation, Windows 95, Windows for Workgroups, or LAN Manager and also is running a file or print service would send server announcement packets.

The roles of the *domain master browser* and the master browser are dependent upon the protocols you are running on your network and whether your network has been *subnetted*.

*Subnetting your network means that you have different physical network segments that are connected through routers.*

Depending on whether you are running TCP/IP or NWLink IPX/SPX compatible transport, NT handles browsing services differently.

Browsing services work through broadcasts that identify computers within the domain. With NWLink IPX/SPX protocol these broadcasts are passed through routers by default. On TCP/IP networks these packets are filtered through most routers.

On an NWLink IPX/SPX network, a domain master browser is able to track all computers within the domain even if the domain is subnetted, because the browser broadcasts are passed through the internetwork routers to the master browser. The domain master browser is always located on the domain's PDC. With NWLink IPX/SPX, browsing services are not very complicated and require no additional configuration.

On TCP/IP networks, browsing services become more complex due to the fact that the browsing broadcasts do not pass through most TCP/IP routers by default. Assume that you have a domain that spans an internetwork, as shown in Figure 7.10 .

**FIGURE 7.10**

Browsing an
internetwork on a
TCP/IP network

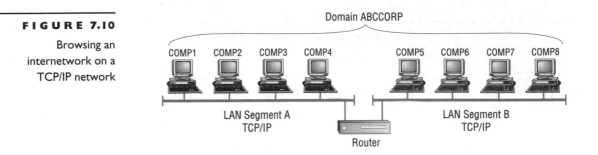

Without a mechanism to overcome the limitation of filtered browse broadcasts, the computers on LAN segment A would only see the computers from segment A on their browse lists, and the computers on LAN segment B would only see the computers from segment B on their browse lists.

The way TCP/IP internetworks deal with browsing is to configure the PDC as the domain master browser and configure a machine known as a master browser on each subnet. The master browsers then swap browse lists with the domain master browser. The combination of the swapped browse lists provides a complete browse list to the browser clients on each subnet.

### Backup Browser

A *backup browser* receives copies of the browse list from the master browser. The function of the backup browser is to offload traffic from the master browser by responding to browse requests from browser clients.

Within the domain, all BDCs will automatically function as backup browsers. The exception to this rule is if the PDC is unavailable and one of the domain's BDCs has to act as a master browser for the domain. All other BDCs continue to act as backup browsers.

Depending on the number of BDCs and computers within the domain, NT automatically calculates and configures the appropriate number of backup browser computers. For every 32 computers in the domain, a backup browser is required. If there are not at least three backup browsers, then the potential browsers will become backup browsers.

### Potential Browser

A *potential browser* is a computer that could become a browser computer. A potential browser participates in browser elections, and, based on the browser election criteria, becomes a browser or remains a browser candidate.

### Non-Browser

A *non-browser* computer is a computer within the domain that cannot be a browser computer because of its configuration. If you had a server that was already overloaded, you could configure it to be a non-browser so that it would never use its resources to maintain browse lists.

## How Browser Computers Are Chosen

By default, the PDC is always the domain master browser and BDCs are backup browsers. If the domain master browser becomes unavailable or you don't have enough BDCs to support the number of backup browsers the network requires, NT will automatically assign browser computers based on the following criteria:

- Computer has NT Server configured as a domain controller (PDC wins over BDC)

- Computer has NT Server configured as a member server

- Computer has NT Workstation

- Computer has Windows 95

- Computer has Windows for Workgroups

Let's say that you have two machines with the same software, then the criteria is based on the OS version. For example, a BDC running NT Server 4.0 would win over a BDC running NT Server 3.51.

If the OS type and version are the same the computer that has been active on the network the longest time would win. In the event of a tie at this level, the computers alphanumeric name is used to determine which will be the browser machine.

It is possible to rig the browser elections through something called *preferred master browser*. A preferred master browser is a browser server that has been configured through its Registry to always win a browser election.

## Browsing within an Enterprise Network

As mentioned earlier, if you are using TCP/IP in a subnetted network within a WAN or enterprise network, browsing services can have problems because of the fact that the browse-related broadcasts do not pass through TCP/IP routers. To allow WAN browsing to be successful, you need to implement one of the following solutions:

- Use the WINS service

- Use LMHOSTS files

- Configure UDP port 137 to forward browser related broadcasts on your routers

I cover the WINS service and LMHOSTS file in more detail in Chapter 11, "TCP/IP and Related Services."

## Browser Failures

Browser services work through broadcasts announcing a computer's presence on, or removal from the network. When a computer is shut down properly, part of the shut down process is to send a "see ya later" packet to the master browser. When the master browser receives the announcement letting it know that a computer is shutting down, it gracefully removes that computer from the master browser's browse list.

Problems occur when a computer does not shut down properly (for example, a user powers off the computer without shutting it down first, or the computer crashes). If the computer does not send an announcement that it is shutting down, the master browser thinks it's still there and leaves it on the browse list. In order for a computer to be dropped from the browse list, it has to miss three announcement periods. Because announcement periods occur every 12 minutes for a non-browser computer, this means that the computer could appear on the browse list inaccurately for up to 36 minutes plus the (up to) 15 minutes it may take to update the backup browsers.

If a backup browser fails it must miss three announcement periods, 15 minutes apart, to be removed from the browse list. If the master browser fails, action will be taken more quickly. The first time a backup browser detects that the master browser is no longer present, an election is forced immediately and a new master browser is elected.

# Chapter Summary

N THIS CHAPTER you learned about Server Manager, PDC/BDC synchronization, and the computer browser service.

The Server Manager utility is used to manage computer and domain functions. Through Server Manager you can manage the properties of a computer by managing the users that are connected to the computer, the shares that have been implemented on the computer, the resources that are currently being used on the computer, replication, and alerts generated on the computer.

Through Server Manager you are also able to create shared directories on the local computer or remote computers, and send messages to all users who are currently connected to a specific computer.

The Server Manager utility allows you to manage domain functions such as promoting a BDC to a PDC or manually synchronizing the SAM databases of the PDC and BDC computers. You are also able to add computers to a domain through Server Manager.

The next main topic that you learned about in this chapter was PDC/BDC synchronization. Domain synchronization controls how often the BDCs are sent updates of the PDC's SAM database. The synchronization rate is controlled through the PDC's Registry values.

The final topic in this chapter was browser services. You learned that browser services provide the lists that allow computers within the domain to view what network resources are available. You also learned that browser computers can play different roles within browser services, and that browser computers are selected through a browser election procedure.

# Review Questions

1. Which utilities can be used to share a directory on a remote computer? Choose all that apply.

   **A.** My Computer

   **B.** Network Neighborhood

   **C.** Server Manager

   **D.** Share Manager

   **E.** Windows NT Explorer

2. Your domain consists of a PDC and 3 BDCs all on the same LAN. Sometimes when your users log on they access their logon script successfully, and sometimes their logon scripts don't run at all. What is the most likely solution to your problem?

   **A.** You need to configure directory replication between the PDC and the BDCs; the PDC should be the export computer and the BDCs should be the import computers.

   **B.** You need to configure directory replication between the PDC and the BDCs; the PDC should be the import computer and the BDCs should be the export computers.

   **C.** Within the User Environment profile box, make sure you have checked the Make logon script available from the network option.

   **D.** Use Server Manager to configure the Logon Script Replication Service.

3. If you wanted to configure the PDC to send SAM database updates to the BDCs every three minutes, which utility would you use?

   **A.** Server Manager

   **B.** Registry Editor

   **C.** PDC Editor

   **D.** ReplicationGovernor

**4.** What two groups should the replicator service account belong to?

   **A.** SERVER OPERATORS

   **B.** REPLICATORS

   **C.** BACKUP OPERATORS

   **D.** ADMINISTRATORS

**5.** Which of the following tasks cannot be completed from Server Manager? Choose all that apply.

   **A.** Creating shared directory resources

   **B.** Creating shared print resources

   **C.** Disconnecting network users from a computer

   **D.** Configuring directory replication

   **E.** Configuring SAM database replication

**6.** Which of the following groups have rights to access the Server Manager utility? Choose all that apply.

   **A.** DOMAIN ADMINS

   **B.** SERVER OPERATORS

   **C.** BACKUP OPERATORS

   **D.** ACCOUNT OPERATORS

   **E.** REPLICATOR

**7.** Which of the following utilities can be used to view browse lists? Choose all that apply.

   **A.** File Manager

   **B.** Browser Manager

   **C.** Network Neighborhood

   **D.** My Computer

   **E.** User Manager for Domains

   **F.** Print Manager

   **G.** Windows NT Explorer

8. If you wanted to control SAM database synchronization to BDCs over a slow WAN link, what would you configure?

   **A.** The ReplicationGovernor on the BDC

   **B.** The ReplicationGovernor on the PDC

   **C.** The NetLogon Parameters Registry key on the BDC

   **D.** The NetLogon Parameters Registry key on the PDC

9. Which of the following machines would have the highest priority in a browser election?

   **A.** NT Server configured as a domain controller

   **B.** NT Server configured as a member server

   **C.** NT Workstation

   **D.** Windows 95

10. Which of the machines would be considered a potential browser machine? Choose all that apply.

   **A.** NT Server configured as a domain controller

   **B.** NT Server configured as a member server

   **C.** NT Workstation

   **D.** Windows 95

   **E.** Windows for Workgroups

   **F.** Windows 3.1

   **G.** DOS client with the MS redirector

# Printing

ONE OF THE main goals of networking is resource sharing. Two of the most common resources that are shared are file resources and print resources. Because it's usually not practical or cost effective to place a printer on each user's desk, the ability to share network printers is a must in any network environment. Printing should also be easy to setup and to manage. In this chapter you will learn how to manage NT printing. The main topics I will cover are:

- Introduction to printing
- Creating printers
- Managing the NT printing environment

# Introduction to Printing

IN ORDER FOR you to understand the print process, I will begin this section by defining the NT printing terms, giving an overview of the NT print process, listing NT print clients, and introducing the print utility used in NT 4.0.

## Printing Terminology

Before you learn about the mechanics of setting up NT printing, it's a good idea to review the terms that are used throughout this chapter. This section will use the following terms:

**Printer:** In NT terminology, a *printer* is the software interface between the *physical printer* (see print device) and the operating system. You can create printers through the Printers folder.

**Print Device:** A *print device* is the actual physical printer or hardware device you will print to.

**Print Server:** *Print servers* are the computers on which the printers have been defined. When you send a job to a network printer, you are actually sending it to the print server first.

**Print Spooler (Print Queue):** The *print spooler* is a directory or folder on the print server that actually stores the print jobs until they can be printed. It's very important that your print server and print spooler have enough hard disk space to hold all of the print jobs that could be pending at any given time.

**Print Processor:** Once a print job has been sent to the spooler, the *print processor* looks at the print job and determines whether or not the job needs further processing. The processing (also called rendering) is used to format the print job so that it can print correctly at the print device.

**Printing Pool:** *Printing pools* are created when you have more than one printing device associated with a single printer. Printing pools can be used when you have printers that all use the same print driver that are in the same location. By using printing pools, you are then able to send your print job to the first available printer.

**Print Driver:** Each printing device has it's own command set. The *print driver* is the specific software that understands your print device. Each print device has an associated print driver.

**Physical Port:** Printers can be connected directly to a computer through a serial (COM) or parallel (LPT) port. If a printer is connected in this manner, it is using a *physical port*.

**Logical Port:** Printers can also be attached to a network through a *logical port*. A logical port uses a direct connection to gain access to the network. This is done by installing a network card on the printer. The advantages to using logical ports are that they are much faster than physical ports and that you are not limited to the cabling limitations imposed by parallel and serial cable distances allowed when connecting a printer to a PC's parallel or serial ports.

**Local Printer:** A *local printer* is a printer that uses a physical port and that has not been shared. If a printer is defined as local, the only users who can use the printer are the local users of the computer that the printer is attached to.

Network Printer: A *network printer* can use physical or logical ports. By defining a printer as a network printer, you make the printer available to local and network users.

## Overview of the NT Printing Process

It's important to understand how the NT print process works so that if you need to troubleshoot the printing process, you have an idea of the steps involved in NT printing. The print process is as follows:

1. From the print client, the user chooses to print. On any Windows platform, the print request is passed to the graphics device interface (GDI). The GDI calls for the print driver. If the user is accessing the printer for the first time, the print driver is loaded into the client's memory from the print server. The print driver will stay in memory until the computer is turned off or a newer print driver is detected at the print server. The GDI is also responsible for rendering or processing print jobs for the appropriate print device.

2. The print job is sent to the computer's local spooler, which in turn sends the job over the network to the print server.

3. The router at the print server receives the print job.

4. The router takes the print job and passes the job to the spooler on the print server which spools the print job to a disk.

5. The print processor on the spooler analyzes the print job and if the job needs any further processing, the print processor processes the job so that the job will print correctly.

6. If specified, the separator page processor adds a separator page to the front of the print job.

7. The print job is passed to the print monitor which determines when the job should print and directs the print job to the correct port.

8. The print job goes to the print device, and the job prints.

# NT Print Clients

One of the main benefits of NT is its ability to support a wide variety of client platforms. Heterogeneous print support is provided for the following client platforms:

- Windows NT clients
- Windows 95 clients
- 16-bit Windows clients
- DOS clients
- UNIX clients
- NetWare clients
- Macintosh clients

### Windows NT Clients

The NT print server provides print drivers to NT clients automatically. When an NT client sends a print job to an NT printer, the client is polled for the print driver and the version of print driver they are using. If the client does not have the print driver, or the print server has a more updated print driver, the print driver is automatically downloaded into the client's memory from the print server.

*You will run into problems if your NT print client is running NT 4.0 and your NT print server is running NT 3.5x. An NT 4.0 client cannot use print drivers used with NT 3.5x. However, an NT 4.0 print server can provide print drivers to NT 3.5x and NT 4.0 clients.*

### Windows 95 Clients

Windows 95 clients can send print jobs to the NT print server through the Windows NT Server service.

### 16-Bit Windows Clients

16-bit Windows clients can send print jobs from DOS applications or Windows 16-bit applications. In order to print to an NT print server, the client must use an MS network client redirector.

### DOS Clients

DOS clients can print to NT print servers assuming that they are using MS network client redirector software. Beware that each DOS application requires its own internal print driver instead of using a single print driver like the Windows environment uses.

### UNIX Clients

UNIX clients are supported through the TCP/IP LPD (line printer daemon) service. To print to an NT printer, UNIX users would then use the `lpr` command to submit print jobs.

### NetWare Clients

If you buy an optional software called File and Print Services for NetWare, your NT print servers can support NetWare clients. Without File and Print Services for NetWare, NetWare clients cannot participate in NT printing.

### Macintosh Clients

Assuming the Services for Macintosh has been installed and configured on NT Server, NT can support Macintosh clients in the NT printing environment.

## NT 4 Print Utilities

If you have used previous versions of Windows NT or Windows, you are probably familiar with the Print Manager. Print Manager has been replaced in NT 4.0 with the Printers folder. Through the Printers folder, you are able to create and manage your NT printing environment. The Printers folder can be accessed by making any of the following selections:

- Start ➢ Settings ➢ Printers

- Start ➢ Settings ➢ Control Panel ➢ Printers

- My Computer ➢ Printers

# Creating Printers

N T 4.0 PROVIDES a printer wizard to help you install new printers, or to connect to printers that have already been created on the network. To access the printer wizard, you open the Printers folder and click Add Printer in the Printers dialog box, shown in Figure 8.1.

**FIGURE 8.1**

The Printers dialog box

In order to create a printer, you must first know how the print device is configured. Table 8.1 describes the configuration options that are available when you are creating a printer.

In Exercise 8.1, you will create a printer. You should be logged into PDC1 as ADMINISTRATOR.

| **TABLE 8.1**<br>Printer wizard<br>configuration options | **CONFIGURATION OPTION** | **DESCRIPTION** |
| --- | --- | --- |
| | My Computer or Network Print Server | The first option you must choose through the printer wizard is whether you are creating a new printer, or connecting to an existing printer. If you are creating a new printer, choose My Computer. If you are connecting to a networked printer, choose Network Print Server. |
| | Port | The ports dialog box allows you to choose whether you are using a local physical port or a network port. Two vendors are included in the network ports, Digital through TCP/IP and Lexmark through DLC or TCP/IP. You also have the option to enable printer pooling or to add new ports. |
| | Printer Manufacturer and Model | Allows you to specify the manufacturer and model of your printer. NT provides a very comprehensive list, or you can use a vendor-supplied installation disk. |
| | Printer Name | Allows you to specify a printer name of up to 31 characters. If you will be providing print services for DOS or Win-16 clients, you should keep the names to eight characters or less for backwards compatibility. There is also the option of making this your default printer. |
| | Shared or Not Shared | Allows you to specify whether or not the printer should be available to network users or whether it should only be available to local users of the computer that the printer is attached to. |
| | Select Operating Systems that Will Print to this Printer | Allows you to choose which platforms will use this printer, so the proper print drivers can be installed. You can choose from Windows 95, Windows NT *x*86, MIPS, Alpha, or PPC for NT 4.0, 3.51, 3.5, or 3.1. This option is only available if the printer is shared. Be sure to have the appropriate source files for the other operating systems because you will need these to complete installation. |
| | Print Test Page | Allows you to print a test page so that you can verify that the printer and print device have been correctly configured. |

**EXERCISE 8.1**

## Creating a Printer

**1.** Click Start ➤ Settings ➤ Printers.

**2.** Double-click Add Printer.

**3.** The Add Printer Wizard dialog box, shown below, appears.

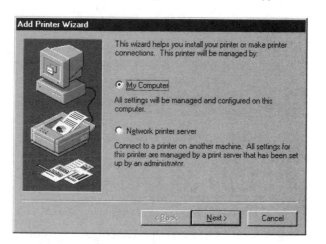

**4.** Choose My Computer and click Next.

**5.** Check LPT1: Local Port and click Next.

**6.** The Manufacturers and Printers boxes, shown below, will appear.

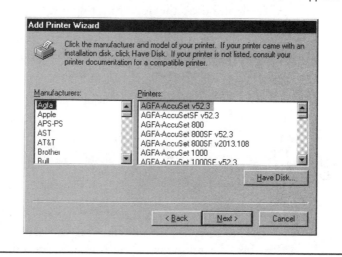

**7.** Choose HP for the Manufacturer and HP LaserJet 5Si for the Printer model and click Next.

**8.** The next dialog box within the Printer Wizard will prompt you for a printer name. Type in **HPLJ5Si** and click Next. At the bottom of this dialog box, click Yes to make this your default printer.

**9.** In the next dialog box, click Not Shared and click Next.

**10.** Specify that you do not want to print a test page in the last dialog box because you probably don't have the printer you just defined hooked up to your computer, and click Finish. Your printer has now been created.

# Sending Print Jobs to Network Printers

ONCE YOU HAVE created a printer, you are able to send the printer print jobs. Two of the ways that you can submit a print job are:

- Send the print job through an applications print option.

- Drag and drop the document to the Printer icon.

After you send a print job to the printer, a printer icon will appear on the NT taskbar next to the clock. This means that your job is printing. Once the print job is complete, this icon will disappear.

# Managing NT Printers

IN THIS SECTION you will learn how to manage NT printers. This allows you to have a great deal of control over your printing environment. One of the benefits of print management is that all printing management can be done by using the Printers folder as opposed to using multiple utilities like you do with other forms of NT management (policies and profiles, for example).

## Managing Printers

Using the printer management functions, you can pause a printer, set your default printer, set document defaults, share your printer, purge all print documents from your printer, and set properties of your printer. Each of these functions will be covered in more detail in the following subsections.

### Pausing the Printer

When a printer is paused, the user can still send jobs to the printer, but the jobs are held and are not sent to the print device. The most common reason a printer would be paused is for maintenance on the printing device, for example, to replace toner or add paper.

### Setting the Default Printer

Each user can have multiple printers to which they can print. For example, Penny in the Accounting department might need to use a laser printer for her normal daily printing needs, a dot matrix printer for continuous feed checks, and a color laser printer for her presentation documents. Since Penny uses the standard laser printer for most of her print jobs, she would choose the laser printer as her default printer.

### Document Defaults

Each printer can be configured with default document properties. The options that you see through document defaults are dependent on the printing device and driver that you are using. For default document properties, you can choose Page Setup and advanced options.

Page Setup allows you to choose your paper size and paper source. The paper size options that you see are the options supported by your print device. You are also able to choose portrait or landscape paper orientation through Page Setup.

The advanced options of default document properties are also dependent on the print device and print driver you are using. The example shown in Figure 8.2 is using the HP DeskJet 660C printer.

**FIGURE 8.2**

The Default Document
Properties dialog box

To access the dialog box shown in Figure 8.2, you select the printer you want to manage through the Printers folder and go to Printer ➤ Document Defaults and click the Advanced tab. Notice in our example that among the options you can configure are Paper/Output options, Graphic resolution and color appearance options, and Document options.

## Sharing Printers over the Network

Printers can be used locally or shared over the network. Depending on the circumstances printers can be setup either way. Consider these examples.

In the first example, you have Michael, the VP of Sales. He has a laser printer directly attached to his computer in his office. It's not likely that Michael wants users coming in and out of his office all day to pick up their printed documents. In this example, you would leave the printer as a local, or unshared printer.

In the second example, you have a high-speed laser printer attached to the network through its own Ethernet card. The printer was chosen based on its ability to support high-volume, fast printing. In this example, you would want to configure the printer as a shared network printer.

In Exercise 8.2, you will share the printer you created in Exercise 8.1.

---

**EXERCISE 8.2**

## Sharing an Existing Printer

**1.** Click Start ➢ Settings ➢ Printers.

**2.** Double-click HPLJ5Si to open the HPLJ5Si dialog box.

**3.** Click Printer ➢ Sharing to open the Sharing tab of the HPLJ5Si Properties dialog box, shown here.

HPLJ5Si Properties

General | Ports | Scheduling | Sharing | Security | Device Settings

HPLJ5Si

○ Not Shared
○ Shared
Share Name: HPLJ5Si

You may install alternate drivers so that users on the following systems can download them automatically when they connect.

Alternate Drivers:
Windows 95
Windows NT 4.0 x86 (Installed)
Windows NT 4.0 MIPS
Windows NT 4.0 Alpha
Windows NT 4.0 PPC
Windows NT 3.5 or 3.51 x86

To modify the permissions on the printer, go to the Security tab.

OK | Cancel

**4.** Click Shared and accept the default share name of HPLJ5Si. Click OK. The printer is now shared.

### Purging Print Documents

You can purge all documents in the printer's print queue by choosing Printer ➤ Purge Print documents. This allows you to delete all of the documents that are currently queued to the printer.

### Printer Properties

For each printer you can define printer properties. Printer properties include general properties, ports configurations, scheduling, sharing, security, and device settings. I cover these options in more detail in the following subsections. In Exercise 8.3, you will open the Printer properties dialog box.

---

**EXERCISE 8.3**

## Accessing Printer Properties

**1.** Click Start ➤ Settings ➤ Printers.

**2.** Double-click HPLJ5Si to open the HPLJ5Si dialog box.

**3.** Click Printer ➤ Properties to open the HPLJ5Si Properties dialog box, shown here.

Notice that the HPLJ5Si dialog box has configuration tabs for General, Ports, Scheduling, Sharing, Security, and Device Settings and that the General tab is selected.

**GENERAL** The General tab defines general properties of a printer that include options for a comment, location, driver, separator page, print processors, and printing test pages. Table 8.2 defines these options.

| **TABLE 8.2**<br>General properties<br>of a printer | **GENERAL PROPERTY** | **DESCRIPTION** |
|---|---|---|
| | Comment | The comment field is for informational purposes. Any text can be inserted into this field—for example, the user account and date that the printer was created. |
| | Location | Used to supply information regarding the physical location of the printer. |
| | Driver | The driver drop-down list is associated with the General printer property and allows you to specify the print driver that should be used with the printer. |
| | New Driver | Allows you to to install or update a newer print driver for an existing printer. |
| | Separator Page | If you choose to use separator pages, it causes a separator page to print prior to each print job. Separator pages are used mainly on shared printers to identify which jobs belong to which users. |
| | Print Processor | Allows you to choose the data type that the printer will use. By default, the print processor should not need to be changed. |
| | Print Test Page | Allows you to determine whether printing has been correctly configured. |

**PORTS** The Ports tab page of a printer's Properties dialog box allows you to add, delete, and configure ports. A port is defined as a location that is used to pass data in and out of a computing device. Ports can be through network interface cards, parallel ports, or serial ports. You are also able to specify on the Ports tab page whether you want to use bi-directional printing or enable printer pooling.

On the Ports tab page, you see all of the currently defined ports. On this page, you can add, delete or configure ports. Adding ports allows you to create network ports (for printers attached to the network through network interface cards) or new local ports. Deleting ports allows you to remove ports that are currently defined in the Ports Properties dialog box. Configuring ports allows you to configure each port's configuration properties. Depending on the type of port you are configuring, you will see different options. For example, a serial (or COM) port has more complex configuration options than a parallel (LPT) port has.

Bi-directional print support is enabled by default; this allows the printer to send information to the print device and to receive information from the print device regarding setting and status information.

**ASSOCIATING MULTIPLE PRINT DEVICES WITH A SINGLE PRINTER (PRINTER POOLING)** Enabling printer pooling allows you to associate multiple print devices with a single printer, as shown in Figure 8.3. To use printer pooling, the printers that will be in the print pool must be the same model, or at least be able to use the same print driver. The printer should also be in the same physical location, because any printer in the printer pool could potentially service the print job.

**FIGURE 8.3**

Associating multiple print devices with a single printer

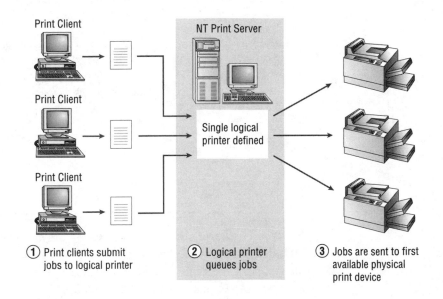

Printer pooling is useful in situations where you have multiple printers that share the same configuration and are in the same location. By creating a printer pool, your print jobs can be serviced by the first available print device. An example of how this might be used is in a secretarial pool, where all of the secretaries are in the same location with multiple printers that are the same model.

### ASSOCIATING MULTIPLE PRINTERS WITH A SINGLE PRINT DEVICE

The flip side of printer pools is associating multiple printers with a single print device. As shown in Figure 8.4, one possible configuration would be to have three logical printers that pointed to the same physical print device. This scenario is often used in conjunction with scheduling—the next subtopic.

**FIGURE 8.4**

Associating multiple printers with a single print device

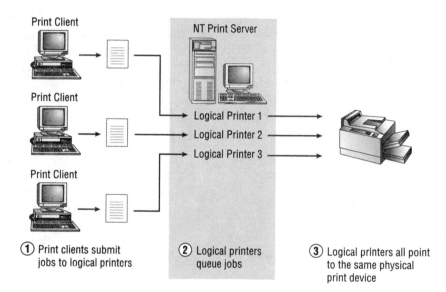

**SCHEDULING** On the Scheduling tab page in the printer's Properties dialog box, you can configure a printer's availability, the priority of the printer, how print jobs are spooled, and how documents should be processed. Table 8.3 defines the printer scheduling properties.

| | PRINT SCHEDULING PROPERTY | DESCRIPTION |
|---|---|---|
| **TABLE 8.3** Printer scheduling properties | Availability | Availability specifies whether the printer should be available 24 hours a day, or limited to certain hours. This is often used when associating multiple printers with a single print device. For example, in Figure 8.4, assume that logical printer 1 is used for short, quickly printed documents, and logical printer 3 is used for longer jobs that should be done overnight. By scheduling logical printer 1 to be available 24 hours a day, and logical printer 3 to be available from 10:00PM-4:00AM, you can control when the long print jobs are sent. |
| | Priority | Priority determines which jobs print first. Priority can be set from 1-99, with 1 being the lowest priority and 99 being the highest priority. Printer Priority is also associated with using multiple printers that share a single print device. Again looking at Figure 8.4, you could make logical printer 1 have a priority of 1 and logical printer 3 have a print priority of 99. Jobs from logical printer 3 would always be processed first. |
| | Spooling print documents | Spooling stores the print document on hard drive while it is waiting to be printed. You can choose to print the job as soon as it is submitted, or you can force the job to finish spooling before it begins to print. |
| | Print directly to the printer | Print directly to the printer allows you to bypass the spooling process. This is useful in troubleshooting if you just want to verify that you have a valid connection to the printer without having to go through the print spooler. |
| | Hold mismatched documents | Hold mismatched documents allows you to use alternate forms when printing a document. If, by default, the correct form is not loaded, the printer will wait for the form to load before the job will be printed, which could potentially back up the print queue. This option directs the queue to hold the mismatched jobs, but to continue to print jobs that are submitted using the current form. |

| **TABLE 8.3** Printer scheduling properties (continued) | **PRINT SCHEDULING PROPERTY** | **DESCRIPTION** |
|---|---|---|
| | Print spooled documents first | Print spooled documents first specifies that jobs that have completed spooling should be allowed to print before jobs that are still spooling. Assume that you have a 500-page print job that comes in with a higher priority than a two-page print job. If this box is not checked, the two-page print job has to wait until the 500-page job spools and prints. By using this option, you are better able to utilize your printer's efficiency. |
| | Keep documents after they have printed | Keep documents after they have printed specifies that the print jobs should not be deleted from the spooler after they have printed. The benefit of this option is that print jobs can be resubmitted from the print queue, not the original sending application. The disadvantage of this option is that you could potentially use a large amount of disk space to accommodate the print jobs in the spooler. |

**SHARING** The Sharing tab page within a printer's Properties dialog box allows you to define whether the printer should be shared or not shared. If you choose the not shared option, then the printer can only be accessed by the user who is logged in at the computer where the printer is physically attached.

If the printer is shared as a network printer, you can specify that alternate drivers be loaded so that if a user from the alternate platform accesses the printer, the correct driver will be downloaded. NT allows you to specify alternate drivers for the following platforms:

- Windows 95

- Windows NT 4.0:*x*86, MIPS, Alpha, or PPC

- Windows NT 3.5*x*:*x*86, MIPS, Alpha, or PPC

- Windows NT 3.1:*x*86, MIPS, or Alpha

**SECURITY** Through the Security tab page in printer properties, you can specify permissions, auditing, and ownership. I cover each of these topics here in more detail.

**Permissions:** Group EVERYONE gets the Print permission on all NT printers by default. You can control who is able to have Full Control, Manage Printers, and Send Print Documents to the Printer through Printer permissions. For example, assume that your company just bought a color laser printer. This printer is expensive to buy and maintain, so you probably don't want employees printing their personal party flyers on it. You want to give only qualified people permission to print on this machine. The printer permissions are defined in Table 8.4, and they can be applied to a user or to a group.

| | | | |
|---|---|---|---|
| **TABLE 8.4**<br>Printer permissions<br>defined | **PRINTER PERMISSION** | **DESCRIPTION** | **DEFAULT ASSIGNMENT** |
| | Full Control | Allows you to create, manage, and delete printers | ADMINISTRATORS, SERVER OPERATORS, PRINT OPERATORS |
| | Manage Documents | Allows you to manage print documents by pausing, restarting, resuming, and deleting queued documents | CREATOR OWNER |
| | Print | Allows you to print documents and manage jobs you have sent to the queue as owner | EVERYONE |
| | No Access | Denies any access to the queue or printer | not assigned by default |

In Exercise 8.4, you will create a printer that can only be accessed by members of the MIS group. You should complete this exercise from PDC1 while logged on as ADMINISTRATOR.

---

**EXERCISE 8.4**

### Managing Printer Permissions

**1.** Use User Manager for Domains to create BUZZ and WOODY. Make sure that you uncheck the User Must Change Password at Next Logon box.

**2.** Use User Manager for Domains to create a global group called MIS. Add BUZZ and WOODY.

**3.** Create a new printer called MISPRINTER. The printer should be configured as follows:

Port:  LPT3

Printer:  HP Deskjet

Shared:  Share name MISPRINTER

**4.** Double-click Misprinter in the Printers folder. Open Printer ≻ Properties, and click the Security tab page. Click Permissions to see the dialog box shown below.

**5.** Click Everyone and click Remove so that the group EVERYONE can no longer print to the Misprinter.

**6.** Click the MIS group and click Add. Leave the type of access at Print and click OK. Click OK in the Printer Permissions dialog box.

**7.** Log off and log on again as KATIE.

**8.** Click Start ≻ Settings ≻ Printers, and double-click MISPRINTER. You should see "Access denied, unable to connect" next to MISPRINTER.

**9.** Log off and log on again as BUZZ.

**10.** Click Start ≻ Settings ≻ Printers, and double-click MISPRINTER. You should not see the same error message you saw in Step 8.

**11.** Log off and log on again as ADMINISTRATOR.

**12.** Click Shared and accept the default share name of HPLJ5Si. Click OK. The printer is now shared.

**Auditing:** Print auditing allows you to audit printing events on the specified printer. You can choose who you want to audit—for example, Everyone or a specific group or user. You can audit the success or failure of the following events:

- Print
- Full Control
- Delete
- Change Permissions
- Take Ownership

Let's assume that you chose to audit print events. For each audited event, you can tell the date and time the document was printed, who sent it, and the computer it was sent from. You can also see the document name and the number of pages that were printed. This information can be used to determine how heavily a printer was being used.

*You use the Event Viewer to see the audit logs. It's interesting to note that audited user policies are tracked in the Security Log and audited print events are tracked in the System and Security Log.*

**Ownership:** The Take Ownership option within a printer's security properties allows a user with appropriate permissions to take ownership of the printer. Taking ownership of the printer would then allow the owner to change the current permissions.

**DEVICE SETTINGS** The Device Settings option of a printer's properties allows you to specify device settings for your computer. These options are based on your computer model. Some of the settings you could select are:

- Form to tray assignment
- Installed font cartridges
- Halftone setup

# Chapter Summary

N THIS CHAPTER you learned the NT printing terms, NT print clients, and the steps involved in the NT print process. You also learned how to create and manage printers. Through printer management you learned how to:

- Pause printers

- Set the default printer

- Set document defaults

- Create a shared network printer

- Purge all print documents from the printer

- Set properties of a printer

# Review Questions

1. The _____ is the directory or folder that stores print jobs until they can be printed.

   **A.** Print Processor

   **B.** Logical Port

   **C.** Print Spooler

   **D.** Printing Pool

2. The _____ is responsible for determining if the print job needs rendering before it is sent to the printing device.

   **A.** Print Processor

   **B.** Logical Port

   **C.** Print Spooler

   **D.** Printing Pool

3. What is required for a NetWare client to print to an NT printer?

   **A.** GSNW

   **B.** CSNW

   **C.** File and Print Services for NetWare

   **D.** Printer Gateway for NetWare

4. Which UNIX command is used to send print jobs to an NT printer?

   **A.** LPQ

   **B.** LPR

   **C.** UPRINT

   **D.** Net Print

5. If you did not want anyone except the SALES group to use the LASER printer, which tab page should you use in the Printer Properties dialog box?

   **A.** General

   **B.** Sharing

   **C.** Security

   **D.** Ports

6. Which tab page would you use in the Printer Properties dialog box to set a printer's priority?

   **A.** General

   **B.** Sharing

   **C.** Security

   **D.** Scheduling

7. By default, which groups have Full Control over networked printers? Choose all that apply.

   **A.** ADMINISTRATORS

   **B.** SERVER OPERATORS

   **C.** PRINT OPERATORS

   **D.** PRINT MANAGERS

**8.** Which of the following tasks can be completed by a user who has the Manage Documents print right? Choose all that apply.

**A.** Create a printer

**B.** Delete a printer

**C.** Delete any user's print jobs

**D.** Reorder print jobs

**E.** Pause print jobs

**9.** Which of the following tasks can be audited through print auditing? Choose all that apply.

**A.** Print

**B.** Take Ownership

**C.** Delete

**D.** Create

**E.** Change Permissions

# NetWare Connectivity

TRADITIONALLY NETWARE HAS held a large share of the network operating system market. This is changing rapidly as NT is becoming a market leader. One of the strategies Microsoft has used since the early days of Windows NT is interoperability with other operating systems. NT is able to interoperate with Novell NetWare through the NWLink IPX/SPX Compatible Transport protocol stack, Client Services for NetWare (CSNW) service and Gateway Services for NetWare (GSNW) service. If you decide that you want to convert your NetWare file servers to Windows NT, Microsoft provides a migration tool called Migration Tool for NetWare that allows you to migrate your NetWare users, groups, data, and security. In this chapter you will learn about:

- NWLink (IPX/SPX)

- Client Services for NetWare

- Gateway Services for NetWare

- Migration Tool for NetWare

# NWLink IPX/SPX Compatible Transport

NWLINK IPX/SPX COMPATIBLE TRANSPORT is Microsoft's implementation of Novell's IPX/SPX protocol stack. IPX/SPX stands for Internetwork Packet Exchange/Sequenced Packet Exchange. The NT implementation adds support for NetBIOS which is used for NT browsing services. (See Chapter 7, "NT Domain Management," for more information on browsing.)

NWLink IPX/SPX Compatible Transport is a transport protocol. The purpose of a transport protocol is to route packets across an internetwork. NWLink IPX/SPX Compatible Transport by itself does not provide access to NetWare file and print services. It does provide a method of transporting data to the NetWare server. One way to think of transport protocols is in terms of language. NetWare servers speak IPX/SPX, and in order to communicate with them our NT environment needs to speak the same language, in this case NWLink IPX/SPX Compatible Transport. This protocol is comparable to the TCP/IP protocol stack.

In order to install Client Services for NetWare or Gateway Services for NetWare you must be running NWLink IPX/SPX Compatible Transport already. If the protocol stack has not been installed, it will auto-install during Client Services or Gateway Services installation. If you used the default protocol selections when you installed NT, you chose NWLink IPX/SPX Compatible Transport by default. NT Workstation, however, does not have NWLink IPX/SPX Compatible Transport as its default protocol.

One of the advantages of using the NWLink IPX/SPX Compatible Transport protocol is that it is very easy to configure. The only configuration options you have to choose from are the *internal network number* and the *frame* type. The internal network number is used to uniquely identify NetWare file servers. This option is left at the default of 00000000 unless you are using File and Print Services for NetWare or are using IPX routing.

*File and Print Services is an add-on product you can purchase from Microsoft; it allows NetWare clients to access NT resources. It is not covered on this exam, so it is not covered in this book.*

A frame is a piece of data that is transmitted over the network. Different LAN cards support different frame types. For example, if you are using Ethernet, you can use the following frame types:

- Ethernet_II

- Ethernet_802.2

- Ethernet_802.3

- Ethernet_SNAP

Frame types are not compatible with each other, so your network needs to use common frame types. When configuring NWLink IPX/SPX Compatible Transport you can choose to configure your frame types through auto-detection or manually. If you choose auto-detection, NT will auto-detect what frame types are currently being used on your network. If NT detects Ethernet_802.2, the industry standard, that is the frame type it will use. Otherwise it will select the first frame type it detected. Manual frame-type detection allows you to specify what frame type or types you will use. In Exercise 9.1 you will cover the options for configuring NWLink IPX/SPX Compatible Transport.

---

**EXERCISE 9.1**

### Viewing NWLink IPX/SPX Compatible Transport Options

This exercise should be completed from PDC1 while logged on as ADMINISTRATOR.

**1.** Select Start ≻ Settings ≻ Control Panel.

**2.** Double-click Network.

**3.** Click the Protocols tab.

**4.** Select the network protocol NWLink IPX/SPX Compatible Transport and click Properties to call up the NWLink IPX/SPX Properties dialog box, shown below.

There is not really anything you need to configure at this time. The purpose of this exercise was to show you that NWLink IPX/SPX Compatible Transport Protocol is installed by default, and how it can be viewed or modified.

# Client Services for NetWare

C LIENT SERVICES FOR NetWare (CSNW) is only available on NT Workstation. CSNW is a NetWare redirector that allows NT Workstations to access NetWare servers. NT Workstation comes with the CSNW software that you can install if your NT Workstations require access to NetWare file and print resources.

*A redirector is a program that intercepts program or user requests and directs them to the appropriate environment. For instance, a networking redirector can direct requests to DOS or to the Network Interface Card for transmission to the server.*

Figure 9.1 shows how CSNW can be used to access NetWare resources. Assume you are a user sitting at NTWS2 in Figure 9.1. You need to access the WP resource on the NetWare file server NWFS. You may want to use this solution temporarily as you migrate to Windows NT, or if you have existing NetWare servers that you need to share resources such as directories and/or printers.

**FIGURE 9.1**

Accessing NetWare resources through CSNW

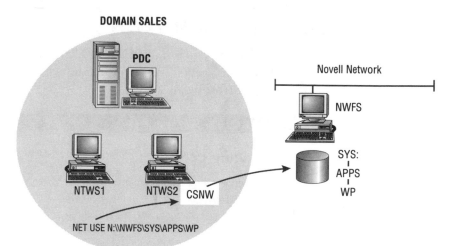

In order to access NetWare resources using CSNW the following conditions must be met:

- To access the directory, you must have a valid user account with appropriate permissions on the NetWare file server.

- Your logon account and password on the NT side must match the logon account and password on the NetWare side.

- NWLink IPX/SPX Compatible Transport must be running on NT Workstation.

- CSNW must be running on NT Workstation.

- The user sitting at NTWS2 connects to the desired resource through Network Neighborhood or the NET USE command line utility.

*One of the nice things about NT 4.0 is that it supports accessing NetWare servers in NetWare Directory Services (NDS) mode or in bindery mode. If you are accessing NetWare 4.x file servers, you will be using NDS. If you are accessing NetWare 2.x or NetWare 3.x file servers you are using bindery mode. NT 3.51 and earlier versions only supported bindery mode.*

## Installing Client Services for NetWare

You will be able to install CSNW in Exercise 9.2, but because you most likely won't have a NetWare server in your test environment, you will not be able to test it (but trust me, it works).

---

**EXERCISE 9.2**

### Installing CSNW

This exercise should be completed from your NT Workstation while logged on as ADMINISTRATOR.

**1.** Select Start ➢ Settings ➢ Control Panel.

**2.** Double-click Network.

**3.** Click the Services tab.

**4.** Click Add.  The Select Network Service dialog box will appear. Choose Client Service for NetWare and click OK. Insert the Windows NT Workstation CD if necessary.  After the file copy, close the Network Services box.

**5.** You will now see a dialog box prompting you to restart the computer for changes to take effect. Click Yes to restart your computer.

**6.** The Startup menu will appear as your computer reboots, choose to start NT Workstation again and log on as ADMINISTRATOR.

**7.** After you log on notice that you see the Select NetWare Logon dialog box.  This dialog box allows you to specify your preferred server, default tree and context, and whether to run the NetWare logon script. Close this box for now. You will see how these options can be configured in Exercise 9.3.

## Configuring Client Services for NetWare

CSNW is configured the first time a user logs on after installing CSNW or at anytime by accessing Control Panel. Table 9.1 defines the options for configuring CSNW.

| TABLE 9.1 | CSNW OPTION | DESCRIPTION |
|---|---|---|
| CSNW configuration options | Preferred Server | Used for accessing bindery-mode servers. Allows you to specify which NetWare server you want to connect to by default. |
| | Default Tree and Context | For use in an NDS environment. Allows you to specify the NDS name and context (where the user account resides within a NetWare NDS tree) the user will use when accessing the NetWare server. |

| | CSNW OPTION | DESCRIPTION |
|---|---|---|
| **TABLE 9.1**<br>CSNW configuration<br>options (continued) | Print Options | Allows you to specify how to handle print requests. Add form feed tells the printer to eject a blank page after each document. Notify when printed ensures that the user receives a pop-up message letting them know when their document has printed. Print banner specifies whether or not a banner page should be printed with each document. A banner page identifies the user who sent the job, and gives a job description. |
| | Login Script Options | Specifies whether the NetWare logon script should run when the user logs on to a NetWare server or NDS tree. |

In Exercise 9.3, you will assume that you are attaching to a NetWare 3.12 file server called NETWARE312. You will then configure the Client Services for NetWare. As noted before, CSNW is only available on NT Workstations. If you need to access NetWare file and print resources through NT Server, use Gateway Services for NetWare (GSNW), which I cover in detail in the next section. GSNW is used on NT Servers in place of Client Services for NetWare, and in addition to providing the functionality of CSNW on a NT Server, it allows other clients to access NetWare file and print resources through its gateway.

---

### EXERCISE 9.3

## Configuring CSNW

Complete this exercise from your NT Workstation while logged on as ADMINISTRATOR.

**1.** Select Start ➢ Settings ➢ Control Panel.

**2.** Double-click CSNW.

---

**3.** Click the Services tab to access the Client Service for NetWare dialog box, shown below.

**4.** Click Preferred Server and in the Select Preferred Server box type in **NETWARE312**.

**5.** Under the Print Options box click Add Form Feed.

**6.** Under Login Script Options click Run Logon Script.

**7.** Click OK to save your changes. You will receive an error message letting you know the NETWARE312 file server could not authenticate you (because it doesn't exist). Click Yes to specify it as your default server anyway. You will receive a message letting you know the changes you have made will take effect the next time you log on.

# Gateway Services for NetWare

G ATEWAY SERVICES FOR NetWare (GSNW) is used for accessing NetWare file and print resources through an NT Server. You would use GSNW for the following reasons:

- Your NT Server needs to access NetWare file or print resources.

- Your NT Workstations do not have CSNW installed and they want to access NetWare file or print resources.

- You have MS-DOS, Windows for Workgroups or any other client that needs to access the NetWare file server through your NT server.

Figure 9.2 shows three users who want to access the EMAIL resource on the NetWare file server, NWFS.

**FIGURE 9.2**

Using Gateway Service for NetWare

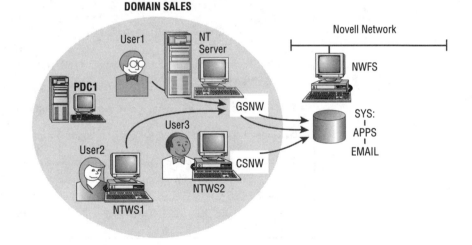

USER1 is sitting at the NT Server. NT Server does not support CSNW. His only choice in this scenario is to use GSNW. USER2 is sitting at NT Workstation NTWS1. CSNW has not been installed on her machine. She can use GSNW to access the NetWare file server. USER3 is sitting at NT Workstation NTWS2. Because CSNW has been installed on his machine he would access the NetWare file server through CSNW.

## Benefits of Using GSNW

There are two main benefits to using GSNW over CSNW. The first benefit is that by using GSNW you don't have to install CSNW on every NT Workstation. There are two sides to this issue. If you install CSNW on NT Workstation, you will have better performance between NT Workstation and the NetWare Server; this is because you are making a direct connection to the NetWare Server instead of having to go through the gateway. The flip side of this argument is that you take up system resources on NT Workstation when you install CSNW on it. The most important factor to consider when deciding whether to use GSNW or CSNW is how much access to the NetWare file server the workstation will require. For workstations that have to access the NetWare resources frequently, CSNW is a better choice. For workstations that require occasional access, GSNW is a better choice.

The second benefit of using GSNW is a licensing issue. NetWare licenses access to its file servers on a per-server basis. That means that if 10 users will connect to the NetWare file server at any given time, you need a 10-user license. If you use CSNW, you need a license for each CSNW connection.

If you use GSNW you are using a single gateway connection. Let's say you have 10 NT Workstations that are accessing the NetWare file server through CSNW and 10 NT Workstations that are accessing the NetWare file server through GSNW. The CSNW users would take up 10 connections. The GSNW users would only take up one connection through the gateway account.

# *Setting Up GSNW*

GATEWAY SERVICES FOR NetWare can only be installed on NT Server. NWLink IPX/SPX Compatible Transport is required. If it hasn't already been installed, NWLink IPX/SPX Compatible Transport will be installed automatically when you install GSNW. In order for GSNW to work, you will first need to configure the NetWare file server and the NT Server. The following sections cover the setup on each platform.

## Configuring the NetWare File Server for GSNW

In order for GSNW to work, you must have access to the NetWare file server. The NetWare file server must have a user account that will be the gateway account. If you do not have administrative rights or are not familiar with NetWare administration utilities, see your NetWare administrator.

The requirements for the NetWare file server are as follows:

1. You will need a user account that has all the access rights the gateway users will need. Let's assume your gateway user is NTUSER. If your NT user accounts require access to the SYS:APPS NetWare file resource, the NTUSER user account needs the appropriate NetWare access rights to access SYS:APPS.

2. You must have a group called NTGATEWAY. The user you created in step 1 must be a member of this group.

3. If you want to support NT long file names on the NetWare file server you must have OS/2 name space on the NetWare volumes that will store long file names. If you do not use OS/2 name space on the NetWare volume, you are limited to the DOS FAT 8.3 naming conventions. If you have NetWare 4.11 then you would use Long Name Space.

## Installing GSNW on NT Server

After the NetWare file server has been prepared you are ready to install GSNW. In Exercise 9.4 you will install GSNW on NT Server.

---

**EXERCISE 9.4**

### Installing GSNW

Complete this exercise from NT Server while logged on as ADMINISTRATOR.

1. Select Start ➢ Settings ➢ Control Panel.

2. Double-click Network.

3. Click the Services tab.

---

EXERCISE 9.4 (CONTINUED FROM PREVIOUS PAGE)

**4.** Click Add and select Gateway (and Client) Services for NetWare. Click OK. If necessary provide the Windows NT Server CD and click Continue.

**5.** Click Close to save the changes. Click Yes on the Network Settings dialog box; this will restart your computer.

**6.** Restart the computer as NT Server and log on as ADMINISTRATOR.

**7.** You will see a Select NetWare dialog box. Click OK to close this box.

## Configuring GSNW

After GSNW has been installed, the Control Panel will have a new icon, GSNW. When you click this item you will see the dialog box in Figure 9.3.

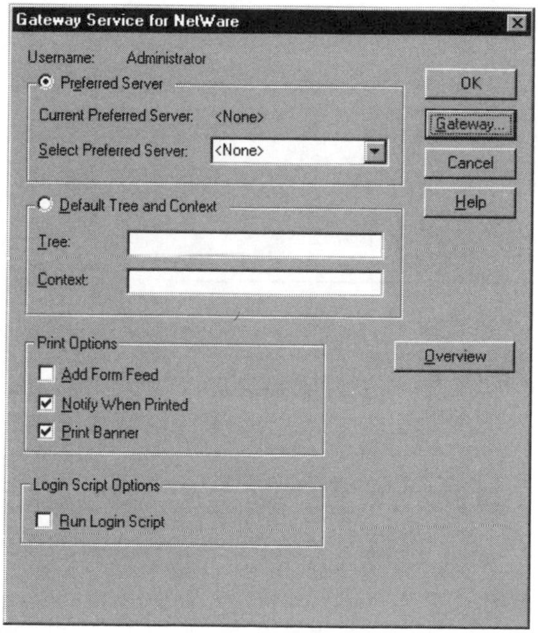

**FIGURE 9.3**

The Gateway Service for NetWare dialog box

You will notice that the Gateway Service for NetWare dialog box is very similar to the CSNW dialog box, shown back in Exercise 9.3. With the exception of the Gateway button, all of the options presented in this dialog box are the same as CSNW. For the options that are the same, refer back to Table 9.1. To configure GSNW, click the Gateway button, and you will see the GSNW Configure Gateway dialog box, as shown in Figure 9.4.

**FIGURE 9.4**

The GSNW Configure Gateway dialog box

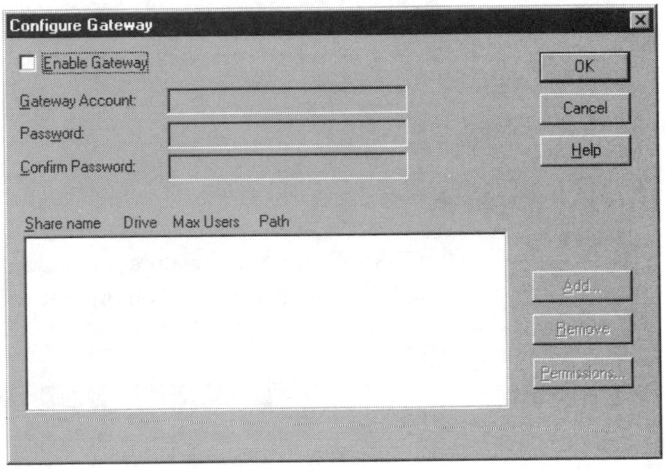

The configuration options available in the GSNW Configure Gateway dialog box are defined in Table 9.2

| TABLE 9.2<br>The Configure Gateway<br>dialog box options | CONFIGURE<br>GATEWAY OPTION | DESCRIPTION |
|---|---|---|
| | Enable Gateway | Enables the gateway. Required for GSNW to be functional. |
| | Gateway Account | This is the user account that was setup on the NetWare file server. This user must be a member of the NTGATEWAY group on the NetWare file server. |
| | Password and Confirm Password | This establishes and confirms the NetWare side password that the NetWare user account has been assigned. |

| | | |
|---|---|---|
| **TABLE 9.2** | **CONFIGURE GATEWAY OPTION** | **DESCRIPTION** |
| The Configure Gateway dialog box options (continued) | Share Name | Lists the shares that have been created on the NT Server that access NetWare resources. |
| | Add | Allows you to create additional shares on NetWare volumes or directories. |
| | Delete | Removes shares that have been created on NetWare volumes or directories. |
| | Permissions | Used to control how NT users can access NetWare resources. |

Once the gateway has been configured, NT users can access NetWare file and print resources through the Network Neighborhood utility.

# Migration Tool for NetWare

N THE PREVIOUS sections, you learned how to operate in a mixed environment of Windows NT and Novell NetWare. In this section, you will learn how to migrate an existing NetWare File Server to an NT PDC using Migration Tool for NetWare; this is assuming that now that you've worked with a mixed environment, have come to see what a superior product NT is over NetWare, and you want to convert everything to NT.

*It is important to note that this is a migration, not an upgrade. An upgrade would assume that you were going to use the NetWare file server and upgrade it to an NT Server (basically using the same machine). It is not possible to upgrade a NetWare file server to an NT Server, only to migrate. In a migration you leave the NetWare file server intact and copy the information to an existing NT Server.*

## Items That Can Be Migrated

If you've been supporting a mixed environment of NetWare and NT you probably have a lot of time invested in your NetWare file servers. When converting to an NT environment you don't want to throw away the work you've already done, and you don't have to. Using the migration tool, you can migrate the following items:

- User accounts

- Groups Accounts

- Selected directories and files

- Effective rights on files and directories

The Migration Tool for NetWare can be used to migrate a NetWare file server or multiple NetWare file servers to a single NT PDC. For example, you might have three NetWare file servers that you want to incorporate into a single NT server. Figure 9.5 diagrams the migration model.

**FIGURE 9.5**

Migration from
NetWare to NT

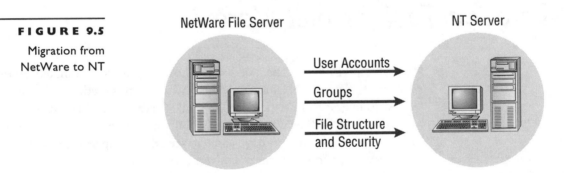

## Items That Cannot Be Migrated

While the NetWare migration will preserve important items like users, groups, and data, it will not migrate everything. Specifically, the following items will not be migrated from the NetWare environment.

- User passwords

- Workgroup and User Account Managers (this is not commonly used in a NetWare environment)

- Logon Scripts

- Print Server and Print Queue information

## Prerequisites for Running a NetWare Migration

In order to run Migration Tool for NetWare you need a NetWare file server and an NT server. If you are transferring user and group information, the NT Server needs to be a PDC. If you are transferring directory and file information, the NT Server can be a member server or a domain controller.

When preparing to migrate from NetWare to NT, you want to be aware of the following conditions:

- You can migrate from NetWare 2.*x*, 3.*x*, or 4.*x*.

- On the NetWare side you have to have Supervisor rights (for Net-Ware 2.*x* or 3.*x*) or Admin rights (for NetWare 4.*x*).

- On the NT side you need to be a member of the DOMAIN ADMINS group.

- You must be running NWLink IPX/SPX Compatible Transport on your destination NT server.

- GSNW must be running.

- If you are migrating directory and file information and you want to preserve NetWare permissions, the destination NT drive must be NTFS.

Another prerequisite to the migration is your careful planning of what will and will not be migrated from the NetWare file server. I think of a migration like moving from one house to another. We all have junk in our houses that we don't need (some of us more than others). Many file servers are the same. We have data and applications that are not being used. During a migration you probably do not want to bring the junk, so by planning out your migration before the event, you only transport what you will need at your new home.

## Using Migration Tool for NetWare

Without a NetWare file server you will not be able to complete a sample migration. If your test environment does not have a NetWare file server, you will not get past the first dialog box on the Migration Tool for NetWare. With that in mind, this section will provide the steps to access the dialog boxes used to configure the Migration Tool for NetWare and, will show you through figures the dialog boxes you would encounter during the migration process.

### Accessing the Migration Tool for NetWare

The Migration Tool for NetWare does not have an icon GUI utility associated with it. To access the migration tool, you run the NWCONV command line utility. This utility is located in the \WINNT\SYSTEM32 directory. You can access it by clicking Start ➤ Run ➤ NWCONV. The Migration Tool for NetWare dialog box will appear, as shown in Figure 9.6.

**FIGURE 9.6**

The Migration Tool for
NetWare dialog box

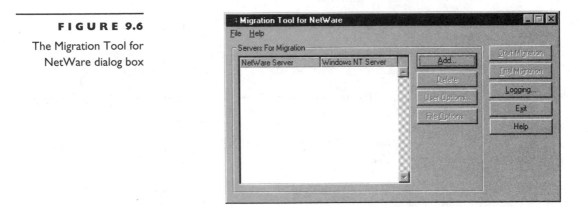

### Selecting NetWare File Server and NT Server for Migration

After you access the Migration Tool for NetWare, the first step in the configuration is to choose the NetWare file server that you will migrate from and the NT Server that you will migrate to. The file servers must be up and running and you must have administrative privileges on both sides.

To select the file servers, click Add in the Migration Tool for NetWare dialog box. The Select Servers For Migration box, shown in Figure 9.7, will appear.

At this point you will need to select the NetWare file server and the NT server.

**FIGURE 9.7**

The Select Servers For
Migration dialog box

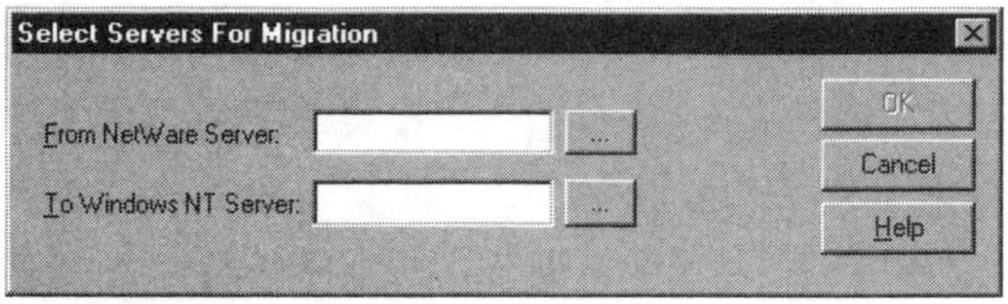

**Select Servers For Migration**

From NetWare Server: [        ] [...]

To Windows NT Server: [        ] [...]

OK

Cancel

Help

*You can type in the name of the server you are selecting or use the ellipsis button to the right of the selection box. It's easier to choose the ellipsis button so you are guaranteed the server is up and running. You eliminate the possibility of misspelling the server's name.*

After you select your servers, all of the buttons within the Migration Tool for NetWare will become active and you are ready to configure the migration options. The migration options are covered in detail in the next subsection.

### Configuring User Options for Migration

The default option during migration is that all user and group accounts are migrated from the NetWare file server to the NT Server domain controller that you specified. The User and Group dialog box allows you to customize how users and groups will be transferred. You should keep the following issues in mind when configuring users and groups for migration:

- Passwords will not transfer. The default is that users will not have a password, but other options are available and will be defined in this section.

- It is possible to have duplicate user and group names between the Net-Ware and NT servers. You can choose how duplicate names will be handled.

- Whether you want to use the default NetWare account policies or to use the default NT domain account policies.

- Whether NetWare administrators will have administrative rights in the NT domain.

To access the User and Group Options dialog box, click the User Options in the Migration Tool for NetWare dialog box. The User and Group Options dialog box, shown in Figure 9.8, will appear.

You will notice that at the top of the box the Transfer Users and Groups box is checked by default. If you do not want to migrate users and groups, you should uncheck this box and click OK. Each of the other options and tabs within the User and Group Options dialog box are defined in the following sections.

**PASSWORDS** The Passwords tab page allows you to make choices about user passwords in a very general fashion. You will see the Passwords tab when you access the Users and Groups Options dialog box. Table 9.3 defines the password options.

**TABLE 9.3**

Password options
available during migration

| OPTION | DESCRIPTION |
|---|---|
| No Password | This is the default option. After a migration, users will have no password the first time they log on. |
| Password is Username | Users use their logon account name for their first password. |
| Password is: | Allows you to specify a general password that will be used by all migrated users for their first logon. |
| User Must Change Password | This box is checked by default. It specifies that after the initial logon, the users must change the password in order to complete subsequent logons. |

None of the options are great choices if you are in an environment that requires any kind of security. The initial logon is basically unprotected. In order to provide a more secure initial logon, you can use a mapping file. This allows you to specify each user's initial password. I will cover the mapping file in the Use Mappings in File subsection.

**USERNAMES** From the User and Group Options dialog box, you can check the Usernames tab page and you will see the options shown in Figure 9.9.

**FIGURE 9.9**

The Usernames tab page of the User and Group Options dialog box

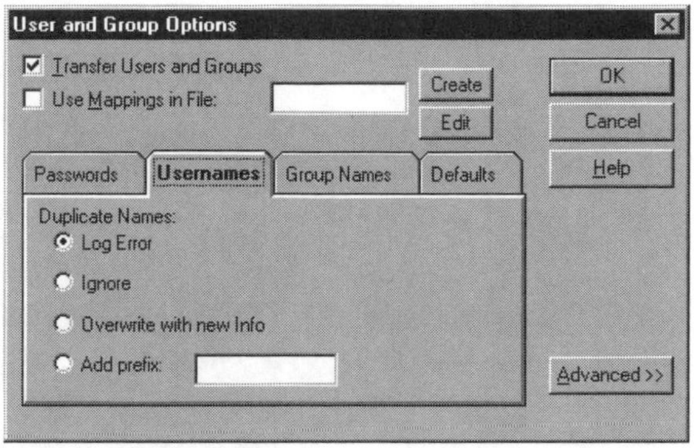

The function of the Usernames tab page is to specify how to handle duplicate names that might be encountered during the migration. This is a fairly common problem. Let's assume that Kevin has been accessing the NetWare file server and the NT domain. On the NetWare side his user account is KDONALD. On the NT domain his user account is also KDONALD. This will be especially common in environments where you have been using CSNW. The problem is that if you already have an existing KDONALD account, you can't create another account with the same name. So what do you do? Table 9.4 defines the options for handling duplicate account names.

**TABLE 9.4**

Username conflict options

| DUPLICATE USERNAME OPTION | DESCRIPTION |
| --- | --- |
| Log Error | Records the error in the ERROR.LOG file. This file will be covered in more detail in the Logging Options During Migration section. |
| Ignore | Causes no action to be taken if there is a conflict. |
| Overwrite with new Info | Replaces the existing NT account information with the NetWare account information. |
| Add Prefix | Allows you to specify a prefix to be added to the duplicate name. For example, if you choose NW as your prefix and you had duplicate KDONALDs, the NetWare account would become NWKDONALD. |

**GROUP NAMES** The Group Names tab page specifies how to handle duplicate group names. You access the window shown in Figure 9.10 by clicking the Group Names tab page of the User and Group Options dialog box.

**FIGURE 9.10**

The Group Names tab
page of the User and
Group Options dialog box

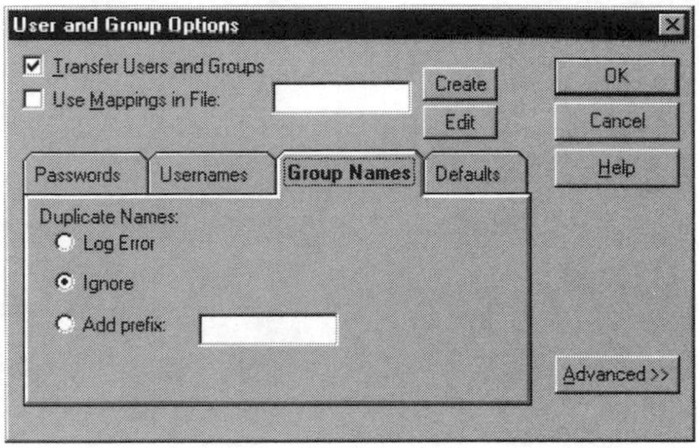

The options for handling duplicate group names are similar to the options for handling duplicate user names. Table 9.5 defines the options on the Group Names tab page.

**TABLE 9.5**

The Group Name
conflict options

| DUPLICATE GROUP NAME OPTION | DESCRIPTION |
| --- | --- |
| Log Error | Records the error in the ERROR.LOG file. This file will be covered in more detail in the "Logging Options During Migration" section. |
| Ignore | Causes no action to be taken if there is a conflict. |
| Add Prefix | Allows you to specify a prefix to be added to the duplicate group name. For example, if you choose NW as your prefix and you had a duplicate group named SALES, the NetWare group would become NWSALES. |

**DEFAULTS** The Defaults tab page specifies how default account restrictions should be handled. You can choose the NetWare default account restrictions or you can use the default NT domain account policies. To access the Defaults tab page from the User and Group Options dialog box, shown in Figure 9.11, click it.

The two options you have under the Defaults tab page are as follows:

- Use Supervisor Defaults

- Add Supervisors to the ADMINS Group

You will notice that the first option, Use Supervisor Defaults, is checked by default. In NetWare, you can set default account restrictions. It is a similar concept to the NT account policies that were covered in Chapter 5, "User Profiles, System Policies and Hardware Profiles." This means that if your NetWare account restrictions required five-character passwords that needed to be changed every 45 days and your NT account policy required seven-character passwords to be changed every 30 days, the default option is that the NetWare defaults apply.

The Add Supervisors to Administrators option specifies whether or not NetWare users who have administrative rights on the NetWare side should have administrative rights on the NT side. If you check this box, administrative rights are retained during migration. The default option is that NetWare administrators do not become members of the DOMAIN ADMINS global group, and administrative rights are lost.

**USE MAPPINGS IN FILE** The Use Mappings in File checkbox option allows you to create a mapping file that specifies how migrated accounts should be treated. Specifically, you can specify how usernames will be transferred, what passwords the new user accounts will use, and what groupnames groups will use.

Let's assume your NetWare File Server used first names for user accounts. On the NT domain controller, you are using first initial–last name as your naming scheme. The mapping file allows you to specify a new name for each NetWare account. You can also specify a password for each user account. This is much more secure than using the options listed on the Passwords tab page of the User and Group Options dialog box. You can also specify new names for groups that will be used.

To create a mapping file you would:

1. Check the Use Mapping File option in the User and Group Options dialog box.

2. Type in the name of the file you want to create. In this example, **NW312**. You will use the User and Group Options dialog box, shown in Figure 9.12.

**FIGURE 9.12**

The User and Group Options dialog box with the Use Mappings in File option checked

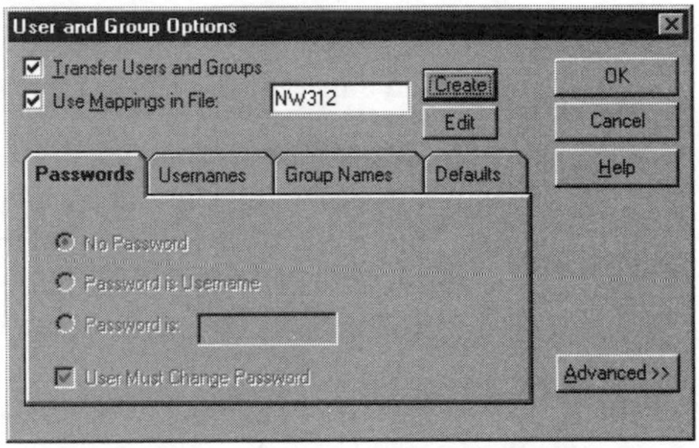

**User and Group Options**

☑ Transfer Users and Groups
☑ Use Mappings in File: NW312   [Create]
                                 [Edit]

[Passwords] [Usernames] [Group Names] [Defaults]

○ No Password
○ Password is Username
○ Password is: [        ]

☑ User Must Change Password   [Advanced >>]

[OK]
[Cancel]
[Help]

3. Click the Create button to the right of the mapping file. You will see the Create Mapping File dialog box, shown in Figure 9.13.

**FIGURE 9.13**

The Create Mapping File dialog box

**Create Mapping File**

Use Mappings in File: NW312   [...]

☑ Include User Names
Default Password:
○ No Password
○ Password is Username
○ Password is: [        ]

☑ Include Group Names

[OK]
[Cancel]

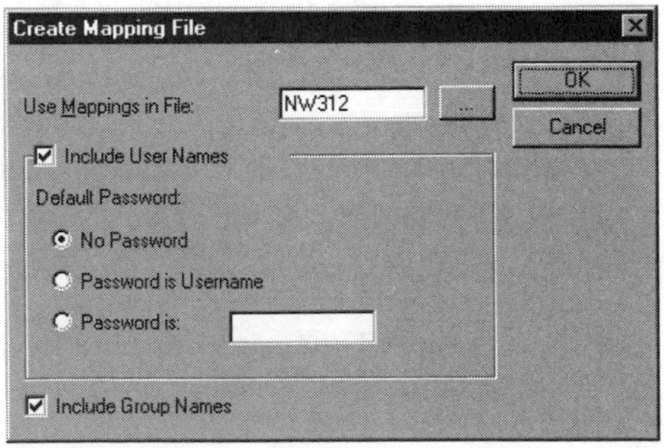

**4.** Click OK to create the mapping file. You will see a message box letting you know the mapping file was created successfully. When asked if you want to edit, click Yes. The mapping file, shown in Figure 9.14, will appear.

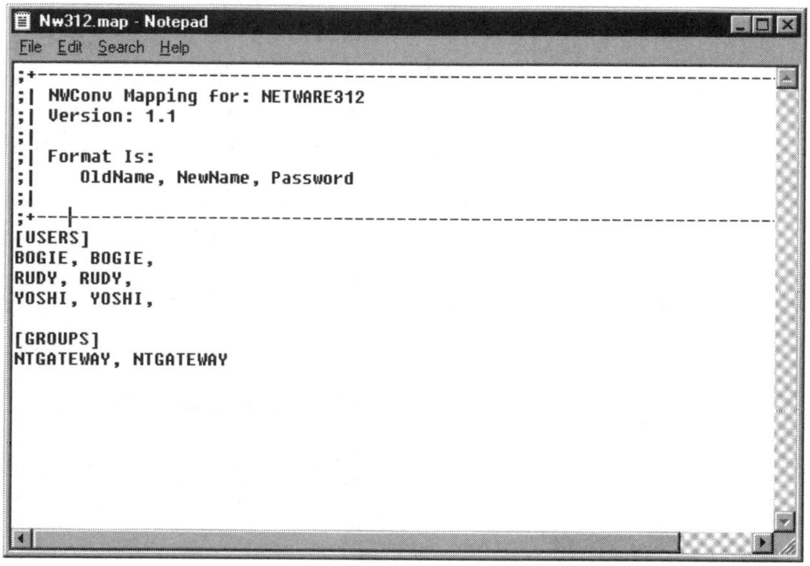

FIGURE 9.14

The Mapping File for NetWare to NT migration

```
Nw312.map - Notepad
File  Edit  Search  Help

;+-----------------------------------------------------
;| NWConv Mapping for: NETWARE312
;| Version: 1.1
;|
;| Format Is:
;|    OldName, NewName, Password
;|
;+---+-------------------------------------------------
[USERS]
BOGIE, BOGIE,
RUDY, RUDY,
YOSHI, YOSHI,

[GROUPS]
NTGATEWAY, NTGATEWAY
```

At this point all of the decisions for configuring your users and groups for migration have been made. In the next section, you will see how the file options can be configured for migration.

## Configuring File Options for Migration

The File Options portion of the NetWare migration allows you to specify how the NetWare volumes, directories, and files will be transferred. The options within the File Options box allow you to:

- Specify whether you want to transfer files.

- Select which directories and files will be transferred.

- Set the resource share name on the NT side.

By default the following files and directories are not migrated from NetWare.

- \SYSTEM directory, containing program files specific to the NetWare OS.

- \LOGIN directory, containing files specific to the NetWare login environment.

- \ETC directory, containing files specific to the NetWare TCP/IP environment.

- All hidden and system files; these are files that have been flagged with the NetWare file attributes of hidden and system. The rationale is that the files will most likely be NetWare related, and thus not needed on the NT side.

The File Options dialog box allows you to select the NetWare source volume and the destination NT directory. If you click the File Options button in the Migration Tool for NetWare dialog box, you see the File Options dialog box, as shown in Figure 9.15.

**FIGURE 9.15**

The File Options
dialog box

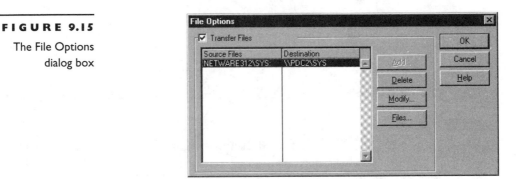

The Transfer Files option is not selected by default, but once this box is checked, the options within this dialog box become active. The default source files are the NetWare root volumes. The default destination directory is the NTFS partition with the most free space.

*If you migrate files to a FAT partition instead of an NTFS partition, your NetWare file permissions will not migrate.*

**MODIFYING DESTINATION DIRECTORY** The default destination directory is the NTFS partition with the most free space. To specify a different destination directory, click Modify within the File Options dialog box. The Modify Destination dialog box, shown in Figure 9.16, will appear.

The volume name, SYS, is automatically shared on the NT Server. If you
click Properties within the Modify Destination dialog box, you see the Share
Properties dialog box, as shown in Figure 9.17.

The Path text box of the Share Properties dialog box allows you to edit the
destination path of the migrated files.

**SPECIFYING FILES TO TRANSFER**   In the File Options dialog box, shown
in Figure 9.15, click Files. If you click this option, you see the Files to Transfer
dialog box, shown in Figure 9.18.

The Files To Transfer dialog box allows you to specify the directories and files that you want to migrate to the NT Server. Notice back in Figure 9.17 that the ETC, LOGIN, and SYSTEM directories are not selected by default.

### Trial and Actual Migration

After you have completed all of the configuration regarding your migration, you can choose to do a trial migration or an actual migration. A trial migration allows you to go through all the steps that you would for an actual migration, but you do not complete the last step, which is writing the data.

It is a really good idea to run a trial migration before you run an actual migration. If you encounter any problems at this stage, you have an opportunity to correct the problem(s) before you make any commitments. You might even run several trial migrations until you have zero or unavoidable errors.

After you are satisfied with the results of the trial migration, you can run an actual migration. At this point, all the options you had configured for the migration will be transferred from the NetWare file server to the NT server.

### Logging Options during Migration

During the migration process you can log information that relates to success or failure of the migration process. This information is very helpful in troubleshooting and for confirming that the trial or actual migration was successful. You will always have summary information regarding your migration in a file called LOGFILE.LOG. If you require more detailed information, you can configure the logging options. Configuring the logging options allows you to get more complete information on a trial or actual migration. The three options that you can choose from are:

- Pop-up on Errors

- Verbose User/Group Logging

- Verbose File Logging

Table 9.6 defines these options.

| **TABLE 9.6**<br>Logging options defined | **LOGGING OPTION** | **DESCRIPTION** |
| --- | --- | --- |
| | Pop-up on Errors | This option causes a pop-up box to appear every time an error occurs. This is a good option to use once you have eliminated all known errors. |

| TABLE 9.6 | LOGGING OPTION | DESCRIPTION |
|---|---|---|
| Logging options defined (continued) | Verbose User/Group Logging | Provides more complete information regarding user and group migrations. |
| | Verbose File Logging | Provides more complete information regarding file and directory migrations. |

# Chapter Summary

NETWARE HAS BEEN a dominant force in the network operating system market for many years. Many environments are now faced with the challenge of supporting a mixed networking environment of NetWare and NT. Microsoft has addressed this issue and provides connectivity solutions through NWLink IPX/SPX Compatible Transport, Client Services for NetWare, Gateway Services for NetWare, and Migration Tool for NetWare.

NWLink IPX/SPX Compatible Transport is a transport protocol that is used to transfer packets across a network. Because NetWare uses the IPX/SPX protocol by default, using the NWLink IPX/SPX Compatible Transport allows you to use a transport protocol that is compatible with the NetWare environment.

The CSNW utility is a NetWare redirector that can be installed on NT Workstation. Once installed the CSNW utility can be used to access NetWare file and print resources. Each NT Workstation using CSNW takes up one connection on the NetWare file server.

The GSNW utility is used with NT Server. It is used to provide NetWare connectivity for NT Servers. It also provides gateway services for NT Workstations that do not have CSNW installed. The gateway connection to the NetWare file server only takes up one NetWare connection, regardless of the number of users accessing the gateway.

The Migration Tool for NetWare allows you to migrate NetWare file servers to NT Server domain controllers. This utility allows you to migrate users, groups, and data. One nice feature of this utility is that you can perform a trial or practice migration without actually making any changes. Once you are satisfied with the way that the migration is working, you can perform an actual migration.

# Review Questions

1. If you were configuring NWLink IPX/SPX compatible transport protocol, and you weren't sure which frame type to use, what is your best option?

   **A.** Ethernet_802.2 because it's the industry standard

   **B.** Scan the network for frame type option

   **C.** Auto-detect option

   **D.** Choose all frame types

2. Which of the following statements are true of NWLink IPX/SPX Compatible Transport protocol? Choose all that apply.

   **A.** It is Microsoft's implementation of Novell's IPX/SPX protocol stack.

   **B.** It is completely compatible with Novell's IPX/SPX protocol stack.

   **C.** It is suggested, but not required, for use with CSNW and GSNW.

   **D.** Microsoft's implementation of IPX/SPX has built-in support for NetBIOS.

3. You are sitting at NT Workstation and want to access a NetWare file server so that you can access file and print resources. Which of the following options could be installed at your workstation to allow you access? Choose all that apply.

   **A.** CSNW

   **B.** GSNW

   **C.** File and Print Services for NetWare

   **D.** Microsoft Services for NetWare

4. In order for GSNW to work, what group must be created?

   **A.** NTGATEWAY on the NetWare file server

   **B.** NTGATEWAY on the NT Server

   **C.** NWGATEWAY on the NetWare file server

   **D.** NWGATEWAY on the NT Server

**5.** Which of the following items can be migrated through Migration Tool for NetWare? Choose all the apply.

**A.** Users

**B.** Groups

**C.** Login scripts

**D.** Print queues and print servers

**E.** User passwords

**F.** File structures and permissions

**6.** Which versions of NetWare can be migrated with Migration Tool for NetWare?

**A.** NetWare 2.*x*

**B.** NetWare 3.*x*

**C.** NetWare 4.*x*

**D.** NetWare 2.*x* and NetWare 3.*x*

**E.** NetWare 2.*x*, NetWare 3.*x*, and NetWare 4.*x*

**7.** For the highest level of password security after migrating your NetWare user accounts to NT, which option should you choose?

**A.** Preserve NetWare password

**B.** Password Is:

**C.** Assign Random password

**D.** Use the mapping file

# Macintosh Connectivity

MANY NETWORK ADMINISTRATORS face the challenge of having to integrate PCs and Apple Macintosh computers on the same network. Windows NT makes it easy to support this mixed environment through Services for Macintosh (SFM). SFM is an optional software service that ships with NT Server. The goal of SFM is to provide NT file and print services to Macintosh users.

In this chapter you will learn:

- SFM benefits

- SFM system and networking requirements

- How to install SFM

- How to share files with SFM

- How to configure SFM

# Benefits of Services for Macintosh

SERVICES FOR MACINTOSH allows Macintosh users to participate in an NT environment when they install the AppleTalk Filing Protocol (AFP) onto an NT server. After SFM is installed, the NT server is a fully compliant AFP server. Macintosh users can then access the NT server as if it were a Macintosh AFP server. The benefit of being fully AFP compliant is that you get better performance than if you were doing translation functions associated with gateway solutions.

Services for Macintosh provides three main benefits.

- File sharing

- Print sharing

- AppleTalk routing

## Services for Macintosh File Sharing

One of the main benefits of SFM is its ability to share file structures between PC users and Macintosh users. It is important to understand that NT provides a means for storing data, but not for translating data. In order to support cross-platform sharing of data, you must have cross-platform applications that translate data for you.

The following example illustrates how SFM works. You have an NT Server running SFM. Rick is a Macintosh user who has just created a Microsoft Word document called BUDGET and has stored it on the NT Server. Kevin is a PC user who wants to access this document. Kevin is using the Windows 95 version of Microsoft Word. He is able to access the document because Microsoft Word has cross-platform support.

In other words, NT itself does not do anything to make data translation possible from one platform to another; that is solely up to the application you are using. If your application supports cross-platform conversion, you will have no problem translating data.

SFM is basically providing a way of storing files so that PC users and Macintosh users can both share the data.

## Services for Macintosh Print Sharing

SFM print sharing provides users with three main benefits. The first benefit is that Macintosh users can send their PostScript print jobs to non-PostScript printers that are attached to NT servers. These printers appear on a Macintosh screen as shared printer icons. The second benefit is that PC users can send PostScript print jobs to PostScript printers attached to Macintosh clients. The third benefit is that NT uses the spooling function to provide print services. Spooling allows a job to be stored on disk as it waits its turn to be processed. By spooling documents, the computer can begin the next task instead of waiting its turn for the printer.

The advantage of cross-platform printing is that it allows you to make maximum use of your resources. For example, assume your network is primarily made up of PCs, but that you support two Macintosh computers in the marketing department. It might be hard to justify an expensive, high-end printer for just two users. Through SFM, the Macintosh users are able to access a high-end printer that is already connected to an NT network.

## Services for Macintosh Routing Services

Through SFM, you can create an AppleTalk internet by connecting AppleTalk physical networks through NT Server. In this way, NT Server would function as an AppleTalk router.

Now you have been introduced to the three main benefits of SFM. The rest of the chapter will focus in greater detail on configuring and using SFM.

# System Requirements for Services for Macintosh

BEFORE YOU BEGIN to install Services for Macintosh, you want to make sure that the system prerequisites for installing SFM have been met. The three areas of concern are:

- NT Server requirements

- Macintosh requirements

- Networking requirements

## NT Server Requirements for Services for Macintosh

In order to install SFM, you must be running NT Server; SFM is not supported by NT Workstation. The NT server must have at least 2MB of free disk space in order to store the SFM files. You must also have an NTFS partition.

The NTFS partition is required to store Macintosh files. The FAT file system supports a data fork. The NTFS file system supports a data fork and a resource fork. The data and resource forks are required to support Macintosh files. If no NTFS partition is present, SFM will install, but only print services will be available; file services will not be available. Before SFM is installed, you can view which partition types your NT Server is using through the Disk Administrator utility in the Administrative Tools group.

*To convert an existing partition to NTFS, you can use the* CONVERT *command line utility. You can type* **CONVERT/?** *at the command prompt for correct command syntax.*

## Macintosh Requirements for Services for Macintosh

You can use any Macintosh computer on your NT network that supports AppleShare. AppleShare is the networking software that ships with all late-model Macintoshes. The Macintosh XL and the Macintosh 128 computers are the exception, and are not supported in an NT network. These computers are practically obsolete, so if you don't have one, you should not have a problem. In addition, a Macintosh must be running System 6.0.7 or later to support SFM. Most likely, your Macintoshes are running System 7 or higher (System 7 came out in 1990). At this writing, the current Macintosh operating system is System 7.55.

*If you are running Macintosh system software older than System 7.5, your system cannot access volumes greater than 2GB. If you are running Macintosh System 7.5 or later, the limitation is 4GB.*

## Networking Requirements for Services for Macintosh

In order to support a mixed environment of Macintoshes and PCs, you will need to have a common network system. Macintoshes can use LocalTalk, EtherTalk, TokenTalk, or FDDITalk.

You may be familiar with Ethernet, Token Ring, and FDDI. EtherTalk, TokenTalk, and FDDITalk are the Macintosh implementations of these common networking cards. If you come from a PC background, you may not be familiar with LocalTalk. LocalTalk is integrated with every Macintosh. It provides a simple, no-extra-cost method of networking Macintoshes. The problem with LocalTalk is that it is slow. In the PC world, ARCnet has always been considered a slow but steady network card. ARCnet transmits at 2.5Mbps (megabits per second). By contrast, Ethernet transmits at 10Mbps (there is also a 100 Mbps specification). Token Ring transmits at 4/16Mbps. FDDI transmits at 100Mbps. LocalTalk transmits at 230.4Kbps. That is 10 times slower than ARCnet.

If you have high-end Macintoshes (Quadra 700 or above) you will likely have on-board EtherTalk cards. If you have a network of LocalTalk connections, you will need to provide some method of connecting them with your PC NT environment. The preferable solution would be to upgrade them to EtherTalk; that may not be an option due to cost. The other options involve using a router. You can use a stand-alone router that has a LocalTalk port and an EtherTalk port, or you can add a LocalTalk card to your NT server to make it the router.

# Installing Services for Macintosh

N THIS SECTION, you will learn how to install SFM. You will also learn about changes that occur in some utilities with the installation of SFM. It is very easy to install SFM. Assuming that you have met the prerequisites, the installation is similar to that of any other service. In Exercise 10.1 you will install Services for Macintosh.

# Utilities Modified by Services for Macintosh

NCE SERVICES FOR Macintosh has been installed on NT Server, you will notice that Server Manager and File Manager (from command line WINFILE) are now modified to reflect that SFM has been installed. These utilities are modified in order to support SFM. In Figure 10.1, notice the options along the top of the File Manager window.

**FIGURE 10.1**

File Manager on NT
Server without SFM

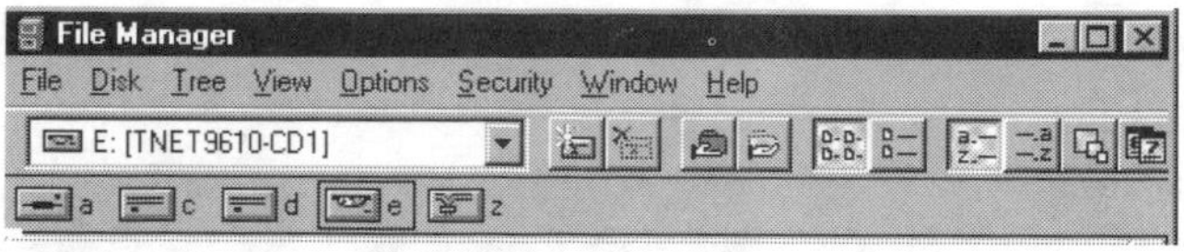

**EXERCISE 10.1**

**Installing Services for Macintosh**

This exercise should be completed from PDC1 while you are logged on as ADMINIS-TRATOR. It assumes that you have completed Exercise 4.1, and that you have an NTFS partition on drive `D:`.

**1.** Select Start ➢ Settings ➢ Control Panel.

**2.** Double-click Network.

**3.** Click the Services tab.

**4.** Click Add to open the Select Network Service dialog box.

**5.** Select Services for Macintosh and click OK.

**6.** You will need to specify from where the distribution files should be copied (CD `drive:\i386\`). Click OK.

**7.** After the file copy is complete, click Close.

**8.** Binding analysis will occur and you will be returned to the Microsoft AppleTalk Protocol Properties window. Click OK.

**9.** A Network Settings Change dialog box will appear. Click Yes to restart your computer.

**10.** Reboot your NT server and log on as ADMINISTRATOR.

Now look at Figure 10.2. This NT server is running SFM. Between the Security and Window options, there is a new option, MacFile. SFM extends the schema of the listed utilities as it is installed.

**FIGURE 10.2**

File Manager on an NT
server running SFM

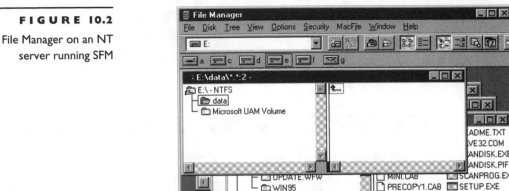

Now you have installed SFM and have seen the changes it makes to your utilities. The next sections will concentrate on configuring SFM through SFM file sharing and SFM properties.

# File Sharing and Services for Macintosh

THIS SECTION WILL explore how to configure SFM file sharing. The specific areas you will learn about are:

■ NTFS Prerequisite

■ File name translation

■ Macintosh-accessible volumes

## NTFS Prerequisite

As mentioned earlier, the NT server that is running SFM must have an NTFS partition to store the Macintosh files. Macintosh files are different from PC files because each Macintosh file is made up of two pieces, or forks. The two types of forks that Macintosh files use are data forks and resource forks. A data fork contains the data associated with the file. A resource fork contains Macintosh Operating System information relating to the file, such as icon definitions, font, menu, and code.

The NTFS partition is required to run SFM because it supports both the resource and data forks, while a FAT partition can store only a data fork. A FAT partition is useless to a Macintosh user. A Macintosh user cannot identify FAT partitions using the Chooser function, because you can't make a FAT partition Macintosh accessible.

## File Name Translation

Different environments support different naming conventions. The diversity of NT clients makes this an issue, as a client on one platform can create a file name that exceeds the length that another client who wants to access that file can support. The common naming conventions supported are shown in Table 10.1.

| **TABLE 10.1** <br> File-naming conventions supported on different platforms in an NT environment | | |
|---|---|---|
| **NT CLIENTS** | **FILE SYSTEMS SUPPORTED** | **FILE-NAMING CONVENTION USED** |
| NT Workstation <br> NT Server | NTFS <br> FAT with LFN <br> (long file name) | 256 characters <br> 256 characters |
| Macintosh | Mac File system | 32 characters |
| Win16 and DOS clients | Regular FAT | 8.3 naming convention |
| Win95 | FAT with LFN | 256 characters |

With Macintosh clients, there are two different problems you can encounter.

- Macintoshes can create file names up to 32 characters without truncation, but DOS and Win16 clients cannot access these files.

- If an NT client creates a file name with more than 32 characters, a Macintosh client cannot access the file without truncation.

To overcome this problem, NT auto-generates short file names for any file over the 8.3 character limitation imposed on DOS and Win16 clients. If you are not sharing files with DOS and Win16 clients, this is not a critical issue. If you are sharing files with DOS and Win16 clients, it is best to keep your file names short to avoid any confusion.

## Macintosh-Accessible Volumes

One of the main functions of Services for Macintosh is that it allows NT file services for Macintosh users. A Macintosh-accessible volume is space on the NT server used to store Macintosh files and folders. You can create Macintosh-accessible volumes through File Manager or through Server Manager.

A Macintosh user will see only Macintosh-accessible volumes through the Chooser (for those of you who aren't Macintosh people, the Chooser is how Macintoshes access network resources).

In this section and the following subsections you will learn about these topics:

- How to create a Macintosh-accessible volume

- Rules for creating a Macintosh-accessible volume

- Properties of Macintosh-accessible volumes

- Macintosh permissions on Macintosh-accessible volumes

- Macintosh file associations

In Exercise 10.2, you will create a Macintosh-accessible volume on the NTFS partition you created in Exercise 4.1.

---

**EXERCISE 10.2**

### Creating a Macintosh-Accessible Volume

This exercise should be completed from PDC1 while you are logged on as ADMINISTRATOR. It assumes that you have already completed Exercise 10.1.

**1.** Select Start ➤ Run.

**2.** At the Run dialog box, type in **WINFILE** and click OK.

**3.** Notice that the MacFile option now appears.

---

**4.** Click drive D: and create the directory structure shown below.

**D:\ (NTFS Partition)**

MAC APPS

WP          SS

MAC DATA

WP DOCS     SS DOCS

**5.** Click the MAC APPS directory so that it is highlighted.

**6.** Click MacFile ➢ Create Volume.

**7.** The Create Macintosh-Accessible Volume dialog box shown below appears.

Create Macintosh-Accessible Volume

Volume Name: MAC APPS
Path: D:\MAC APPS
Password:
Confirm Password:

OK
Cancel
Permissions...
Help

**Volume Security**
☐ This volume is read-only
☑ Guests can use this volume

**User Limit**
◉ Unlimited
○ Allow [    ] Users

**8.** Leave the values at default and click OK. You now have created a Macintosh-accessible volume.

## No-Nesting Rule for Macintosh-Accessible Volumes

A Macintosh-accessible volume is like a network share for Macintosh users. The difference between Macintosh-accessible shares and regular NT shares is that you cannot nest Macintosh-accessible volumes.

The no-nesting rule means that when you create a Macintosh-accessible volume at any level, you cannot create another Macintosh-accessible volume above or below the level of the volume you have already created. For example, assume you have the directory structure created in Step 4 of Exercise 10.2.

Let's say you have created a Macintosh-accessible volume on MAC APPS. You cannot make the root of drive D: a Macintosh-accessible volume because it is above MAC APPS, which makes it nested. You would get an error message if you tried to create a volume at D:\. You would also get an error message if you tried to create a Macintosh-accessible volume at D:\MAC APPS\WP because it is below MAC APPS.

In Exercise 10.3, you will see what happens when you try to nest Macintosh volumes.

---

**EXERCISE 10.3**

## Attempting to Nest Macintosh Volumes

This exercise assumes that you have completed Exercise 10.2 and that you are still in the File Manager utility.

**1.** Under D: click D:\NTFS.

**2.** Click MacFile ➢ Create Volume.

**3.** Type in **TEST** for the volume name and click OK. You will get the error message shown below.

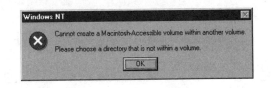

This error message occurs because the Macintosh-accessible volume you created in Exercise 10.2 is under drive D:.

### Volume Security on Macintosh-Accessible Volumes

When you create a Macintosh-accessible volume, you see the Macintosh-Accessible Volume dialog box. Under Volume Security you have two options to choose from. (This volume is read-only and guests can use it.)

The This volume is read-only option specifies that the volume can be read but not edited. Even if the logged-on user has more access permission to the resource that is within a read-only Macintosh-accessible volume, they are still restricted by the read-only security. This option would be used for application folders or folders that contain data you would never want your Macintosh users to modify or delete.

The Guests can use this volume option allows users who are logged on with Guest access to use the Macintosh-accessible volume. In order for Guest access to be granted, you first have to enable the GUEST account through User Manager for Domains.

### Properties of Macintosh-Accessible Volumes

When creating a Macintosh-accessible volume, you are able to specify a password associated with it as well as a user limit. The password option specifies a password that any Macintosh user trying to access the volume must know. The user-limit option defines how many concurrent users can access the volume. One instance in which you would limit user access is if you had a Macintosh application with a limited number of client licenses. You could impose a user limit for the volume that contained the Macintosh application.

### Permissions on Macintosh-Accessible Volumes

During the creation of a Macintosh-accessible volume, you can specify what Macintosh permissions you want applied to the volume. These permissions allow you to be more restrictive than the NT permissions that have already been applied. If you use the Macintosh permissions, the Macintosh users will be governed by the most limited security imposed through:

- NTFS security

- Macintosh permissions

The concept is the same as network share permissions on the PC side that were covered in Chapter 4, "Resource Management." The difference is that the Macintosh permissions are different from the share permissions. In the Macintosh world, permissions can be applied to the owner, primary group, or to group EVERYONE. The owner is the user who created, or has taken ownership of, the directory on which the Macintosh-accessible volume was created. Each Macintosh-accessible volume can have one primary group associated with it. The primary group would be the group that uses the files and folders within the Macintosh-accessible volume. You can specify which primary group you want each user to associate with through User Manager for Domains.

*The concept of a primary group is unique to the Macintosh environment.*

The Macintosh permissions that are associated with a Macintosh-accessible volume are:

- See Files
- See Folders
- Make Changes

These permissions are defined and mapped to NT permissions in Table 10.2.

| TABLE 10.2 Macintosh directory permissions | PERMISSION | DESCRIPTION | NT EQUIVALENT |
|---|---|---|---|
| | See Files | User or group can list and read files within the folder | Read |
| | See Folders | User or group can see what folders are contained within the current folder | Read |
| | Make Changes | User or group can list and read files within a folder, rename files, move files, and create and delete files | Write and Delete |

In Exercise 10.4, you will create a user and group account, and then apply Macintosh permissions to the Macintosh-accessible volume you created in Exercise 10.2.

**EXERCISE 10.4**

## Assigning Macintosh Permissions to Macintosh-Accessible Volumes

This exercise should be completed from PDC1 while you are logged on as ADMINISTRATOR. It assumes that you have completed the previous exercises in this chapter.

In the first part of this exercise, you will create a new Macintosh user and global group, then you will associate the new user with a primary group.

**1.** Click Start ➤ Programs ➤ Administrative Tools (common) ➤ User Manager for Domains.

**2.** Click User ➤ New User.

**3.** In the New User dialog box, type in **MACDUDE** in the Username field, uncheck the User Must Change Password at Next Logon option, and click OK.

**4.** Click User ➤ New Global Group.

**5.** In the New Global Group dialog box, type in **MACUSERS** in the Group Name field. From the Not member of box, select MACDUDE and click Add to place him in the Member of box. Click OK.

**6.** You should now be at the User Manager for Domains dialog box. Double-click MACDUDE to bring up the User Properties dialog box.

**7.** Click Groups to bring up the Group Memberships dialog box, shown below.

**8.** The PRIMARY GROUP option is set to DOMAIN USERS by default. In the Member of box, click MACUSERS and click Set. MACDUDE is now associated with the MACUSERS Primary Group.

In the second part of this exercise, you will assign Macintosh access rights to MACDUDE.

**9.** Select Start ➢ Run.

**10.** At the Run dialog box, type in **WINFILE** and click OK.

**11.** Click drive D: and choose the MAC APPS directory that you created as a Macintosh-accessible volume in Exercise 10.2.

**12.** Select MACFILE ➢ Permissions. The Macintosh View of Directory Permissions dialog box, shown below, will appear.

**13.** Click the Ellipsis (...) button next to the Primary Group option. Select the MACUSERS global group and click Add. Click OK.

**14.** Uncheck the Make Changes option for MACUSERS and EVERYONE. Click OK.

Within the Macintosh View of Directory Permissions dialog box, there are two other options: Replace Permissions on Subdirectories and Cannot Move, Rename, or Delete. The Replace Permissions on Subdirectories option is not checked by default. This means that even though you restricted the MACUSERS group to Seeing Files and Seeing Folders at the MAC APPS folder, the MACUSERS group would have Make Changes at the WP and SS subfolders due to the unchecked default setting of Replacing Permissions on Subdirectories. The Cannot Move, Rename, or Delete option means that even if Macintosh users have other access rights, they cannot move, rename, or delete any files or folders within the Macintosh-accessible volume if this box is checked.

### Macintosh File Associations

Macintosh applications do not use file extensions the way PC applications do. Macintosh applications embed the application information within the file name as the Macintoshcreator. This could lead to problems when a Macintosh user tries to access a PC-created document. To overcome this problem, you can associate MS-DOS extensions with a Macintosh document creator. To create a Macintosh file association, choose MacFile from the File Manager utility and open the Associate dialog box shown in Figure 10.3.

**FIGURE 10.3**

The MacFile Associate
dialog box

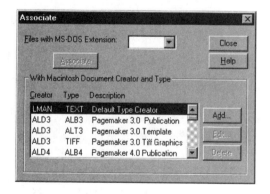

Now you have learned to configure Macintosh file services. The next section will focus on configuring Services for Macintosh through the MacFile icon and Services for Macintosh properties.

# Configuring Services for Macintosh

A FTER YOU HAVE installed Services for Macintosh, you will need to configure it. In this section you will learn how to configure the MacFile properties. The MacFile properties allows you to configure and view the status of Macintosh user sessions.

## MacFile Properties

The MacFile Properties dialog box allows you to configure the properties of the Macintosh users' logon environment and the accessibility they have to the NT file system. The options that you can view or configure through the MacFile dialog box are:

- View usage summary

- View which Macintosh users are currently connected and what they are accessing

- Configure Macintosh-accessible volumes

- See files currently in use by Macintosh users, and view and set attributes that govern Mac logons

### MacFile Usage Summary

After you install Services for Macintosh, you will see a new icon in the Control Panel called MacFile. If you double-click MacFile you will see the MacFile Properties dialog box, shown in Figure 10.4.

**FIGURE 10.4**

The MacFile Properties
dialog box

**MacFile Properties on PDC1**

Usage Summary

Active AppleTalk Sessions:     0
Open File Forks:               0
File Locks:                    0

Close
Help

Users    Volumes    Files    Attributes

In the main screen of this box, usage statistics are defined. These statistics are informational and cannot be edited. Table 10.3 defines the usage properties.

**TABLE 10.3**

Usage summary statistics defined

| USAGE SUMMARY STATISTIC | DEFINITION |
| --- | --- |
| Active AppleTalk Sessions | Indicates the number of Macintosh clients who are currently logged on. |
| Open File Forks | A file fork is one of two subfiles associated with a Macintosh file. One subfile is a data fork and the other is a resource fork. Open File Forks indicates the combination of open data forks and resource forks. |
| File Locks | A lock is used to manage files and subdirectories. If a file or subdirectory is locked, it prevents further access. File Locks reflects the number of locks currently in use. |

## Macintosh Users Currently Connected

If you click Users, you access the Macintosh Users dialog box, shown in Figure 10.5. This dialog box shows you which Macintosh users are currently connected and what resources they are using. This information can be very useful. For example, at any given time, you can see exactly how many Macintosh users are accessing your server, which number can be used to determine licensing requirements. It's also a way to play Big Brother; you can see exactly which files each user is accessing.

The Macintosh Users dialog box is divided into two sections: the top half and the bottom half of the screen.

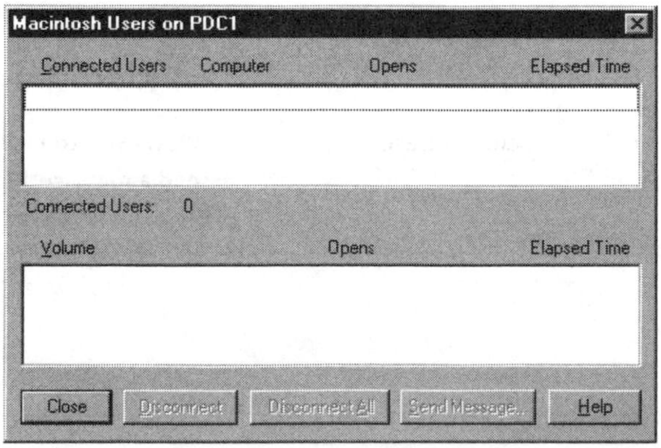

**FIGURE 10.5**

The Macintosh Users dialog box

The top half of the screen shows you statistics regarding the Macintosh users who are currently logged on. The bottom half shows you specific information as to what resources each user is accessing.

Table 10.4 defines the options within the Macintosh Users dialog box.

| | | |
|---|---|---|
| **TABLE 10.4** Macintosh Users dialog box options defined | **MACINTOSH USERS OPTION** | **DEFINITION** |
| | Connected Users | Displays all Macintosh users who are currently logged on. The bottom half of the screen shows the current connections in use for whoever is highlighted under Connected Users. |
| | Computer | The name of the computer at which the Macintosh user is logged in. |
| | Opens | The number of file opens for each Macintosh user. |
| | Elapsed Time | The number of minutes that each Macintosh user has been logged on. |
| | Connected Users | In the middle of the screen, displays the total number of connected users. |
| | Volume | The Macintosh volumes being accessed by the specified user in the top half of the screen. |
| | Opens | The number of file opens for the specified Macintosh user. |
| | Elapsed Time | For each Macintosh volume being accessed, displays the number of minutes the volume has been open. |
| | Disconnect | Allows you to select a Macintosh user whom you want to disconnect from the NT server. |
| | Disconnect All | Allows you to disconnect all Macintosh users who are currently connected to your NT server. |
| | Send Message | Allows you to pick a Macintosh user to whom you want to send a message. Normally, if you are going to disconnect a user, you first send them a warning message. |

### Macintosh Volumes

In order for Macintosh users to access NT file resources, a Macintosh-accessible volume must first be created. Macintosh-accessible volumes were covered earlier in this chapter.

Once Macintosh-accessible volumes are created, you can view which users are currently accessing the volumes by clicking Volumes in the MacFile Properties dialog box. If you have more than one volume, you can see which users are accessing which volume by clicking each specific volume.

This information display is similar to what you saw through the Users button. It is just presented in a different format. Depending on what type of information you are seeking, both formats are useful. For example, let's assume you have 100 Macintosh users and 10 Macintosh-accessible volumes. If you want to see what RICK is accessing, you do not want to click 10 different volumes to see if he is accessing them. Rather, you look under RICK's name. On the other hand, if you want to see who is accessing the Applications volume, you do not want to click each of 100 different user names to determine who has access. Instead, you click the volume.

### Files Opened by Macintosh Users

The Files Opened By Macintosh Users option with MacFile provides specific information on files that are currently being accessed by Macintosh users. Through this dialog box you can determine which files users have open, who has them open, and what type of access the user has to the file. You can also see whether the file has been locked. This dialog box also lets you manage files by selectively closing file forks, or by closing all file forks.

### MacFile Attributes

The MacFile Attributes dialog box allows you to control the sessions of Macintosh clients. Through this dialog box you can specify the server name and greeting message to be displayed to Macintosh clients. You also can control security and session information. When you click Attributes in the MacFile Properties dialog box, shown in Figure 10.4, you see the MacFile Attributes dialog box shown in Figure 10.6.

**FIGURE 10.6**

The MacFile Attributes
dialog box

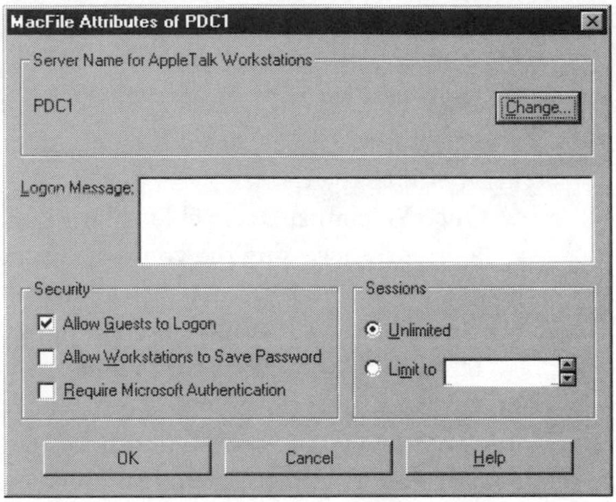

**SERVER NAME AND LOGON MESSAGE** The Server Name for Macintosh Workstations option allows you to specify the server name that will be broadcast to Macintosh users. By default, this name is the NetBIOS name of the NT server. In order to avoid confusion, it is best to leave this option at default.

The Logon Message option allows you to specify a greeting message that Macintosh users will see when they log on to the NT server. It is similar to the greeting message that PC users see when they log on, as covered in Chapter 5, "User Profiles, System Profiles, and Hardware Profiles."

**SECURITY** The level of Macintosh security you will get depends upon three circumstances: whether guest logons are allowed, whether Macintosh workstations can save passwords, and whether Microsoft authentication is required.

Table 10.5 defines these MacFile security options.

**TABLE 10.5**

MacFile security options

| MACFILE SECURITY OPTION | DESCRIPTION | DEFAULT SETTING |
|---|---|---|
| Allow Guests to Logon | Specifies that Macintosh users who do not have an NT user account can still access Macintosh-accessible volumes through a Guest logon. This assumes that the Guest account has been enabled through User Manager for Domains. | Enabled |

| TABLE 10.5 | MACFILE SECURITY OPTION | DESCRIPTION | DEFAULT SETTING |
|---|---|---|---|
| MacFile security options (continued) | Allow Workstations to Save Password | Allows Macintosh users to save their NT account password, so that a password prompt does not appear during the logon sequence. This feature is not recommended for high-security networks. | Disabled |
| | Require Microsoft Authentication | Macintosh users can log on in two ways: with clear-text passwords, or through Microsoft Authentication. Clear-text passwords can be only eight characters in length and can be read by protocol analyzers. Microsoft Authentication encrypts the password and support passwords up to 14 characters in length. This feature should be enabled in security-conscious environments. | Disabled |

*If Macintosh users are not required to use Microsoft Authentication during logon, the Macintosh requires no additional software. The Microsoft User Authentication software for Mac users is placed on the NTFS partition with the most free space during installation of SFM. This software must be copied to the Macintosh computer if Microsoft Authentication is required.*

**SESSIONS** The Sessions option allows you to specify whether you will allow unlimited Macintosh users to access your NT server, or whether you want to limit the concurrent number of Macintosh users who can access your NT server.

In Exercise 10.5, you will configure the MacFile Attributes for your server.

**EXERCISE 10.5**

### Configuring MacFile Attributes

This exercise should be completed from PDC1 while you are logged on as ADMINISTRATOR.

**1.** Click Start ➢ Settings ➢ Control Panel ➢ Network ➢ MacFile.

**2.** From the MacFile Properties dialog box, click Attributes.

**3.** In the Logon Message box, type **"Hello Mac Users"**.

**4.** In the Security area, uncheck Allow Guests to Logon and check the Require Microsoft Authentication option. Click OK.

**5.** At the MacFile Properties dialog box, click Close.

# Chapter Summary

NT SERVER COMES with an optional service called Services for Macintosh (SFM). SFM allows Macintosh users to participate in an NT domain. It does this by allowing them to share file resources on an NT server that is running SFM, and that has created Macintosh-accessible volumes. SFM also allows print sharing and routing services.

In this chapter you learned that there are minimum NT Server requirements, Macintosh requirements, and networking requirements that have to be met in order to successfully implement SFM.

File resources can be shared once SFM has been installed by creating Macintosh-accessible volumes. Macintosh-accessible volumes can be configured with passwords, volume security, user connection limitations, and Macintosh permissions.

You also get a new icon, MacFile, in the control panel once SFM has been installed. Through MacFile you can view which Macintosh users are connected to your NT server, which file resources are being accessed, as well as who is accessing them. Through the Attributes option of MacFile, you can configure the Macintosh users' logon environment.

# *Review Questions*

1. Your boss has heard that Services for Macintosh provides support for Macintosh users on an NT server. He wants to know exactly what SFM will do. Which of the following benefits can you tell him are available with Services for Macintosh? Choose all that apply.

   **A.** Macintosh files stored on Macintosh computers are available to NT-PC users.

   **B.** Macintosh files stored on NT servers can be shared by Macintosh and PC users.

   **C.** Macintosh users can send their print jobs to non-PostScript printers attached to NT servers.

   **D.** PC users can send print jobs to PostScript printers attached to Macintosh clients.

2. Which of the following requirements must be met on an NT server to support SFM? Choose all that apply.

   **A.** Must have 2MB of free disk space

   **B.** Must have an NTFS partition for file services

   **C.** Must have installed AFP through Control Panel Network option

   **D.** Must have 4MB of free disk space

3. Which option could be used to connect an NT network running Ethernet with a Macintosh network running LocalTalk? Choose all that apply.

   **A.** Upgrade the Macintoshes to EtherTalk cards.

   **B.** Add a LocalTalk card to the NT server to make it a router.

   **C.** Use an external router with LocalTalk and Ethernet.

   **D.** Use a LocalTalk-to-Ethernet converter cable on the NT server.

**4.** Which of the following utilities are modified by SFM? Choose all that apply.

    **A.** Server Manager

    **B.** User Manager for Domains

    **C.** Event Viewer

    **D.** File Manager

**5.** Which of the following utilities can be used to create a Macintosh-accessible volume? Choose all the apply.

    **A.** Server Manager

    **B.** MacFile applet

    **C.** User Manager for Domains

    **D.** File Manager

**6.** Which of the following properties can be associated with Macintosh-accessible volumes? Choose all that apply.

    **A.** User limit

    **B.** Volume password

    **C.** File-level security

    **D.** Guest access

**7.** If you want to disconnect a Macintosh user who is attached to your NT server, which utility do you use? Choose all that apply.

    **A.** Server Manager

    **B.** MacFile applet

    **C.** User Manager for Domains

    **D.** File Manager

# TCP/IP and Related Services

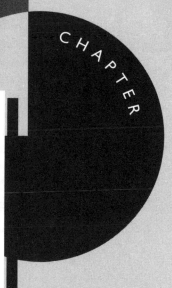

O F THE MANY transport protocols available, Transport Control Protocol/ Internet Protocol (TCP/IP) is the de facto industry standard. TCP/IP is a collection of protocols used on the Internet to connect systems around the world into a public global data network. Using TCP/IP, you can connect to a wide variety of computers, from mainframes to Macintoshes to UNIX workstations. Enterprising computer enthusiasts have even used TCP/IP to connect such dissimilar devices as coke machines and video cameras to the Internet. This versatile collection of protocols can be configured to transfer files to or from any computer, or even to monitor the status of TCP/IP systems on a network and send an alert when a computer goes down.

Since NT version 3.51, Microsoft has made TCP/IP one of its default protocols. Microsoft NT Server 4.0 also includes several services which run with TCP/IP, including the Dynamic Host Configuration Protocol, the Windows Internet Naming Service, and the Domain Name Service. In this chapter you will learn about:

- the TCP/IP protocol suite

- Dynamic Host Configuration Protocol (DHCP)

- Windows Internet Naming Service (WINS)

- Domain Name Service (DNS)

# The TCP/IP Protocol Suite

T CP/IP IS THE name given to a collection (or suite) of protocols developed in conjunction with the Internet. The predecessor to today's Internet was the ARPANET (Advanced Research Projects Agency

Network), which was developed by the United States Department of Defense Advanced Research Projects Agency, or DARPA. In 1984, the ARPANET was split into two separate networks, ARPANET and MILNET (Military Network). MILNET was for unclassified military traffic and the ARPANET, or the ARPA Internet, was designated for nonmilitary communication and research. Universities and corporations evolved beyond research and used the Internet for everyday communications. As the Internet has become more popular, the TCP/IP protocol suite has also gained popularity.

Microsoft provides full TCP/IP protocol stack support through core protocols, programming interfaces, connectivity utilities, and diagnostic utilities.

# TCP/IP Core Protocols

TCP and IP are only two of the protocols developed in the early seventies to tie the Internet together. The TCP/IP protocol suite is actually made up of many protocols that together are referred to as the TCP/IP protocol suite. NT supports many of these protocols including TCP, IP, Address Resolution Protocol (ARP), Internet Control Message Protocol (ICMP), and User Datagram Protocol (UDP).

In order to understand how these protocols work, it helps to have a simple understanding of the Open Systems Interconnection (OSI) model to which these protocols can be mapped.

The OSI model is a conceptual model consisting of seven layers. Each layer is responsible for managing different portions of a network's task. In Table 11.1, the OSI layers are defined.

| | LAYER | FUNCTIONALITY |
|---|---|---|
| **TABLE 11.1**<br>OSI model layers defined | Application | The Application layer is a user interface to network services such as file transfer and management and document and message retrieval services. |
| | Presentation | The Presentation layer is responsible for the syntax or representation of data to be transferred between two Application-layer protocols. The Presentation layer also provides data security through encryption services. |
| | Session | The Session layer is used to synchronize data and manage data exchange between two Application-layer protocols. |

| | LAYER | FUNCTIONALITY |
|---|---|---|
| **TABLE 11.1**<br>OSI model layers defined<br>(continued) | Transport | The Transport layer is used to provide reliable message delivery services. Transport services range from basic services used to make a simple connection to services which provide full error and flow control. |
| | Network | The Network layer routes packets across an internetwork. |
| | Data Link | The Data Link layer provides the information used to route the packets to the correct host once the packets have reached the correct network segment. Basic error control is also provided by the Data Link layer. |
| | Physical | This layer is concerned with the physical connection to the network. |

*The traditional mnemonic for remembering the OSI layers from the top to the bottom layers is All People Seem To Need Data Processing. The updated version for remembering each layer starts from the bottom and is People Don't Need To See Paula Abdul.*

The core protocols that are covered in this subsection pertain to the Network and Transport layers of the OSI model and are shown in Figure 11.1.

**FIGURE 11.1**
TCP/IP core protocols
and the OSI model

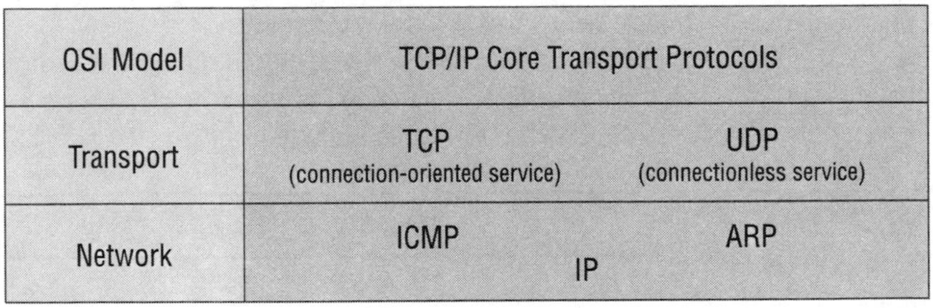

| OSI Model | TCP/IP Core Transport Protocols | |
|---|---|---|
| Transport | TCP<br>(connection-oriented service) | UDP<br>(connectionless service) |
| Network | ICMP      IP | ARP |

## TCP and UDP

At the Transport layer of the OSI model, programmers can specify either TCP or UDP. TCP is used for connection-oriented, reliable network service. UDP provides connectionless datagram service and provides no built-in reliability.

When developing a TCP/IP based application, the choice to use TCP or UDP is determined by two main factors. The factors that are used in protocol selection are reliability and speed. If reliability is more important—for example, in domain logons—then programmers will use TCP. If speed and performance are more important—for example, in domain broadcasts—then they will use UDP with its minimal overhead.

### IP

IP is the Network layer protocol that is used to route packets across an internetwork. IP works by determining the source and destination network addresses. If the destination address is not on the same network segment as the source address, IP routes the packet on a best-try delivery system. If your packet requires reliable service, IP should be used in conjunction with TCP.

*A common analogy for TCP and IP is that TCP provides connection-oriented services like a telephone connection and IP provides connectionless services like the post office.*

### ARP

The ARP protocol works by mapping the IP address, which is a logical, software address, to the Media Access Control (MAC) address, which is the physical address on a network interface card (NIC).

### ICMP

ICMP is used to detect errors in IP transmissions. As previously noted the IP protocol is connectionless and is like mail delivery. If an IP packet encounters a problem—for instance, if its destination is unreachable, or if the packet has timed-out—ICMP is used to provide the sender with some form of error message.

ICMP is also used by a popular TCP/IP utility called PING (which stands for Packet InterNet Groper). PING is usually used to test an IP address to make sure it is working.

## TCP/IP Programming Interfaces

The Microsoft TCP/IP protocol suite can use two different network application programming interfaces (API), Windows Sockets and NetBIOS (Network Basic Input Output System), to access the Transport layer.

Windows Sockets is the more traditional programming interface; it is a two-way interface, used to transport incoming and outgoing application data. By implementing Windows Sockets, you are able to use dynamic-link libraries to bind and run applications and to run transport services at the same time. Connectivity over the Sockets interface is established using an IP address or an optional name called a *Host name*. TCP/IP utilities like FTP and Telnet use Windows Sockets. FTP and Telnet are covered in the next subsection.

NetBIOS is an API that is used by application programs. The function of NetBIOS is to provide a uniform set of commands to application programs in order to provide lower-level services with transmission services.

In NT, all resources on the network are identified by a NetBIOS name. NetBIOS names can be up to 15 characters long. A computer's NetBIOS name is registered each time the computer starts, services start, or a user logs on.

*Don't confuse Host names with NetBIOS names. Host names are a convenient substitute for tedious numeric addresses but are not required for connecting sockets-based applications. NetBIOS names are mandatory unique names used for most Microsoft network functions.*

## TCP/IP Connectivity Utilities

The TCP/IP connectivity utilities that are supported by NT are `finger`, `ftp`, `lpr`, `rcp`, `rexec`, `rsh`, `telnet`, and `tftp`. The purpose of these utilities is to allow NT users to access resources on non-Microsoft hosts, like UNIX. These utilities are only available if the TCP/IP protocol stack has been installed. Table 11.2 defines the TCP/IP connectivity utilities.

| **TABLE 11.2**<br>TCP/IP connectivity<br>utilities defined | **TCP/IP CONNECTIVITY UTILITY** | **DESCRIPTION** |
|---|---|---|
| | `finger` | Allows you to retrieve information from a remote computer. |
| | `ftp` | File Transfer Protocol. This is one of the most widely used TCP/IP utilities. FTP uses TCP to provide connection-oriented file transfer capabilities. |
| | `lpr` | Line Printer. Used to print to a computer running the Line Printer Daemon (LPD) service. |

| TABLE 11.2 | TCP/IP CONNECTIVITY UTILITY | DESCRIPTION |
| --- | --- | --- |
| TCP/IP connectivity utilities defined (continued) | rcp | Remote Copy Program. Used to copy files between an NT computer and a UNIX computer running the Remote Shell Daemon (RSHD). |
| | rexec | Remote Execution. Used to execute commands on a remote computer. |
| | rsh | Remote Shell. Invokes a command interpreter on a remote UNIX host. |
| | telnet | Used to provide remote terminal service, or terminal emulation. |
| | tftp | Trivial File Transfer Protocol. This is similar to FTP in that it provides file transfer capabilities. However, while FTP is connection oriented, TFTP is connectionless and uses the UDP transport protocol. |

## TCP/IP Diagnostic Utilities

In addition to the TCP/IP connectivity utilities, you also get the TCP/IP diagnostic utilities when you install the TCP/IP protocol. These utilities include arp, hostname, ipconfig, lpq, nbtstat, netstat, ping, route, and tracert. These utilities can be used to troubleshoot TCP/IP problems. Table 11.3 defines the TCP/IP diagnostic utilities.

| TABLE 11.3 | TCP/IP DIAGNOSTIC UTILITY | DESCRIPTION |
| --- | --- | --- |
| TCP/IP diagnostic utilities defined | arp | Address Resolution Protocol. ARP displays the results of the ARP protocol's work which is an IP address mapped to the MAC node address. |
| | hostname | Displays the current computer's host name. |
| | ipconfig | Displays the computer's current IP configuration. |

| TABLE 11.3 | TCP/IP DIAGNOSTIC UTILITY | DESCRIPTION |
|---|---|---|
| TCP/IP diagnostic utilities defined (continued) | lpq | Shows the status of a print queue on a computer running the LPD service. |
| | nbtstat | NBT is NetBIOS over TCP/IP. NBTSTAT shows NBT statistics. |
| | netstat | Used to show current TCP/IP status and statistics. |
| | ping | Packet Internet Groper. PING is used to test Used to test and verify network connections. |
| | route | Displays current local routing tables. |
| | tracert | Traces routes used by TCP/IP by using ICMP packets. |

# IP Addressing

At the Internet layer, IP uses a numeric address to deliver data to its intended destination. Every device, or *host*, on a TCP/IP network must be given an IP address that contains the network number on which the host resides, and the unique number assigned to that host on that network. The binary number is composed of 32 ones and zeroes, for example:

10000011 01101011 00000010 11001000

For ease of use, this number is usually divided into four groups of eight bits and converted to its base-10 decimal equivalent. The decimal equivalent is called *dotted decimal notation*, with four decimal numbers ranging from 0 to 255 separated by periods. For example, 131.107.2.200 would be the decimal equivalent of the above address.

| 10000011 | 01101011 | 00000010 | 11001000 |
|---|---|---|---|
| 131 | 107 | 2 | 200 |

In order to identify which part of the above address is the network number and which part is the host number, the IP address also requires a *subnet mask*, which is also a 32-bit binary number displayed in dotted decimal notation. Every time a one appears in the subnet mask it means that binary place is part of the network number. A zero means that number is part of the host address. A typical subnet mask for the above address might be

```
11111111 11111111 11111111 00000000
```

which would translate to 255.255.255.0. In this example, the first 24 places are all ones, which translates to 131.107.2, so this would be the network number. The last eight places are all zeroes, which translate to 200. 200 would be the host number on the network 131.107.2.0. (Zero in the last place means we don't care what the host number is; all we are looking at is the network number.)

If you are not connecting to the public Internet, you can make up any addresses as long as all the hosts on the same physical network segment get the same network number and each host on that segment gets a unique host number. If you are connecting to the Internet, you will need to get a registered IP address from the *InterNIC*, the agency that governs IP addresses, or from an Internet Service Provider who has already obtained a block of addresses from the InterNIC. Usually just a few people at each organization are responsible for deciding what IP addresses and subnet masks to use. If you choose your addresses and subnet masks properly, neither will need to be changed for a long time.

## Installing and Viewing TCP/IP Configuration Information

If you chose the default protocol selection during the installation of NT Server (in Exercise 2.1), then you should already have TCP/IP installed. In Exercise 11.1, you will view your current TCP/IP configuration.

---

**EXERCISE 11.1**

### Viewing the Microsoft TCP/IP Protocol Stack

This exercise should be completed from PDC1 while logged on as ADMINISTRATOR.

**1.** Select Start ➢ Settings ➢ Control Panel.

**2.** Double-click Network.

**3.** Click the Protocols tab.

---

**4.** Click the TCP/IP protocol and then click Properties. You will see a screen similar to the graphic below.

**5.** To test your TCP/IP configuration, go to a command prompt and type **PING 131.107.2.1**.

**6.** You should receive four echo responses, indicating your TCP/IP protocol has been correctly installed.

**7.** To see your MAC address, type **IPCONFIG/all**.

# Using Dynamic Host Configuration Protocol (DHCP)

A S MENTIONED IN the first section, every device that will use TCP/IP must have a valid, unique IP address on that network. Trying to keep track of which host has which address has proved to be a monumental task. Companies have used databases and spreadsheets and even sticky labels to manage which host has which IP address.

## The Need For DHCP

The methods used to manage IP addresses manually are unfortunately only as good as their last update. If an administrator forgets to note that an address is already assigned, the same address could be assigned twice and result in tremendous confusion. Just imagine if the telephone company assigned two people the same phone number in the same area code! It is also possible for administrators to mistype an address in the configuration dialog box, which could result in either an accidental duplicate address or a completely wrong address. Sometimes users unwittingly contribute to the problem by copying configuration files off a coworker's computer or by trying to guess at an IP address.

Duplicate IP addresses can cause problems ranging from the malfunctioning of a single workstation to the downing of an entire network. Microsoft TCP/IP tries to minimize problems resulting from duplication by sending an ARP broadcast before the TCP/IP stack is initialized. If another machine replies to the ARP, it means the address is already in use and TCP/IP will not be initialized on the new machine. Both machines also receive a warning notice that an IP address has been duplicated.

Another common problem is caused by computers being moved from one subnet to another without reconfiguring the IP address. If a computer moves from one subnet to another, then the IP address must be modified to reflect the new subnet address. Failure to provide the correct subnet address will result in TCP/IP initializing but the computer will not be able to communicate with anybody else because it will think local traffic is remote and remote traffic is local. Sometimes even moving a computer from its cubicle to the one next door can change the physical subnet and require an IP address change.

## DHCP Fundamentals

In order to help alleviate the problem of tracking and assigning valid IP addresses, the Internet Engineering Task Force (IETF) has worked with vendors to develop the Dynamic Host Configuration Protocol (DHCP). As with all development on the Internet, this protocol has been discussed in a series of RFCs (Requests for Comments) which are available at numerous Internet sites.

*The RFCs that are relevant to DHCP are 1533, 1534, 1541, and 1542. These RFCs can be found at* `http://www.internic.net/ds/dspg1intdoc.html`.

DHCP is implemented as a client/server service. DHCP works in the following manner:

- When the client computer starts up, it sends a broadcast message requesting a DHCP server. The request includes the hardware address of the requesting client.

- Any DHCP server receiving the broadcast will send out its own broadcast to the client offering an IP address for a set period of time or *lease period*. The address offered by the server is marked as unavailable and will not be assigned to any other client in the meantime.

- The client selects one of the offers and again broadcasts that it has made a selection. This allows any DHCP offers that were not selected to be returned to the pool of available IP addresses.

- The DHCP server that was selected sends back a broadcast acknowledgment indicating the IP address, subnet mask, and duration of the lease for that IP address. It may also be configured to include additional information in the lease, such as the address of the default gateway or the DNS server.

*You can remember the four-step process of obtaining an IP address by using the mnemonic device ROSA.*

*IP Lease **R**equest*
*IP Lease **O**ffer*
*IP Lease **S**election*
*IP Lease **A**cknowledgment*

# DHCP Clients

NT Workstation, NT Server, Windows 95, Windows for Workgroups, and the MS DOS 3.0 Network Client can all be DHCP clients. Use Control Panel ➢ Network ➢ Protocols ➢ TCP/IP Properties to enable a client to use DHCP. To make a computer a DHCP client, you would choose the Obtain an IP address from a DHCP server option of the Microsoft TCP/IP Properties dialog box, shown in Figure 11.2.

When changing from a static IP address to a DHCP address, you won't have to reboot your computer for the change to take effect but if you change back to a static IP address, you must reboot for the change to take effect.

**FIGURE 11.2**

The Microsoft TCP/IP Properties dialog box

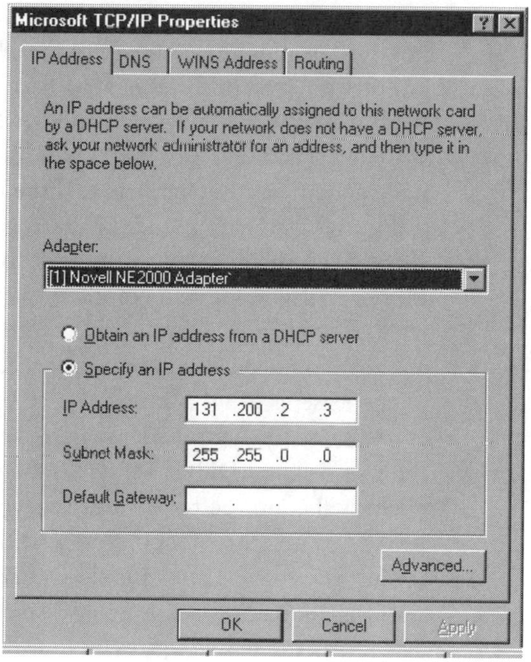

## DHCP Client Lease Period

After the client has obtained the IP address, the lease information is visible using the IPCONFIG/all command line utility. The DHCP lease is defined as the amount of time that the DHCP client can use the IP address that has been assigned by the DHCP server. The IPCONFIG/all command will list the assigned IP address, the DHCP server, the start of the lease and the end of the lease period.

If no DHCP server is available to grant a lease, the IPCONFIG/all command will display an IP address of 0.0.0.0 and a DHCP server address of 255.255.255.255, which is a broadcast address (we will see how to do this in Exercise 11.2). It will continue to attempt to obtain an IP lease at 9, 13, and 16-second intervals and at a random backoff time between 0 and 1000 milliseconds. After four unsuccessful requests, the client will display a message that no DHCP server was available to validate the request; but it will still continue to attempt to lease an address every five minutes until it is successful.

IPCONFIG can also be used with the /release switch to give up a lease or the /renew switch to obtain a new lease. IPCONFIG /release is not automatically performed when the computer shuts down in order to increase the likelihood of keeping the same address as long as possible. Instead, the assigned IP address is noted in the Registry of an NT or 95 machine, or in the DHCP.BIN file on Windows for Workgroups or DOS clients. When the client computer starts up, it will request a renewal of its leased address and the DHCP server will send an acknowledgment. If the client has moved to a new physical network, the server will send a negative acknowledgment (NACK) and force the client to go through the entire lease process from the beginning (which means that even if you move a computer to a new network segment, you will not have a problem with an incorrect address). Even if the client doesn't receive an acknowledgment, it can continue to use its assigned address for the duration of the lease as long as it hasn't received a NACK.

Halfway through the lease period, the client will attempt to renew the lease with its original DHCP server. If the server is unavailable at that time, the client will continue to attempt renewal with the same server until the lease is 87.5% complete (7/8 complete). At the 87.5% mark, the client will resort to broadcasting for any available DHCP server that can extend a lease. If the client is unable to obtain a new lease, all communication over TCP/IP ceases as soon as the lease expires.

If the amount of traffic generated by this lease process is a problem, consider using longer lease periods so clients will not have to renew as frequently. Traffic can be monitored using Network Monitor and Performance monitor. If you have a limited number of IP addresses, you might consider making your lease period shorter so that unused IP addresses can be returned to the DHCP pool.

### Installing a DHCP Client

In Exercise 11.2, you will attempt to install a DHCP client. Because you have not yet configured a DHCP server you will receive an error. The purpose of this exercise is to show you how to setup a DHCP client and the messages you will see because you have the incorrect configuration.

---

**EXERCISE 11.2**

### Configuring a DHCP Client

This exercise should be completed from NT Workstation while logged on as ADMINISTRATOR.

**1.** Select Start ➤ Settings ➤ Control Panel.

**2.** Double-click Network.

**3.** Click the Protocols tab.

**4.** Click TCP/IP Protocol and click Properties.

**5.** Select Obtain an IP address from a DHCP server. You will see a message stating "DHCP protocol will attempt to automatically configure your workstation during system initialization. Any parameters specified in these property pages will override any values obtained by DHCP. Do you want to enable DHCP?" Click Yes. Click OK.

**6.** Log off and log on again as ADMINISTRATOR. Unless you are on a LAN with active DHCP servers, you might get a message telling you that a DHCP server could not be found. Click Yes to see future DHCP messages.

**7.** To see your current configuration, access a Command Prompt and type **IPCON-FIG /all**.

**8.** Respond to "What is your IP address?" (It should be 0 . 0 . 0 . 0.)

**9.** Respond to "What is the address of your DHCP server?" (This should be blank.)

**10.** Write down the physical (hardware) address of your network card for future reference.

# DHCP Servers

Starting with NT 3.5, Microsoft has bundled a DHCP server with NT Server at no extra cost. The service is installed through Control Panel ➤ Network ➤ Services. Once you install DHCP, you must configure it through the DHCP server manager.

The most important part about DHCP configuration is assigning one or more *scopes* of valid IP addresses for the server to lease. Because it is not possible to create multiple scopes for a subnet on a single DHCP server (meaning multiple ranges of IP addresses), all addresses that the server will lease must be configured on one scope for that server. A DHCP server assumes that any addresses in its scope are available for lease unless they have been excluded. If there are any addresses within that scope that cannot be leased for any reason, they must be excluded. Some reasons for excluding IP addresses within the scope are:

- the address is already in use by a host using manual configuration

- the address is assigned to a non-DHCP client like a UNIX box or a printer

- the address is set aside for future use

Assume that you have TCP/IP addresses 131.107.2.1 through 131.107.2.255 that have been allocated as shown in Table 11.4.

*131.107.2.0 and 131.107.2.255 are not available because these are reserved addresses used by TCP/IP for network and broadcast addresses.*

| TABLE 11.4 | IP ADDRESS(ES) | ASSIGNMENT |
|---|---|---|
| IP address availability example | 131.107.2.1 - 131.107.2.10 | Reserved for static routers |
| | 131.107.2.11 - 131.107.2.199 | Available for lease (note exclusions in last two boxes of this table) |
| | 131.107.2.200 - 131.107.2.254 | Reserved for servers with static IP addresses |
| | 131.107.2.100- 131.107.2.120 | Reserved for UNIX machines |
| | 131.107.2.75 | Reserved for a TCP/IP-based printer |

Figure 11.3 shows how the scope would be set up based on the example shown in Table 11.4.

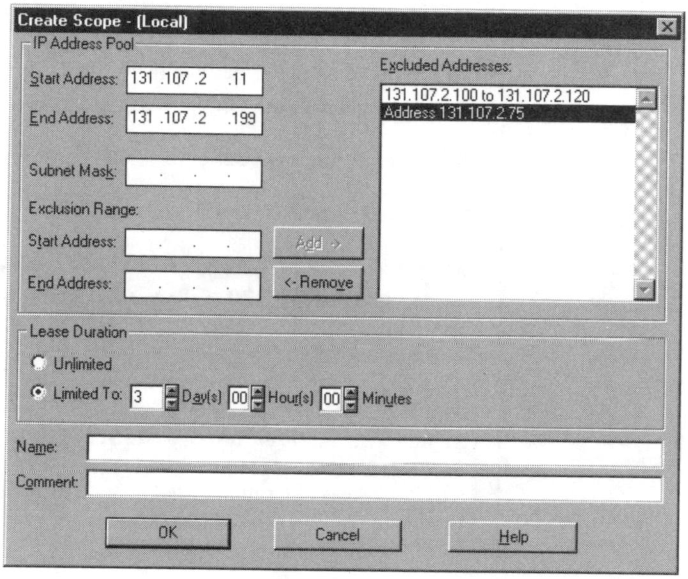

**FIGURE 11.3**

A sample TCP/IP scope

In Exercise 11.3, you will install a DHCP server on PDC1.

**EXERCISE 11.3**

**Installing a DHCP Server**

This exercise should be completed from PDC1 while logged on as ADMINISTRATOR.

**1.** Select Start ➤ Settings ➤ Control Panel.

**2.** Double-click Network.

**3.** Click the Services tab.

**4.** Click Add. The Select Network Service dialog box will appear. Choose Dynamic Host Configuration Protocol and click OK. Insert the Windows NT Server CD if necessary. Once the files copy, close the Network Services box.

**5.** You must now restart the computer for the changes to take effect. Click Yes when prompted to restart your computer.

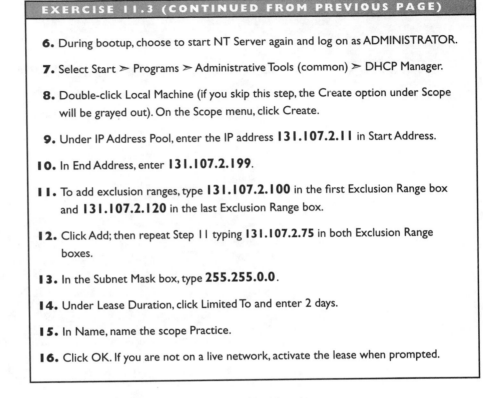

**EXERCISE 11.3 (CONTINUED FROM PREVIOUS PAGE)**

**6.** During bootup, choose to start NT Server again and log on as ADMINISTRATOR.

**7.** Select Start ≻ Programs ≻ Administrative Tools (common) ≻ DHCP Manager.

**8.** Double-click Local Machine (if you skip this step, the Create option under Scope will be grayed out). On the Scope menu, click Create.

**9.** Under IP Address Pool, enter the IP address **131.107.2.11** in Start Address.

**10.** In End Address, enter **131.107.2.199**.

**11.** To add exclusion ranges, type **131.107.2.100** in the first Exclusion Range box and **131.107.2.120** in the last Exclusion Range box.

**12.** Click Add; then repeat Step 11 typing **131.107.2.75** in both Exclusion Range boxes.

**13.** In the Subnet Mask box, type **255.255.0.0**.

**14.** Under Lease Duration, click Limited To and enter 2 days.

**15.** In Name, name the scope Practice.

**16.** Click OK. If you are not on a live network, activate the lease when prompted.

**WARNING**

*If you are on a network with real DHCP clients, do not activate your scope when prompted to do so.*

# Windows Internet Name Service (WINS)

Windows Internet Name Service (WINS) is a name resolution service used in a TCP/IP network. The main function of WINS is to map the computer's NetBIOS name to an IP address. The benefit of using the WINS service is that it resolves the NetBIOS name to IP mapping dynamically without the administrator having to manage configuration files manually. The main functions of WINS are to:

- resolve NetBIOS names to IP addresses

- register NetBIOS names on all subnets

- facilitate browsing across internetworks

## NetBIOS Name Registration

Anytime you use NET commands or Explorer, you are using the NetBIOS interface. Because the NetBIOS name space is flat, not hierarchical, there is no way to distinguish between a server called CORP1 in the NORTH domain and a different server called CORP1 in the SOUTH domain.

For this reason, every computer must have a unique name on the network. When a computer using NetBIOS-based protocols initializes, by default it will send out a broadcast asking to register its name. If no other computer responds to the registration request, the computer is allowed to use that name for the duration of its session (until it is shut down). If another computer has already registered the name in question, then the registration is denied and the second computer will not be able to start network services until it is reconfigured with a unique name.

This is especially important when a client is trying to locate a server, because the client will send a NetBIOS broadcast looking for the server name; if more than one machine could answer, there would be a problem connecting to the proper server. When a machine is shut down properly using the Shut Down command on the Start menu, it sends a NetBIOS broadcast to release its name. If a machine is not shut down properly, it will not release its name on the network, which really isn't a problem because it won't be online to deny another computer the right to use the name.

As you can see, NetBIOS can generate quite a bit of broadcast traffic. With the protocol NetBEUI, you are loaded down by all the broadcasts. When using NetBIOS over TCP/IP, however, WINS will help to greatly reduce the amount of broadcast traffic.

## WINS Name Registration

Instead of broadcasting its name registration request, a WINS client will send a message directly to the WINS server. When it is ready to shut down, it again sends a directed message to the WINS server to release the NetBIOS name. When clients need to locate the server in question, they also contact the WINS server first rather than broadcasting.

In addition to reducing broadcast traffic, WINS also facilitates communication across subnets. By default, NetBIOS broadcasts don't cross IP routers. While it is possible to enable this on many routers, it is not advisable because it will use too much bandwidth to perpetuate the broadcasts all around the network. When TCP/IP is used in an internetworked environment, we have to enable some way for clients to find servers without broadcasts.

## LMHOSTS Files

Originally, Microsoft used a text file called an LMHOSTS file in the LanManager operating system to allow clients to find servers without having to broadcast across the entire network. The LMHOSTS file would have listings matching IP addresses with NetBIOS names as seen in the following format:

```
131.107.10.207    Server2
131.107.5.223     CORP5
```

When clients using NetBIOS resources over the Microsoft TCP/IP protocol suite attempt to find a server, they will start broadcasting by default. If the broadcast is unsuccessful, however, they will look for the name in question in their LMHOSTS file. If the name is present, the client will establish communication directly with that IP address across whatever routers are in between. There are two major disadvantages with LMHOSTS files:

- an LMHOSTS file must be configured on each and every client that will use NetBIOS resources

- all of those LMHOSTS files must be constantly updated as the names and addresses on the network change

While it is possible to alleviate some of this hassle by creating a centralized LMHOSTS file and using each local LMHOSTS file on the client to point to the master file, this solution is still of no help when we consider DHCP. In a DHCP environment, addresses may be changing daily, or even hourly. Trying to maintain an accurate record in a static text file would be impossible.

## WINS as an Alternative to *LMHOSTS* Files

As previously noted, manually managing a static text file can be an overwhelming task. This makes WINS a vital part of any network using NetBIOS resources. Clients are configured to use the WINS server before using a broadcast so traffic is reduced. Furthermore, each WINS client is configured with the exact IP address of its WINS server so it doesn't depend on NetBIOS broadcasts crossing routers.

## WINS and DHCP as Companion Services

Because each client computer registers its name with the WINS server every time it turns on and renews that name, it can also inform the WINS server of any change to its IP address should the DHCP-assigned address change.

There are similarities between the WINS service and the DHCP service. The similarities are:

- Both are implemented as databases on an NT Server machine.

- Both are installed through the Network Control Panel ➤ Add Service option.

- Both update their information dynamically.

After that, the similarities diminish. The WINS server requires no additional configuration once it is installed; the DHCP server must be configured before it can be used.

Each WINS client is configured with the IP address of a WINS server and, if desired, a backup WINS server for fault tolerance. Because we are sending directly to an address rather than via a broadcast, we don't have to worry about routers being BOOTP/DHCP relay agents. In fact, because it doesn't matter which subnet the WINS server is on, and because a WINS server can process 1,500 name registrations per minute and 4,500 queries per minute, one WINS server can conceivably service 10,000 computers on an internetwork. (You would, however, want a backup WINS server for fault tolerance.)

## WINS Name Registration Database

As the clients check in and register with the WINS server, it begins to build a database of registered names. Many names in the database *look* like they've been registered two or three times, but the 16th character (the one in the brackets) is what makes each name different. For example, CSTRAIN-NT has three listings. [00h] stands for the Workstation (client) service. [03h] stands for the messenger service so we can reach it with NET SEND commands or with server announcements. The Server service is represented by [20h].

The 16th character also designates domain roles like PDCs and BDCs and browsing roles like master browser. WINS servers can also be configured to replicate their databases through WINS manager.

*Earlier it was noted that you can specify NetBIOS computer names of up to 15 charac-ters. Microsoft reserves a 16th character for registration purposes. The NT Server Resource Kit contains an appendix that lists all of the 16th bit designators.*

In Exercise 11.5, you will install WINS and view the registration database that is created through the WINS service.

---

**EXERCISE 11.5**

### Installing WINS

This exercise should be completed from PDC1 while logged on as ADMINISTRATOR.

**1.** Select Start ➤ Settings ➤ Control Panel.

**2.** Double-click Network.

**3.** Click the Services tab.

**4.** Click Add. The Select Network Service dialog box will appear. Choose Windows Internet Name Service and click OK. Insert the Windows NT Server CD if neces-sary. Once the files copy, close the Network Services box.

**5.** You must now restart the computer for changes to take effect. Click Yes to restart your computer.

**6.** Choose to start NT Server again and log on as ADMINISTRATOR.

**7.** Select Start ➤ Programs ➤ Administration Tools ➤ WINS Manager. Examine the database.

**8.** On the NT Workstation, access the Network Control Panel.

**9.** On the Protocols tab, select TCP/IP and click Properties.

**10.** Select the WINS tab and enter the address of the WINS server **131.200.2.1** in the WINS field. Click OK.

**11.** Click OK again and restart the machine when prompted to do so.

**12.** After the workstation has restarted, check the database on the WINS server to see the workstation's name registration.

# Domain Name Server

T HE DOMAIN NAME SERVER (DNS) is used to resolve host names to IP addresses. Unlike NetBIOS names, which are required for all NT computers, host names are optional and merely help to avoid having to remember long IP addresses. When using the World Wide Web, for example, you could either point your browser to 198.137.240.91 or just remember www.whitehouse.gov. The latter is definitely easier to remember.

Originally, host names were kept on each local system in a text file called simply HOSTS. Each machine could have its own HOSTS file or maintain a current copy of a company-wide HOST file. As networks grew larger, and the Internet grew larger, keeping the HOSTS files current on every machine with all the names and IP addresses became a huge task.

To simplify administration, a DNS keeps all the names and IP addresses in one central location. Instead of keeping HOSTS files, DNS keeps a text-based zone file that has all the database information for a domain or a hierarchy of domains.

The top of the domain hierarchy is called the root. The root of the Internet DNS is managed by the InterNIC and it is represented by a single dot (.) Underneath the root are the top level domains, which are either organizationally or geographically based—.com, .edu, .us. The next level has the organization names or the geographical region. For example, microsoft.com, ucla.edu, sanjose.ca.us. To register a domain name with a top level domain, the organization has to either set up its own DNS or hire an ISP to do it. Then each organization can create its own domain hierarchy with its own DNS system.

When locating a host using DNS, we use a *fully qualified domain name* (FQDN) to find it in the DNS tree. For example, server6.dev.microsoft.com is the FQDN representing a server named server6 in the .dev subdomain under the .microsoft domain under the .com top level domain. When a user issues a sockets-based command like ftp (as opposed to a NetBIOS based command like NET USE), DNS finds the host name in the DNS hierarchy and returns the IP address that goes with that name.

Like WINS, DNS is used to resolve names to IP addresses but it has some important differences. The major differences between WINS and DNS are shown in Table 11.5.

| **TABLE 11.5**<br><br>WINS and DNS differences | **WINS** | **DNS** |
|---|---|---|
| | Resolves NetBIOS names to IP addresses. | Resolves host names to IP addresses. |
| | Only translates the NetBIOS name to the IP address. | Can do a reverse lookup, translating the IP address to a host name. |
| | Registers client names and addresses automatically as they initialize. | Must be manually configured by the administrator with name and IP address. |
| | Keeps all the names in one flat name space and only shares them with configured replication partners. | Keeps the names in hierarchical structures called "fully qualified domain names" that are registered and recognized throughout the Internet. |
| | Used primarily for Microsoft clients on Microsoft networks. | Used on the Internet and on intranets for all TCP/IP hosts. |
| | Only lets each client register their name once, though the name may be different in the 16th character, describing what service or function it performs on the network. | Lets the administrator create different aliases for the same host. |
| | Facilitates domain related functions like browsing and logging on to domains. | N/A |

In Exercise 11.6, you will install DNS.

---

**EXERCISE 11.6**

## Installing DNS

This exercise should be completed from PDC1 while logged on as ADMINISTRATOR.

**1.** Select Start ➢ Settings ➢ Control Panel.

**2.** Double-click Network.

**3.** Click the Services tab.

**4.** Click Add. The Select Network Service dialog box will appear. Choose Microsoft DNS Server and click OK. Insert the Windows NT Server CD if necessary. Once the files copy, close the Network Services box.

**5.** Click the Protocols tab.

**6.** Double-click TCP/IP.

**7.** In the TCP/IP Properties box, click the DNS tab.

**8.** In the Domain box, type **MYDOMAIN**. Notice that your host name, by default, is the same as your NetBIOS name.

**9.** In the Network dialog box, click OK. Click OK again.

**10.** You must now restart the computer for changes to take effect. Click Yes to restart your computer.

**11.** Choose to start NT Server again and log on as ADMINISTRATOR.

**12.** Select Start ➢ Programs ➢ Administration Tools ➢ DNS Manager.

**13.** On the DNS menu, click New Server. The Add DNS Server dialog box appears.

**14.** In the DNS Server box, type your computer name and click OK.

**15.** After your server name has been added, right-click the server name and select New Zone.

---

**EXERCISE 11.6 (CONTINUED FROM PREVIOUS PAGE)**

**16.** In the Zone Creation wizard, select Primary and click Next.

**17.** In the Zone Name box, type **MYDOMAIN**.

**18.** Press Tab. Notice that the Zone File Box now reads `mydomain.com.dns`. This is the name of the text file holding the host name records. Click Next.

**19.** Click Finish to create the zone.

**20.** To create a host record, right-click the zone name and select New Host.

**21.** In the Host Name box type **TESTHOST**.

**22.** Enter **131.107.2.9** in the Host IP Address box and then click Add Host.

**23.** Click Done.

---

## Considerations When Using DHCP and DNS

DNS is static and must be manually managed. This could cause problems when using DHCP to assign IP addresses, because every time DHCP dynamically assigns an address, the address has to be changed manually in the static DNS database. If you imagine a network where hundreds of IP addresses could be changing every hour, you'll see why a dynamic system like WINS is helpful. Even though WINS and DNS are used for slightly different things, Microsoft has tried to integrate them. Because WINS can keep track of names and IP addresses dynamically, it tracks the NetBIOS name which will also be used for the host name. Because NetBIOS can't resolve FQDNs, it hands that part over to the DNS server. Using this combination, it is possible to do a NET USE to `\\server6.dev.microsoft.com`. DNS can find the domain `.dev.microsoft.com` anywhere on the Internet or the internal intranet. WINS can find the IP address for SERVER6, even if its address has changed recently due to DHCP. For this to happen, however, a special record must be added to the Microsoft DNS server that tells it to use WINS for its DNS lookups. In Exercise 11.7, you will configure DNS to use WINS.

---

**EXERCISE 11.7**

### Configuring DNS to Use WINS

This exercise should be completed from PDC1 while logged on as ADMINISTRATOR.

**1.** Select Start ➤ Programs ➤ Administration Tools ➤ DNS Manager.

**2.** Right click the zone and select Properties. Click the WINS Lookup tab.

**3.** Check UseWINS Resolution.

**4.** In the WINS Servers box, type the address of your WINS server, **131.200.2.1**.

**5.** Click OK.

---

# Chapter Summary

CP/IP IS A versatile, universal protocol on which businesses, educational institutions, and the Internet solidly rely.

It requires some administration to make sure every client has a proper network number and host number as part of its IP address. To facilitate the administration of a TCP/IP network, NT includes the Dynamic Host Configuration Protocol which can automatically assign IP addresses to DHCP clients.

Because computers may be changing their IP addresses often, NT includes the Windows Internet Name Service which can dynamically register the proper IP address with the NetBIOS name. WINS also helps tremendously in reducing broadcast traffic due to name registration and name resolution queries. Without WINS, NetBIOS-dependent tasks like browsing and domain functions become difficult.

DNS keeps track of a different sort of name called a host name. Unlike NetBIOS names, host names are an optional alternative to remembering IP addresses. DNS uses a static text file to keep track of host names and IP addresses, but in NT 4.0, it can also use WINS to help it resolve IP addresses for hosts whose addresses may be changing. Such changes could be due to DHCP or a change in network configuration.

# Review Questions

1. In order to communicate with a machine on a remote subnet, which of the following must be configured? Choose all that apply.

   **A.** Subnet Mask

   **B.** Default Gateway

   **C.** DNS Server

   **D.** IP Address

2. Which of the following is not part of the TCP/IP protocol suite?

   **A.** ARP

   **B.** NetBEUI

   **C.** UDP

   **D.** ICMP

3. What does the subnet mask do? Choose the best answer.

   **A.** Tells how many bits represent the network address and how many bits represent the host address

   **B.** Combines many physical networks into one logical network

   **C.** Hides the IP address from the user

   **D.** Provides a route to reach remote networks

4. Which of the following best describes a NetBIOS name?

   **A.** An optional name used instead of an IP address

   **B.** An alias programmed into a DNS server

   **C.** The computer name, set in the Network Control Panel

   **D.** The name assigned by the DHCP server

5. Which of the following best describes a host name?

    **A.** An optional name used instead of an IP address

    **B.** An alias programmed into a DNS server

    **C.** The computer name, set in the Network Control Panel

    **D.** The name assigned by the DHCP server

6. Which of the following are differences between DNS and WINS? Choose all that apply.

    **A.** DNS is static and WINS is dynamic.

    **B.** DNS is dynamic and WINS is static.

    **C.** DNS maps NetBIOS names to IP addresses and WINS maps host names to IP addresses.

    **D.** DNS maps host names to IP addresses and WINS maps NetBIOS names to IP addresses.

# Internet Services

CHAPTER

12

HE INTERNET IS the latest evolution in large scale global communications. What began as a way of connecting governmental and educational organizations has grown into a network for businesses and private individuals. The Internet is a global network made up of many networks. Through the Internet, you can post and retrieve information on any subject imaginable.

Today, it is hard to imagine what life would be like without telephones. It's not that hard to imagine that the Internet will someday be as commonly used as the telephone system is today. The era of the Internet has begun, and people from all walks of life (not just the computer geeks) are scrambling to surf the net.

This chapter will focus on the Internet Information Server (IIS). IIS is a file and application server that provides World Wide Web (WWW), File Transfer Protocol (FTP), and Gopher services. IIS is included with NT Server for the first time with version 4.0. Through WWW, FTP, and Gopher, IIS supports services that are used to get and provide services on the Internet. In this chapter you will learn:

- The difference between an intranet and the Internet

- Terms associated with Internet services

- Internet tools provided with NT Server

# Intranet versus the Internet

WO TERMS USED to describe networks are *intranet* and *Internet* (Internet, as it refers to the world-wide network, is always capitalized). An intranet is a TCP/IP network that uses Internet technology. An intranet is used for internal purposes, and does not necessarily connect to the outside world.

The Internet is a world-wide computer network that uses the TCP/IP protocol and services. When connecting to the Internet, you must use standardized protocols and procedures. For example, you must use registered IP addresses.

The services covered in this chapter apply to intranets and the Internet.

# Terminology Used in Internet Services

F YOU ARE new to the Internet, the following are terms you should be familiar with because they will be used throughout this chapter:

- **Dial-up Client**: A computer with a temporary connection to the Internet that cannot act as a server because its IP address is temporary.

- **Domain Name**: The textual identifier of a specific Internet host. Domain names are in the form of: `server.organization.type` (`www.microsoft.com`) and are resolved to Internet addresses by Domain Name Servers.

- **Domain Name Server**: An Internet host dedicated to the function of translating fully-qualified domain names into IP addresses.

- **File Transfer Protocol (FTP)**: A protocol that serves files independent of operating system type. FTP is also a command line utility useful for downloading files via the FTP protocol when you can't or don't want to use Internet Explorer. Most Web browsers support FTP as well as HTTP, eliminating the need for a separate FTP client. RFC 765 describes the FTP protocol in detail.

- **Gopher**: A text-based service that links to other Gopher sites. Gopher pre-dates HTTP by about a year, but has been made obsolete by the richer format provided by HTTP.

- **Home Page**: The default page returned to by an HTTP server when a URL containing no specific path or filename is requested. Home Page also refers to the default page you see when you launch your Internet browser.

- **Host**: An Internet Server. Hosts are constantly connected to the Internet.

- **Hyperlink**: A link embedded in text or graphics that has an embedded Web address. By clicking the link, you jump to another Web address. You can identify a hyperlink because it is a different color from the rest of the Web page.

- **HyperText Markup Language (HTML)**: The language of Web documents. A human-readable language describing both the presentation characteristics and content of Web documents.

- **HyperText Transfer Protocol (HTTP)**: The client/server interprocess communication protocol served by Internet servers and requested by Internet browsers. HTTP serves Web pages consisting of text, graphics, and links to other Web pages.

- **Internet**: The public global interconnection of networks based on the TCP/IP protocol suite.

- **Internet Explorer**: An industry leading Web browser, with which you can take full advantage of all popular Internet protocols. Internet Explorer supports the use of modular components so new protocols (like voice and multimedia support) can be supported without upgrading.

- **Internet Information Server (IIS)**: Software used to serve higher-level Internet protocols like HTTP and FTP to clients using Web browsers.

- **Intranet**: A privately owned network which uses the TCP/IP protocol suite.

- **Request For Comment (RFC)**: The standards describing each of the Internet protocols developed by the Internet Engineering Task Force (IETF), among other Internet related topics. RFCs contain complete details and specifications for the TCP/IP protocol suite. They are freely available on the Internet at many different Web sites.

- **Search Engine:** A tool which allows users to find the information they are looking for by requesting specific information using keywords. The engines search massive locally stored Web page databases, and respond with the URLs of pages that fit the search phrase.

- **Simple Mail Transfer Protocol (SMTP):** An Internet protocol for transferring mail between Internet Hosts. SMTP is often used to upload mail directly from the client to an Intermediate host, but can only be used to receive mail by computers constantly connected to the Internet.

- **Site:** A related collection of HTML documents at the same Internet address, usually oriented toward some specific information or purpose.

- **Surf:** To browse the Web randomly looking for interesting information.

- **Uniform Resource Locator (URL):** Information embedded in a HyperText Link that uniquely identifies a resource on the Internet. URLs contain the domain name of the Internet host serving the resource, the path to the resource, and the resource name. URLs are defined in RFC 1738. For example, Cable News Network's URL is http://www.cnn.com.

- **Web Browser:** An application that makes HTTP requests, and formats the resultant HTML documents for users to view and read. The preeminent Internet clients, most Web browsers understand all standard Internet protocols.

- **Web Page:** Any HTML document on an HTTP server.

- **World Wide Web (WWW or the Web):** A graphical easy-to-use collection of rich-content documents maintained by millions of Internet servers around the world.

# Internet Tools Provided with NT Server

MICROSOFT HAS RECOGNIZED the personal and business potential of using the Internet as a form of communication. Their goal is to provide products and services that support Internet technology. NT Server 4.0 ships with two services to support Internet technology—Internet Explorer and the Internet Information Server (IIS).

The Internet Explorer is a client Web browser and IIS is a Web server. The two services are complimentary to each other. For example, in Figure 12.1, assume that you heard that ABCCorp has a really neat home page and you want to check it out. You, the client, would use the Internet Explorer to access the Internet and contact the ABCCorp server that would be running IIS.

**FIGURE 12.1**

Internet Explorer
and IIS example

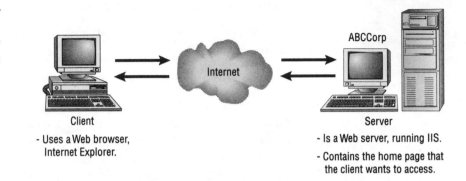

Internet Explorer and IIS are described in the following subsections.

## Internet Explorer

The Internet Explorer client software is used to browse the Internet. It is a fully functional Web browser, which means that it allows you to surf the Web, read HTML format documents, and run Common Gateway Interface (CGI) scripts, and Java and ActiveX applications. The Internet Explorer is also available for:

- Windows 3.1

- Windows for Workgroups

- Windows 95

- Windows NT Workstation

## Internet Information Server

IIS is server software that is used to publish information on an internal intranet or on the world-wide Internet. Clients make requests of IIS and IIS responds with an HTML page.

The key features of IIS are:

- **Performance:** IIS maximizes speed while reducing RAM requirements. To run all three IIS services you only need 400K of memory.

- **File Publication:** IIS allows you to publish files on a Web server.

- **Security:** Allows secure access to Internet resources.

- **Network Management:** Allows you to manage and monitor network access.

- **Support for common Internet standards:** Supports common languages for developing Web applications such as CGI and PERL.

### The Internet Information Servers Integrated Services

IIS is made up of three main service protocols. They are Hypertext Transfer Protocol (HTTP), File Transfer Protocol (FTP), and the Gopher service. The purpose of these service protocols is to provide publishing services for an intranet or the Internet. Once IIS has been installed, anyone with an Internet connection can access Web pages or interactive applications that you have published.

*Anyone who accesses your Web pages or interactive application is subject to your security measures.*

The HTTP service is a client/server interprocess communication protocol served by Internet servers and requested by Internet browsers. Through HTTP you can create and navigate WWW applications and hypertext documents. HTTP can serve Web pages consisting of text, graphics, and links to other Web pages.

FTP is a service that supports file transfers between local and remote systems regardless of operating system type. The FTP Server service is installed with IIS. The FTP client software is installed with the TCP/IP connectivity utilities.

The Gopher service is used to provide publishing services on an intranet or the Internet. You use a menu system with Gopher to enable links to other servers. Gopher has been made virtually obsolete through newer technology available through HTTP.

### Installing and Configuring IIS

In this section, you will learn how to install and configure IIS. In order to install IIS, you should first meet the following requirements:

- IIS requires NT Server 4.0 using TCP/IP.

- If you want Internet connectivity, you need some form of connection to the Internet (for example, a leased line from an Internet service provider (ISP). Your ISP will need to provide you with an IP address, subnet mask, and a default gateway IP address.

- You need to be logged on with Administrator rights.

In addition, the NT Server Resource Kit specifies the following minimum and maximum hardware requirements, as noted in Table 12.1.

**TABLE 12.1**

Hardware requirements for IIS

| HARDWARE | MINIMUM REQUIREMENT | RECOMMENDED REQUIREMENT |
|---|---|---|
| CPU | 486/50MHz | Pentium 90MHz |
| RAM | 16MB | 32-64MB |
| Free disk space | 50MB | 200MB |

*If you are concerned with local security, IIS should be installed on a drive that uses the NTFS file system.*

**INSTALLATION OF IIS** In Exercise 12.1, you will install IIS on PDC1.

---

**EXERCISE 12.1**

### Installing Internet Information Server

The following exercise should be completed from PDC1 while logged on as ADMINISTRATOR.

**1.** Select Start ➢ Settings ➢ Control Panel.

**2.** Double-click the Network icon.

**3.** Click the Services tab.

---

**4.** Click Add and choose Microsoft Internet Information Server.

**5.** Choose the CD Drive as your source drive, insert the NT Server CD if it is not already in your CD drive.

**6.** The Microsoft Internet Information Server 2.0 Setup dialog box, shown below, will appear. Click OK to continue installing.

**7.** Check all available options, as shown here, and click OK.

**8.** When prompted to create an installation directory, accept the default directory assignments by clicking Yes.

**9.** The Publishing Directories dialog box will appear. Click OK to accept the default directory assignments. You will see another dialog box prompting you to confirm directory creation. Click Yes.

**10.** Click OK if presented with a "Domain name necessary for Gopher services" message.

**11.** Select SQL Server and click OK in the Install Drivers dialog box.

**12.** Click OK to acknowledge completion of the installation.

Your server is now able to serve HTTP, FTP, and Gopher requests.

**CONFIGURATION OF IIS**  Once you have installed IIS, you can configure it through the Internet Service Manager. The Internet Service Manager can be used to start, stop, and pause the three services (WWW, Gopher, and FTP) that make up IIS.

You can also configure the properties of the:

▪ WWW service

▪ Gopher service

▪ FTP service

There are many similarities in how these services are configured. Because the WWW service is the most commonly used, this section will focus on configuring the WWW service.

To configure the WWW service, go to Start ➤ Programs ➤ Microsoft Internet Server (common) ➤ Internet Service Manager. You will see a screen similar to Figure 12.2.

**FIGURE 12.2**

Microsoft Internet
Service Manager

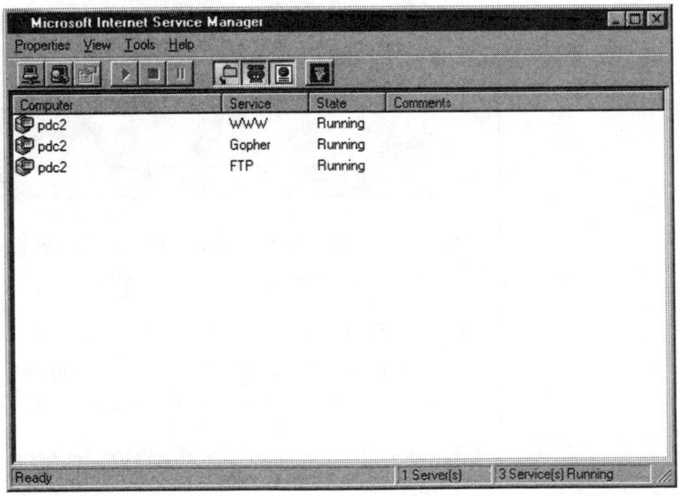

To configure the WWW service, you can double-click the WWW service and you will see the WWW Service Properties dialog box, as shown in Figure 12.3.

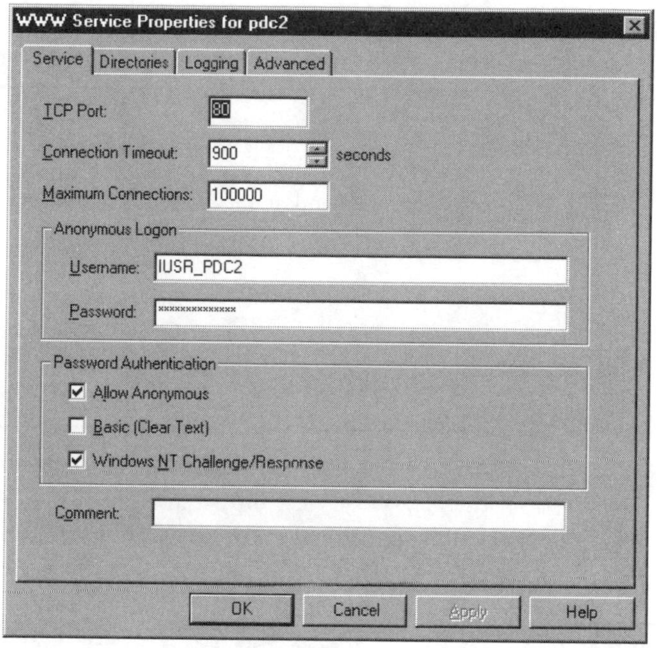

**FIGURE 12.3**

The WWW Service
Properties dialog box

**FIGURE 12.3**

The WWW Service
Properties dialog box

Notice in Figure 12.3 that the WWW Service Properties dialog box has four tab pages: Service, Directories, Logging, and Advanced.

**CONFIGURING SERVICE PROPERTIES**  The Service tab page allows you to define service properties as defined in Table 12.2.

**TABLE 12.2**

Service properties
of WWW

| SERVICE PROPERTY | DESCRIPTION |
|---|---|
| TCP Port | Allows you to specify the TCP port on which you want the WWW service to run. By default WWW uses port 80. |
| Connection Timeout | Specifies how long a connection should be held open without any user activity. By default this value is set at 900 seconds. |
| Maximum Connections | The number of concurrent connections the server will support. |

| TABLE 12.2 Service properties of WWW (continued) | SERVICE PROPERTY | DESCRIPTION |
|---|---|---|
| | Anonymous Logon | The NT user account that will be used if you choose to allow anonymous access. |
| | Password Authentication | Specifies the authentication process you want to use. You can choose from Allow Anonymous, which is no authentication, Basic (Clear Text), which is encoded and supported by most browsers, and Windows NT Challenge/Response, which automatically encrypts usernames and passwords (Internet Explorer 2.0 and later supports this). |

**CONFIGURING DIRECTORIES PROPERTIES** The Directories tab page of the WWW service, shown in Figure 12.4, allows you to specify directories that will be published by the WWW service.

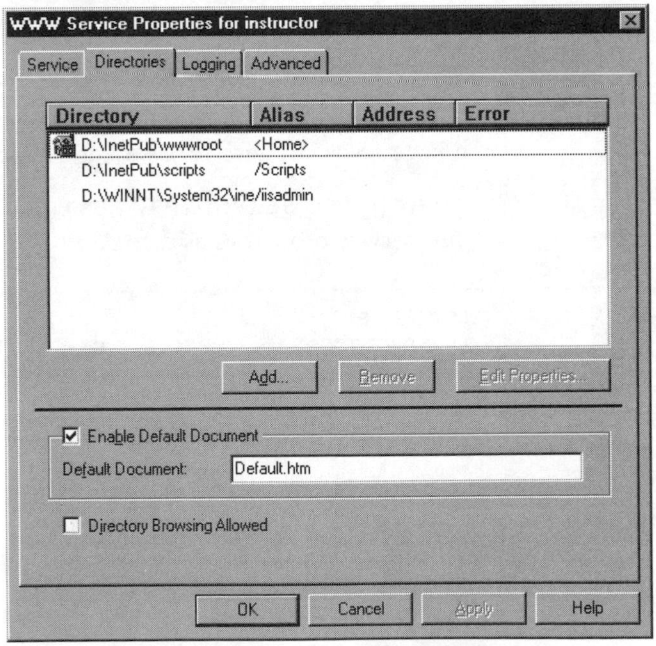

**FIGURE 12.4**

The Directories tab page of the WWW Service Properties dialog box

On the Directories tab page you can specify or view:

- the directories that the WWW service will use

- the alias or path for virtual directories

- the IP address for virtual directories

- any errors associated with the published directories

**CONFIGURING LOGGING PROPERTIES** The Logging tab page of the WWW service is shown in Figure 12.5 and allows you to log to a file. Logging is the process of collecting information as to how a server is being accessed and placing that information in a file for tracking purposes. You can also log to an SQL (Structured Query Language)/ODBC (Open Data Base Connectivity) database.

On the  Logging tab page of the WWW service, you can see how your server is being used and identify possible security violations.

**CONFIGURING ADVANCED PROPERTIES** The Advanced tab page of the WWW service allows you to determine which computers should have access to the WWW service. Note in Figure 12.6 that you can specify that computers should be granted access or denied access with an exceptions box.

Assuming that you wanted all of your users except Terry and Ron to use the WWW service, you would grant access to all users, and list Terry and Ron in the exception box. If you only wanted Ron and Terry to use the WWW service, you would deny access to all users, and again use the exception box to list Ron and Terry. To make an exception, you would provide the IP address and subnet mask for Ron's and Terry's computers.

**CONFIGURING VIRTUAL DIRECTORIES AND VIRTUAL SERVERS** Virtual directories are used to make directories that reside on other computers appear to reside on your computer's Web site. Virtual servers are single servers that have been configured to appear as several physical servers.

Each Internet service can publish multiple directories. The directory uses a local drive letter, a network drive letter, or a universal naming convention

(UNC) name. The published directories are referred to as virtual directories. Virtual directories simplify the Web user's user interface.

You can also configure virtual servers which make a single computer appear to be multiple machines. You might do this if you wanted to use one computer running IIS, but you wanted to have a home page for each department within your company, or you were a consultant managing 15 companies' Web pages, and they did not have the resources to dedicate a machine as a Web server. To create a virtual server, you must:

- Have a unique IP address for the primary server and for each virtual server (you get IP addresses from your ISP).

- Use Control Panel ➤ Network to assign the multiple IP addresses to a single network adapter card.

- Assign a home directory to each IP address (through the Directories tab page of the WWW Service Properties).

# Chapter Summary

A
N INTRANET IS a private TCP/IP network and the Internet is the global, public TCP/IP network. There is special terminology associated with Internet services.

Windows NT Server 4.0 comes with two Internet tools, Internet Explorer and Internet Information Server (IIS). The Internet Explorer is a Web client and IIS is a Web server supporting the HTTP, FTP, and Gopher services.

You have learned how to install and manage IIS. In managing IIS, you use the Internet Service Manager utility. You also learned to recognize and create virtual directories and virtual servers.

# Review Questions

1. Which Internet services ship with NT Server 4.0? Choose all that apply.

   A. Internet Web Surfer

   B. Internet Explorer

   C. Internet Information Server

   D. Internet Information Service

2. Which services make up IIS? Choose all that apply.

   A. HTTP

   B. Gopher

   C. PPP

   D. FTP

3. Which Web browser does Microsoft ship with NT Server 4.0?

   A. Internet Explorer

   B. IIS

   C. Internet Web Crawler

   D. Internet Information Explorer

4. If you had a question about an Internet standard and wanted to get more information, what would you look for?

   A. SMTP

   B. RFC

   C. Internet Documents Standardized

   D. Internet Help

**5.** What is the name of the Web server that ships with NT Server 4.0?

   **A.** Internet Explorer

   **B.** Internet Information Server (IIS)

   **C.** Internet Web Crawler

   **D.** Internet Information Explorer

**6.** Which of the following conditions must be met in order to install IIS? Choose all that apply.

   **A.** Must be running NT Workstation or NT Server 4.0

   **B.** Must be running NT Server 4.0

   **C.** Must be using TCP/IP or NWLink IPX/SPX

   **D.** Must be running TCP/IP

   **E.** Must be logged in as an Administrator

   **F.** Must be logged in as a Server Operator or an Adminitrator

**7.** Which of the following password authentication methods used by IIS offers the highest level of security?

   **A.** Allow anonymous

   **B.** Basic (clear text)

   **C.** C2/ E2 authentication response mode

   **D.** Challenge/response

**8.** Which utility is used to manage IIS?

   **A.** IIS Manager

   **B.** Internet Service Manager

   **C.** User Manager for IIS

   **D.** Server Manager for IIS

**9.** The World Wide Web is based on which protocol?

   **A.** HTTP

   **B.** HTML

   **C.** FTP

   **D.** SMTP

   **E.** PPP

**10.** In order to support a virtual server, which two steps should you complete?

   **A.** Assign an IP address for each virtual server to a single network adapter in Control Panel, Network.

   **B.** Assign a home directory to each IP address through the Directories tab in WWW Service Properties.

   **C.** Assign multiple IP addresses for each virtual server in the General tab of WWW Service Properties.

   **D.** Create a home page for each virtual server and link it to the IP address through Control Panel, Network.

# Internetwork Routing

13

T HESE DAYS, NO network is an island. In order to connect multiple networks, Microsoft has included in NT 4.0 a MultiProtocol Router (MPR) that can dynamically route traffic between subnets over IPX and TCP/IP. MPR can also forward BOOTP relay agents to facilitate the DHCP process. In this chapter you will learn about:

- MultiProtocol Router

- IP Routing

- RIP Protocol for Dynamic IP/IPX Routing

- BOOTP

# MultiProtocol Router

I N AN INTERNETWORK environment, all of the devices on a physical cable segment must share the same network number and have a unique device number. For an intranet, the administrator can make up network numbers. To use TCP/IP on the Internet, the administrator must apply to the InterNIC for a unique, valid network number. For an IP network, the unique device number is part of the IP address. For a device on an IPX network, the device number is the hardware or MAC address.

When information from a computer on one network segment needs to reach a computer on another segment, the data must cross routers which link the subnets together. From the beginning, NT has been capable of performing as a static router over TCP/IP. In order to enable IP routing, you must first install another network adapter card and attach it to a different physical subnet. Computers with multiple network adapters are said to be *multihomed*.

You will enable routing in Exercise 13.1.

**EXERCISE 13.1**

### Enabling IP Forwarding

The following exercise should be completed from PDC1 while logged on as ADMINISTRATOR.

**1.** Select Start ➢ Settings ➢ Control Panel.

**2.** Open the Network icon.

**3.** Click the Protocols tab.

**4.** Choose the network protocol TCP/IP.

**5.** Click Properties.

**6.** Click the Routing tab.

**7.** Click Enable IP Forwarding, as shown here.

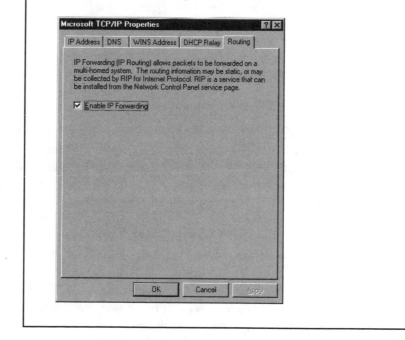

Keep in mind that enabling IP routing could place a significant performance burden on the computer, depending on how much traffic it needs to route and between how many networks it is routing. You can use Performance Monitor to evaluate how much burden routing is placing on the system (the Performance Monitor is covered in Chapter 15) and, if necessary, buy a third-party unit designed specifically for routing.

Once IP routing has been enabled on an NT machine, it can only detect the networks and routes to which it is directly connected. In a large internetwork, though, you may have several networks connected by several different routers. In order to inform your multihomed NT machine about other available routes, you must create static routes to each router using the ROUTE ADD command. Because this process is tedious and potentially inaccurate or outdated, most routers use some sort of dynamic routing protocol that can update the route tables automatically by communicating directly with other routers.

NT 4.0 includes the MultiProtocol Router which can route information over TCP/IP dynamically. MPR also makes it possible to route IPX and to pass the DHCP relay agents which let DHCP clients find the DHCP servers across subnets.

# IP Routing

WHEN ONE HOST attempts to communicate with another over TCP/IP, it must first determine if the destination address is on the same network or a remote network. In the following example, assume we have a host with an IP address of 131.107.2.200 and a subnet mask of 255.255.255.0, so the network number is 131.107.2.0. If this host wants to communicate with a host at 131.107.2.25, the subnet mask says that these two machines are on the same network and sends an ARP broadcast asking for the MAC address that goes with that IP address. The host at 131.107.2.25 sends a reply with its hardware address, and communication is established.

If either of these hosts tries to reach a machine with an IP address of 131.107.10.37, the subnet mask says this address is on network number 131.107.10.0, which is a different network. ARP broadcasts only reach machines on our own physical network segment, so we need to cross over a router that connects our network with the remote network. Machines with the Microsoft TCP/IP stack maintain their own internal route tables that tell them how to reach remote networks. To see the active routes on your network, you can type **route print** from the command prompt as shown in Figure 13.1.

**FIGURE 13.1**

*ROUTE PRINT*
routing tables

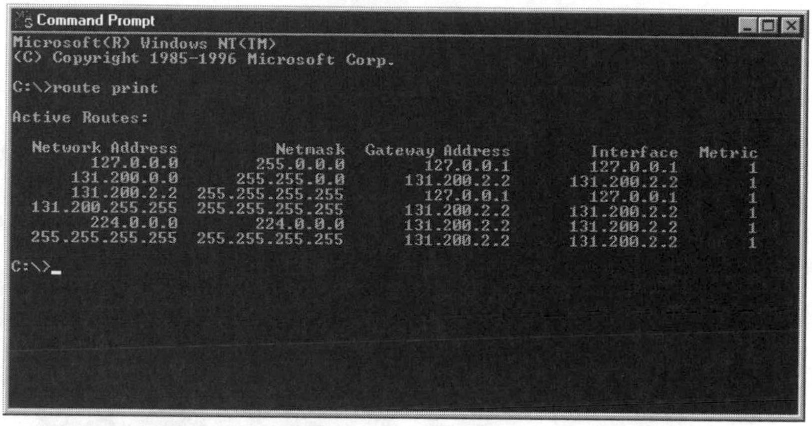

In Figure 13.1, the first column has the network address the host is trying to reach. The second column shows the subnet mask. The Gateway Address is the IP address of a router that can locate that particular network number. Interface is the actual address to which it will send the packet. 127.0.0.1 is a special address called *loopback* that loops back and contacts the local network adapter of the local machine. The metric is how many routers we have to cross to get to our destination. A metric of 1 means that the network is the local network.

Routes can be manually added to this route table using the ROUTE ADD command. Because manually adding gateway addresses for all the possible network destinations on each and every network host would be exhausting, TCP/IP allows you to configure a default gateway to use for any remote traffic not listed in the local route table. If we still wanted to reach 131.107.10.37, rather than building a route entry that specifies the gateway to use to get to 131.107.10.0, we can say that any traffic for *any* remote network can go to a default gateway address of 131.107.2.1, a router that connects our network to other subnetworks.

The default gateway for your LAN connection is set up in the Network Control Panel. It is possible to configure multiple default gateways for fault tolerance. The additional gateway addresses, however, will only be used if the first address is physically unavailable. In Exercise 13.2, you will configure a default gateway.

---

### Configuring the Default Gateway

Unless you are on an internetwork, you won't notice anything different after this exercise. This exercise should be completed from PDCI while logged on as ADMINISTRATOR.

**1.** Select Start ➤ Settings ➤ Control Panel.

**2.** Double-click Network.

**3.** Click the Protocols tab.

**4.** Select the network protocol TCP/IP and click Properties to call up the TCP/IP Properties dialog box, shown here.

**5.** In the field for default gateway, enter **131.107.2.1**.

**6.** Access the command prompt and type **PING 131.107.2.25**.

---

**EXERCISE 13.2 (CONTINUED FROM PREVIOUS PAGE)**

**7.** Document the response:_____

**8.** While you are still at the command prompt, type **PING 131.107.10.37**.

**9.** Document the response:_____

Notice that the two responses are different. This is because the first PING was trying to find the host on the local network. It sent an ARP broadcast, but nothing responded. In the second PING, we tried to reach a remote network. Even though we have a default gateway now, the gateway doesn't know how to reach the network `131.107.10.0`, so it returns "destination host unreachable."

Exercise 13.3 is optional and can be completed if you have access to an Internet Service Provider.

**EXERCISE 13.3**

## Using the Default Gateway

If you have access to an Internet Service Provider (ISP) you can reach remote networks on the Internet. You will first check your route table to verify that you don't have a route to the destination address. Then you will see your TCP/IP configuration, including the default gateway, by using `IPCONFIG`.

**1.** First, dial into your ISP as you usually do.

**2.** While still connected to your ISP, open a command prompt and type **ROUTE PRINT**.

**3.** Examine your local routing table.

**4.** Still at the command prompt, type **IPCONFIG /all**.

**5.** Locate the line for Default Gateway and write it down:

_____

**6.** Test your default gateway by PINGing the number you just wrote down.

**7.** To reach a remote network, try typing the following at the command prompt: **PING 198.137.240.91**.

This is the IP Address for the White House. Did your PING work?

# RIP Protocol for Dynamic IP/IPX Routing

A S PART OF the MPR, NT 4.0 comes with the Routing Information Protocol (RIP) to enable dynamic routing. RIP comes in two flavors, RIP for Internet Protocol and RIP for NWLink IPX/SPX compatible protocol. If you are routing TCP/IP you would use RIP for Internet Protocol. If you are routing NWLink IPX/SPX, you would use RIP for NWLink IPX/SPX compatible transport. You could use both forms of RIP if you were using TCP/IP and NWLink IPX/SPX, and you wanted to route both protocols. RIP routers send broadcasts every 30 seconds by default so other RIP enabled routers can build route tables based on that information.

*You can change the amount of time in the registry through* HKEY_LOCAL_MACHINE\ SYSTEM\CurrentControlSet\Services\IpRip\Parameters\ UpdateFrequency. *The range is from 15 to 88440 seconds.*

*RIP routers and static routers will not be able to share any information with each other.*

In Exercise 13.4, you will install RIP.

---

**EXERCISE 13.4**

### Installing RIP

**1.** Select Start ➤ Settings ➤ Control Panel ➤ Network.

**2.** Click the Services tab.

**3.** Click Add, choose RIP for Internet Protocol or RIP for NWLink IPX/SPX compatible transport and click OK. Insert the NT Server CD if necessary.

**4.** Click Close, and restart your computer for the changes to take effect.

---

No additional configuration is required after RIP for Internet Protocol is installed. If you are installing RIP for NWLink IPX/SPX then you will see another dialog box asking if you want to enable NetBios broadcast propagation. You should keep the default unless you only have the IPX protocol on the network and you need to use servers on other networks. If necessary, either service can be stopped if you click Start ➤ Settings ➤ Control Panel ➤ Services. If you want them removed, then click Start ➤ Settings ➤ Control Panel ➤ Network.

Once RIP is working, you can use the ROUTE PRINT command and look for listings in the Metric column that are larger than 2. Such listings indicate that the local router has exchanged routing information with other RIP-enabled routers.

*After you install RIP, you will start to exchange routing information with other RIP-enabled routers on the network. If you have made up addresses, used invalid addresses, or mis-configured any addresses, this could cause serious malfunctions on the network. Do not install RIP for IP or IPX unless you completely understand how it will interact with all of the routers on your network.*

## BOOTP and DHCP

DHCP is partially based on an earlier RFC called the Bootstrap Protocol or BOOTP (see RFC 951 and 1533). BOOTP was designed for diskless workstations that had no way to hold on to their own IP configurations. It required a fair amount of work because the administrator had to create a configuration file that matched each host with a static IP address. If the host changed, the configuration file had to be changed too.

As we saw in the last section, DHCP can respond quickly to changing network conditions, and the length of the lease can be varied to reduce network traffic or to extend a small pool of addresses. We also saw that the broadcasts DHCP clients use when trying to lease an address do not cross routers indiscriminately. Because DHCP was built on the existing BOOTP protocol, routers that are able to forward DHCP client broadcasts are said to be BOOTP relay agents. Routers that will act as BOOTP relay agents conform to RFC 1542. When the IP Address Request packets reach the routers, they will forward the packet on to the next network but mark the packet with the network of origin so the DHCP server can select an address form the proper scope. The MPR included with NT 4.0 will allow a multihomed NT machine to forward BOOTP/DHCP broadcasts.

In addition to including the MPR, NT 4.0 makes it possible for a workstation or a server to function as a relay agent without the installation of

MPR. First the DHCP Relay Agent Service is installed on the designated NT computer. To install the DHCP Relay Agent Service, follow the steps shown in Exercise 13.5.

---

**EXERCISE 13.5**

### Installing the DHCP Relay Agent

**1.** Select Start ≻ Settings ≻ Control Panel ≻ Network.

**2.** Click the Services tab.

**3.** Click Add, and choose DHCP Relay Agent. Click OK. Insert the NT Server CD if necessary.

---

After the computer is restarted, the relay agent is configured using the properties for the TCP/IP protocol, as shown in Figure 13.2. Each relay agent should be configured with the IP address of at least one DHCP server. Once this is configured, the DHCP Relay Agent will act as a proxy to forward DHCP Request packets directly to the appropriate server.

**FIGURE 13.2**

The DHCP Relay Agent tab page of the Microsoft TCP/IP Properties dialog box

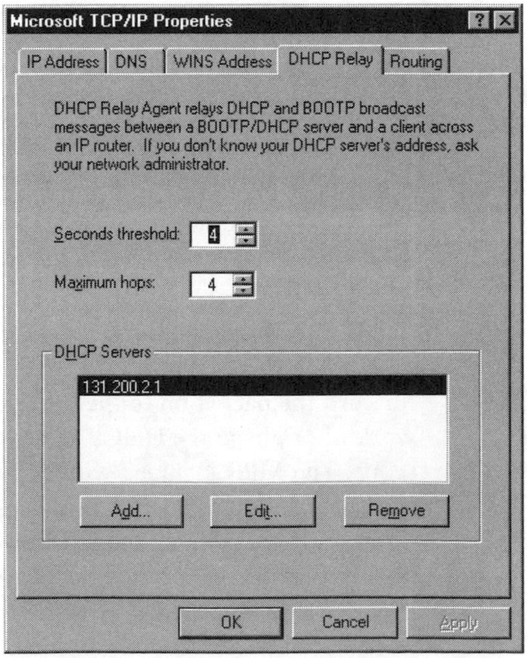

# Chapter Summary

NT ALLOWS A user to install multiple network cards. A machine with more than one network adapter is said to be multihomed. By enabling the IP routing feature in the TCP/IP configuration properties, NT can route between networks. While a multihomed NT machine may not provide optimum routing performance, it can be convenient. A simple multihomed machine, however, must have all of its route tables manually configured.

NT 4.0 also provides a Multiprotocol Router which allows NT to dynamically route IPX and IP. Dynamic routing is enabled by installing the RIP protocol in the Network Control Panel. To assist in the DHCP process, MPR routers can pass BOOTP relay agents. With this feature, DHCP clients can reach DHCP servers on remote networks. If the router cannot be enabled for BOOTP, NT also provides a service that can be installed on an NT Server or Workstation to function as a BOOTP proxy and forward the DHCP requests to a DHCP server.

# Review Questions

**1.** What two tasks configure an NT machine as a DHCP Relay Agent?

    **A.** Install the TCP/IP protocol. Enable IP Routing.

    **B.** Install the DHCP Relay Service. Configure the TCP/IP properties with the IP address of a DHCP server.

    **C.** Install the DHCP Relay Service. Configure the IP address of a DHCP server in the DHCP Manager.

    **D.** Enable IP Routing. Create an LMHOSTS file.

2. Which protocols is NT 4.0 capable of routing? Choose all that apply.

   A. IPX

   B. NetBEUI

   C. TCP/IP

   D. NetBIOS

3. If you have a combination of dynamic NT routers using RIP and static NT routers, what will you have to do so all routers can see all network routes?

   A. Do nothing. The routers will automatically share information.

   B. Manually add the static routes to the dynamic routers and manually add the routes from the dynamic routers to the static routers.

   C. Install the RIP protocol on the dynamic routers.

   D. Install the DHCP relay agent on the dynamic routers.

# Remote Access Service

REMOTE ACCESS SERVICE (RAS) is used to connect remote users to the network. Users who are working from home or are traveling on business can access network services through telephone lines, Integrated Services Digital Network (ISDN), X.25 networks, or Point to Point Tunneling Protocol (PPTP).

The purpose of RAS is that it allows you to efficiently use your dial-up resources. Just as users can share mass storage and printers, users can share dial-in and dial-out resources (for example, modems) through RAS.

In this chapter you will learn about:

- Fundamentals of RAS

- Overview of RAS servers and RAS clients

- Installing RAS servers

- Wide Area Network (WAN) connectivity options

- Local Area Network (LAN) protocols used with RAS

- Remote access protocols

- Security options available through RAS

- RAS clients

# Fundamentals of RAS

THE REMOTE ACCESS Service in Windows NT was designed to allow you to participate in your organization's network even when you are away from the physical location of your network. RAS allows you to use modems and telephone lines as slow network connections as opposed to using your network card to make a network connection. This type of remote access is called remote node.

Remote node connections allow you to function as a client on the network. You physically participate in the network as if you were locally connected, the difference being that WAN connections are typically slower that LAN connections.

Through RAS you can setup WAN connections through telephone lines, ISDN, X.25, and Internet Service Providers (ISPs) through PPTP. Remote users can then access network files such as e-mail, word processing, and other data and application files.

# RAS Servers and RAS Clients

YOU CAN APPROACH RAS from two points of view: the RAS client and the RAS server. RAS clients are the users who are accessing the network through a remote connection, and RAS servers are the computers on the local network providing local network access to the remote RAS clients.

## RAS Clients

RAS clients are the remote computers which participate in the NT network through a WAN connection. In order for you to use RAS in a client computer, you must have networking software installed on that computer. Your computer does not require a network card (such as an Ethernet or Token Ring card), but you do need a transport protocol such as TCP/IP or NetBEUI, and some form of network redirector.

RAS on the client computer will then allow you to use the modem to dial to and establish a connection with a RAS server on your organization's network. Then RAS will emulate a network interface adapter for the transport protocol and allow the network services component (Workstation or Client for Microsoft Networks) to operate just as if your client computer were directly connected to the network.

*Your RAS network connection will not be as fast as if you were directly connected to the network, because most network adapters are much faster than modems.*

The following platforms are able to participate as RAS clients:

- NT Servers and Workstations

- Windows 95

- Windows for Workgroups

- MS-DOS RAS

- LAN Manager

- Any non-Microsoft Point-to-Point Protocol (PPP) client

## The RAS Server

The RAS server, which usually runs on a Windows NT Server, uses modems or other WAN connections with the server to accept connections from client computers and to exchange network data over those connections. NT Server can support up to 256 RAS sessions per server (as opposed to NT Workstation which can only support one RAS session).

Because most computers do not have 256 serial ports available, RAS servers typically use multiport adapter boards. A multiport adapter board is installed in the computer and has multiple external connectors that are used to connect the modems.

You have many options that can be configured to allow you to customize how the RAS server will be accessed. For example you can configure the RAS server to only allow the client to access resources on the RAS server, or you can configure the RAS server to act as a router so that the client computer can access any of the resources on the network.

RAS servers can also support dial-in and dial-out services. By default, both dial-in and dial-out services are supported, although you can limit what access is available. Dial-in connectivity allows users to dial in to your network and access network resources. Dial-out connectivity allows your network to access the outside world through the same hardware used for your dial-in services. For example, a network user dialing out to CompuServe does so using the dial-in hardware.

Once you dial in to the network, you must use a LAN protocol to communicate on the network. RAS supports the TCP/IP, NetBEUI, and NWLink IPX/SPX transport protocols.

To the server computer, the RAS server modems look like network interface adapters. A RAS server, like a RAS client, must have networking components installed in order to use RAS.

RAS servers can also be used to link networks together. For example, if you have a main office downtown in a city, and you have several outlying branch offices, you can connect the networks at each site using modems and telephone lines. The RAS servers on each of the networks will route network traffic destined to another network to that network, and will not send transmissions that are only meant for computers on the local network, thereby minimizing the amount of information that has to be sent over the slow modem lines.

RAS is seldom used for more than temporarily or occasionally linking networks together, however, because a phone line that is constantly dialed in to another location can be expensive to pay for, especially if the call is long-distance. Permanent links between networks are more often made with dedicated digital hardware (unlike the analog technology used in regular modems) and telephone lines that are leased from the telephone company to provide a permanent connection between two places.

# Installing RAS Servers

NSTALLING RAS IS no more difficult than installing any other service in Windows NT. Because the main use of RAS is to connect computers over a asynchronous phone line, you should have access to another computer running RAS or RAS client software (such as Windows NT Workstation or Windows 95) that will connect to your RAS server. Both the RAS server and the RAS client must use the same transport protocol (such as TCP/IP or NWLink).

*Without access to another computer to which you can connect, you will have difficulty understanding the operational nuances of RAS. You really need to use the software in order to understand it.*

Before you install RAS you need to have modems or other WAN connection adapters (such as ISDN or X.25) installed for RAS to use (although for test purposes, you could use a *null modem* cable, a special cable that has the transmit and receive pins reversed and that is used to emulate a modem connection). The following section will cover two common connectivity options— using an analog modem or using an ISDN adapter (in the real world you can use one or both options). You will also learn how to install and configure RAS which is used no matter which connectivity option you choose.

## Configuring Analog Modems for Use with RAS

One of the common connection methods used with RAS is a modem. Microsoft recommends that you use modems of 9600 baud or above. You will probably want to use even faster modems. At the writing of this book I purchased a 33.6 internal modem for under $90. As technology improves, prices drop and you're better off getting faster, better equipment. However, if you are buying a new modem always keep in mind that Microsoft requires that you buy hardware that is on the Hardware Compatibility List (HCL).

If you have a modem, but have not installed it, the following exercises will guide you through the NT setup. Before you install your modem, you need to know what COM port you will be using and the IRQ setting for your modem (you only need to know IRQ if you are using an external modem).

Exercise 14.1 will show you how to identify a free COM port on your computer using the NT Diagnostics, and Exercise 14.2 will show you how to install a modem through your Control Panel.

*If you are not sure how to configure your internal modem, see your modem vendor's documentation.*

---

**EXERCISE 14.1**

## Using NT Diagnostics to Find Available COM Ports

This exercise should be completed from PDC1 while logged on as ADMINISTRATOR.

**1.** Select Start ➤ Programs ➤ Administrative Tools (common) ➤ Windows NT Diagnostics.

**2.** Select the Resources tab.

**3.** Click the IRQ button.

**4.** Note the state of interrupt requests (IRQ) 03 and 04. If they appear on the list, it means they are already in use. If they do not appear on the list, then you can configure your modem to use the free IRQ.

**5.** Select a free IRQ.

- If IRQ 04 is available, set your modem to use IRQ 04 and COM 1.

- If IRQ 03 is available, set your modem to use IRQ 03 and COM 2.

- If both are in use, you will need to set your modem to use another unused IRQ. Check your modem documentation to see if IRQ 05, 07, or 09 are supported. Set the modem IRQ to any IRQ your modem supports that is not shown in the resource list.

**6.** Set your modem to use either COM 3 or COM 4. Make sure you don't have another serial port in your system using these COM ports. Most computers do not.

**7.** Shut down your Windows NT Server and physically install the modem. When you restart, your modem should be available for use. If you have any difficulties or encounter new error messages, call the technical support number provided by your modem manufacturer for assistance.

---

Once your modem has been physically installed in your computer, you need to tell Windows NT about it. Follow the procedure shown in Exercise 14.2 to make your modem available to Windows NT. Before going through this exercise, make certain you've physically installed a modem on a free COM port and IRQ.

---

**EXERCISE 14.2**

### Installing Your Modem

This exercise should be completed from PDC1 while logged on as ADMINISTRATOR.

**1.** Select Start ➤ Settings ➤ Control Panel.

**2.** Double-click the Modems applet.

**3.** If no modem is installed, you can let NT detect your modem. Click Next to detect your modem. Letting Windows NT automatically detect will allow you to confirm that your modem is answering as it should. Detecting will take up to five minutes depending upon the speed of your computer.

**4.** Accept the settings shown in the detected modem window by clicking Next unless you are absolutely certain they will not work with your modem. Windows NT will usually work correctly with a modem it has identified even if the model shown in the window doesn't match the brand name of the modem.

**5.** Click Finish to complete the installation process.

**6.** Click Dialing Properties in the Modem Properties dialog box.

**7.** Enter the country and area code information that is appropriate for you.

**8.** Add the appropriate information if you need to add outside line access or disable call waiting. If you have call waiting and someone calls while a RAS session is active, your RAS connection can be abruptly disconnected.

**9.** Click OK.

**10.** Click Close.

---

Your modem is now available to Windows NT programs such as RAS.

*IRQ conflicts can appear as a number of different problems under Windows NT. If you suddenly begin having problems with your Windows NT installation, remove your modem and verify that the COM port and IRQ are indeed free. Check that no other service (for instance, a fax monitor) is attempting to use the same modem. Check the Event Viewer for Serial events occurring during startup.*

## Configuring ISDN Adapters for Use with RAS

Some ISDN adapters connect to your computer through the regular serial port on the back of your computer and will appear to your computer to be a regular PSTN modem. You can find drivers for many of these ISDN adapters in the Modems Control Panel. Other ISDN adapters (usually adapters that are installed internally to your computer) establish a new *serial interface* in your computer separate from the COM1 or COM2 interface you are familiar with. These ISDN adapters appear to Windows NT to be network interface adapters just like Ethernet and Token Ring cards, and the ISDN drivers for these adapters are installed from the Adapters tab page of the Networking Control Panel.

Configuring an ISDN adapter is a bit more complicated than connecting a regular modem to your phone line. Issues you should consider are as follows:

- You will need to use an ISDN phone line as opposed to a more common analog phone line.

- You may need to have a network termination device (NT-1) to connect your ISDN adapter cards to the ISDN phone line. Some network adapter cards have an NT-1 built in, others do not.

- Not all ISDN services provide the same transmission speeds. Some phone companies provide data channels in increments of 64Kbps transmission speeds, and others provide them in increments of 56Kbps.

- The switch protocol used by your local telephone company may be the N11 protocol, or it may be another type such as that used by AT&T 5ESS switches or Northern Telecom DMS100 switches. You must configure your adapter to use the appropriate switch protocol.

- You should configure your ISDN connection to be Multipoint. This allows you to use each ISDN channel (ISDN Basic Rate allows you two channels) independently or you may combine the ISDN channels to provide greater bandwidth to a single connection.

The installation process for ISDN adapters varies by type and model. Exercise 11.3 will walk you through the process of configuring a typical adapter (the US Robotics Sportster ISDN modem inserted in an ISA slot). You can perform this exercise without actually having an ISDN adapter in your computer.

**EXERCISE 14.3**

## Configuring an ISDN Adapter

This exercise should be completed from PDC1 while logged on as ADMINISTRATOR.

**1.** Select Start ➢ Settings ➢ Control Panel ➢ Network.

**2.** Choose the Adapters tab and then click Add.

**3.** Find the US Robotics Sportster ISDN modem and select it.

**4.** If you have more than one bus in your computer (for example, if you can have both ISA and PCI cards in your computer) you must select the bus that the adapter uses. Select ISA.

**5.** Select the I/O base address and interrupt for the ISDN adapter as installed in your computer (or accept the defaults if you do not actually have an adapter installed).

**6.** Select the Telco Switch option that matches your local telephone company, or accept the default setting.

**7.** Set the number of terminals to two, unless you are limited by your local telephone company to one ISDN channel.

**8.** In the Terminal 1 and Terminal 2 areas, set the phone numbers and SPIDs of your ISDN channels. These will be given to you by the telephone company. If you are just following along with the example, enter 1, 2, 3, 4... the numbers don't matter because you don't actually have an ISDN modem installed.

**9.** Click OK.

**10.** You will be informed that the ISDN installation process is complete. Press OK. You will then be allowed to configure RAS to use the ISDN adapter.

**11.** In the Remote Access Setup window press Add.

**12.** Select ISDN1-USBRI and then press OK.

**13.** Click Continue, and then click Close in the Network window.

**14.** You must restart your computer for the changes to take effect. Press Yes to restart your computer.

## Installing the RAS Server

Installing the RAS server is similar to installing all other network services. If you are using X.25 or an ISDN connection, install those adapters first with the procedures provided by the manufacturer of that device before proceeding with the RAS installation. Rather than selecting the Modem settings, you will use the X.25 PAD button in the RAS setup dialog box or the settings window for the ISDN adapter in the Network Control Panel. Exercise 14.4 shows the standard procedure for installing a RAS server with a regular modem. You should already have installed your modem to work with Windows NT through the Modems Control Panel (see Exercise 14.2) before proceeding with this exercise.

---

**EXERCISE 14.4**

### Installing the Remote Access Server

This exercise should be completed from PDC1 while logged on as ADMINISTRATOR.

**1.** Select Start ≻ Settings ≻ Control Panel ≻ Network.

**2.** Click the Services tab.

**3.** Click Add.

**4.** Select Remote Access Service from the Services list.

**5.** Click OK. Provide the path to your NT Server CD.

**6.** Select the modem you wish to use for RAS and click OK in the Add RAS Device dialog box. If your modem does not appear in the Modem list, click Install Modem and follow the prompts to install your modem.

**7.** Click Configure.

**8.** Select the Dial Out and Receive Calls option if you wish to also be able to dial out using the modem line, otherwise select receive calls only and click OK.

**9.** Click Add and then repeat Steps 8 through 11 if you have another modem or serial port you would like to configure for RAS.

**10.** Click Continue when you are finished adding your modem(s).

**11.** Close the Network dialog.

**12.** Answer Yes when asked if you want to restart your computer.

# Wide Area Network (WAN) Connectivity Options

R AS CURRENTLY SUPPORTS WAN connections over the following media:

- PSTN (Public Switched Telephone Network; regular modems)

- ISDN (Integrated Services Digital Network)

- X.25 (A protocol commonly used with leased-line frame relay and WANs prior to the Internet)

- RS-232 null modem cables

- PPTP (Point-to-Point Tunneling Protocol)

*ISDN and X.25 interfaces are often treated as network adapters rather than modems.*

## PSTN

Regular phone lines use the public switched telephone network. This is currently considered the world's largest network. This is a common method for connecting to RAS servers because mobile users can typically access PSTN.

There are currently around 200 modems on the HCL for NT. You should choose a modem that is on the list because incompatible modems often cause problems that are difficult to trace.

## ISDN

While PSTN is widely available and inexpensive, it also relies on outdated analog technology. Integrated Services Digital Network uses digital technology and is significantly faster. While analog lines can typically transmit at 9600bps (although you do see faster speeds due to compression techniques), ISDN lines are capable of transmitting at 64-128 kilobits per second.

In order to use ISDN, the RAS server and RAS client must be using ISDN services; his requires an ISDN line and ISDN equipment. The ISDN line and equipment are more expensive than PSTN lines and equipment. However, if you are paying long-distance charges on you RAS connections, then ISDN could be less expensive in the long run, due to its increased speed.

ISDN is an attractive choice for users who telecommute from a single location on a regular basis because costs are dropping as the technology is more commonly used.

## X.25

X.25 networks are packet-switching networks that use the X.25 protocol. These networks were commonly used for WAN connectivity prior to the explosion of the Internet.

X.25 networks use public data networks to route data. NT supports X.25 communication through Packet Assemblers/Disassemblers (PADs) and X.25 smart cards.

## RS-232 Null Modem Cables

A null modem cable isn't really a modem. It is a special serial cable that has the transmit and receive pins crossed over so that you can simulate a modem connection using a cable. You could use a null modem cable for the following reasons:

- You want to simulate a RAS connection and you don't have the necessary equipment or two phone lines.

- You want to connect to the network, but you don't have a network adapter (this requires some setup, and is quite slow).

- You want to troubleshoot your RAS software setup and are bypassing the communications hardware.

## PPTP

A new feature of Windows NT version 4.0 is RAS support for the PPTP. PPTP allows you to take advantage of existing Internet connections to allow secure connection to your RAS server from anywhere you can get an Internet connection.

PPTP uses a two-step process to connect the client computer to your RAS server. First the client computer is connected to the Internet (usually by making a regular connection to an Internet Service Provider, ISP) and then you use the PPTP service on the client to make an encrypted link to the RAS server on your network. The RAS server must be connected to the Internet; otherwise the client would not be able to make a connection to it.

The RAS server will take the traffic that it would normally send over a modem connection to the client and encrypt it and send it over the Internet to the client. The client and the RAS server can continue to exchange information in this manner, tunneling the stream of information through the Internet.

The advantage of using PPTP is that it can be less expensive to utilize an existing link with an ISP as opposed to using PSTN or ISDN lines and paying long-distance charges.

# Local Area Network (LAN) Protocols Used with RAS

N CHAPTER 2 you learned that NT uses three main LAN protocols: TCP/IP, NWLink IPX/SPX and NetBEUI. RAS also uses these three primary Windows NT transport protocols to provide network services over a dial-up connection. You must have the protocol already installed for Windows NT's use before you can use it with RAS.

For each device you configure for use with RAS (usually a modem) you can select which of the transport protocols you wish to use. For example, you may wish to configure one modem to use TCP/IP to connect your network to the Internet, and you may wish to configure several more modems to use NWLink so that remote Windows clients can connect to your network with the minimum of communications overhead.

You enable the protocols a modem will use from the RAS item on the Services tab page of the Network Control Panel. TCP/IP, NWLink, and NetBEUI all can be enabled or disabled for a modem for both dial-out and calling in. This allows you to, for example, have the same modem use NetBEUI for incoming calls from remote network clients, and use TCP/IP to connect to an Internet Service Provider.

Each of the protocols are configured for dial-in in a slightly different manner. When you click Configure for each of the protocols, a window requesting the specific settings required for that protocol appears. The following subsections will cover the settings of each of the protocols and then Exercise 14.5 will walk you through the steps of configuring each protocol for a typical RAS installation.

# TCP/IP

TCP/IP is the transport protocol used by the Internet. You can also use TCP/IP to connect remote computers to your network. TCP/IP is a very robust protocol. If you cannot guarantee that the telephone connection will be free of extraneous noise then the error detection and correction characteristics of TCP/IP may make it a better protocol for this purpose than faster transport protocols such as NWLink and NetBEUI.

With TCP/IP you can allow an incoming call to access only the RAS Server computer, or you can allow the computer making the incoming call to access the rest of the network as well. In addition you can configure the incoming connection to be given an IP address via DHCP, you can configure the IP address to come from a pool of addresses maintained on the RAS server, or you can allow the incoming connection to request its own IP address. Figure 14.1 shows the RAS Server TCP/IP Configuration dialog box.

**FIGURE 14.1**

The RAS Server TCP/IP Configuration dialog box

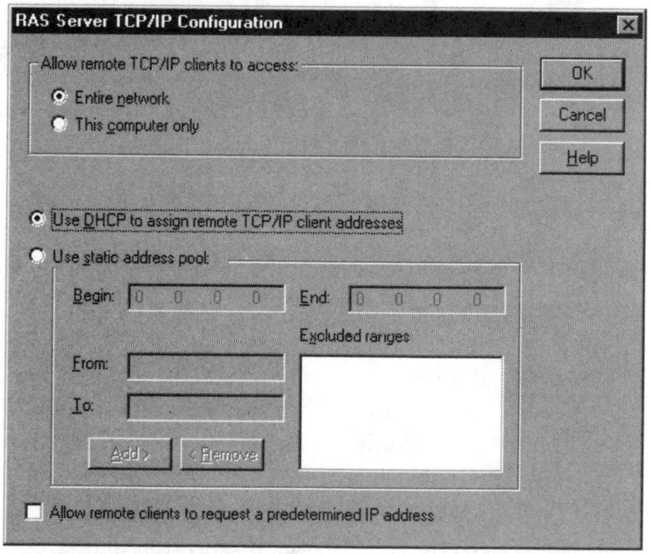

# IPX

IPX or NWLink IPX/SPX is a fast and efficient network transport protocol. If you have NetWare servers in your network you might standardize on NWLink for both LAN communications and dial-up connections, so that you do not have to configure computers to support more than one networking protocol.

NWLink can be configured to allow the connecting computer to access only the RAS server computer or to access the whole network. In addition, the NWLink dial-in configuration window allows you to allocate network numbers automatically or to allocate them starting at a number you specify in the configuration window. You can also set it to assign the same network number to all IPX clients, and you can set it to allow remote clients to request an IPX node number. Figure 14.2 shows the RAS Server IPX Configuration dialog box.

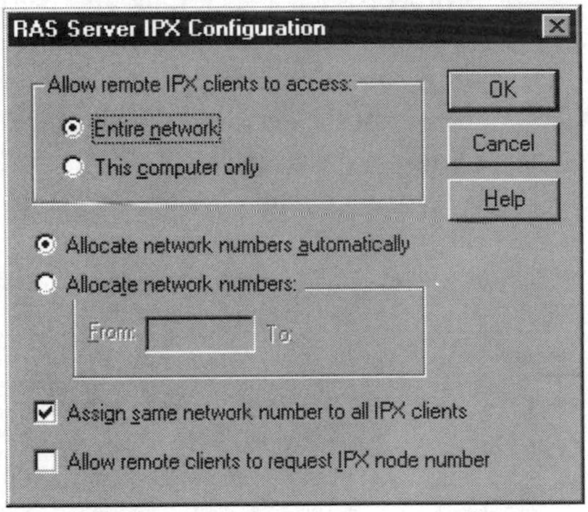

**FIGURE 14.2**

The RAS Server IPX
Configuration dialog box

**RAS Server IPX Configuration**

Allow remote IPX clients to access:
- ⦿ Entire network
- ○ This computer only

[OK] [Cancel] [Help]

- ⦿ Allocate network numbers automatically
- ○ Allocate network numbers:
  - From [    ] To [    ]

- ☑ Assign same network number to all IPX clients
- ☐ Allow remote clients to request IPX node number

# NetBEUI

NetBEUI is the simplest of the network transport protocols, and it is also the most efficient. Microsoft suggests that if you do not require features of NWLink or of TCP/IP then you should use NetBEUI to make dial-up connections to your RAS server so that the maximum amount of bandwidth will be available for use in programs rather than tied up in protocol overhead.

The only setting you can configure from the NetBEUI setup button is whether NetBEUI dial-up clients can access the rest of your network or are limited to accessing only the RAS server computer. Figure 14.3 shows the RAS Server NetBEUI Configuration dialog box.

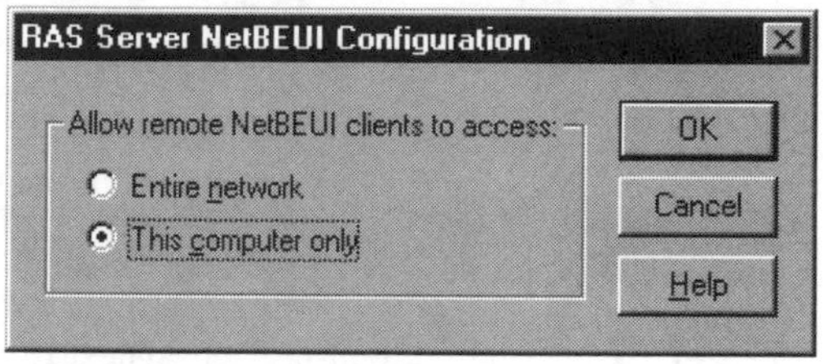

**FIGURE 14.3**

The RAS Server NetBEUI
Configuration dialog box

## Configuring the Protocols for RAS

Windows NT automatically provides settings for the protocols that should work properly in most dial-in situations. In most cases you can simply accept the values and selections that appear in the configuration windows. In Exercise 14.5 you will configure your RAS server to allow access to your network via RAS using any of the supported protocols.

---

**EXERCISE 14.5**

### Configuring RAS Protocols

**1.** Select Start ➤ Settings ➤ Control Panel ➤ Network ➤ Services.

**2.** Select the Remote Access Services entry from the list and then click Properties.

**3.** Select the modem you wish to configure protocols for and then click Network. The Network Configuration dialog box will appear, as shown below.

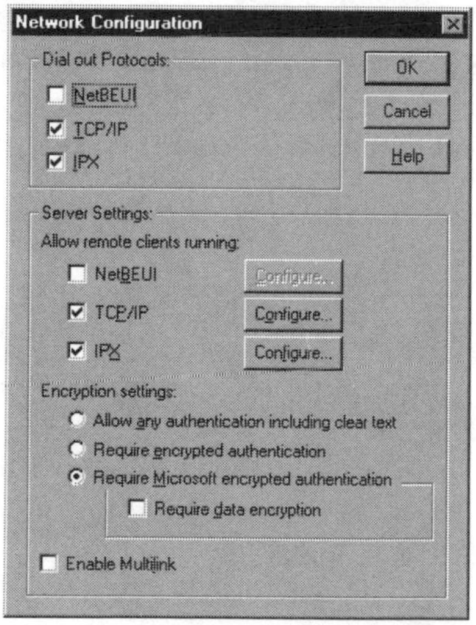

**4.** In the Server Setting box, make sure that the NetBEUI, TCP/IP, and IPX boxes are checked (TCP/IP and IPX should be checked by default).

**5.** Click the Configure button next to NetBEUI and select Entire Network. Click OK.

**6.** Click the Configure button next to TCP/IP. Select Entire Network. Select Use DHCP and select Allow clients to request a predetermined IP address. Click OK.

**7.** Press the Configure button next to IPX. Select Entire Network, and Allocate network numbers automatically. Click OK.

**8.** Click OK in the network configuration window and then click Continue in the Remote Access Setup window.

**9.** Click Close in the network window. You must restart your computer before the changes take effect. Select Yes to restart your computer.

# Remote Access Protocols

RAS CAN USE two protocols—Support for Serial Line Internet Protocol (SLIP) and Point-to-Point protocol (PPP)—in addition to the transport protocols also used for LAN communication. These two protocols perform the same function in a dial-up networking connection that Ethernet or Token ring perform in a LAN environment; they provide a media access protocol that the transport protocol (TCP/IP, NWLink, or NetBEUI) uses to transport information.

## RAS and SLIP

SLIP is an early protocol for the transfer of Internet packets over serial connections such as modems and T1 leased lines. Until recently, SLIP was the most common method of making a modem connection to an Internet Service Provider. PPP is a newer protocol and has many advantages over SLIP; it has made SLIP much less popular.

Although you can configure RAS to dial out and make a connection to another computer using the SLIP protocol, you cannot configure RAS to accept a connection using the SLIP protocol. This means that you cannot use SLIP to connect two computers running RAS, nor can you use SLIP to connect to your RAS server a client computer running another operating system such as Windows 95. Instead you use PPP.

## RAS and PPP

PPP addresses some deficiencies in the SLIP protocol, providing mechanisms for encrypting logon requests and for supporting other transport protocols besides TCP/IP. PPP is optimized for low-bandwidth communications and conveys data between communicating computers more efficiently than does SLIP.

PPP is the default method of making connections to and from a RAS server. PPP is automatically installed when you install the RAS server component, and there is little you can do to directly configure how RAS uses PPP. You do, however, indirectly configure PPP when you select and use PPP security options; this is explained in the following section.

# RAS Security

BEFORE RAS CONNECTS your remote client computers to your network it must ensure that the client computers are not intruders masquerading as regular client connections. RAS security features, including permissions, callback, encrypted passwords, and PPTP protect your RAS connections against intrusion and eavesdropping.

## RAS Permissions

If your network is not connected to the Internet and if it does not provide dial-up connections then you do not have to be concerned about electronic intrusion. Your primary security concerns will be unauthorized physical access to your network and network users that may exceed their authority to read or modify network data.

If, however, you do provide dial-up lines (or Internet connections) then you must ensure that only authorized users access your network. You can configure RAS permissions through the Remote Access Admin utility found in the Administrative Tools group. RAS permissions for users of dial-up connections are shown in Figure 14.4.

The RAS permissions you establish for dial-up connections are your first line of defense against network intruders. You should pay careful attention to how you set up the dial-in permissions of your RAS server so that only users that should access your network over dial-up lines can do so. In addition, if your network contains sensitive information, you should consider disallowing dial-up access for user accounts with extensive permissions to the system (such as the ADMINISTRATOR account) and requiring the users of those accounts, if they require dial-up access, to use an account with less privileges when connecting via RAS.

The permissions that you can set are defined in Table 14.1

**TABLE 14.1**

Remote Access Permissions defined

| REMOTE ACCESS PERMISSION | DESCRIPTION |
| --- | --- |
| Grant dialin permission | If the Grant dialin permission box is checked, the selected user can dial in to the RAS server. If this box is unchecked, the user has no dial-in permission. |

| TABLE 14.1 Remote Access Permissions defined | REMOTE ACCESS PERMISSION | DESCRIPTION |
|---|---|---|
| | Call Back | Allows you to specify the callback option you want to be used in conjunction with RAS dial-ins and can be customized per user. The three choices are No Call Back (default option), Set By Caller, and Preset To. The Set By Caller option is useful if you have a user who travels to multiple sites and wants call back so that the site that contains the RAS server will incur the long-distance charges. The Preset To call back option is useful for user accounts that have access to sensitive information and will always be calling from the same location (for example, from home). |

*You can only set permissions for individual users, not for groups.*

*Network intrusion is a serious threat to any network that is connected to the Internet or that allows dial-up access via the telephone lines.*

## RAS Encryption

When you log on to your network using RAS you must provide a username and a password (this is a normal NT user account created through User Manager for Domains). The password must travel over the telephone lines to your RAS server so that the RAS server can determine if that username has dial-in privileges and if the connection must be made using the RAS *dial-back* feature.

The way the RAS client and the RAS server exchange the username and password (and some other information such as the temporary network address allocated to the client) is called the authentication protocol. RAS Server supports only PPP for dial-in connections, and it supports three encryption options:

- Allow any authentication including clear text

- Require encrypted authentication

- Require Microsoft encrypted authentication

The default setting for RAS password authentication is Require Microsoft encrypted authentication. When you enable this option for a RAS device (such as a particular modem or ISDN adapter) the clients connecting via that device must encrypt the password with MS-CHAP (Microsoft Challenge Handshake Protocol). When you select this option, only Microsoft clients (such as Windows 95, Windows NT Workstation, or other Windows NT Server computers) can connect to your RAS server. MS-CHAP implements the RSA Data Security MD4 (Message Digest Four) algorithm over PPP.

If you use the MS-CHAP protocol then you can also set the RAS device to Require data encryption. This will encrypt the data exchanged between the RAS server and client as well as the password exchanged to establish the connection. Windows NT will handle all of the details of establishing the encrypted communications channel, such as selecting and exchanging encryption keys; you simply have to select that you wish to use the feature.

If you wish to allow computers running other operating systems (such as UNIX) to connect to your RAS server, but you also wish to require that passwords be encrypted, then you can select the Require encrypted authentication option, which will enable the CHAP authentication protocol. CHAP stands for Challenge Handshake Protocol, and implements the RSA Data Security Message Digest Five (MD5) algorithm over PPP.

Some client operating systems do not support encrypted password authentication. For these computers, you can select Allow any authentication including clear text. This option allows users to connect using the PAP protocol, which does not require encryption.

# RAS Clients

THE PREVIOUS SECTION showed you how to set up a RAS server. That, however, is only half the problem of enabling RAS to your network. The other half entails the configuration of clients to connect to your RAS server.

RAS supports the connection of any operating system that supports PPP, one of the three authentication protocols (PAP, CHAP, or MS-CHAP) and one of the three transports (TCP/IP, NWLink, or NetBEUI). If the client is going to access services on the Windows NT Server then they must support a service protocol of Windows NT (such as NetBIOS for file access or HTTP for access to Internet Information Server Web pages).

Just about any computer can connect to your network via RAS. Each operating system has its own methods of configuring the various protocols they support.

*Other books in this series (MCSE: Windows 95 Study Guide and MCSE: NT Workstation Study Guide) explain how to connect Windows 95 and Windows NT Workstation computers to RAS in some detail.*

Windows NT Server is connected as a client to another Windows NT Server using RAS in exactly the same way Windows NT Workstation is. This section will review how you use RAS as a client to connect a Windows NT computer to a RAS server on another computer.

## Installing RAS Client Software

On a Windows NT Workstation computer or on a Windows NT Server computer that does not already have RAS loaded to allow RAS dial-in connections, you may need to install RAS services in order to connect to a RAS server. If you already have RAS configured for dial-in, you do not have to install it again for dial-out, you can simply check the Dial out and receive calls or the Dial out only options in the Configure Port Usage window.

Exercise 14.4 (earlier in this chapter) walks you through the process of installing RAS on a Windows NT Server or Workstation computer.

## Creating a Dial-Up Connection

After installing RAS, you will need to create a dial-up network connection in the RAS phone book that contains the dialing and network information for each different dial-up server to which you will attach. This process is basically the same for Windows RAS servers and UNIX/Internet servers. Follow Exercise 14.6 to create a dial-up networking connection. Repeat this process for each dial-up server to which you need access.

**EXERCISE 14.6**

## Creating a Dial-Up Networking Connection

**1.** Double-click the My Computer icon on the Desktop.

**2.** Double-click the Dial-Up Networking icon.

**3.** Click OK to pass the "The phonebook is empty" notice if it appears. If it does not appear, you already have at least one RAS entry. Click New.

**4.** The New Phonebook Entry Wizard dialog box appears. Type the name of the new phonebook entry, check the I know all about phonebook entries box, and click Next. (Once you choose to enter the phonebook information without the wizard, you must use More/User Preferences/Appearance/Use Wizard to create new phonebook entries to use the wizard again.) Enter the name of the server to which you will be attaching in the Entry name text box.

**5.** Select your modem in the Dial using drop-down menu. If you are using a null modem cable to connect two computers, select the Dial-Up Networking Serial Cable between 2 PCs on the appropriate COM port.

**6.** Click the Use Telephony dialing properties option.

**7.** Enter the area code and phone number of your RAS server in the Phone number input lines. If you are using a Null modem cable, leave these lines blank.

**8.** Click Alternates if your RAS server has alternate phone numbers. Add the alternate phone numbers.

**9.** Click the Servers tab.

**10.** Select the protocol used by the network your RAS server is on (TCP/IP, NetBEUI, or NWLink).

**11.** Click the Security tab.

**12.** Select Allow any encryption including clear text.

**13.** Click OK to accept your settings.

**14.** Click Close. Restarting your computer is not necessary after adding dial-up servers.

## Client Protocols

When you dial in to a network you must use a protocol that the RAS server supports. For a Windows NT RAS server, this will be either TCP/IP, NWLink, or NetBEUI.

You can select a different protocol or set of protocols for each phone book entry, and you can have two phone book entries for the same RAS server, differing only by which protocol is selected. You could use this, for instance, to select TCP/IP when telephone service is bad, and NWLink otherwise.

You can change the protocols a phone book entry uses by clicking My Computer, clicking Dial-up Networking, clicking the phone book entry, and then selecting the Server tab page. Figure 14.5 shows the Server tab page of the phonebook entry.

**FIGURE 14.5**

The Server tab page of the
New Phonebook Entry
window

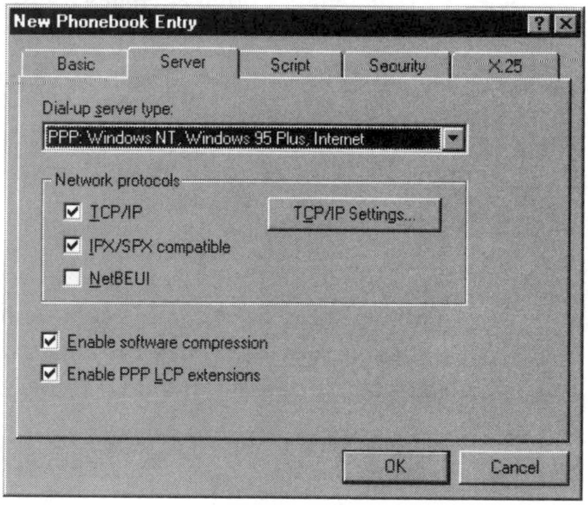

## Security

The RAS client complement to the RAS server security options resides in the Security tab of the phone book entry. From there you can specify what kind of dial-up authentication you will use to connect your RAS client computer to the RAS server. The same options are available from the client side as are from the server side:

- Allow any authentication including clear text

- Require encrypted authentication

- Require Microsoft encrypted authentication

You can also specify that data passing over the RAS connection will be encrypted.

The security you select must match the security selected on the RAS server, except if either side selects Allow any authentication including clear text, then it doesn't matter which protocol the other uses (other than from a security standpoint).

## Scripting

Windows NT Server and Workstation version 4.0 came with a powerful new scripting language. You can use this language to automate connections to non-RAS dial up servers. (The scripting language is not necessary for connecting to RAS servers because the authentication protocols already do all the work of connecting the client to the RAS server.)

Using the scripting language is not difficult. Look at the examples provided with the Windows NT Server CD-ROM and read the documentation about the scripting language (found as <Winnt>\system32\ras\Script.doc) in order to see how it works.

## Testing a RAS Installation

Testing a RAS Installation requires another computer running Microsoft RAS. You may need to ask your network administrator for the phone number of your company's RAS server and what protocols it supports. Exercise 14.7 shows you how to test a RAS connection.

---

**EXERCISE 14.7**

### Testing a RAS Connection

1. Double-click the My Computer Icon on the Desktop.

2. Double-click the Dial-Up Networking Icon.

3. Check whether the server you entered in the previous section appears as the default phonebook entry. If this is not the case, select the entry from the list box. If it does not appear, repeat Exercise 14.6.

---

**EXERCISE 14.7 (CONTINUED FROM PREVIOUS PAGE)**

**4.** Click the Dial button.

**5.** Enter your user name, password, and domain for the remote server in the Connect to window. Click the Save password check box.

**6.** Click OK.

**7.** Listen for the modem to dial and connect. RAS will beep if the connection went through correctly.

After running this procedure, you are connected to the remote RAS host. You will have access to all the resources on the remote network that your security permissions allow.

### Disconnecting a RAS Session

You can disconnect a RAS session through the RAS session dialog box. Exercise 14.8 shows this simple procedure.

**EXERCISE 14.8**

**Disconnecting a RAS Session**

**1.** Right-click the RAS monitor next to the Time in the task bar. (If you already changed the icon into a status window, right-click the window.)

**2.** Select the Hang up connection option.

**3.** Select the name of the server or service provider from which you wish to disconnect.

**4.** Answer Yes when asked if you want to disconnect.

**5.** Listen for a beep to confirm the disconnect.

# Chapter Summary

THE REMOTE ACCESS Service for Windows NT extends the advantages of networking to computers that cannot be directly connected to your network. RAS uses modems or other devices that attach to telephone company lines to call in and share files and services.

In this chapter you learned how to configure analog modems and ISDN adapters to be used in the RAS server. Installing the RAS service is easy and is accomplished through Control Panel ➤ Network.

RAS servers support a wide variety of wide area network connectivity options including PSTN, ISDN, X.25, RS-232 null modem cables, and PPTP.

A RAS server can also support any of the three primary transport protocols of Windows NT (TCP/IP, NWLink, and NetBEUI). It supports PPP for dial-in, and both SLIP and PPP for dial-out. It supports PAP, CHAP and MS-CHAP for password authentication, and if you use MS-CHAP then you can also encrypt the data transferred over a RAS link.

RAS supports the connection of any computer that supports the PPP protocol, PAP, CHAP, or MS-CHAP as an authentication protocol, and IPX, TCP/IP, or NetBEUI as a transport protocol. If the client computer will access services on the RAS server then the client must also support a services protocol that the RAS server also supports, such as NetBIOS or HTTP.

RAS permissions are established on a per-user basis, and include a callback feature. You cannot assign permissions by Windows NT server or domain groups.

Protocols are selected for dial-out from within the phone book entry for that dial-out connection, as is the authentication that will be used for that dial-out connection. RAS also allows you to make a script to automate connection to non-RAS servers.

# *Review Questions*

1. Which WAN connections are supported by RAS? Choose all that apply.

   **A.** PSTN

   **B.** ISDN

   **C.** X.25

   **D.** PPTP

   **E.** V.32

2. Which LAN protocols are supported by RAS? Choose all that apply.

   **A.** AFP

   **B.** TCP/IP

   **C.** NetBEUI

   **D.** DLC

   **E.** IPX

3. Which utility can be used to find available COM ports in NT Server?

   **A.** Control Panel ➤ Modems (detect available COM ports option)

   **B.** NT Diagnostics

   **C.** Dr.Watson for NT diagnostics

   **D.** Control Panel ➤ Network (detect available COM ports option)

4. Which LAN protocol requires the least amount of configuration for use with RAS?

   **A.** AFP

   **B.** TCP/IP

   **C.** NetBEUI

   **D.** DLC

   **E.** IPX

**5.** Which of the following protocols supports RAS dial-out and RAS dial-in capabilities?

**A.** SLIP

**B.** PPP

**C.** NetBEUI

**D.** DLC

**E.** IPX

**6.** Which RAS callback option provides the greatest level of security?

**A.** Set By Caller

**B.** Set by RAS Server

**C.** Preset To

**D.** Callback and Confirm RAS password

**7.** Which RAS encryption option also has an additional option to encrypt data?

**A.** Require encrypted authentication

**B.** Require C2 encrypted authentication

**C.** Require C2/E2 encrypted authentication

**D.** Require Microsoft encrypted authentication

**8.** Where in NT Server do you specify which users have dialin permission to the RAS server?

**A.** User Manager for Domains

**B.** Control Panel ➤ Network ➤ Services ➤ RAS ➤ Properties

**C.** Administrative Tools ➤ Remote Access Admin

**D.** Control Panel ➤ Remote Access Admin

# Monitoring System Performance

ONITORING SYSTEM PERFORMANCE is a way of checking your server's vital statistics. NT Server comes with Performance Monitor and Task Manager, which can be used to monitor your system's performance.

Of the two utilities, Performance Monitor has more capabilities; you can use it to see how efficiently your computer is running, determine whether any components are causing system bottlenecks, plan for future growth, and set alert conditions.

Task Manager is a new utility for NT 4.0. You can use it to see an overview of system CPU and memory usage. Task Manager also provides monitoring capabilities for the more commonly tracked options of Performance Monitor. The nice thing about Task Manager is that it is easy to access and requires no configuration.

This chapter will cover:

- The purpose of Performance Monitor

- The four main areas that should be tracked through Performance Monitor

- The different views that can be created through Performance Monitor

- Configuring system memory usage

- The Task Manager utility

# Performance Monitor

ERFORMANCE MONITOR IS a very powerful reporting utility that can be used to track and monitor system performance, and entire books have been written on it. In order to really understand Performance

Monitor, the best thing to do is play with it. In this chapter, my goal is to provide you with an introduction to Performance Monitor, and to give you an idea of its usefulness.

This section will examine the purpose of Performance Monitor, the main areas that you should track in Performance Monitor, and the four views that can be created through Performance Monitor.

## Performance Monitor's Purpose

Performance Monitor allows you to view your system's current health. Consider the following scenario. The accounting department has just implemented a new accounting application. The application is memory intensive and the users are expressing that they need new computers. You decide to approach the problem scientifically and use Performance Monitor to see why the application is running so slowly. After charting the application through Performance Monitor, you see that the CPU utilization is actually very low, but the system is using excessive paging, and memory is actually the problem. Armed with this information, you order memory upgrades for the accounting department, as opposed to new computers, saving the company money. And, because it's the accounting department you're dealing with, they actually appreciate it.

The main uses of Performance Monitor are to create baselines, determine system bottlenecks, create charts to plan for future growth, and create alert thresholds to notify you of potential problems.

### Creating Baselines

A *baseline* is a snapshot of how your system is currently performing. Let's assume that the network hardware has not changed in the last three months, and the users are saying that the network seems slow. If I have been using Performance Monitor to track system performance and saving my reports, I can tell if the server's performance has changed. The server's performance can change as a result of higher usage or a change in the type of processing it is doing. Based on this information, I can determine what changes should be made to fix the server so that performance is again at an acceptable level.

Baselines are also useful for determining the effect of changes you make to your system. For example, if I upgrade the CPU in the server, or add another processor to a multi-processor computer, I can run Performance Monitor before the hardware is added and after the hardware is added, and compare the two reports to measure change.

You should also use Performance Monitor baselines to determine the effect of system configuration changes. For the most part, NT is self-tuning, and you don't need to tweak any configuration. But, if you do tweak configuration, it is highly recommended that you baseline before the tweak and after the tweak. If you don't see a noticeable performance improvement, it may be best to go back to the original configuration

Some of the common counters that would be included in a system baseline are listed in Table 15.1.

| **TABLE 15.1** Useful counters for baselines | OBJECT | COUNTER |
|---|---|---|
| | Cache | Data Map Hits % |
| | LogicalDisk | %Free Space |
| | Memory | Pages/Sec |
| | Memory | Available Pages |
| | Paging File | %Usage |
| | Physical Disk | Disk Queue Length |
| | Physical Disk | Average Disk sec/Transfer |
| | Processor | %Processor Time |
| | Server | Bytes Total/sec |
| | System | File Read Operations/sec |
| | System | File Write Operations/sec |

### Determining System Bottlenecks

A *bottleneck* is a system resource that is inefficient compared to the rest of the computer system as a whole. The bottleneck can cause the rest of the system to run slowly. Consider a computer that is a 486/100 with 16MB of RAM. If the applications are memory intensive and the memory is the bottleneck, upgrading your CPU isn't going to fix the problem.

The advantage of using Performance Monitor is that you have a tool that can measure system performance and allow you to pinpoint system bottlenecks scientifically.

### Planning for Future Growth

Many of us tend to manage life reactively instead of proactively. Reactive management means that when we actually have a problem and the fires are burning, then our attention will be focused on the problem. Proactive management means that we avoid the problems in the first place. In a perfect world, we would manage life proactively.

Performance Monitor is a great tool for proactive network management. If you are creating baselines on a regular basis, it will help you identify network trends. For example, if you notice CPU utilization increasing by 5% every month, you can assume that within the next six months, you're going to have a problem. Before performance becomes so slow that users are complaining, you can upgrade the hardware.

### Creating Alerts for Problem Notification

Through Performance Monitor you can specify alert thresholds. That means you can ensure that an alert is generated if a counter reaches a certain value.

For example, you could specify that if the free space on your logical disk is under 10%, you want to be alerted. Once alerted, you can add more disk space or delete unneeded files before your users run out of disk space. You will learn how to create an alert later in this chapter.

## Tracking Performance through Performance Monitor

In this section you will learn how Performance Monitor is organized and the main areas you should track through Performance Monitor.

### Organization of Performance Monitor

When you first access Performance Monitor, you will notice that, by default, nothing is tracked. In order for Performance Monitor to be useful, you must configure it to track something. In this section, you will learn how Performance Monitor is organized, so you can use it to track system events.

Through Performance Monitor, you can define what you want to track through Computer, Object, Instance and Counter, as shown in Figure 15.1.

**FIGURE 15.1**

The Add to Chart
dialog box

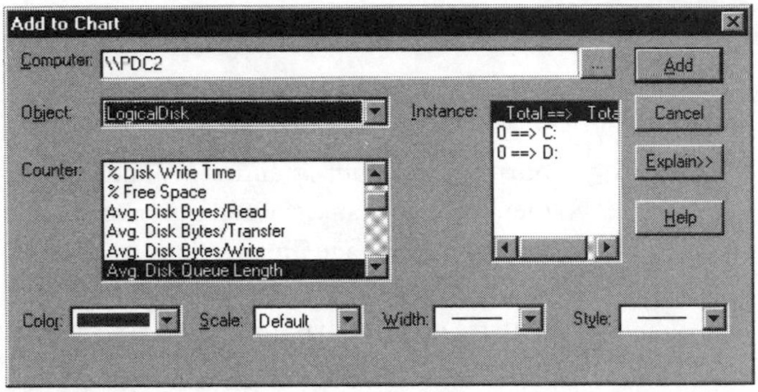

**COMPUTER** As you add counters to Performance Monitor, the default computer that is tracked is the computer that Performance Monitor is being run on. However, you can specify that you want to track events on a remote system. This is especially useful if you do not want the overhead of running Performance Monitor on the machine you are trying to measure.

Assuming that you have administrative rights, you can specify the computer on which you want to track system events. You could use Performance Monitor to track the events of an NT Server from a remote computer, or you could track events from multiple computers on a single chart in Performance Monitor.

**OBJECT** NT system resources are organized as *objects*. The sum of all objects represents your total system. You see object lists in Performance Monitor. Certain objects appear on all NT computers, and other objects only appear if the process or service is running. For example, you would only see objects relating to RAS if RAS was installed. Table 15.2 lists the objects that are always available on NT Server (and Workstation).

**INSTANCE** Each object can have a single *instance* or multiple instances. Objects, like memory and cache, will always have one instance. Objects, like processor and physical disks, can have multiple instances if you have multiples of the same object running.

**COUNTER** Each object has an associated set of *counters*. Counters are used to track specific information regarding your objects.

| | OBJECT | DESCRIPTION |
|---|---|---|
| **TABLE 15.2**<br>NT objects defined in<br>Performance Monitor | Cache | Area of system memory used to hold recently accessed data. |
| | Logical Disk | Disk partitions that logically organize your physical disk space. For example, if you have drive 0, that is your physical disk. Drive C : and drive D : as defined on drive 0 are the logical disks. |
| | Memory | Physical memory installed on the computer. |
| | Objects | System defined software objects. |
| | Paging File | Special file on the hard disk that is used as virtual memory. |
| | Physical Disk | Physical hard drive on your computer. |
| | Process | Software that is currently running. |
| | Processor | CPU and how it is currently operating. |
| | Redirector | Used to redirect requests to the network, as opposed to processing locally. |
| | System | Counters used to track system hardware and software. |
| | Thread | Objects within a process that run program instructions. |

*Notice that when you choose an object, a counter is always pre-selected for you. Instead of presenting you with an alphabetical list, the most commonly used counter will be pre-selected for you.*

In Exercise 15.1, you will create a simple chart to track your system performance.

In the next section, you will learn how to use Performance Monitor to identify possible bottlenecks.

---

**EXERCISE 15.1**

**Tracking System Performance through Performance Monitor**

This exercise should be completed from PDC1 while logged on as ADMINISTRATOR.

**1.** Select Start ➤ Programs ➤ Administrative Tools (common) ➤ Performance Monitor.

**2.** Select Edit ➤ Add to Chart.

**3.** Choose Object: Processor and Counter: %Processor Time and click Add.

**4.** Repeat Step 3 and add the following to your chart:

| Object | Counter |
|--------|---------|
| Logical Disk | Ave. Disk Queue Length |
| Memory | Pages/Sec. |
| Paging File | %Usage |

**5.** Click Done.

---

# Identifying Bottlenecks with Performance Monitor

There are four main areas that cause bottlenecks in your system. They are:

- Memory
- CPU
- Disk access
- Network access

### Memory

Memory is usually the most likely cause of system bottlenecks. If you have no idea what is causing a system bottleneck, memory is usually a good place to start checking. To determine how your memory is being used, there are two areas you need to examine: physical memory and logical memory (the page file).

Physical memory is the physical RAM that is installed in the computer. You can't have too much memory. It's a good idea to have more memory than you think you need just to be on the safe side. Now that RAM prices keep dropping, it's easier to do that.

The page file is logical memory that exists on the hard drive. If you are using excessive paging (swapping between logical RAM—on a hard disk—and physical RAM), it's a clear sign that you need to add more physical RAM.

Specific counters that should be checked if you suspect a memory problem are listed in Table 15.3.

**TABLE 15.3**

Counters used to define memory-related problems

| OBJECT | COUNTER | DESCRIPTION |
|--------|---------|-------------|
| Memory | Available Bytes | Virtual memory available for system use. Less than 4MB indicates a need for more RAM. |
| Memory | Pages/sec | Number of pages being written between physical memory and the paging file. This number should be below 20. |
| Memory | Committed Bytes | Memory that is allocated and currently being used by applications. Should be less than the physical memory installed on your computer. |

If you detect a memory shortage, the best fix is to add more RAM, plain and simple.

## CPU

You can track how busy your CPU is through the System object, which tracks your processor(s) on a system-wide basis, and through the Processor object, which allows you to track processor use on an individual processor basis. If you only have a single processor, these values will be the same.

Processors aren't as likely to be bottlenecks as memory is, but you can determine if the processor is the bottleneck by watching the %Processor Time counter.

When tracking performance, Performance Monitor will display minimum, maximum, and average statistics for the current monitored session. You shouldn't be overly concerned with temporary spikes in %Processor Time, but if the average %Processor Time is consistently at or above 80%, you should consider upgrading your processor, or adding an additional processor if your computer supports multiprocessors. Your decision on whether to add an additional processor or to upgrade your processor should be based on which applications you are running. Multiple processors will only help if you are running more than one process or you have a multi-threaded application.

### Disk Access

Disk access is the amount of time your disk takes to retrieve data from the drive. The two factors that determine how quickly your disk will respond to requests are the average disk access time and the speed of your disk controller.

By default, the disk activity counters are not activated. This is because using disk counters on older 386 computers degraded system performance by about 1.5%. For newer systems, the performance degradation is very minimal. To turn your disk counters on, you must run the command DISKPERF -Y from the command line and reboot your computer.

Once disk activity counters are enabled, you can monitor your disk through the Physical Disk object and the Logical Disk object. It's a good idea to track Physical Disk and Logical Disk counters in your baseline so you know what is average for your system.

The %Disk Time counter and the Current Disk Queue Length in the Physical Disk object point out bottlenecks. If the %Disk Time counter reads over 90% or the Current Disk Queue Length is over 2 then your disk is probably a bottleneck.

If you detect that your disk performance is inadequate, the following steps will help you improve it:

- Use disk striping to take advantage of multiple I/O channels

- Balance heavily used files on multiple I/O channels

- Use faster disks and disk controllers

- Add another disk controller for load balancing

*Excessive paging can look like you have a disk I/O problem, when in fact, excessive paging is caused by a shortage of RAM.*

In Exercise 15.2, you will enable the disk counters for Performance Monitor.

*To disable your disk counters, you would use* DISKPERF-N *and restart your computer.*

---

**EXERCISE 15.2**

### Enabling Your Disk Counters

This exercise should be completed from PDCI while logged on as ADMINISTRATOR.

**1.** Select Start ➤ Programs ➤ Command Prompt.

**2.** Type **DISKPERF -Y**.

**3.** Select Start ➤ Shut Down. Restart your computer.

Your disk counters will now be active.

---

### Network Access

You can monitor network access through Performance Monitor, or through Network Monitor, which is covered in Chapter 16, "Network Monitor." To take advantage of all of the network counters, you must first run the network monitoring agent.

You can see how busy your network segment is by watching the Network Segment object, %Network Utilization counter. This should be below 40% in Ethernet networks and below 80% on Token Ring networks.

Other components that generate network statistics are the workstation service, the server service, and your network protocols (TCP/IP, NWLink IPX/SPX, and NetBEUI).

One recommendation for optimizing network performance is to buy network adapter cards that can use the full bus width of your system. It's a very good investment to buy 32-bit network adapter cards for your servers as opposed to 16-bit network adapter cards. The performance of a 32-bit card is 1.14MB as opposed to 700K for a 16-bit card. Just be sure that your 32-bit card is on the hardware compatibility list and that there is an NDIS 4 driver.

# Views Available through Performance Monitor

Performance Monitor has four different ways, or views, of tracking system data. The views that Performance Monitor uses are:

- Chart
- Alert

- Log

- Report

Each of these views is described in the following subsections.

### Chart

The default view that is used with Performance Monitor is the Chart view. The Chart view shows how the system is running in real time. The two modes that the Chart view uses are graph and histogram. Graphs show system data tracked over time. Histograms are vertical bar charts and can be used to look at data in real time without the historical perspective of a graph. Either mode allows you to see multiple counters at once.

**GRAPH CHART VIEW** The Graph Chart view tracks the counters you have selected over time. By default, the counters are updated every second and the chart displays 0-100 data points. Even while you are running the Graph Chart view, it is constantly being updated. You can tell where the current update is occurring because there is always a vertical red line moving across the view, which indicates the last update.

Figure 15.2 shows an example of the Graph Chart view. Notice that under the graph you have a value bar which displays statistics for the counter that is currently highlighted within the legend. The legend is at the bottom of the screen and shows colors associated with the counters you have chosen. In Figure 15.2, the value bar is showing values for %Processor Time.

*By choosing a counter within the legend and pressing Backspace, you highlight the corresponding chart line for easier viewing.*

**HISTOGRAM CHART VIEW** The Histogram Chart view, shown in Figure 15.3, displays the counters you have chosen in real time, but not in a historical perspective as the Graph Chart view does. The Histogram Chart view can be useful if you are charting so many values that the graph becomes hard to read.

In Exercise 15.3, you use Performance Monitor to create a chart using the Graph Chart mode, and then view the same chart through the Histogram Chart mode.

*Once you have created a chart, you can save the settings to be used by future charts by going to File ➢ Save Chart Settings or File ➢ Save Chart Settings As. By default, the following views are saved with the following extensions:*

| | | | |
|---|---|---|---|
| *Chart File* | `* .pmc` | *Alert File* | `* .pma` |
| *Log File* | `* .pml` | *Report File* | `* .pmr` |

**FIGURE 15.2**

Performance Monitor's Graph Chart view

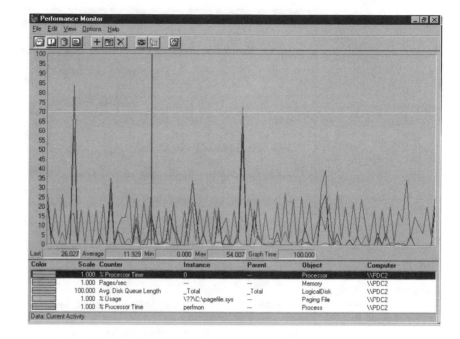

**FIGURE 15.3**

Performance Monitor's Histogram Chart view

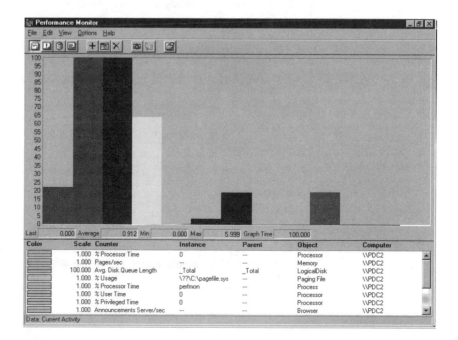

---

**EXERCISE 15.3**

## Using Performance Monitor's Chart View

This exercise should be completed from PDC1 while logged on as ADMINISTRATOR.

**1.** Select Start ➣ Programs ➣ Administrative Tools (common) ➣ Performance Monitor.

**2.** Choose Edit ➣ Add to Chart.

**3.** Add the following objects and counters to your chart:

| Object | Counter |
|--------|---------|
| Processor | %Processor Time |
| LogicalDisk | Ave. Disk Queue Length |
| Memory | Pages/Sec |
| Paging File | %Usage |
| Process | %Processor Time (instance:perfmon) |

**4.** In the legend section of your chart, click the %Processor Time counter and hit the Backspace key to highlight the counter.

**5.** To switch to the Histogram Chart view of your chart, select Options ➣ Chart to call up the Chart Options dialog box as shown here.

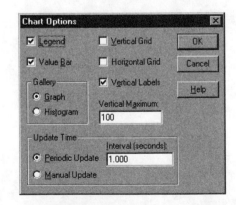

**6.** In the Gallery section of the Chart Options dialog box, choose Histogram and click OK. Your chart should now be in the Histogram Chart mode.

### Alert

The Alert view allows you to create system alerts based on counters exceeding thresholds that you specify. Alerts can be used to identify potential network problems so that you can correct them before they become major problems.

For each alert counter that you choose, you must specify:

- Computer

- Object

- Counter

- Threshold Value (Alert if over or under value)

You can also choose to run a program if an alert is triggered.

Performance Monitor will track up to 1,000 alerts before the newer alerts start to overwrite the oldest alerts.

In Exercise 15.4, you will use Performance Monitor to create an Alert view.

---

**EXERCISE 15.4**

### Using Performance Monitor's Alert View

This exercise should be completed from PDC1 while logged on as ADMINISTRATOR.

**1.** Select Start ➤ Programs ➤ Administrative Tools (common) ➤ Performance Monitor.

**2.** Choose View ➤ Alert.

**3.** Choose Edit ➤ Add to Chart.

**4.** Select the following counters:

| Computer | Object | Counter | Alert If |
|----------|--------|---------|----------|
| PDC1 | LogicalDisk | %Free Space | If Under 10 |
| PDC2 | LogicalDisk | %Free Space | If Under 10 |
| PDC1 | Processor | %Processor Time | If Over 90 |

If you have more than 10% free space on your logical disk, you can manipulate the If under alert threshold number for logical disk to generate an alert.

## Log

The Log view of Performance Monitor is used to save data to a file which can be used as a baseline and for future analysis.

To create a Log file, you specify which objects you want tracked in the Log file. You can only specify objects, as opposed to specific counters. For each object you track, all of the associated counters for that object will also be tracked. Once you choose your objects to log, you then start the Log file. After you collect your data, you can stop the Log file, and view the data through Performance Monitor, or you can export the data to some other application, such as a spreadsheet or a database.

## Report

The Report view within Performance Monitor allows you to display real-time Performance Monitor statistics in a report format. The Report view isn't as exciting as the Chart view, but it is useful to show a large number of objects and counters at once.

The Report view is shown in Figure 15.4.

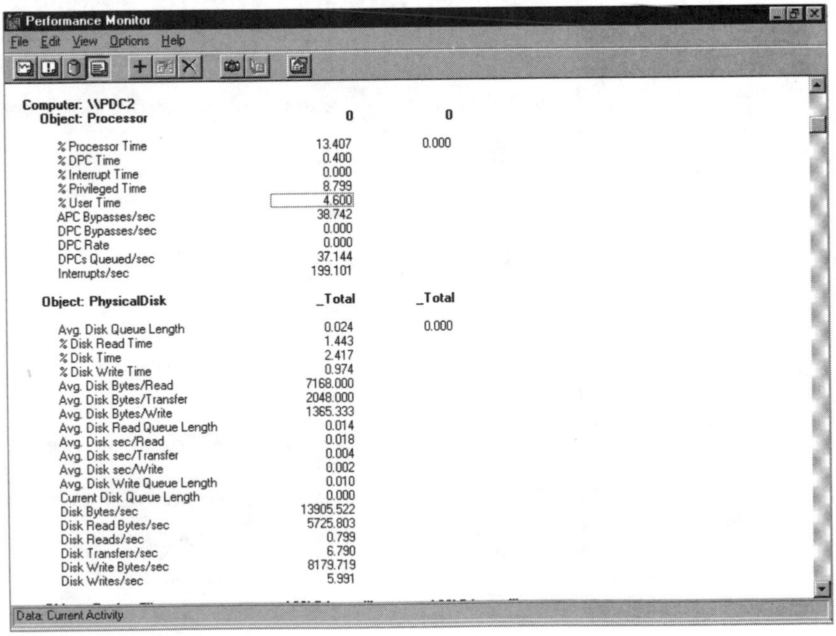

**FIGURE 15.4**

Performance Monitor's Report view

# Optimizing NT Server

YOU CAN MANIPULATE how NT Server allocates memory between network connections and applications by choosing the optimization option that is right for your server. As shown in Figure 15.5, you can choose from the following options:

- Minimize Memory Used

- Balance

- Maximize Throughput for File Sharing

- Manage Throughput for Network Applications

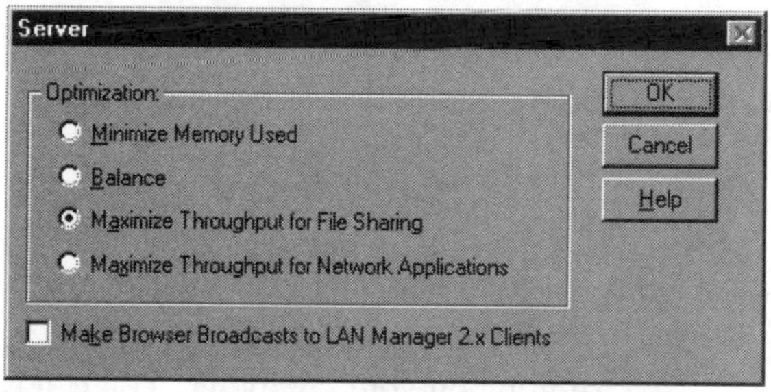

**FIGURE 15.5**

The Server Optimization dialog box

To access the dialog box shown in Figure 15.5, select Start ➤ Settings ➤ Control Panel ➤ Network ➤ Services ➤ Server ➤ Properties.

Table 15.4 defines your options for server optimization.

**TABLE 15.4**

Server optimization options defined

| SERVER OPTIMIZATION | DESCRIPTION |
| --- | --- |
| Minimize Memory Used | Provides best performance if you will have under 10 users. |
| Balance | Provides best performance if you will support 10-64 users. |

| TABLE 15.4 | SERVER OPTIMIZATION | DESCRIPTION |
| --- | --- | --- |
| Server optimization options defined (continued) | Maximize Throughput for File Sharing | Default selection. Used to support servers with 64 or more users. Maximum memory is allocated to file-sharing applications. |
| | Maximize Throughput for Network Applications | Used for servers supporting distributed applications that use memory caching—for example, SQL server. |

*You should baseline your performance with Performance Monitor prior to changing your server optimization. Baseline your server's performance after changes have been made to confirm that your server is properly tuned.*

# Task Manager

T HE TASK MANAGER utility is new to NT 4.0. Task Manager is the new generation version of Task List that the Windows 3.x interface used. Through Task Manager, you can view and control what is currently running on your computer. You can see:

- Applications (programs) that are currently in use

- Processes that are currently running on your computer

- General information regarding your computer's performance

To access Task Manager, you press Ctrl+Alt+Del to access the Windows NT Security dialog box. Click the Task Manager button to see the Task Manager utility, shown in Figure 15.6.

Each of the three Task Manager tabs (Applications, Processes, and Performance) are defined in the following subsections. There is a menu selection called Update Speed available throughout Task Manager. Select View ➢ Update Speed to access it. You are able to change this to High, Normal, Low, or Paused. The default is Normal. There are also other menu selections available on each individual tab page.

**FIGURE 15.6**

The Windows NT Task
Manager dialog box

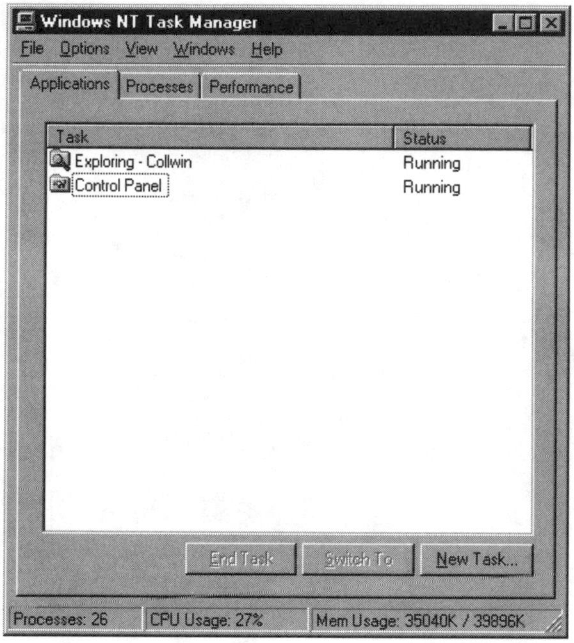

## Applications

The Applications tab page in Task Manager shows the status of all of the programs or tasks currently running on your computer. On the Applications tab page, you can end tasks, switch to a currently running task, or open a new task.

## Processes

The Processes tab page, shown in Figure 15.7, displays all processes that are currently running on your computer. This is a quick way to check on all the processes that are running, as well as their CPU and memory usage. You can also selectively end processes on this tab page.

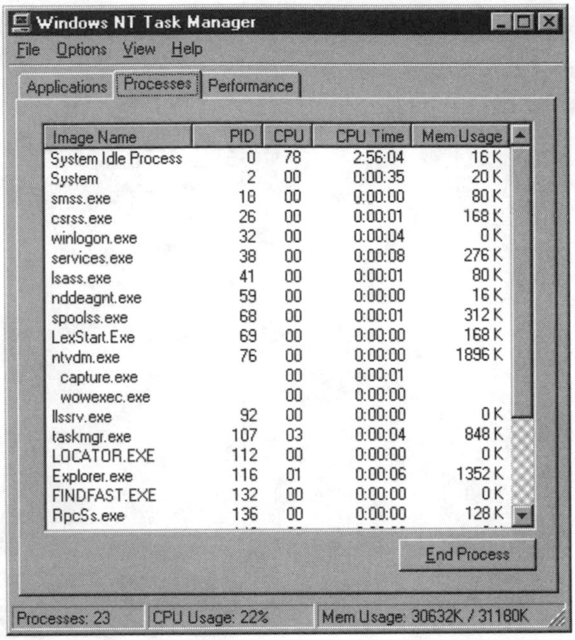

**FIGURE 15.7**

The Task Manager
Processes tab page

**FIGURE 15.7**

The Task Manager
Processes tab page

## Performance

Through the Performance tab page of Task Manager, shown in Figure 15.8, you can see an overview of your computer's performance. This is the same kind of information that you can see through Performance Monitor. Task Manager differs from Performance Monitor in that the Task Manager utility is pre-configured to show you commonly used statistics, and Performance Monitor requires some form of configuration (although through Performance Monitor you can see much more information).

The Performance tab page of Task Manager displays real-time information on:

- CPU usage (graph and real-time)

- Memory usage (graph and real-time)

- Totals for handles, threads, and processes

- Physical memory statistics

- Commit charge memory statistics (commit charge memory is memory allocated to programs or the system)

- Kernel memory statistics

**FIGURE 15.8**

The Task Manager Performance tab page

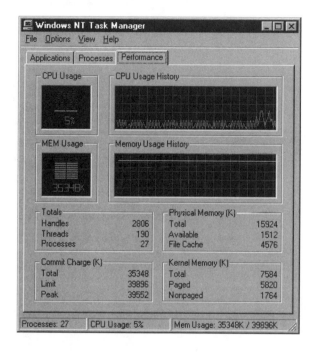

# Chapter Summary

N THIS CHAPTER you learned how to manage system performance through the Performance Monitor and Task Manager.

Through the Performance Monitor you can create baselines, determine system bottlenecks, plan for future growth, and create alerts for problem notification. By using Performance Monitor you can manage your network proactively instead of reactively.

Performance Monitor allows you to take the computer system which, as a whole, could be overwhelming, and break it up into manageable pieces which can then be measured through computer, object, and counters. You can monitor a local computer or a remote computer with Performance Monitor.

Through Performance Monitor, you can also identify system bottlenecks. A bottleneck is a resource that is inefficient compared to the rest of the system; it slows down the entire system. The four most common bottlenecks are memory, CPU, disk access, and network access.

Through Performance Monitor, you can display system data in different formats, called views. The four views that Performance Monitor uses are Chart, Alert, Log, and Report.

NT 4.0 also comes with a new utility called Task Manager. With Task Manager you can view tasks that are currently in use, information on processes currently in use, and general information regarding your computer's overall performance.

# Review Questions

**1.** What needs to be done in order to enable disk counters in Performance Monitor?

**A.** Enable disk counters through Tools in Disk Administrator.

**B.** Enable disk counters through Tools in Performance Monitor.

**C.** Run the DISKMON command.

**D.** Run the DISKPERF command.

**2.** Which utilities can be used to display your CPU's current utilization? Choose all that apply.

**A.** Performance Monitor

**B.** Network Monitor

**C.** Task Manager

**D.** Windows NT Diagnostics

**3.** Which of the following views is not available through Performance Monitor?

   **A.** Chart

   **B.** Report

   **C.** Log

   **D.** Graph

**4.** Which view through Performance Monitor would you choose if you wanted to create a baseline for future reference?

   **A.** Chart

   **B.** Report

   **C.** Log

   **D.** Graph

**5.** Which Server Optimization method is recommended if your server supports under 10 users?

   **A.** Minimize Memory Used

   **B.** Balance

   **C.** Maximize Throughput for File Sharing

   **D.** Manage Throughput for Network Applications

**6.** Which Server Optimization method is recommended if your server supports distributed applications such as SQL server?

   **A.** Minimize Memory Used

   **B.** Balance

   **C.** Maximize Throughput for File Sharing

   **D.** Manage Throughput for Network Applications

# Network Monitor

NE OF THE new features that comes with NT Server 4.0 is a limited version of Network Monitor, which ships with the Systems Management Server (SMS) software. Network monitors are used to capture all those packets whizzing around the cable on your network. By capturing this information, you can troubleshoot network problems. This chapter will cover:

- Overview of Network Monitor

- How to install Network Monitor

- How to capture data with Network Monitor

- How to filter data with Network Monitor

- Network Monitor security features

# Introduction to Network Monitor

ETWORK MONITORS ARE designed to monitor the data that is sent over a network. Data is sent through the network in *frames*, or *packets*. Each frame contains a header which identifies the protocol being used to send the frame, a destination address, a source address, and the data.

Sending packets is very similar to the way we send packages. When I send a package, I can send it through the Post Office, UPS, or Federal Express. These modes of transmission are the regular mail equivalents of the protocols used to send the packet—for example, Transmission Control Protocol (TCP), Server Message Blocks (SMB), or NetBIOS over TCP (NBT). Just as there are other ways of sending packages, there are also other protocols that can be used. Packages sent in the mail contain source and destination addresses. Packets must also contain this information to be correctly delivered. Finally, each package sent through the mail has something in it, otherwise why would you bother? Packets contain the network data.

Normally, we don't go around opening everyone else's packages. A network is the same way. By default, a network card will not look at any information on a packet beyond the packet's source and destination addresses. If the packet is not addressed to the computer's network adapter, then the packet is ignored.

Network monitors really don't care to whom a packet is sent; they are able to capture all packets on a network. As noted, network cards normally only look at the packets that are addressed to the network card in the computer. Network monitors work by using network cards in *promiscuous mode*. Promiscuous mode drivers work by capturing the data of every packet as opposed to packets that are only addressed to the computer network card.

The Network Monitor that ships with NT Server 4.0 is not a fully functional network monitor. It is a limited version of the Network Monitor that ships with SMS (a BackOffice application that can be purchased separately). Instead of being able to capture all of the networks packets, this version of Network Monitor can only capture:

- Frames sent from the server

- Frames sent to the server

- Broadcast frames

- Multicast frames

Because the Network Monitor that ships with NT Server 4.0 is not fully functional and does not capture every network packet, the server's network card driver does not have to run in promiscuous mode. Network Monitor is able to use the network driver interface specification (NDIS) 4.0 that your network card uses anyway. The frames that are detected are then copied to the server's memory in a capture buffer. By using the NDIS 4.0 standard instead of using promiscuous mode, your CPU load is reduced by as much as 30%.

In contrast, the Network Monitor that ships with the SMS product is able to capture all packets on a network, regardless of the source or destination computer address. This requires that the SMS use a promiscuous mode network driver.

# Installing Network Monitor

THE NETWORK MONITOR is installed as a service through Control Panel ➤ Network. In Exercise 16.1, you will install Network Monitor on PDC1.

---

**EXERCISE 16.1**

### Installing Network Monitor

This exercise should be completed from PDC1 while logged on as ADMINISTRATOR.

**1.** Select Start ➤ Settings ➤ Control Panel.

**2.** Double-click Network.

**3.** Click the Services tab.

**4.** Click Add and choose Network Monitor Tools ➤ Agent.

**5.** Click OK. (Insert and provide path for NT Server CD.)

**6.** Click Close in the Network dialog box.

**7.** The Network Settings dialog box will appear prompting you to restart your computer so that the changes can take effect. Click Yes to restart your computer.

---

Once the Network Monitor has been installed you will notice that the following utilities are added to your NT Server:

- Control Panel will include an icon for Monitoring Agent
- Administrative Tools will contain Network Monitor

# Capturing Data with Network Monitor

NCE THE NETWORK Monitor has been installed, you can capture data. You can only capture as much data as will fit into system memory. In this section you will learn how to:

- Manually execute a data capture

- View information generated by a data capture

- Save captured data

## Manually Executing a Data Capture

You can capture data manually at any time by running the Network Monitor and choosing to start a capture. When you are done capturing data, you can simply stop the capture and view the data at a later time, or you can stop and view the data within a single menu choice. In Exercise 16.2, you will execute a data capture manually.

---

**EXERCISE 16.2**

### Executing a Data Capture Manually

This exercise should be completed from PDC1 while you are logged on as ADMINIS-TRATOR. It assumes that you have completed Exercise 16.1.

**1.** Select Start ➢ Programs ➢ Administrative Tools (common) ➢ Network Monitor. You will see the Network Monitor user interface dialog box (see Figure 16.1).

**EXERCISE 16.2 (CONTINUED FROM PREVIOUS PAGE)**

**2.** Select Start from the Capture menu, as shown here.

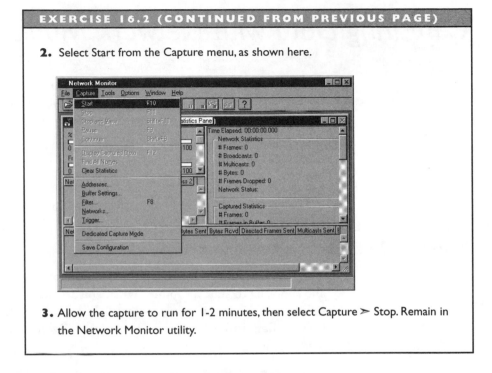

**3.** Allow the capture to run for 1-2 minutes, then select Capture ➢ Stop. Remain in the Network Monitor utility.

The next subsection describes what information is available from the capture session.

## Information Captured by Network Monitor

The Network Monitor is able to provide information in real time and as cumulative, saved data. Notice that the Network Monitor user interface dialog box, shown in Figure 16.1, has four main sections:

- Bar graphs
- Session statistics
- Station statistics
- Summary statistics

FIGURE 16.1

FIGURE 16.1

The Network Monitor
user interface dialog box

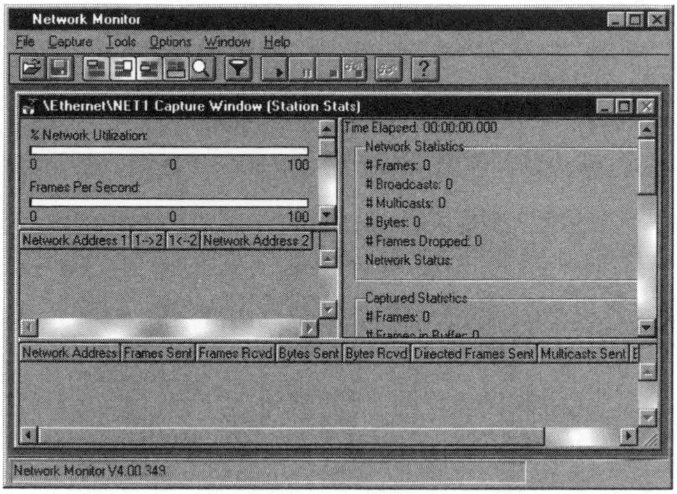

Each of the Network Monitor user interface sections are described in
Table 16.1.

| TABLE 16.1<br><br>Network Monitor<br>user interface<br>sections described | NETWORK MONITOR USER INTERFACE SECTION | DESCRIPTION |
|---|---|---|
| | Bar graphs | Bar graphs provide real-time information on network activity. The bar graphs that are provided are network utilization, frames per second, bytes per second, broadcasts per second, and multicasts per second. The network utilization statistic is especially useful because it can help identify how traffic to and from the server is affecting segment performance. |
| | Session statistics | The session statistics section shows the conversations that are taking place on the network. This information is real-time and cumulative for the capture session. Due to the limitations placed on this utility, you will only see sessions that include the NT Server. |

| TABLE 16.1 | NETWORK MONITOR USER INTERFACE SECTION | DESCRIPTION |
|---|---|---|
| Network Monitor user interface sections described (continued) | Station statistics | Station statistics are a cumulative number and provide information on the network conversations. You can see the network address, frames sent, frames received, bytes sent, bytes received, directed frames sent, multicasts sent, and broadcasts sent. |
| | Summary statistics | Summary statistics are cumulative statistics and include network statistics, captured statistics, per second statistics, network card media access control (MAC) statistics, and network card MAC error statistics. |

During the network capture, all packets that are sent or received by the server are saved in the server's memory buffer. To see the frames that have been captured, you choose Capture ➤ Display Captured Data from the Network Monitor dialog box. You will see a screen similar to that shown in Figure 16.2.

**FIGURE 16.2**

The Network Monitor Capture window

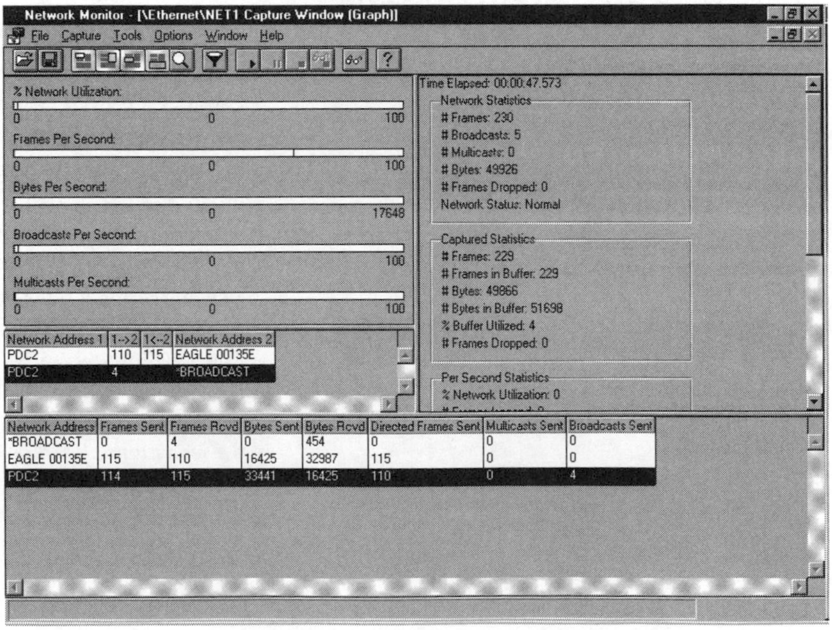

For specific information regarding a packet, you can double-click the packet to see a frame detail screen similar to that in Figure 16.3.

**FIGURE 16.3**

Network Monitor
Capture—Frame detail

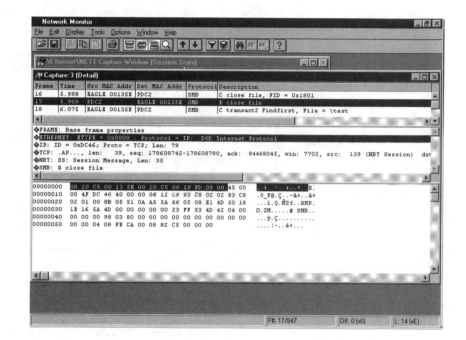

Notice in Figure 16.3 that each frame detail screen consists of three sections:

- Top section: Summary pane

- Middle section: Detail pane

- Bottom section: Hex pane

The summary pane lists all of the frames in the current capture. By highlighting specific frames, the information in the detail pane and hex pane reflects the highlighted frame's information. The summary pane lists columns for the frame number, the time (relative to the capture process), the source MAC address, the destination MAC address, the protocol used to transmit the frame, and a description which is a summary of the frame's content.

The detail pane gives more detailed information on the current frame. It shows all of the protocol information associated with the specific frame. If there is a plus sign (+) to the left of the protocol, then you can click the protocol for more detailed information.

The *hex pane* shows the hexadecimal information associated with the selected frame. The hex values appear to the left of this pane, and the corresponding ASCII character appears to the right of this pane.

In Exercise 16.3, you will examine a frame from the capture you executed in Exercise 16.2.

---

**EXERCISE 16.3**

### Examining Captured Data

This exercise should be completed from PDC1 while you are logged on as ADMINISTRATOR. It assumes that you have completed Exercise 16.2. You should still be in the Network Monitor main dialog screen.

**1.** Select Capture ➢ Display Captured Data.

**2.** The Capture dialog box will appear. Select a frame and double-click anywhere on the frame. You should see something similar to Figure 16.3.

---

## Saving Captured Data

Once data has been captured, you can save it to a file; it can be used for archiving purposes, or it can be sent off to be analyzed by another source. To save captured data, go to File ➢ Save As. You are then prompted to supply a file name. By default, captured data is saved in the root directory that NT Server has been installed to under \SYSTEM32\NETMON\CAPTURES, and the file is saved with a .CAP extension. In Exercise 16.4, you will save the data that was captured in Exercise 16.2.

---

**EXERCISE 16.4**

### Saving Captured Data

This exercise should be completed from PDC1 while you are logged on as ADMINISTRATOR. It assumes that you have completed Exercise 16.2. You should still be in the Network Monitor main dialog screen.

**1.** Select File ➢ Save As.

**2.** The Save Data as... dialog screen will appear. Type **TESTCAPT** and click OK. Your captured data has now been saved.

---

# Filtering Captured Data

I T IS VERY easy to accumulate a large amount of data in a very short amount of time during data captures. In my little test capture, I captured data for 1 minute and 47 seconds. I did some file copies to generate network traffic. This test generated 846 frames. Imagine if you captured data on a production server for a longer period of time. Looking for specific information could be like looking for a needle in a haystack. Luckily, the Network Monitor comes with a filtering capability that allows you to filter displayed frames based on:

- Protocols

- Computer address

- Protocol properties

By default, the filter displays all protocols, all computer addresses, and all protocol properties.

To filter network data, you choose Display ➤ Filter. The Network Monitor Display Filter dialog box will appear, as shown in Figure 16.4. Configure the filter to display frames that match the values you specify.

The following examples illustrate why you would filter data. Assume that you suspect that the network card in Pam's machine is failing and is causing excessive network traffic to the server, even though Pam is not currently using her machine. You can filter and view all of the packets that are being sent from Pam's network card by choosing her network and node address through the Capture filter.

I've also seen documentation that states that if you're not sure what protocol to use (TCP/IP, NWLink IPX/SPX, or NetBEUI) you should install all of them. This isn't such a great idea because it can generate unnecessary network traffic. But, if you did install multiple protocols and you wanted to see what impact each protocol had on server traffic, you could create a filter for each specific protocol and see how many packets each protocol was generating.

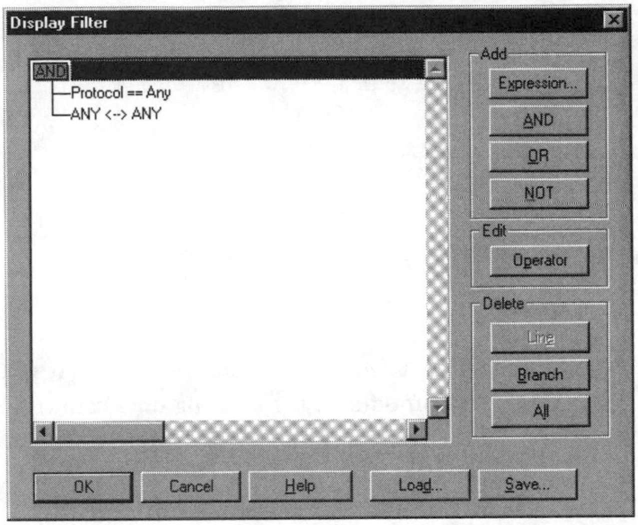

FIGURE 16.4

The Network Monitor
Display Filter dialog box

# Network Monitor Security

A S PREVIOUSLY NOTED, the Network Monitor allows you to view network packets that are transmitted or received by the NT Server. These packets could potentially contain sensitive data that you want to protect. Two security features guard against unauthorized use of Network Monitor.

- Password protection
- Detection of other Network Monitor installations

## Password Protection

In order for Network Monitor to capture packets, the Network Monitoring Agent must first be running. The Network Monitoring Agent is capable of using dual-level passwords that can control who views captured data and who captures and views captured data files.

To access the Network Monitoring Agent configuration screen, you would go to Start ➤ Settings ➤ Control Panel ➤ Monitoring Agent. Once you open the Monitoring Agent applet, you see the Configure Network Monitoring Agent dialog box, shown in Figure 16.5.

**FIGURE 16.5**

The Configure Network Monitoring Agent dialog box

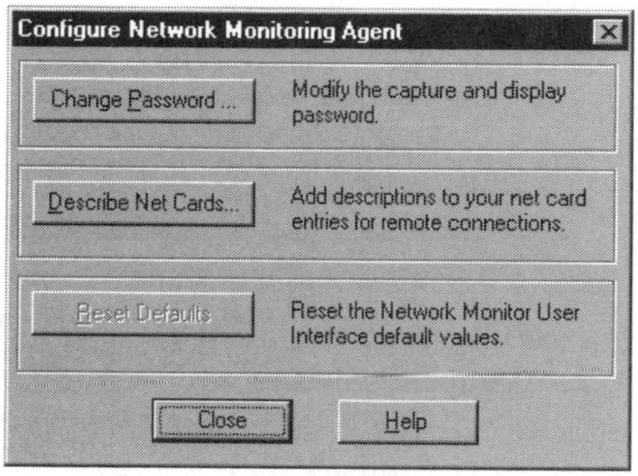

To configure, capture, and display passwords, click Change Password. The Network Monitoring Password Change dialog box, shown in Figure 16.6, will appear.

**FIGURE 16.6**

The Network Monitoring Password Change dialog box

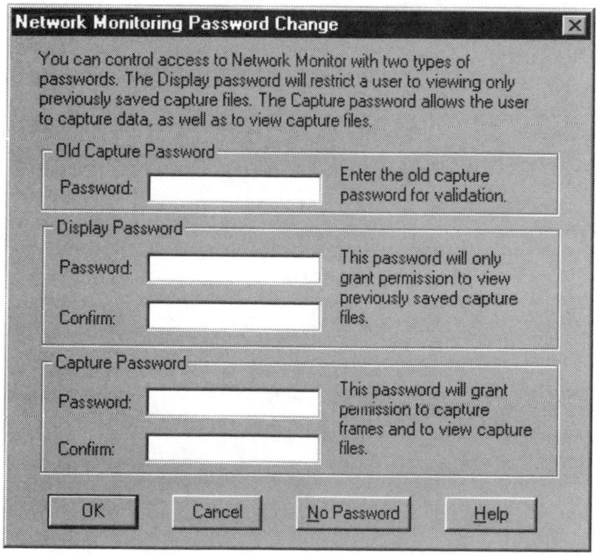

## Detection of Other Network Monitor Installations

Detection of other network monitor installations is very important because if someone else has a network monitor they will be able to see the contents of the packets on the network. Some of these packets may not be encrypted and they may see things like SQL Server user passwords and names. If you monitor the existence of other users capturing and viewing packets, then you will be one step ahead. Through Network Monitor, you are able to detect if others are running Network Monitor (through SMS or NT Server's Network Monitor). If others are running Network Monitor, you will see:

- The computer name from where Network Monitor is running

- The user who is currently logged on to the computer running Network Monitor

- The MAC address of the computer running Network Monitor

- The state of Network Monitor (running, capturing, or transmitting)

- The version of Network Monitor

To detect if others are running Network Monitor, access Network Monitor from the Administrative Tools group and select Tools ≻ Identify Network Monitor Users. Notice, as shown in Figure 16.7, that there are currently two instances of Network Monitor running and that PDC1 is currently running a network capture.

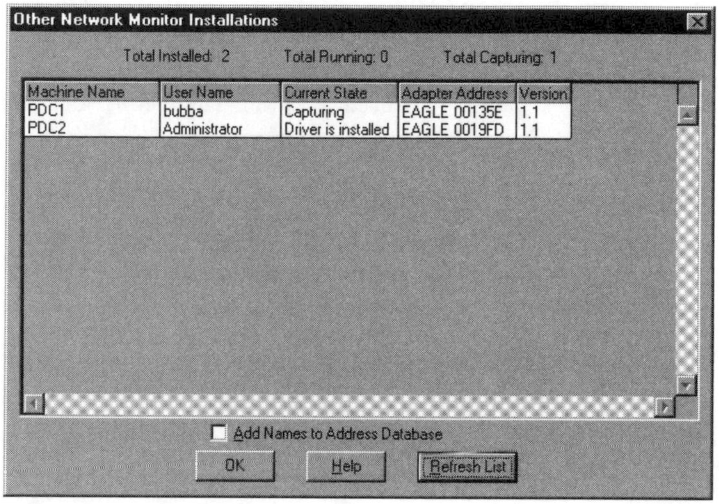

**FIGURE 16.7**

The Other Network
Monitor Installations
dialog box

# Chapter Summary

ETWORK MONITOR IS used to capture packets being sent to or
from NT Server, or to broadcast or multicast frames. It is a limited version of Network Monitor which ships with SMS and is
able to capture network packets from an entire network.

You install the Network Monitor through Control Panel ➤ Network. Once
Network Monitor is installed, you can capture data, and manage Network
Monitor through the Network Monitor utility which appears in the Adminis-
trative Tools group.

You are able to capture as much data as you can fit into your system
memory. Through Network Monitor you can manually execute data captures,
view information generated by a data capture, and save captured data to a file
for future reference or to be analyzed by another source.

Once data has been captured, you can filter it by looking at the protocol it
used, its computer address and its protocol properties. The data filter allows
you to take a large amount of information, and display only the frames that
match your criteria, thus reducing the amount of information presented and
making it more manageable.

Network Monitor also provides some basic security features through password protection and Network Monitor detection. Password protection is two-tiered. The first password can be used to allow a user only to view a previously captured data file. The second level can be used to allow a user to initiate and view a data capture. Through Network Monitor detection you are able to find other instances of Network Monitor that are running on your network. If Network Monitor detects that someone else is running Network Monitor, it will identify the computer, user, network card address, state, and version of Network Monitor.

# Review Questions

1. Which of the following can be tracked with Network Monitor in NT Server? Choose all that apply.

   **A.** Any packet sent over the local network

   **B.** Any packet sent over the network, even packets across a router

   **C.** Packets sent to or from the server

   **D.** Broadcast packets

2. If you want to use a fully functional Network Monitor, which additional package should you purchase?

   **A.** SQL

   **B.** SMS

   **C.** Network Monitor v2.0

   **D.** Network Monitor v3.0

3. Assuming that NT Server has been installed to `C:` in the `WINNT` directory, what is the default directory that captured data is saved in by default through Network Monitor?

   **A.** `C:\WINNT\SYSTEM32\NETMON\CAPTURES`

   **B.** `C:\WINNT\NETMON\CAPTURES`

   **C.** `C:\WINNT\SYSTEM32\REPL\NETMON\CAPTURES`

   **D.** `C:\NETMON\CAPTURES`

4. Which properties can be filtered through the Network Monitor filter process? Choose all that apply.

   **A.** Hex strings

   **B.** Protocols

   **C.** Computer address

   **D.** Protocol properties

5. Where would you set a password that could only be used to view previously saved network captures with Network Monitor?

   **A.** Network Monitor through Administrative Tools

   **B.** Network Monitor through Control Panel

   **C.** Monitoring Agent through Administrative Tools

   **D.** Monitoring Agent through Control Panel

# Hard Disk Configurations for Fault Tolerance

An important area of network management is planning for fault tolerance. Fault tolerance ensures data integrity in the event of hardware failure. In this chapter you will learn about the fault tolerance NT Server provides through the two levels of *Redundant Arrays of Inexpensive Disks* (RAID) it supports. You will also learn how to recover from hard disk failure when using RAID.

# RAID Support

RAID is an industry standard that defines fault tolerance for disk subsystems. The idea is that hard drives are not 100% reliable (can you believe that?), and by implementing RAID systems, you are able to increase your fault tolerance. RAID can be implemented through hardware or software solutions.

Hardware implementations of RAID are vendor-specific and usually very expensive. The advantage of using vendor-specific RAID subsystems is that you will typically get better performance, and some vendors offer plug-and-play recoverability through hot-swappable drives. The negative aspects of hardware RAID implementations are the cost and the fact that you become married to a single vendor.

NT comes with a software RAID implementation; this means that you can use any vendor's hardware and your expense is less. Though it's flexible and cost efficient, you do trade performance and convenience.

## Levels of RAID

There are six levels of RAID. Each level offers different price, performance and reliability features. Table 17.1 defines the six levels of RAID.

| TABLE 17.1 | RAID LEVEL | DESCRIPTION |
|---|---|---|
| Six levels of RAID | RAID 0 | Disk striping without parity. Provides performance enhancements, but no fault tolerance. |
| | RAID 1 | Disk mirroring. |
| | RAID 2 | Disk striping with error-correction code. Not currently implemented. |
| | RAID 3 | Disk striping with error-correction code stored as parity. Not currently implemented. |
| | RAID 4 | Disk striping, all parity is stored on one drive. Not currently implemented. |
| | RAID 5 | Disk striping, parity is distributed across all drives in stripe set. |

# RAID Supported by NT

NT Server supports RAID 0, RAID 1, and RAID 5. RAID 0 is not considered a fault tolerant RAID solution. RAID 1 and RAID 5 are considered to be fault tolerant. We will never use RAID levels 2, 3, and 4; they are part of the evolution of the RAID standard, but are not used today.

RAID 1 and RAID 5 are supported on NT Server, but are not available on NT Workstation. To implement RAID, use Administrative Tools ➢ Disk Administrator ➢ Fault Tolerance.

I explain RAID 1 and RAID 5 in the next sections.

### RAID 1: Disk Mirroring

*Disk mirroring* is the process of mirroring one hard drive to another. The mirrored drive contains an exact duplicate of the data stored on the primary disk. The purpose of disk mirroring is to ensure that the secondary drive will continue to function without any loss of service if the primary drive fails. This is the fastest form of data recovery because the mirror set contains the exact data from the primary drive, and there is no need to regenerate the data, as there is in using RAID 5.

Any partition can be mirrored, including the system and boot partition. The only requirement is that the primary and mirrored partition must be the same size. Figure 17.1 illustrates disk mirroring.

**FIGURE 17.1**

Disk mirroring

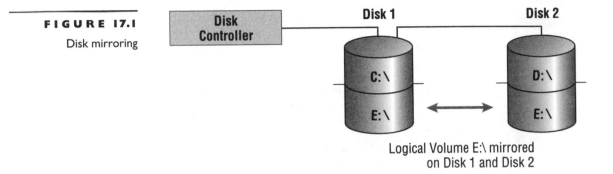

Logical Volume E:\ mirrored on Disk 1 and Disk 2

Disk mirroring assumes that you have one controller and two hard drives. The driver that is responsible for making sure that the two drives are mirrored is called FTDISK.SYS. The disadvantage of disk mirroring is that you will have a performance decrease on write operations because one controller has to write to both hard drives.

*Disk mirroring is not fault tolerant if your disk controller fails.*

*Disk duplexing* is an extension of disk mirroring and provides more fault tolerance by adding a second disk controller to your mirrored set. Disk duplexing has two advantages over disk mirroring. Because it uses two controllers, disk duplexing provides more fault tolerance and offers better write performance. The disadvantage of disk duplexing is that it's more costly than disk mirroring. Both disk mirroring and disk duplexing are configured the same way through NT Server. Figure 17.2 illustrates disk duplexing.

### RAID 5: Disk Striping with Parity

RAID level 5 is *disk striping with parity*. In order to support RAID 5, you need to have at least three drives and a maximum of 32 drives. Each drive must have a logical partition with free space on it that is equal in size to the free space on the other drives that will be a part of the stripe set. For example, if you had three drives, two with 150MB of free space and one with 100MB of

**FIGURE 17.2**

Disk duplexing

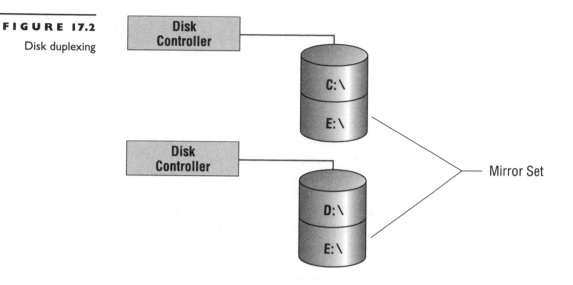

free space, you would only be able to use 100MB from each drive (as you are limited by the smallest partition). Your stripe set would be assigned a single drive letter, and the data would be written evenly across all the stripe sets. This allows for better performance because you are able to utilize multiple I/O channels.

The parity information is mathematical calculations of the data contained on a disk. If any single disk within the stripe set fails, the parity information can be used to regenerate the data once the failed drive has been replaced.

In Figure 17.3, the RAID 5 implementation is using a four-drive system. Each of the four drives contains a parity stripe.

**FIGURE 17.3**

Disk striping with parity

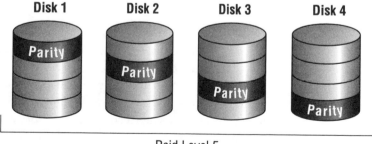

Raid Level 5
Disk Array

If one drive in the array fails you can still access the data through reconstructed parity information. Due to the parity recalculation, you will need approximately three times as much memory for the parity recalculation. Read performance is also slower on a system with a failed drive. If two or more drives fail, you are out of luck, and will need to replace the drives and restore from tape backup.

When you set up disk striping with parity you can use three to 32 drives. As you use more drives in your array, parity striping becomes more efficient. The parity stripes are equal to one drive's space in the array. Assume that you are using four drives in your RAID 5 set. Each drive must dedicate 25% of its space for the parity stripe. The four drives multiplied by 25% space they allocate then equals one drive. With five drives, each drive would only give up 20% of its space for parity. If you implemented 20 drives, then the ratio would drop to 5%.

*The system and boot partition cannot be contained within a striped partition.*

*After configuring either Raid 1 or 5, be sure to use the menu option Commit Changes now or your changes will not be saved right away.*

# Recovering from Disk Failure in a RAID Environment

THE PURPOSE OF using RAID is that in the event of hard drive failure, you are able to recover fairly easily. It is not enough just to set up the fault tolerance and consider your task complete. You must also have a tried-and-true disaster recovery plan. The purpose of a disaster recovery plan is to prepare you to cope with trouble when it strikes. You should also test that your recovery plan will work; in this instance that means testing your RAID 1 or RAID 5 implementation.

Successful disaster recovery relies on two things—that you have some form of fault tolerance implemented and that you have a viable recovery plan. This is especially important in an environment where you are using RAID for fault tolerance. The next two subsections will examine recovery from a failure in an environment using RAID 1 (disk mirroring) and RAID 5 (striping with parity).

# Recovering from Disk Mirroring Failure

As noted earlier, disk mirroring can be done on a system or boot partition or on a regular data partition. Depending on what has been mirrored, there are different steps to take to recover from a hard drive failure. In the next two subsections, you will learn how to recover if the data partition fails, and how to recover if the system or boot partition fails.

### Disk Mirroring Failure on a Data Partition

If the disk drive that fails is a data partition, it is fairly easy to repair the mirror set. Follow these steps:

1. Using the Disk Administrator utility, break the mirror set (breaking the mirror set disables disk mirroring and allows each drive to function independently) and delete the failed partition.

2. Replace the failed hardware.

3. Using the free space on the replaced hardware, use the Disk Administrator utility to establish a new mirrored set.

### Disk Mirroring Failure on a System or Boot Partition

If the disk drive that fails is a system or boot partition, the mirroring recovery process becomes more complex. Here's why. While booting, NT accesses a file called BOOT.INI. The BOOT.INI file is responsible for pointing to the location of the NT boot partition through an Advanced RISC (Reduced Instruction Set Computing) Computing (ARC) name. By default, this file points to the ordinal number of the partition where you installed the NT system files. If your boot partition fails, the mirrored drive contains an exact copy of the BOOT.INI file that points NT to the failed partition. In this case, NT will not boot and the mirroring is not fault tolerant.

To overcome this problem, create an NT startup floppy disk that can be used to boot NT from the mirrored drive. In order to create a startup floppy disk, you will first need to determine what the mirrored drive's ARC name is, and create an alternate BOOT.INI file. The following is an example of an ARC name:

```
Multi(0)Disk(0)Rdisk(0)Partition(1)
```

Table 17.2 defines the ARC naming conventions and refers to the following structure:

```
Multi/SCSI(w)Disk(x)Rdisk(y)Partition(z)
```

| **TABLE 17.2**<br>ARC naming conventions | **ARC CONVENTION** | **DEFINITION** |
| --- | --- | --- |
| | Multi/SCSI | Multi is used to define Integrated Drive Electronics (IDE) controllers or SCSI controllers with the BIOS enabled. SCSI is used to define SCSI controllers with the BIOS disabled. |
| | (w) | Ordinal number of the hardware adapter. |
| | Disk(x) | SCSI bus number. This number is only applicable if using the SCSI convention. If you use MULTI this number is always 0. |
| | Rdisk(y) | In an IDE environment it is the ordinal of the disk on the controller and will be 0 or 1. On a SCSI controller it is the SCSI logical unit number (LUN) of the disk that contains the boot partition. |
| | Partition(z) | The partition number on the disk where the boot partition is contained. This number starts with 1 unlike all other entries, which begin with 0. |

Once you have determined the ARC path for your mirrored drive, you need to create an NT startup floppy disk that can be used to boot the mirrored drive. Create the NT startup disk by following these steps (assuming you are using an Intel platform):

1. While running NT, format the floppy disk through the My Computer option or through Run ➤ Format.

**2.** Copy the following files from the root of your active partition to the floppy (these files are flagged hidden, system, and read-only and will need to be unflagged in order to be copied):

- NTLDR

- NTDETECT.COM

- BOOTSECT.DOS (if dual-booting to another OS)

- NTBOOTD.SYS (if using the SCSI option in BOOT.INI)

- the BOOT.INI file you edited to reflect the mirrored partition

After you have created the NT startup boot disk, test it by booting the NT computer with it before a problem occurs. Once you have tested the floppy, put it in a safe place.

Now if your primary system or boot partition fails, you can boot with the NT startup boot diskette, break the mirror and delete the failed partition. After the hardware is replaced, you can create a new volume and reestablish the mirror. Assuming the hardware is in the same configuration as the replaced hardware, you can now boot without the floppy disk, and the BOOT.INI file should point to the correct location of the boot partition. If the new hardware is not in the same configuration as the replaced hardware, edit the BOOT.INI file to reflect the proper location of the boot partition.

## Recovering from Disk Failure on a Stripe Set with Parity

If a drive within a stripe set with parity fails, you can still access the data by reconstructing it from the parity stripes. To return the system to full working condition, you will first need to replace the failed drive. The new drive must have free space equal to the original failed drive. From the Disk Administrator utility you can then select Fault Tolerance ➤ Regenerate and regenerate the data on the new drive.

When using stripe set with parity you might consider installing an extra drive in the server and leaving the free space available. This way if you have a failure, all you need to do is regenerate the stripe set without any down time. At the very least, you should consider keeping a spare hard drive around. The cost of hard drives is so low compared to what down time costs, that it makes sense to keep spare hardware.

If two or more of the drives within your stripe set fail, you are out of luck. At this point, you would need to replace your hardware and restore your data from your normal backup system. A stripe set with parity does not replace the need to perform regular backups.

# Chapter Summary

I N THIS CHAPTER you learned about disk configurations that can be used in a fault tolerant environment. You learned that, through NT software and your hardware, your hard drives can be configured for disk mirroring (RAID 1) or for disk striping with parity (RAID 5).

Disk mirroring involves duplicating the information within one partition on a disk to another partition on another disk. This exact copy can be used in the event of a hard drive failure. The benefits of disk mirroring are that you can mirror any partition type and performance is not affected in the event of failure. The drawback of disk mirroring is that you have a 50% disk-space overhead, meaning that if you have two 100MB partitions, only 100 of the 200MB is actually useful; the second 100MB contains the mirror.

Disk striping with parity is another form of disk fault tolerance. In the event of hard drive failure, data can be regenerated with the parity information. This affects performance and requires more system RAM. Disk striping with parity can be done on data drives, but it cannot contain a system or boot partition. If you use disk striping with parity you are able to use between three and 32 drives. As the number of drives increases, the cost in MB used for parity information decreases, which makes it a more cost efficient means of fault tolerance.

# Review Questions

1. You have a system and boot partition on drive C:. You want to protect them with disk fault tolerance. Which options of RAID can you use through NT Server software? Choose all that apply.

   **A.** RAID 1

   **B.** RAID 2

   **C.** RAID 3

   **D.** RAID 4

   **E.** RAID 5

2. Your primary drive in a mirrored set has just failed. The drive contains the boot partition. What is the best way to recover from the failure?

   **A.** Replace the failed hardware, use the NT startup disk you created prior to failure, regenerate the mirror set.

   **B.** Replace the failed hardware, use the NT emergency repair disk, regenerate the mirror set.

   **C.** Replace the failed hardware and boot to the Last Known Good option and then regenerate the failed set.

   **D.** Replace the failed hardware and restore your system through your tape backup.

3. One of your drives fails in your stripe set with parity. What do you do?

   **A.** Replace the failed hardware, use the NT startup disk you created prior to failure, regenerate the stripe set.

   **B.** Replace the failed hardware, use the NT emergency repair disk, regenerate the stripe.

   **C.** Replace the failed hardware and use Disk Administrator to regenerate the stripe set.

   **D.** Replace the failed hardware and restore your system through your tape backup.

**4.** Two of your drives fail in your stripe set with parity. What do you do?

    **A.** Replace the failed hardware, use the NT startup disk you created prior to failure, regenerate the stripe set.

    **B.** Replace the failed hardware, use the NT emergency repair disk, regenerate the stripe.

    **C.** Replace the failed hardware and use Disk Administrator to regenerate the stripe set.

    **D.** Replace the failed hardware and restore your system through your tape backup.

**5.** Which RAID levels are supported through NT Server software? Choose all that apply.

    **A.** RAID 1

    **B.** RAID 2

    **C.** RAID 3

    **D.** RAID 4

    **E.** RAID 5

# NT
# Troubleshooting

TROUBLESHOOTING AN NT network is one of the most challenging tasks of NT administration. Troubleshooting is a four-step process that involves identifying a problem, diagnosing a problem, implementing a solution, and verifying that the solution has solved the problem.

Because NT is such a feature-rich product, there are many areas you need to check when you encounter a problem (but hey, that's why they pay us the big bucks). In this chapter, we will cover many of the common areas to check when troubleshooting. The four main areas of NT Troubleshooting are as follows:

- Hardware configuration troubleshooting

- Resource troubleshooting

- Repair strategies

- Advanced problem resolution

The hardware configuration troubleshooting section will address errors that occur during installation, boot failures, errors in the BOOT.INI file, and configuration errors. We will explore some of the most common errors, such as media errors, misspellings during configuration, incorrect or outdated drivers, and missing or corrupted system files. We will examine the BOOT.INI file in detail, and we will discuss using the NT Diagnostics utility.

In the resource troubleshooting section, we will look for reasons and solutions for problems in the following categories: Printing, Remote Access Service (RAS), Connectivity, and File and Resource Access. Printing problems can surface after a network has been running successfully for a period of time. Solving printing problems will include examining the physical connections, printer definitions, spooling service, and disk space. We will look at protocols, frame types, and encryption to solve connectivity issues. In troubleshooting Files and Resources, we will refer to File and Directory rights, and Security Access Manager use.

Once an administrator identifies a problem, they can move on to the next level, repair strategies. In this section we will look at solutions to problems. Problems you may encounter include deleted or corrupted files that you need to restore from a previous version; these files are available from multiple sources.

Some methods that can be used as repair strategies are as follows. The Last Known Good configuration represents the set of parameters that existed during the most recent successful logon. The Emergency Repair Disk allows the restoration of many critical system files needed for NT to start. Specific files, or the entire system, can be restored from a backup. Aside from restoring specific files, the Registry can be edited to correct specific problems. The Event Log can also assist in identifying common errors.

Advanced problem resolution includes Blue Screen interpretation (the Blue Screen occurs when NT fails to boot successfully or encounters a serious failure), Kernel debugging, and Memory Dump examination. Only an experienced support engineer can interpret the results of these tools. This section will provide assistance in explaining specific items from the Blue Screen. We will also discuss how to use the Kernel Debugger and how to configure and use the Memory Dump.

# *Hardware Configuration Troubleshooting*

I N HARDWARE CONFIGURATION troubleshooting, we will cover media errors, dependency services errors and other issues. We will also cover boot failures with all the primary files on the system partition. One important file in particular will be covered separately—the BOOT.INI file. This file is responsible for informing the NT Loader file (NTLDR) where the boot partition is to load Windows NT. The final subsection covers general configuration error troubleshooting.

## Installation

During installation, you may encounter various errors, such as the following:

- Media errors

- Problems connecting to the domain controller

- Blue Screen or stop message errors

- Incorrect hardware configuration

Here are some suggestions for dealing with the above problems.

If Media Errors are displayed during installation, it could mean that there are problems with your CD-ROM player or your network connection. Try another media type, such as another CD-ROM, or copy the contents of the CD-ROM onto your hard drive manually. If either of these processes are successful, then the corrective step would be to replace the original media type for future installations.

The message "Inability to connect to the Domain controller" is usually a result of one of the following problems: incorrect spelling of the domain, incorrect network settings, or the domain controller being offline. If you are not sure the domain controller is functioning properly as an NT server, then check it physically and make sure it is. If the other clients are connected to the domain controller, then check to see if the network settings are correct. These settings can be verified with the original setup disk provided by the network interface card manufacturer.

If you are unable to bypass the Blue Screen when booting NT, check the screen contents to ensure that the proper drivers are being utilized. A typical error would be an incorrect or outdated driver for a SCSI controller. Ensure that the driver is the most current one available from the manufacturer. Most major manufacturers make their latest drivers available on their corporate Web sites. For more information, please see the Blue Screen subsection.

After installation, one or more of the dependency services may fail to start. For example, if the network interface card driver doesn't start, then the *dependency services*—the server service, the workstation service and several other services—will not start either. If this occurs, check the Event Log with the event viewer and find the oldest error. If you cannot find an error in the log, then check all your system's hardware components.

# Boot Failures

Now that installation is complete, you may encounter additional challenges. Perhaps after months of successful NT server operation, an error is suddenly displayed during the boot process. One reason for this may be because the boot process may not be able to locate a critical file that is relied upon to successfully start NT. The primary files that are located on the system partition are:

- NTLDR: The "NT Loader" file takes control of the entire boot process until it passes control to the NTOSKRNL.EXE application once the NT operating system menu option is selected.

- BOOT.INI: This initialization file contains the information that includes the location of the NT boot partition. It is also responsible for the menu choices displayed on bootup.

- BOOTSECT.DOS: This file takes control from NTLDR if you are running an operating system other than Windows NT.

- NTDETECT.COM: This application detects the hardware installed and adds the hardware list to the registry.

The following are the common error messages that you may receive if any of these files are missing.

### NTDRL Error Message

If NTLDR is missing or if the floppy drive A: contains a diskette, you will see the following error message:

"BOOT: Couldn't find NTLDR. Please insert another disk."

If NTLDR is missing, go through the repair process described at the end of this subsection. If you have a diskette in drive A:, then remove the diskette and press any key to continue the boot process.

### NTOSKRNL Missing Error Message

The file NTOSKRNL.EXE can be perceived as missing because of corrupted files or, more commonly, because the BOOT.INI file points to the wrong partition, disk or controller. If the NTOSKRNL.EXE file is perceived as missing, you will see the following error message:

"Windows NT could not start because the following file is missing or corrupt:

> \winnt root\system32\ntoskrnl.exe

Please re-install a copy of the above file."

Use the repair process to fix this error if the NTOSKRNL.EXE file is in fact corrupt. If the BOOT.INI settings are incorrect, refer to the BOOT.INI subsection in this chapter for information on how to correct them.

### BOOT.INI Missing Error Message

If the BOOT.INI file is missing, the NTLDR will try to boot NT from the default directory of the active partition \WINNT. If this fails, then the NTLDR error message will appear. This is because NTLDR will not be able to find NTOSKRNL.EXE without the proper path. The BOOT.INI file is covered in more detail in the "BOOT.INI Configuration File" section of this chapter.

### BOOTSECT.DOS Missing Error Message

If the BOOTSECT.DOS file is missing while attempting to boot to MS-DOS or another operating system (other than Windows NT), you may receive this error message:

"I/O Error accessing boot sector file

> multi (0) disk(0) rdisk (0) partition (1):\bootsect.dos"

You can use the repair process described below to fix this error.

### NTDETECT.COM Missing Error Message

If the NTDETECT.COM file is missing, the following error message will appear:

"NTDETECT V1.0 Checking Hardware . . .
NTDETECT failed"

The NTDETECT.COM file error can be corrected with the repair process as well.

### Repair Process

You can repair all of the failures discussed above with the Emergency Repair Disk (ERD). If you have previously made an ERD, and you have the Windows NT setup disks, then you can perform the repair process described below (see Exercise 18.1 to create an ERD):

**1.** Boot with the Windows NT setup disks 1 & 2.

**2.** Choose R for repair.

**3.** Insert the Windows NT disk 3.

**4.** Insert the ERD when requested to do so.

**5.** Select "Verify Windows NT system files."

**6.** Choose the components you want to restore.

*If you do not already have the Windows NT setup boot disks, then you can create them on another machine with the WINNT/ ox command.*

*The ERD is unique for each computer; you should not use an ERD created from any machine except your own.*

## BOOT.INI Configuration File

The BOOT.INI file is a very important file to understand because it informs NTLDR of the location for the boot partition. If this file is edited incorrectly, or if system changes are made without corresponding changes being made to this file, then the NT operating system will not be able to start. Here is an example of a BOOT.INI file.

```
[boot loader]
timeout=15
default=multi(0)disk(0)rdisk(0)partition(1)\WINNT
[operating systems]
```

```
multi(0)disk(0)rdisk(1)partition(1)\WINNT="Windows NT
   Server Version 4.00"
```

```
multi(0)disk(0)rdisk(0)partition(1)\WINNT="Windows NT
   Server Version 4.00 [VGA mode]"
```

```
/basevideo /sos
```

```
C:\="MS-DOS"
```

Let's examine each section of this file in detail. The timeout variable represents the number of seconds NT will wait before executing your default choice. Under the [operating systems] header are the choices of operating systems available to boot. When the server starts up, a menu listing these operating systems will be displayed. In this example, you see three choices.

■ "Windows NT Server Version 4.00"

■ "Windows NT Server Version 4.00 [VGA mode]"

■ "MS-DOS"

The information preceding the menu choices tells the NTLDR application where the operating system is located. Here are some location examples:

```
scsi(0)disk(0)rdisk(0)partition(1)\WINNT="Windows NT
   Server Version 4.00"
```

This statement shows:

■ The SCSI controller does not have the BIOS enabled.

■ The boot partition is on SCSI ID 0.

■ RDISK is on 0 because we are using SCSI without the BIOS enabled.

■ The boot partition is located on partition 1.

```
multi(0)disk(0)rdisk(1)partition(1)\WINNT="Windows NT
   Server Version 4.00"
```

This statement shows:

■ Multi means that we may have a SCSI controller with the BIOS enabled, or a non-SCSI controller without the BIOS enabled.

■ The disk parameter should remain 0 because it is not a SCSI controller without the BIOS enabled.

- The boot partition is on the primary controller if it is SCSI, and on Logical Unit Number (LUN) 2 if it is EIDE.

- The boot partition is located on partition 1.

The naming scheme used above is called *Arc naming*. Let's break this down into its individual components.

The first component is the type of disk controller installed in the system—multi or scsi. scsi is selected only when a SCSI device is installed and when the BIOS has not been enabled. Multi is used in all alternate configurations.

The second component is the disk value. The default value for disk is 0. This value changes only if a SCSI controller is used. In this case, the disk value should be set to the SCSI ID of target disk.

The third component is rdisk. The default value for rdisk starts with 0 and it is changed only if a multi disk controller is used. The allowed values are 0-1 if the disk is connected to the primary controller, and 0-3 if the disk is on a dual-channel EIDE controller. The value will refer to the LUN of the disk that contains the boot partition.

The fourth component refers to the partition number that serves as the boot partition for the system. The default value for partition is 1. This number is determined during installation and should only be changed if you are creating a fault tolerance disk as discussed in Chapter 17, "Hard Disk Configurations for Fault Tolerance," or if you are advised to do so when using Disk Administrator.

*When using Disk Administrator, be sure to pay careful attention to the pop-up messages. If you have used Disk Administrator to create or delete logical partitions, you might see a pop-up message letting you know that you need to edit the BOOT.INI file to reflect new ordinal numbers. If any of the ordinal numbers are changed by manipulating the partitions, you will not be able to restart Windows NT.*

## Configuration Errors

If there are configuration errors, a pop-up dialog box will probably appear to inform you of it and instruct you to check the event viewer. If the system's configuration has been modified recently, you could try to use the Last Known Good configuration. If not, you will need to investigate further to determine the source of the error.

One useful place to check for information is Windows NT Diagnostics. To run this application, click Start ➢ Programs ➢ Administrative Tools (common) ➢ Windows NT Diagnostics. From this utility, you can print out a report, or go through each tab page manually to determine where the problem is. The first place I would check is the Resources tab page. This shows you all the devices one by one, the drivers loaded, the IRQs (interrupts) used, and more. This process is easier if the event viewer has already identified the possible problem. Table 18.1 is a guide to the information available on each tab page of Windows NT Diagnostics.

| **TABLE 18.1**<br><br>Windows NT diagnostic information | **TAB PAGE** | **INFORMATION AVAILABLE** |
|---|---|---|
| | Version | Operating system version, type of processor |
| | System | Type of system, which hardware abstraction layer (HAL), BIOS date, type of CPU |
| | Display | BIOS version, display setting, driver used and all the components |
| | Drives | Logical partitions, network connections |
| | Memory | How much physical memory, file cache amount, memory currently available |
| | Services | The setting of the services that are running (automatic, manual) |
| | Resources | Which drivers are loaded and the setting (manual, automatic, boot, system), IRQs used, devices used, and the memory address and length, direct memory access (DMA) used |
| | Environment | System and current user environment variables |
| | Network | User access information, bindings, settings on network parameters |

Remember, if the event viewer states that something cannot be started because of a dependency service, you need to keep looking at previous messages until you find out which driver failed. For example, if the network interface card driver fails, then the server service, and the workstation service and many more services will fail to start because they all depend on network access, and rely on the network interface card to work before they can be initialized.

*It's a good idea to keep a log of diagnostic printouts to document what has changed.*

# Resource Troubleshooting

G ENERAL RESOURCE TROUBLESHOOTING includes: Printing problems, RAS problems, Connectivity problems and File and Resource Access problems.

## Printing Problems

Printing problems are frequent on a network that has been in operation for a lengthy period. Here are a few areas to check if you are having trouble with your printers.

- Check the physical connections first. Next, you will need to logically follow the printing process flow, as shown in Chapter 8, "Printing." If the printing problem still persists, look into the following areas to continue your diagnosis.

- If there is a problem with the print manager, check the printer. Print manager problems include the inability to create a local printer or to install a particular type of printer. If you have either of these problems, then delete and recreate the printer.

- If a job seems to disappear, and no one can print to the printer, start and restart the spooler service. The spooler is in charge of routing the job, so if the job disappears, then it was probably routed incorrectly, or is stuck in the spooler.

- Always check if there is enough disk space where you are spooling. A lack of disk space will produce error messages, because the machine will not be able to spool the job to the hard disk. If you have large print jobs and you choose to retain them, this is a very common error.

- Be sure to use the correct printer driver. An incorrect printer driver will cause output that does not meet the users' expectations. This scenario is commonly found with individual users (running another operating system) who access the printer as a shared network printer or choose the wrong printer driver.

## Troubleshooting Remote Access Server (RAS)

The following are some of the common errors which may occur with RAS:

- If you have problems with Point-to-Point Protocol (PPP), then turn the PPP log on by changing the Registry parameter from 0 to 1. The Registry parameter is located in:

  `\HKEY_LOCAL_MACHINE\System\CurrentControlSet\`
  `Services\Rasman\PPP\Logging.`

- The PPP log will be stored in:

  `\Winnt_root\System32\Ras\PPP.Log`

- If you are having problems connecting to a remote server, try changing the encryption level to clear text. If that works, then try increasing each side's authentication until you find the highest level that works.

- Check the Dial-up Networking Monitor for the number of errors.

## Connectivity Troubleshooting

If you are having problems connecting to another machine over the network, check the following items:

- For NWLink, check the frame type. There may be a mismatch.

- You may be using a different protocol from the server or the rest of the network.

- The network may have a high load resulting in slow network traffic.

- Check for a correct TCP/IP address if you are not using a DHCP server.

## File and Resource Access

If your users are having trouble accessing any resources, including files and directories, check the following areas:

- If a user is having problems accessing certain files or directories, check the share rights versus the local rights (for NTFS). Remember that your user will receive the more restrictive of the two options.

- For file and directory access, also check the subdirectories and files rights versus the parent directories rights. While assigning rights, you may have forgotten to check the Apply to subdirectories option.

- Also, check to verify that the particular user does not belong to any groups without access rights. Remember that group rights override any other sets of rights you may give to that user.

- Is it possible that the access token has not been refreshed? You can force an automatic refresh of the token by logging off the network and logging on again.

- If the above steps still do not permit the user to access the resource, try logging on as a different user to determine if they can access the resource. This allows you to narrow down the scope of the problem. If another user is able to access the resource, then you can focus your efforts on the access rights of the client. If no one is able to access the resource, then the problem lies with the rights assigned at the server.

- The final task to try is restoring the SAM database. You may need to do this if the SAM database is corrupt. You could use the ERD and the repair process to restore the SAM database.

# Repair Strategies

N TRYING TO repair the Windows NT system, there are many methods available. Some methods can be undone and some are more permanent. The first place to look if you are having errors is in the Event Log. You can do this through the Event Viewer. If the problem lies in a driver you have just installed, then you can reboot and use the Last Known Good configuration. If the problem persists, then you can try looking in the registry for clues.

If you are still unsure what the problem could be, or if you can narrow it down to the registry, then try using the ERD to restore and check the files on your machine. If that doesn't work, then restore from your backup.

This is the order in which we will be covering these topics:

- Event Log
- Last Known Good
- Registry
- ERD
- Restore from backup

## Event Log

Within the Event Viewer, you can see Event Logs from three different areas of NT: System, Security and Application. There are five different types of events recorded: Error, Information, Warning, Success Audit, and Failure Audit. Depending on which log you are checking and which services are enabled, you will see different event types.

The System Log would have information about general system health, including items such as services not starting, a browsing election, printing problems, and hardware conflicts. The System Log is shown in Figure 18.1.

**FIGURE 18.1**

The Event Viewer showing a System Log

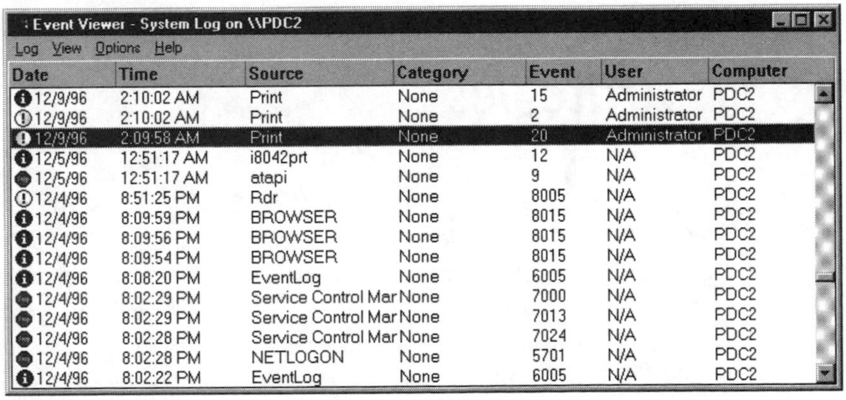
Event Viewer - System Log on \\PDC2
Log View Options Help
Date Time Source Category Event User Computer
12/9/96 2:10:02 AM Print None 15 Administrator PDC2
12/9/96 2:10:02 AM Print None 2 Administrator PDC2
12/9/96 2:09:58 AM Print None 20 Administrator PDC2
12/5/96 12:51:17 AM i8042prt None 12 N/A PDC2
12/5/96 12:51:17 AM atapi None 9 N/A PDC2
12/4/96 8:51:25 PM Rdr None 8005 N/A PDC2
12/4/96 8:09:59 PM BROWSER None 8015 N/A PDC2
12/4/96 8:09:56 PM BROWSER None 8015 N/A PDC2
12/4/96 8:09:54 PM BROWSER None 8015 N/A PDC2
12/4/96 8:08:20 PM EventLog None 6005 N/A PDC2
12/4/96 8:02:29 PM Service Control Mar None 7000 N/A PDC2
12/4/96 8:02:29 PM Service Control Mar None 7013 N/A PDC2
12/4/96 8:02:28 PM Service Control Mar None 7024 N/A PDC2
12/4/96 8:02:28 PM NETLOGON None 5701 N/A PDC2
12/4/96 8:02:22 PM EventLog None 6005 N/A PDC2

Table 18.2 explains each column of the Event Viewer.

| TABLE 18.2 | COLUMN | DEFINITION |
|---|---|---|
| Definition of Event Viewer columns | Date | Date of event |
| | Time | Time of event |
| | Source | Service Source |
| | Category | Type of event (used especially in the Security Log) |
| | Event | Event ID |
| | User | User associated with event |
| | Computer | Computer name where event occurred |

The Security Log, shown in Figure 18.2, contains the Audit trail, and Success and Failure event types. In order for these events to appear in this log, be sure to turn auditing on for the events and resources you wish to examine.

**FIGURE 18.2**

The Event Viewer showing a Security Log

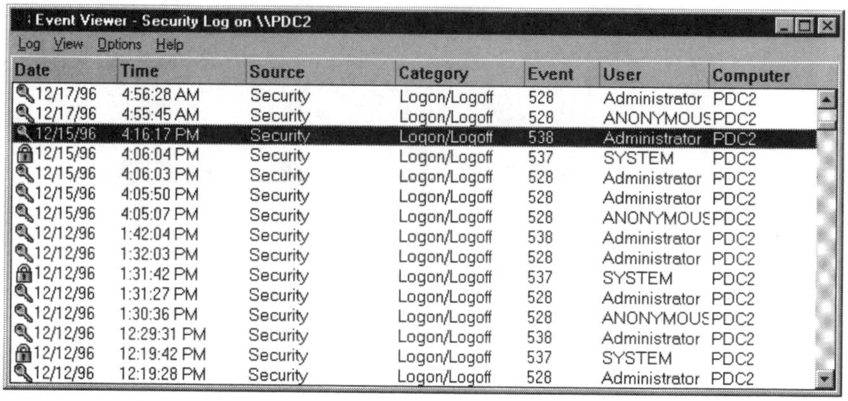

The Application Log, shown in Figure 18.3, contains errors from applications such as SQL server, Dr. Watson, and other applications that send their error messages to this log.

**FIGURE 18.3**

The Event Viewer showing
an Application Log

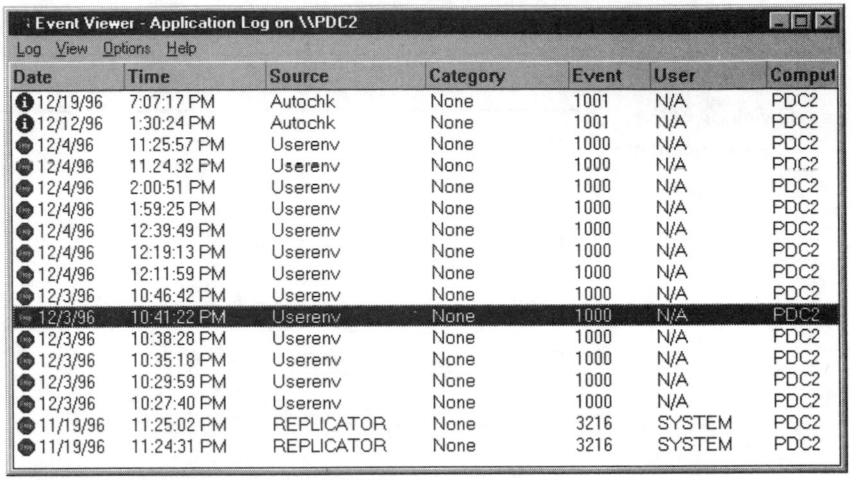

| Date | Time | Source | Category | Event | User | Comput |
|------|------|--------|----------|-------|------|--------|
| 12/19/96 | 7:07:17 PM | Autochk | None | 1001 | N/A | PDC2 |
| 12/12/96 | 1:30:24 PM | Autochk | None | 1001 | N/A | PDC2 |
| 12/4/96 | 11:25:57 PM | Userenv | None | 1000 | N/A | PDC2 |
| 12/4/96 | 11:24:32 PM | Userenv | None | 1000 | N/A | PDC2 |
| 12/4/96 | 2:00:51 PM | Userenv | None | 1000 | N/A | PDC2 |
| 12/4/96 | 1:59:25 PM | Userenv | None | 1000 | N/A | PDC2 |
| 12/4/96 | 12:39:49 PM | Userenv | None | 1000 | N/A | PDC2 |
| 12/4/96 | 12:19:13 PM | Userenv | None | 1000 | N/A | PDC2 |
| 12/4/96 | 12:11:59 PM | Userenv | None | 1000 | N/A | PDC2 |
| 12/3/96 | 10:46:42 PM | Userenv | None | 1000 | N/A | PDC2 |
| 12/3/96 | 10:41:22 PM | Userenv | None | 1000 | N/A | PDC2 |
| 12/3/96 | 10:38:28 PM | Userenv | None | 1000 | N/A | PDC2 |
| 12/3/96 | 10:35:18 PM | Userenv | None | 1000 | N/A | PDC2 |
| 12/3/96 | 10:29:59 PM | Userenv | None | 1000 | N/A | PDC2 |
| 12/3/96 | 10:27:40 PM | Userenv | None | 1000 | N/A | PDC2 |
| 11/19/96 | 11:25:02 PM | REPLICATOR | None | 3216 | SYSTEM | PDC2 |
| 11/19/96 | 11:24:31 PM | REPLICATOR | None | 3216 | SYSTEM | PDC2 |

You can filter events by type, date, username, computer name or event ID. You can also sort or view additional details about events. When you are viewing the details of the event, you should look up the event, user, or computer ID to find what the actual error was and what may have caused it.

Another important thing to remember is that the oldest error is usually the one that causes the other dependency errors. After viewing the oldest error, work your way to the newer events to see if there are other clues about the problem.

You can even view another computer's Event Log remotely by choosing Log ➤ Select Computer in Event Viewer.

# Last Known Good Configuration

NT saves several versions of your past configurations. One of the most valuable configurations is the Last Known Good configuration. This configuration is saved when a successful login has occurred. It is saved in the Registry, and is only activated in two instances:

1. Whenever there is a critical error from which NT cannot recover

2. When it is initiated by the user during startup

Last Known Good configuration can assist in troubleshooting if you installed a driver that was incorrect and need to revert back to the last set of successful settings. However, this means all changes made after the Last Known Good configuration being saved are lost.

The system Registry HKEY_LOCAL_MACHINE\SYSTEM\Select contains a value named LastKnownGood. Within this value, is a number which refers to one of the CurrentControlSets saved within the Registry. For example, If the value is 001 it would refer to CurrentControlSet001, or if the value were 002, it would be referring to CurrentControlSet002. Figure 18.4 shows the Registry Editor HKEY_LOCAL_MACHINE.

**FIGURE 18.4**

The Registry Editor
*HKEY_LOCAL_MACHINE*

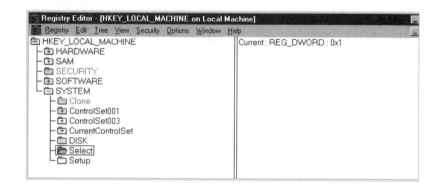

To use the Last Known Good configuration, while the system is booting,

**1.** Press the spacebar.

**2.** Press L for the Use Last Known Good configuration option.

# Registry

The Registry is a combination of the .ini files, the configuration of hardware and software components, and user configuration options. There are 5 subtrees in the Registry: HKEY_CURRENT_USER, HKEY_USERS, HKEY_CLASSES_ROOT, HKEY_CURRENT_CONFIG, and HKEY_LOCAL_MACHINE. Each of these subtrees has a particular purpose.

■ HKEY_CURRENT_USER keeps all the configuration information for the specific user who is logged on.

- `HKEY_USERS` keeps all the users information that have ever logged on to this machine.

- `HKEY_CLASSES_ROOT` contains information pertaining to the OLE and file associations.

- `HKEY_CURRENT_CONFIG` contains information pertaining only to the current settings.

- `HKEY_LOCAL_MACHINE` contains information pertaining to the hardware settings.

Whenever you install software or change hardware you are changing the Registry. It's a good idea to use front-end tools to change the Registry rather than editing it manually through the `REGEDT32` command because you could accidentally make a parameter change that stops your machine. Examples of front-end tools are the Control Panel and installation programs.

Use the `regedt32.exe` utility to edit the Registry. Be sure to make a backup of the Registry because reinstalling or manually repairing it may not fix the damage to it. You will need to reinstall the operating system from scratch. The System Policy Editor is another front-end tool you can use to change the Registry. Within the System Policy Editor you would choose Open Registry and then Save.

The Registry often provides keys to how something, a service for example, is set up, and provides valuable troubleshooting hints. For example, you could look into the Registry and examine previous hardware settings and compare them to the current settings. This comparison would be useful if you just made a recent change and noticed an error message in the System Log.

For dependency errors, you can check `HKEY_LOCAL_MACHINE\SYSTEM\CurrentControlSet\Control\ServiceGroupOrder` for a list of which services will load and in what order. To find out which services depend on which other services, you can check `HKEY_LOCAL_MACHINE\SYSTEM\CurrentControlSet\Services\,<service>` under the `DependOnGroup` entry or the `DependOnService` entry.

Some things can only be changed through the Registry. For example, the replication governor is changed on BDCs whenever you are replicating over slow links.

Back up the Registry regularly. When inadvertent changes or corruption occurs, the backup is necessary for recovery. Use the `regback.exe` and `regrest.exe` utilities to perform a backup. These utilities are included in the

Windows NT Workstation Resource Kit CD. You can also save each key or *hive* (part of the Registry that contains keys, subkeys, and values) to be loaded back into the Registry at a later date. You can even save the subtree as a text file as documentation to be used for troubleshooting. Parts of the Registry are saved with the ERD, providing extra protection for your Registry.

## Emergency Repair Disk

To create an Emergency Repair Disk (ERD), use the `Rdisk.exe` utility. `Rdisk` can either save the critical system files to your hard disk or save them to a floppy. The reason these files are important is that if your Registry, default profile, or configuration files for DOS (`Autoexec.nt` and `Config.nt`) get corrupted or are missing, you will have a way to recover from it. If not, you may need to reinstall Windows NT and start over if you do not have a regular backup. Table 18.3 defines the ERD contents.

| **TABLE 18.3** ERD contents | **FILE ON ERD** | **CONTENTS** |
| --- | --- | --- |
| | `System._` | `HKEY_LOCAL_MACHINE\SYSTEM` Registry hive, compressed |
| | `Software._` | `HKEY_LOCAL_MACHINE\SOFTWARE` Registry hive, compressed |
| | `Security._` | `HKEY_LOCAL_MACHINE\SECURITY` Registry hive, compressed |
| | `Sam._` | `HKEY_LOCAL_MACHINE\SAM` Registry hive, compressed |
| | `Ntuser.da_` | Compressed version of the default profile `%Winntroot%\profile\default user\ntuser.dat` |
| | `Autoexec.nt` | `%winntroot%\system32\autoexec.nt` |
| | `Config.nt` | `%winntroot%\system32\config.nt` |
| | `Setup.log` | Contains a list of which files were installed and their CRC |
| | `Default._` | `HKEY_USERS\DEFAULT` Registry hive, compressed |

In Exercise 18.1, you will update the ERD you created in Exercise 2.1 for PDC1.

**EXERCISE 18.1**

## Creating an Emergency Repair Disk

Complete this exercise from PDC1 while logged on as ADMINISTRATOR. You will need a blank pre-formatted high density disk.

**1.** Click Start ➤ Run.

**2.** In the Run dialog box, type **RDISK**. The dialog box shown here will appear.

**3.** Choose Update Repair Info. Because we created an ERD in Exercise 2.1, the Repair Disk Utility dialog box lets you know that previous information will be deleted. Click Yes when it asks if that is okay, and continue the operation.

**4.** The Repair Disk Utility dialog box will now prompt you to create an Emergency Repair Disk. Click Yes to continue.

**5.** You will be prompted to place a disk in the floppy drive. Click Yes to continue.

**6.** Click Exit to exit the Repair Disk Utility.

The ERD is now updated.

To use the ERD, boot from the original setup disks. You will be asked if you want to repair the disk. At that point, insert the ERD to start restoring information.

# Advanced Resolution

ADVANCED RESOLUTION INCLUDES Blue Screen interpretation, Kernel debugging, and Memory Dump examination. The reason these are considered advanced resolution is because an experienced support engineer is needed to interpret the results of any of these tools. For example, the support engineer would need to be able to determine in which drive the memory address of the error resides, or to determine whether a driver supports a specific hardware component. In the following subsections you will learn about the:

- Blue Screen

- Kernel Debugger

- Memory Dump

## Blue Screen

The dreaded Blue Screen appears when the computer encounters a fatal error. In this section, you will see a sample Stop message (shown on the Blue Screen) and learn how to interpret it:

```
*** STOP:   0x0000000A

(0x00000000,0x0000001A,0x00000000,0x00000000)

IRQL_NOT_LESS_OR_EQUAL***
```

There are five parts to Stop messages:

- The first part identifies debug port status if the Kernel Debugger is used.

- The second part identifies the location of the error, the memory address that may be involved, and the type of error.

- The third part identifies which modules have already loaded successfully.

- The fourth part identifies which modules were due to be loaded and were on the stack.

- The fifth part provides confirmation of the communications parameters and whether a dump file was created; it is displayed when using the Kernel Debugger.

We will concentrate on the second part because identifying the error location will most likely point us to the problem. The second part can be divided into four main parameters. The parameters vary depending on the Stop error.

For example, if the error is the one shown above, we can interpret the four parameters as follows. The invalid address referenced is the first parameter. The interrupt request level (IRQL) is the second parameter. The third parameter is access type (0 for read, and 1 for write). The fourth parameter is the code address.

To find out what the parameters mean in your Stop message, examine the dump analysis that is shown on the Blue Screen. Each parameter will be labeled, and you will see more information regarding the possible source, and more troubleshooting information. Table 18.4 defines common stop codes.

| | STOP CODES | DESCRIPTION | PROBLEM/ SUGGESTED RESOLUTION |
|---|---|---|---|
| **TABLE 18.4**  Example stop codes defined | 0x00000000 | DIVIDE_BY_ZERO_ERROR | An application tried to divide by zero. If you get this error, you should examine a Memory Dump to examine what the cause might be. |
| | 0x0000000A | IRQL_NOT_LESS_OR_EQUAL | An application tried to access memory and was not allowed to because the IRQL was too high. A typical cause for this error is a device driver that uses improper addresses. In this case you should replace or update your device driver. |
| | 0X0000001E | KMODE_EXCEPTION_NOT _HANDLED | Typically caused by a bug within a driver. Look at the second parameter to find what driver and exception address generated the message. |
| | 0x00000051 | REGISTRY_ERROR | The Registry may be corrupt. Restore the Registry from backup. |
| | 0x0000007B | INACCESSIBLE_BOOT _DEVICE | This could be because of a driver problem, hardware failure, or a virus. Replace defective hardware device. |

| | | | PROBLEM/ |
|---|---|---|---|
| **TABLE 18.4** | **STOP** | | **SUGGESTED** |
| Example stop | **CODES** | **DESCRIPTION** | **RESOLUTION** |
| codes defined | | | |
| (continued) | 0x0000007F | UNEXPECTED_KERNEL_MODE _TRAP | Could indicate a hardware problem with the RAM or BIOS, or corrupted system drivers. Replace defective hardware device. |

# Kernel Debugger

The Kernel Debugger displays files being loaded during the boot sequence. Use the Kernel Debugger when Stop errors and crashes occur, and when you have trouble identifying the source.

Two computers are required to run the Kernel Debugger. The target computer reports the Stop errors or crashes. The hose computer receives files and messages while the target computer is booting. Because the debugging software cannot run on the target computer, you need two machines. In order to use the debugger at run time, a host computer is required to receive information from the target computer. The Kernel Debugger will create a Memory Dump file that you can examine for hints about the source of the error.

Requirements for using the Kernel Debugger:

- Both computers running the same version of Windows NT

- A host computer and a target computer

- The host computer needs symbol files for the target computer from `support\debug\platform\symbols` on the Windows NT CD-ROM. If service packs are installed, you will also need to find the symbols from them and include them on the host computer. Copy them in order from oldest to newest. (This procedure ensures that the newest ones are not overwritten.)

- The host computer also needs the debugging software from `\support\debug\platform`

- The host computer must have the environment variables set. The environment variables should be set under Control Panel ➤ System ➤ Environment, and would be specified with the following variables and values.

| VARIABLE | VALUE |
|---|---|
| _NT_DEBUG_PORT | COM1 or COM2 |
| _NT_DEBUG_BAUD_RATE | Initial baud rate |
| _NT_SYMBOL_PATH | The directory to which you copied the SYMBOLS directory (by default \systemroot\symbols) |

- The target computer needs to have its BOOT.INI file modified with the /DEBUG option. Place the /DEBUG option at the end of the line for the menu choice you will be running with the Kernel Debugger. For intermittent problems, use the /CRASHDEBUG option instead.

*Be sure to use the correct version of the SYMBOL files. The SYMBOL files contain the debugging code. Using the wrong files is a common mistake. Without the correct symbols, the debugger cannot give you the correct information.*

To perform remote debugging, connect the host and target computer through RAS or through a null modem cable. If you are connecting via RAS, then you need to run a special command called REMOTE. REMOTE needs to be started on both the host and target computers. REMOTE uses named pipes to provide remote network access.

The syntax for the host computer is:

```
REMOTE /s "I386KD -v" DEBUG
(/s means server, -v means verbose, DEBUG is the unique ID)
```

The syntax for the target computer is:

```
REMOTE /C computername DEBUG
(/c means client, debug is the unique ID to match the server)
```

### Using the Kernel Debugger

Follow these steps to use the Kernel Debugger:

1. After meeting all the requirements listed above (including using the REMOTE command if you are using RAS), restart the target computer with the Debug Option menu choice.

2. When the target computer starts, it will send information about an activity to the host computer.

**3.** You may examine the Memory Dump later with `dumpexam.exe`; this is optional.

Before using these advanced resolution techniques or Kernel Debugger, have an idea of what items you want to look for. If you need help prior to using these tools, refer to the Resource Kit, then call Microsoft for assistance.

## Memory Dump

Creating a Memory Dump causes NT to write the contents of system memory to a file if a Stop error occurs; this information can be used to help troubleshoot a Stop error. To enable Windows NT to save what is in memory after an NT crash, use the following menu selections: Settings ➤ Control Panel ➤ System ➤ Startup/Shutdown tab page. Choose the check box for writing debug information to: `%systemroot%\memory.dmp`, as shown in Figure 18.5.

**FIGURE 18.5**

The System Properties Startup/Shutdown tab page

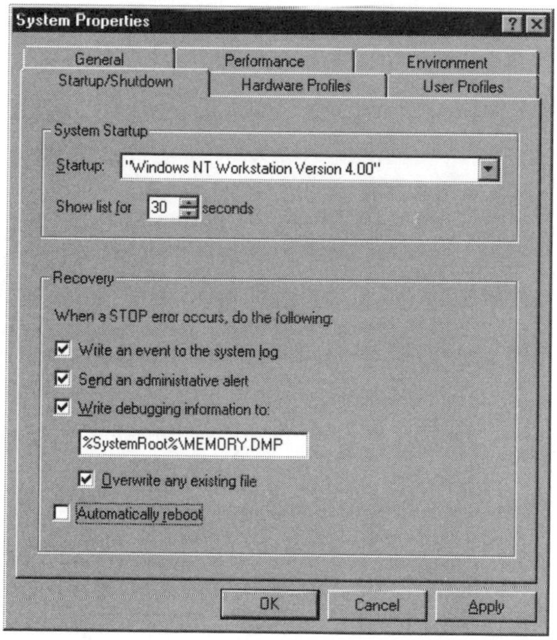

The requirements for enabling this are:

- The paging file must be on the system partition and must be at least 1MB larger than physical RAM.

- The system partition must contain free space to accommodate the paging file.

If configured before a stop message occurs, then the contents of the memory is dumped to the paging file, and from the paging file to `%systemroot%\memory.dmp`. You can examine this file later with `dumpexam.exe`.

Once you have created a Memory Dump file, then you can use the `dumpchk` application. `dumpchk` will allow you to make sure the dumpfile has been made correctly. `dumpchk` will perform a complete check by validating the integrity of the `PSLoadedModuleList`, and by verifying the addresses in the Memory Dump. The syntax is:

```
dumpchk [options] CrashDumpFile
```

| | |
|---|---|
| -? | Help on syntax |
| -p | Prints the header only (no validation) |
| -v | Verbose mode |
| -q | Performs a quick test |

Once you are sure the Memory Dump has been created correctly, then you can use the `dumpexam` application to examine the dump file, extract data, and write it to a text file. It will create a file named `systemroot\memory.txt`.
The syntax is:

```
dumpexam [options] [CrashDumpFile]
```

| | |
|---|---|
| -? | Help on syntax |
| -v | Verbose mode |
| -p | Prints header only |
| -f | Filename output filename (specify only if you've moved the dump file path) |
| -y | Path to where the symbols directory is (only if you are using an alternate path) |

In the rare case that you would save the Memory Dump on floppies to send to Microsoft for examination, use the `dumpflop` utility.

The syntax for storing on floppies is:

```
dumpflop [options] <drive>: [<CrashDumpFile>]
```

The syntax to restore from floppies is:

```
dumpflop [options] [<CrashDumpFile>] <drive>:
```

| | |
|---|---|
| ? | Help on syntax |
| p | Prints crash dump header if assembling |
| v | Compression statistics |
| q | Formats the floppy if storing, overwrites already created crash dump file if assembling |

The `dumpchk`, `dumpexam` and `dumpflop` utilities are located on the Windows NT CD-ROM in the `\support\debug\platform` directory.

# Chapter Summary

I N THIS CHAPTER we discussed the background and solutions for many problems that occur during NT network administration. The first two sections documented problems that occur with system hardware and system resources. The next section discussed multiple repair techniques using tools available from Windows NT. The final section covered information on using the Advanced Resolution tools.

## Hardware Troubleshooting

The following is a list of topics covered under Hardware Troubleshooting:

**Installation**—Media errors can prevent a successful NT installation. Using an alternate media device successfully will prove that the original media was faulty and in need of replacement. If the message "Inability to connect to the domain controller" appears, the following should be examined: incorrect spelling, incorrect network settings, and the status of the domain controller. Outdated or incorrect device drivers will also prevent an installation from being completed. Usually, the most current drivers are available on the manufacturer's Web pages. If dependency services fail to start, checking the Event Log will help identify and isolate the problem.

**Boot failures**—Four critical files are necessary for NT to complete its booting process: NTLDR, BOOT.INI, botsect.dos, ntdetect.com. If these files are missing or corrupted, the system will display corresponding error messages. Also, a disk in drive A: can cause a "missing file" message as NT searches the disk for the system files. NT will interpret the ntoskrnl file as missing if the BOOT.INI file is missing or points to a wrong partition, disk, or controller.

*BOOTSECT.DOS*—This file takes control from the NTLDR if you are running an operating system other than Windows NT. A missing boot-sect.dos file will report "I/O Error accessing boot sector file." Missing files can be restored using the ERD.

*BOOT.INI*—This file informs the NTLDRNTLDR of the boot partition location. If this file is edited incorrectly, the user will not be able to start Windows NT or other operating systems through the initial menu. Each component of a menu selection—for example,

```
scsi(0)disk(0)rdisk(0)partition(1)\WINNT="Windows NT
    Server Version 4.00)
```

—is explained in this section.

**Configuration errors**—In most cases, these types of errors will be displayed in the form of a dialog box, and instruct the user to check the Event Viewer. One remedy may be to use the Last Known Good configuration if a change was made recently. Also, the NT Diagnostics application is a very useful tool to explore the current settings recognized by Windows NT.

# Resource Troubleshooting

The following is a list of topics covered under Resource Troubleshooting:

**Printing**—Printing problems can occur during or after an installation has been completed. Checking the physical connection to the printer, and examining the printing process flow are the first diagnostic steps. If a local printer cannot be created, or if a specific printer cannot be installed, you will need to delete and recreate the printer. Problems with the spooler can cause print jobs to disappear or remain suspended indefinitely. Restarting the spooler often corrects these problems. Monitoring disk space is important as error message will result if adequate disk space is unavailable for the spooler.

**Connectivity**—If users encounter problems when attempting to log on to a remote server, the PPP log may provide details pointing to why they are not able to log on. A common technique is to set the encryption to clear text and gradually move to stronger encryption levels to isolate the problem. The Dial-Up Networking monitor is a tool that also provides valuable diagnostic information.

Problems on the local area network can be solved by examining specific network parameters. If NWLink is used, ensure that the frame type on the client matches the server. Also, identical protocols should be used between the client and the rest of the network. The TCP/IP settings should be checked to be compatible with the local area network. Finally, if the server is experiencing a heavy load of users or network traffic, the end user may perceive that the network is not available.

**File and Resource Access**—Users may report trouble accessing resources, including files and directories. Check the share rights versus the local rights. If subdirectory rights are different than the parent directory's rights, verify that the "apply to subdirectories" option has been checked. If a user belongs to a group with more restrictive rights, it will override their individual rights. To refresh the access token automatically, log off the system then log on again. If a specific user is experiencing problems, try logging on as a different user. This will allow you to narrow the problem to a client or server issue. One final remedy may be to restore the Security Accounts Manager with the Emergency Repair Disk.

## Repair Methods

The following are methods for repairing items within the NT operating system:

**Last Known Good**—NT saves several versions of past system configurations. One of the most valuable is the Last Known Good configuration file which is written after the most recent successful logon. This file is used if NT is unable to recover from a critical error during the boot process. Also, it is available to the user as a choice during startup.

**Emergency Repair Disk** —The `Rdisk` utility is used to create the Emergency Repair Disk. The critical system files can be saved to the hard disk or the floppy. Examples of these critical system files include the Registry, default profile, and configuration files for DOS.

**Restore from Backup**— If neither of the above procedures solve your problem, the final step may be to restore individual files or the operating system from backup copies.

**Registry** —The Registry contains a combination of `.ini` files, hardware and software configuration components, and user configuration options. Editing the Registry can help to solve specific problems. Be careful to use front-end tools like the Control Panel or installation programs to make Registry changes. Inadvertent manual changes can cause more damage to the system and prevent NT from starting. If you do have a good understanding of the Registry, the `regedt32.exe` utility allows manual editing of the Registry. Make sure that the Registry is backed up on a regular basis with the `regback.exe` and `regrest.exe` utilities.

**Event Log**—The Event View allows you to examine three different Event Logs: System, Security, and Application. The System Log contains information relating to general system health. It can report on services that are not started, printing problems, and hardware configuration problems. The Security Log contains the audit trails and the success and failure event types. The Application Log contains information from applications such as SQL Server, Dr. Watson, and other applications.

## Advanced Resolution

Advanced Resolution includes Blue Screen interpretation, Kernel Debugging, and Memory Dump examination. These three resolution modes are characterized as follows:

**Blue Screen**—The Blue Screen contains clues such as the details in stop messages that are displayed. The stop messages contain four major components including port status, location and type of error, modules loaded successfully, and modules due to be loaded. If the Kernel Debugger is used, a fifth parameter will confirm communication parameters and whether a dumpfile was created. In this section, we examined specific stop codes and their corresponding descriptions and potential causes.

**Kernel Debugger**—Use this tool when stop errors and crashes are occurring. The Kernel Debugger is able to create a Memory Dump file for examination. In this section, we discussed what requirements are necessary to set up a host and target computer. Remote debugging can be done using RAS or a null modem cable.

**Memory Dump**—Windows NT can be enabled to save memory contents after a system crash. The `dumpchk` utility is used to check whether the dump file was created correctly. The `dumpexam` application is used to examine the dump file, extract data, and write the contents to a text file. The file is named `systemroot\memory.txt`. This file can be sent to Microsoft in case you need additional assistance.

# Review Questions

1. If you were dual-booting to DOS and DOS would not load, which boot file would you check first?

   **A.** `NTLDR`

   **B.** `BOOT.INI`

   **C.** `BOOTSECT.DOS`

   **D.** `NTDETECT.COM`

2. Which file is used to specify the location of the boot partition during NT system startup?

   **A.** NTLDR

   **B.** BOOT.INI

   **C.** BOOTSECT.DOS

   **D.** NTDETECT.COM

3. You just added a new driver to NT and now your computer won't reboot successfully. What should be your first course of action?

   **A.** Use the ERD.

   **B.** Restore from tape backup.

   **C.** Use the Last Known Good configuration.

   **D.** Do a cold boot on your computer so NTDETECT can attempt to fix the problem.

4. Which registry subtree contains information regarding the computers configuration and hardware settings?

   **A.** HKEY_CURRENT_USER

   **B.** HKEY_USERS

   **C.** HKEY_CURRENT_CONFIG

   **D.** HKEY_CLASSES_ROOT

   **E.** HKEY_LOCAL_MACHINE

5. Your NT Server keeps crashing. You have called Microsoft for help and they tell you to send them a Memory Dump. How do you create this file?

   **A.** Configure the recovery option to write debugging information to a file through Startup/Shutdown Properties in Control Panel ➢ System.

   **B.** Through NT diagnostics, configure Create a crash debug file under the Memory tab.

   **C.** Use the Event Viewer to view the Memory Dump automatically.

   **D.** Use Dr. Watson for NT to create the Memory Dump file.

**6.** Which utility do you use to create an emergency repair disk?

   **A.** ERD

   **B.** REPAIRDSK

   **C.** Windows NT Diagnostics

   **D.** RDISK

**7.** Which of the following statements is true of the ERD?

   **A.** The ERD is bootable.

   **B.** You can copy needed files from the ERD to a hard drive.

   **C.** To use the ERD, you must first boot to the NT setup disks.

   **D.** To restore from the ERD, use the RDISK utility.

# Answers to Review Questions

## Chapter I Answers

1. You have two domains, Domain A and Domain B. Kevin is a user in Domain A and he wants to be able to access a resource in Domain B. What is the minimal trust relationship you need to establish for Kevin to access resources in Domain B?

   **A.** Configure Domain A to trust Domain B.

   **B.** Configure Domain B to trust Domain A.

   **C.** Configure a two-way trust between Domain A and Domain B.

   **Answer:** B

2. Your company has two offices, one in San Francisco and one in Los Angeles. Your company has decided to place a high speed WAN link between the two locations and use a single domain model. They have also decided to put a PDC at the San Francisco location and a BDC at the Los Angeles location. You are the manager of the Los Angeles location and have decided to install the BDC even though the WAN link has not yet been installed. You receive an error message during the installation telling you that the domain controller for this domain cannot be located. What do you do?

   **A.** Choose bypass error message. The BDC will complete the installation, and when the PDC becomes available it will automatically synchronize.

   **B.** Install the BDC as a member server and upgrade it to BDC when the WAN link is installed.

   **C.** Install the BDC as a PDC in it's own domain. After the WAN link becomes available you can merge the two domains together.

   **D.** Wait until the WAN link becomes available before installing the BDC.

   **Answer:** D

3. You have been experiencing very heavy traffic to your PDC during the morning hours and when users are returning from lunch. You decide to add another machine to help offload the logon authentication from the PDC. Which is the best solution?

**A.** Add a BDC to your existing domain and manually migrate the SAM database.

**B.** Add a member server to your existing domain, copy the SAM database, and start the Netlogon service.

**C.** Add a BDC to your existing domain and specify an administrative account and password during installation.

**D.** Add a BDC to your existing domain and stop the Netlogon service on your PDC.

**Answer:** C

4. Your company has two main divisions, East and West. Each division implemented Windows NT without any coordination from MIS. Now they want to be able to share network resources between the EAST and WEST domains. What is the easiest way to configure the domains?

**A.** Configure EAST to trust WEST.

**B.** Configure WEST to trust EAST.

**C.** Setup a two-way trust between EAST and WEST.

**D.** Start from scratch and implement a master domain model.

**Answer:** C

5. You installed an NT server for the Sales department. The server was supposed to be installed into the SALES domain, but the WAN link to SALES was down during the installation. You installed the server as a member server in the MIS domain. What do you do now?

**A.** When the WAN link comes up, change the configuration of the server so it is now part of the SALES domain.

**B.** Upgrade the server to a BDC so it can be moved to the SALES domain.

**C.** Wait until the WAN link comes up and reinstall the server so it can be associated with the proper domain.

**Answer:** A

**6.** Your network has four domains, NORTH, EAST, WEST, and SOUTH. All domains contain users and resources. The NORTH domain contains all the corporate resources that users in all domains need to access. The resources in WEST, EAST and SOUTH are all local resources and do not require access to users outside their domains. What are the minimum trust relationships that need to be established?

**A.** Establish one-way trust relationships in which EAST, WEST, and SOUTH trust NORTH.

**B.** Establish one-way trust relationships in which NORTH trusts EAST, WEST, and SOUTH.

**C.** Establish a two-way trust between NORTH and SOUTH, NORTH and WEST, and NORTH and EAST.

**D.** Establish two-way trusts between all four domains.

**Answer:** B

**7.** Your company is in a single location. You have six NT servers and 200 users. Your company wants to centralize management and wants users to be able to access resources from other departments. Which of the following options is the best solution?

**A.** Create a single domain and install one server as a PDC and another server as a BDC, then setup the remaining servers as part of the domain.

**B.** Use the master domain model. In the master domain install one server as PDC and another server as a BDC. Put each department in its own resource domain and install their department server as PDC.

**C.** Create a single domain that has a PDC and a BDC, and install the departmental servers as member servers in their own workgroup.

**D.** Set up each department in its own domain. Use the complete trust domain model to ensure that users can access resources in other domains.

**Answer:** A

8. Your domain currently has a PDC that is a Pentium with 32MB of RAM. You want to install a new server that is an Alpha with 64MB of RAM. You prefer that the new machine be the PDC. What do you do?

   **A.** When installing the new machine specify the machine as PDC, this will automatically make the old machine a BDC.

   **B.** When installing the new machine configure it as a BDC, then after the installation, you can promote it to a PDC.

   **C.** Install the new machine as a member server, copy the SAM from the PDC, configure the old machine as a BDC, and promote the new machine to PDC.

   **D.** Install the new machine as the PDC, then copy the SAM from the original PDC, then demote the original PDC to BDC.

   **Answer:** B

9. Your PAYROLL domain contains resources that users in other domains will never need to access. Your SALES and MARKETING domains frequently need to share resources across the SALES and MARKETING domains. Occasionally users in PAYROLL also need to access resources in the SALES and MARKETING domains. What do you need to do to set up the trust relationships?

   **A.** Configure a one-way trust from SALES and MARKETING to trust PAYROLL, then configure a two-way trust between SALES and MARKETING.

   **B.** Configure a one-way trust from PAYROLL to trust SALES and MARKETING, then configure a two-way trust between SALES and MARKETING.

   **C.** Set up a two-way trust between SALES and MARKETING, create duplicate user accounts in the domains for PAYROLL users who need to access resources in domains other than PAYROLL.

   **D.** Set up two-way trust relationships between PAYROLL, SALES, and MARKETING.

   **Answer:** A

## Chapter 2 Answers

**1.** To create a computer account at a domain controller, which utility do you use?

**A.** Server Manager

**B.** Control Panel ➤ Network

**C.** User Manager for Domains

**D.** Computer Account Manager

**E.** License Manager

**Answer:** A

**2.** Which utility is used to implement a trust relationship?

**A.** Server Manager

**B.** Control Panel ➤ Network

**C.** User Manager for Domains

**D.** Computer Account Manager

**Answer:** C

**3.** To install NT Server, the minimum requirement for your processor is:

**A.** 386/16

**B.** 486/25

**C.** 486/33

**D.** 486/100

**E.** Pentium Processor

**Answer:** C

**4.** To install NT Server, the minimum requirement for your RAM is:

**A.** 12MB

**B.** 16MB

**C.** 32MB

**D.** 64MB

**Answer:** B

**5.** The NT 4.0 partitions that can be created during the WINNT installation process are (choose all that apply):

**A.** FAT

**B.** HPFS

**C.** NTFS

**D.** CDFS

**Answer:** A and C

**6.** If you were concerned about local security, which file system would be your best choice?

**A.** FAT

**B.** HPFS

**C.** NTFS

**D.** CDFS

**Answer:** C

**7.** If you wanted to dual-boot to NT Server and Windows 95, which file system(s) would be supported on both platforms? Choose all that apply.

**A.** FAT

**B.** HPFS

**C.** NTFS

**Answer:** A

**8.** The two licensing modes NT Server can use are:

**Answer:**

**a.** per-seat licensing

**b.** per-server licensing

**9.** The default protocols you can select during NT installation are:

**Answer:**

**a.** NetBEUI

**b.** NWLink IPX/SPX

**c.** TCP/IP

**10.** The two methods of joining a domain are:

**Answer:**

**a.** Use Server Manager to create the computer account, then add it through Control Panel ➤ Network at the workstation

**b.** Add it through Control Panel ➤ Network at the workstation and supply a user name and password for a user that has rights to add a workstation to the domain

## Chapter 3 Answers

**1.** You have decided to put all of your home directories on a shared directory on the CORP server in the MASTER domain. The shared directory is called USERS. You want to create the home directories for the users as the users are created. You use the User Environment Profile dialog box in User Manager for Domains. Which option do you choose?

**A.** Click the connect radio button and type in a drive letter. In the path specify \\MASTER\USERS\%LOGONNAME%.

**B.** Click the local path radio button and type in the shared path of \\MASTER\CORP\USERS\%USERNAME%.

**C.** Click the connect radio button and type in a drive letter. In the path specify \\CORP\USERS\%USERNAME%.

**D.** Click the connect radio button and type in a drive letter. In the path specify \\CORP\USERS\%LOGONID%.

**Answer:** C

**2.** Local groups can reside on (choose all that apply):

   **A.** Windows 95 Workstations

   **B.** NT Workstations

   **C.** NT member servers

   **D.** NT domain controllers (PDC and BDCs)

   **Answer:** B, C, D

**3.** Global groups can reside on (choose all that apply):

   **A.** Windows 95 Workstations

   **B.** NT Workstations

   **C.** NT member servers

   **D.** NT domain controllers (PDC and BDCs)

   **Answer:** D

**4.** You have a user named Katie who needs to manage user and group accounts. What are the minimum rights you can give her so she will be able to manage users and groups?

   **A.** Add her to the ADMINISTRATORS local group.

   **B.** Add her to the DOMAIN ADMIN global group.

   **C.** Add her to the SERVER OPERATORS local group.

   **D.** Add her to the ACCOUNT OPERATORS local group.

   **E.** Add her to the ACCOUNT OPERATORS global group.

   **Answer:** D

**5.** Your company has been using the NT Workgroup model. You have now decided that you want your users to participate in a domain model. You install NT Server as a PDC in Domain CORP. Now one of your junior technicians needs to go to each NT Workstation and add it to the domain. What are the minimum rights you can give him to accomplish his task?

    **A.** Add him to the ADMINISTRATORS local group.

    **B.** Add him to the DOMAIN ADMIN global group.

    **C.** Add him to the SERVER OPERATORS local group.

    **D.** Add him to the ACCOUNT OPERATORS local group.

    **E.** Assign him the Add Workstations to Domain user right.

    **Answer:** E

6. Your company is using the master domain model. All of your user accounts are in the CORP domain. Your CORP domain has a PDC and two BDCs. Your resource domains are EAST and WEST and they each have one PDC and one BDC. Your users are forced to change passwords every 30 days, but some users are using the same password every time their old password expires. What can you do to fix this problem?

    **A.** Configure the account policy on the CORP domain's PDC to set password uniqueness to 5.

    **B.** Configure the account policy on the PDC and the two BDCs in the CORP domain to set minimum password age to 30.

    **C.** Configure the account policy on the PDC and the two BDCs in the CORP domain to set password uniqueness to 5.

    **D.** Click the require unique passwords button in the account policy box on the PDC in the CORP domain.

    **Answer:** A

7. The home directory variable used to substitute a logon name for the home directory is:

    **A.** %LOGONNAME%

    **B.** %USERNAME%

    **C.** %USER%

    **D.** %LOGONID%

    **Answer:** B

**8.** Your company uses a master domain model. The user accounts are in the CORP domain, which has one PDC and two BDCs. The resources are in the resource domains of EAST and WEST. EAST and WEST each have one PDC and one BDC. Everyday you back up the network servers between 2:00AM and 5:00AM. You don't want your users to log on during the backup period. What do you do?

**A.** Configure each account's user properties so the users cannot log on between 2:00AM and 5:00AM.

**B.** Configure CORP's domain policy to not allow any domain user to log on between 2:00AM and 5:00AM.

**C.** Configure the accounts policy on each domain controller in the CORP domain to disallow logon between 2:00AM and 5:00AM.

**D.** Configure the accounts policy on each domain controller in the CORP, EAST and WEST domains to disallow logon between 2:00AM and 5:00AM.

**Answer:** A

**9.** You use the master domain model. All user accounts are in the ABC domain and all resources are in the SALES and ACCT domains. You hire a user named Terry and you want her to be able to manage all of the printers in the resource domains, and also be able to create new users and groups in the accounts domain. What are the minimum assignments you can make so that Terry can perform these actions?

**A.** Make Terry a member of the DOMAIN ADMIN global group on the ABC domain and make her a member of the global group PRINT OPERATORS on the SALES and ACCT domains.

**B.** Make Terry a member of the ACCOUNT OPERATORS global group on the PDC in the ABC domain and make her a member of the global group PRINT OPERATORS on the SALES and ACCT domains.

**C.** Make Terry a member of the ACCOUNT OPERATORS local group on the PDC in the ABC domain and make her a member of the local group PRINT OPERATORS on the SALES and ACCT domains.

**D.** Make Terry a member of the ADMINISTRATORS local group on the ABC domain and make her a member of the PRINT OPERA-TORS global group on the SALES and ACCT domains.

**Answer:** C

10. Your company has been using the NT domain model. You have just hired a new MIS employee. You want the new employee to be able to share and stop share resources as well as back up and restore the server. You also want her to be able to down the server if needed. You do not want her to be able to do any account management. What do you do?

    **A.** Add her to the ADMINISTRATORS local group.

    **B.** Add her to the DOMAIN ADMIN global group.

    **C.** Add her to the SERVER OPERATORS local group.

    **D.** Add her to the ACCOUNT OPERATORS local group.

    **E.** Assign her the Manage Server user right.

    **Answer:** C

11. Your company uses the master domain model. You have a master domain, CORP, and three resource domains, MIS, SALES, and ACCT. The MIS, SALES, and ACCT domains trust the CORP domain. The MIS domain has an e-mail application on the APP server. All users need to access this application. What do you do?

    **A.** Create a local group on the APP server called EMAIL USERS and assign the permissions that the e-mail users will need, then add the global group DOMAIN USERS from the CORP domain to the local group EMAIL USERS.

    **B.** Add trust relationships, so that CORP trusts MIS, SALES, and ACCT. Create a global group called EMAIL USERS on the MIS domain and add users. Assign the necessary rights to access the e-mail application to EMAIL USERS.

    **C.** Add a trust relationship so that MIS trusts SALES and ACCT. Create a global group on MIS called EMAIL USERS and add users. Assign the necessary rights to the EMAIL USERS group.

    **D.** Create a global group on the APP server called EMAIL USERS and assign the permissions that the EMAIL USERS group will need, then add the global group DOMAIN USERS from the CORP domain to the global group EMAIL USERS.

    **Answer:** A

**12.** Your boss read an article on how programs could be written to break into your domain. The program worked by generating random passwords until it was able to log on. What option should be set in account policies to prevent this from happening?

**A.** Set minimum password age to 5.

**B.** Set password uniqueness to 7.

**C.** Set minimum password length to 15.

**D.** Configure account lockout.

**Answer:** D

**13.** You have just hired Rick to take care of your backups. You want him to be able to back up files and directories, but you don't want him to be able to restore the backup. What do you do?

**A.** Add him to the DOMAIN ADMIN global group.

**B.** Add him to the BACKUP OPERATORS local group.

**C.** Assign him the Backup file and directories user right.

**D.** Make him a member of the SERVER OPERATORS local group.

**Answer:** C

# Chapter 4 Answers

**1.** TERRY is a member of the SALES and MIS groups, the APPS share has the following rights assigned:

| USER/GROUP | ASSIGNMENT |
|------------|------------|
| EVERYONE | No Access |
| MIS | Full Control |
| TERRY | Change |

What are TERRY's rights at APPS?

**A.** Full Control

**B.** Change

**C.** Change and Full Control

**D.** No Access

**Answer:** D

2. You have just created a share on the DATA folder. You have not assigned any permissions. What can PEONUSER do at the DATA folder?

**A.** Nothing, no rights have been assigned

**B.** Read

**C.** List

**D.** Full Control

**Answer:** D

3. LARS is a member of the MIS group and is working at the APPS server. The APPS folder is on a FAT partition on the APPS server. The MIS group has Change permissions to a share called APPS in the APPS folder. The EVERYONE group has Read permission. What is(are) LARS' permission(s)?

**A.** Change

**B.** Read

**C.** Read and Change

**D.** Full Control

**Answer:** D

4. You want to create a network share for your DATA folder. Which of the following groups are able to create a network share? Choose all that apply.

**A.** Any user can create a share.

**B.** ADMINISTRATORS

**C.** SERVER OPERATORS

**D.** ACCOUNT OPERATORS

**Answer:** B and C

5. Auditing file resources allows you to determine which file resources are being accessed. Which of the following conditions must be met to enable auditing? Choose all that apply.

   **A.** You must be logged on as a user who is part of the ADMINISTRA-TORS group.

   **B.** Under the Policies menu of User Manager for Domains, you must go to the audit menu and select audit File and Object Access.

   **C.** The auditing service must be started.

   **D.** The partition you want to audit has to be NTFS.

   **E.** The partition you want to audit has to be shared.

   **F.** The partition type must be FAT or NTFS.

   **Answer:** A, B and D

6. What rights are needed to view the audit logs generated by file auditing? Choose all that apply.

   **A.** You must be logged on as a user who is part of the ADMINISTRA-TORS group.

   **B.** You must be logged on as a user who originally enabled the auditing.

   **C.** You must be logged on as a user who has the Manage Auditing and Security Log right.

   **D.** You must be logged on as a user who has the Manage Auditing right.

   **Answer:** A and C

7. What utility is used to view the audit logs generated by file auditing?

   **A.** Server Manager

   **B.** Event Viewer

   **C.** Audit Manager

   **D.** User Manager for Domains

   **Answer:** B

**8.** Which utilities can be used to create a network share? Choose all that apply.

**A.** Server Manager

**B.** My Computer

**C.** Windows NT Explorer

**D.** User Manager for Domains

**Answer:** A, B and C

**9.** If you wanted to assign local permissions so that a user could add, delete, or read a file, what would be the minimum assignment you could make?

**A.** Write

**B.** Read and Delete

**C.** Change

**D.** Full Control

**Answer:** C

# Chapter 5 Answers

**1.** Where are user profiles stored by default?

**A.** `%WINNTROOT%\PROFILES`

**B.** `%WINNTROOT%\POLICIES`

**C.** `%WINNTROOT%\SYSTEM32\REPL\IMPORT\SCRIPTS`

**D.** `%WINNTROOT%\SYSTEM32\REPL\EXPORT\SCRIPTS`

**Answer:** A

**2.** Which folder does the system check by default when looking for system policies?

**A.** `%WINNTROOT%\PROFILES`

**B.** `%WINNTROOT%\POLICIES`

   **C.** `%WINNTROOT%\SYSTEM32\REPL\IMPORT\SCRIPTS`

   **D.** `%WINNTROOT%\SYSTEM32\REPL\EXPORT\SCRIPTS`

   **Answer:** C

**3.** What is the name of the system policy file that NT Server looks for by default?

   **A.** `CONFIG.POL`

   **B.** `NTCONFIG.POL`

   **C.** `NTUSER.DAT`

   **D.** `USER.DAT`

   **Answer:** B

**4.** What is the name of the file used to store user profiles?

   **A.** `CONFIG.POL`

   **B.** `NTCONFIG.POL`

   **C.** `NTUSER.DAT`

   **D.** `USER.DAT`

   **Answer:** C

**5.** KATIE is a member of the SALES group and the MANAGERS group. The system policy defines that DEFAULT USER uses the Blue and Black color scheme. The SALES system policy defines the Blues 256 color scheme. The MANAGERS system policy defines the Celery 256 color scheme. KATIE's system policy defines the Rose 256 color scheme. What will KATIE's color scheme be when she logs on?

   **A.** Blue and Black

   **B.** Blues 256

   **C.** Celery 256

   **D.** Rose 256

   **Answer:** D

**6.** Which of the following configuration options can be specified through a user profile? Choose all that apply.

**A.** Network printer connections

**B.** Taskbar settings

**C.** Whether display settings should be restricted

**D.** Desktop color scheme

**E.** Whether to disable the Registry editor

**Answer:** A, B, and D

**7.** Which of the following configuration options can be specified through a user system policy? Choose all that apply.

**A.** Network printer connections

**B.** Taskbar settings

**C.** Whether display settings should be restricted

**D.** Desktop color scheme

**E.** Whether to disable the Registry editor

**Answer:** C, D, and E

**8.** Which Registry keys are updated through system policies? Choose all that apply.

**A.** HKEY_CURRENT_USER

**B.** HKEY_CURRENT_CONFIG

**C.** HKEY_CLASSES_ROOT

**D.** HKEY_USERS

**E.** HKEY_LOCAL_MACHINE

**Answer:** A and E

**9.** If KEVIN is a member of the SALES group and the MANAGERS group, and both groups have system policies defined, how does the system know which policy to apply?

   **A.** It's based on KEVIN's primary group as defined in User Manager for Domains.

   **B.** You can specify group priority in System Policy Editor.

   **C.** You can specify group priority in User Manager for Domains.

   **D.** Group priority is based on the group names' alphabetical order.

   **Answer:** B

**10.** What utility is used to create and manage system policies?

   **A.** User Manager for Domains

   **B.** System Policy Editor

   **C.** System Policy Manager

   **D.** Server Manager

   **Answer:** B

**11.** How are mandatory profiles specified?

   **A.** By clicking the Mandatory check box in User Manager Editor

   **B.** By renaming the NTUSER.DAT file to NTUSER.MAN

   **C.** By checking the User Mandatory Profiles box in User Manager for Domains

   **D.** By renaming the NTUSER.DAT file to NTUSER.MDT

   **Answer:** B

## Chapter 6 Answers

1. Which of the following options is not available through the Network Client Administrator?

   **A.** Creating installation disk sets

   **B.** Creating NT boot diskettes

   **C.** Making NT network installation startup disks

   **D.** Viewing remoteboot client information

      **Answer:** B

2. Which of the following operating systems can be installed through network installation startup disks? Choose all that apply.

   **A.** Network Client for MS-DOS

   **B.** Windows for Workgroups

   **C.** Windows 95

   **D.** NT Workstation

   **E.** NT Server

   **F.** LAN Manager for MS-DOS

   **G.** LAN Manager for OS/2

      **Answer:** A, B, C, D, and E

3. Which of the following operating systems can have installation disk sets created? Choose all that apply.

   **A.** Network Client for MS-DOS

   **B.** TCP/IP 32 for Windows for Workgroups

   **C.** Windows 95

   **D.** NT Workstation

   **E.** RAS for MS-DOS

**F.** LAN Manager for MS-DOS

**G.** LAN Manager for OS/2

**Answer:** B

4. Which of the following configuration options must be specified for a network startup disk? Choose all that apply.

**A.** Computer name

**B.** User name

**C.** Address of network interface card

**D.** Domain name

**Answer:** A, B, and C

5. Which of the following administrative tools are available on a Windows 95 client? Choose all that apply.

**A.** Server Manager

**B.** User Profile Editor

**C.** User Manager for Domains

**D.** Event Viewer

**E.** DHCP Manager

**Answer:** A, C, and D

6. Which of the following administrative tools are available on an NT Workstation? Choose all that apply.

**A.** Server Manager

**B.** User Profile Editor

**C.** User Manager for Domains

**D.** Event Viewer

**E.** DHCP Manager

**Answer:** A, B, C, D, and E

**7.** Which platforms can the administrative tools be copied to based on what's provided on the NT Server 4.0 CD? Choose all that apply.

**A.** Network Client for MS-DOS

**B.** Windows for Workgroups

**C.** Windows 95

**D.** NT Workstation

**E.** NT member server

**F.** LAN Manager for MS-DOS

**G.** LAN Manager for OS/2

   **Answer:** C, D, and E

## Chapter 7 Answers

**1.** Which utilities can be used to share a directory on a remote computer? Choose all that apply.

**A.** My Computer

**B.** Network Neighborhood

**C.** Server Manager

**D.** Share Manager

**E.** Windows NT Explorer

   **Answer:** C

**2.** Your domain consists of a PDC and 3 BDCs all on the same LAN. Sometimes when your users log on they access their logon scripts successfully, and sometimes their logon scripts don't run at all. What is the most likely solution to your problem?

**A.** You need to configure directory replication between the PDC and the BDCs; the PDC should be the export computer and the BDCs should be the import computers.

**B.** You need to configure directory replication between the PDC and the BDCs; the PDC should be the import computer and the BDCs should be the export computers.

**C.** Within the User Environment profile box, make sure you have checked the Make logon script available from the network option.

**D.** Use Server Manager to configure the Logon Script Replication Service.

**Answer:** A

**3.** If you wanted to configure the PDC to send SAM database updates to the BDCs every three minutes, which utility would you use?

**A.** Server Manager

**B.** Registry Editor

**C.** PDC Editor

**D.** ReplicationGovernor

**Answer:** B

**4.** What two groups should the replicator service account belong to?

**A.** SERVER OPERATORS

**B.** REPLICATORS

**C.** BACKUP OPERATORS

**D.** ADMINISTRATORS

**Answer:** B and C

**5.** Which of the following tasks cannot be completed from Server Manager? Choose all that apply.

**A.** Creating shared directory resources

**B.** Creating shared print resources

**C.** Disconnecting network users from a computer

**D.** Configuring directory replication

**E.** Configuring SAM database replication

**Answer:** B and E

**6.** Which of the following groups have rights to access the Server Manager utility? Choose all that apply.

**A.** DOMAIN ADMINS

**B.** SERVER OPERATORS

**C.** BACKUP OPERATORS

**D.** ACCOUNT OPERATORS

**E.** REPLICATOR

**Answer:** A, B and D

**7.** Which of the following utilities can be used to view browse lists? Choose all that apply.

**A.** File Manager

**B.** Browser Manager

**C.** Network Neighborhood

**D.** My Computer

**E.** User Manager for Domains

**F.** Print Manager

**G.** Windows NT Explorer

**Answer:** A, C, F and G

**8.** If you wanted to control SAM database synchronization to BDCs over a slow WAN link, what would you configure?

**A.** The ReplicationGovernor on the BDC

**B.** The ReplicationGovernor on the PDC

**C.** The NetLogon Parameters Registry key on the BDC

**D.** The NetLogon Parameters Registry key on the PDC

**Answer:** A

**9.** Which of the following machines would have the highest priority in a browser election?

**A.** NT Server configured as a domain controller

**B.** NT Server configured as a member server

**C.** NT Workstation

**D.** Windows 95

**Answer:** A

**10.** Which of the machines would be considered a potential browser machine? Choose all that apply.

**A.** NT Server configured as a domain controller

**B.** NT Server configured as a member server

**C.** NT Workstation

**D.** Windows 95

**E.** Windows for Workgroups

**F.** Windows 3.1

**G.** DOS client with the MS redirector

**Answer:** A, B, C, D and E

# Chapter 8 Answers

**1.** The _____ is the directory or folder that stores print jobs until they can be printed.

**A.** Print Processor

**B.** Logical Port

**C.** Print Spooler

**D.** Printing Pool

**Answer:** C

2. The _____ is responsible for determining if the print job needs rendering before it is sent to the printing device.

   **A.** Print Processor

   **B.** Logical Port

   **C.** Print Spooler

   **D.** Printing Pool

   **Answer:** A

3. What is required for a NetWare client to print to an NT printer?

   **A.** GSNW

   **B.** CSNW

   **C.** File and Print Services for NetWare

   **D.** Printer Gateway for NetWare

   **Answer:** C

4. Which UNIX command is used to send print jobs to an NT printer?

   **A.** LPQ

   **B.** LPR

   **C.** UPRINT

   **D.** Net Print

   **Answer:** B

5. If you did not want anyone except the SALES group to use the LASER printer, which tab page should you use in the Printer Properties dialog box?

   **A.** General

   **B.** Sharing

   **C.** Security

   **D.** Ports

   **Answer:** C

**6.** Which tab page would you use in the Printer Properties dialog box to set a printer's priority?

**A.** General

**B.** Sharing

**C.** Security

**D.** Scheduling

**Answer:** D

**7.** By default, which groups have Full Control over networked printers? Choose all that apply.

**A.** ADMINISTRATORS

**B.** SERVER OPERATORS

**C.** PRINT OPERATORS

**D.** PRINT MANAGERS

**Answer:** A, B and C

**8.** Which of the following tasks can be completed by a user who has the Manage Documents print right? Choose all that apply.

**A.** Create a printer

**B.** Delete a printer

**C.** Delete any user's print jobs

**D.** Reorder print jobs

**E.** Pause print jobs

**Answer:** C

**9.** Which of the following tasks can be audited through print auditing? Choose all that apply.

**A.** Print

**B.** Take Ownership

**C.** Delete

**D.** Create

**Answer:** A, B, C and E

# Chapter 9 Answers

1. If you were configuring NWLink IPX/SPX Compatible Transport protocol, and you weren't sure which frame type to use, what is your best option?

   **A.** Ethernet_802.2 because it's the industry standard

   **B.** Scan the network for frame type option

   **C.** Auto-detect option

   **D.** Choose all frame types

   **Answer:** C

2. Which of the following statements are true of NWLink IPX/SPX Compatible Transport protocol? Choose all that apply.

   **A.** It is Microsoft's implementation of Novell's IPX/SPX protocol stack.

   **B.** It is completely compatible with Novell's IPX/SPX protocol stack.

   **C.** It is suggested, but not required, for use with CSNW and GSNW.

   **D.** Microsoft's implementation of IPX/SPX has built-in support for NetBIOS.

   **Answer:** A, B and D

3. You are sitting at NT Workstation and want to access a NetWare file server so that you can access file and print resources. Which of the following options could be installed at your workstation to allow you access? Choose all that apply.

   **A.** CSNW

   **B.** GSNW

**C.** File and Print Services for NetWare

**D.** Microsoft Services for NetWare

**Answer:** A

**4.** In order for GSNW to work, what group must be created?

**A.** NTGATEWAY on the NetWare file server

**B.** NTGATEWAY on the NT Server

**C.** NWGATEWAY on the NetWare file server

**D.** NWGATEWAY on the NT Server

**Answer:** A

**5.** Which of the following items can be migrated through Migration Tool for NetWare? Choose all the apply.

**A.** Users

**B.** Groups

**C.** Login scripts

**D.** Print queues and print servers

**E.** User passwords

**F.** File structures and permissions

**Answer:** A, B and F

**6.** Which versions of NetWare can be migrated with Migration Tool for NetWare?

**A.** NetWare 2.$x$

**B.** NetWare 3.$x$

**C.** NetWare 4.$x$

**D.** NetWare 2.$x$ and NetWare 3.$x$

**E.** NetWare 2.$x$, NetWare 3.$x$, and NetWare 4.$x$

**Answer:** E

**7.** For the highest level of password security after migrating your NetWare user accounts to NT, which option should you choose?

**A.** Preserve NetWare password

**B.** Password Is:

**C.** Assign Random password

**D.** Use the mapping file

**Answer:** D

## Chapter 10 Answers

**1.** Your boss has heard that Services for Macintosh provides support for Macintosh users on an NT server. He wants to know exactly what SFM will do. Which of the following benefits can you tell him are available with Services for Macintosh? Choose all that apply.

**A.** Macintosh files stored on Macintosh computers are available to NT-PC users.

**B.** Macintosh files stored on NT servers can be shared by Macintosh and PC users.

**C.** Macintosh users can send their print jobs to non-PostScript printers attached to NT servers.

**D.** PC users can send print jobs to PostScript printers attached to Macintosh clients.

**Answer:** B, C and D

**2.** Which of the following requirements must be met on an NT server to support SFM? Choose all that apply.

**A.** Must have 2MB of free disk space

**B.** Must have an NTFS partition for file services

**C.** Must have installed AFP through Control Panel Network option

**D.** Must have 4MB of free disk space

**Answer:** A and B

3. Which option could be used to connect an NT network running Ethernet with a Macintosh network running LocalTalk? Choose all that apply.

**A.** Upgrade the Macintoshes to EtherTalk cards.

**B.** Add a LocalTalk card to the NT server to make it a router.

**C.** Use an external router with LocalTalk and Ethernet.

**D.** Use a LocalTalk-to-Ethernet converter cable on the NT server.

**Answer:** A, B and C

4. Which of the following utilities are modified by SFM? Choose all that apply.

**A.** Server Manager

**B.** User Manager for Domains

**C.** Event Viewer

**D.** File Manager

**Answer:** A and D

5. Which of the following utilities can be used to create a Macintosh-accessible volume? Choose all that apply.

**A.** Server Manager

**B.** MacFile applet

**C.** User Manager for Domains

**D.** File Manager

**Answer:** A and D

6. Which of the following properties can be associated with Macintosh-accessible volumes? Choose all that apply.

   **A.** User limit

   **B.** Volume password

   **C.** File-level security

   **D.** Guest access

   **Answer:** A, B and D

7. If you want to disconnect a Macintosh user who is attached to your NT server, which utility do you use? Choose all that apply.

   **A.** Server Manager

   **B.** MacFile applet

   **C.** User Manager for Domains

   **D.** File Manager

   **Answer:** A and B

## Chapter 11 Answers

1. In order to communicate with a machine on a remote subnet, which of the following must be configured? Choose all that apply.

   **A.** Subnet Mask

   **B.** Default Gateway

   **C.** DNS Server

   **D.** IP Address

   **Answer:** A, B and D

2. Which of the following is not part of the TCP/IP protocol suite?

   **A.** ARP

   **B.** NetBEUI

**C.** UDP

**D.** ICMP

**Answer:** B

3. What does the subnet mask do? Choose the best answer.

**A.** Tells how many bits represent the network address and how many bits represent the host address

**B.** Combines many physical networks into one logical network

**C.** Hides the IP address from the user

**D.** Provides a route to reach remote networks

**Answer:** A

4. Which of the following best describes a NetBIOS name?

**A.** An optional name used instead of an IP address

**B.** An alias programmed into a DNS server

**C.** The computer name, set in the Network Control Panel

**D.** The name assigned by the DHCP server

**Answer:** C

5. Which of the following best describes a host name?

**A.** An optional name used instead of an IP address

**B.** An alias programmed into a DNS server

**C.** The computer name, set in the Network Control Panel

**D.** The name assigned by the DHCP server

**Answer:** A

6. Which of the following are differences between DNS and WINS? Choose all that apply.

**A.** DNS is static and WINS is dynamic.

**B.** DNS is dynamic and WINS is static.

    **C.** DNS maps NetBIOS names to IP addresses and WINS maps host names to IP addresses.

    **D.** DNS maps host names to IP addresses and WINS maps NetBIOS names to IP addresses.

    **Answer:** A and D

# Chapter 12 Answers

**1.** Which Internet services ship with NT Server 4.0? Choose all that apply.

    **A.** Internet Web Surfer

    **B.** Internet Explorer

    **C.** Internet Information Server

    **D.** Internet Information Service

    **Answer:** B and C

**2.** Which services make up IIS? Choose all that apply.

    **A.** HTTP

    **B.** Gopher

    **C.** PPP

    **D.** FTP

    **Answer:** A, B and D

**3.** Which Web browser does Microsoft ship with NT Server 4.0?

    **A.** Internet Explorer

    **B.** IIS

    **C.** Internet Web Crawler

    **D.** Internet Information Explorer

    **Answer:** A

**4.** If you had a question about an Internet standard and wanted to get more information, what would you look for?

**A.** SMTP

**B.** RFC

**C.** Internet Documents Standardized

**D.** Internet Help

**Answer:** B

**5.** What is the name of the Web server that ships with NT Server 4.0?

**A.** Internet Explorer

**B.** Internet Information Server (IIS)

**C.** Internet Web Crawler

**D.** Internet Information Explorer

**Answer:** B

**6.** Which of the following conditions must be met in order to install IIS? Choose all that apply.

**A.** Must be running NT Workstation or NT Server 4.0

**B.** Must be running NT Server 4.0

**C.** Must be using TCP/IP or NWLink IPX/SPX

**D.** Must be running TCP/IP

**E.** Must be logged on as an administrator

**F.** Must be logged on as a server operator or an administrator

**Answer:** B, D and E

**7.** Which of the following password authentication methods used by IIS offers the highest level of security?

   **A.** Allow anonymous

   **B.** Basic (clear text)

   **C.** C2/ E2 authentication response mode

   **D.** Challenge/response

   **Answer:** D

**8.** Which utility is used to manage IIS?

   **A.** IIS Manager

   **B.** Internet Service Manager

   **C.** User Manager for IIS

   **D.** Server Manager for IIS

   **Answer:** B

**9.** The World Wide Web is based on which protocol?

   **A.** HTTP

   **B.** HTML

   **C.** FTP

   **D.** SMTP

   **E.** PPP

   **Answer:** A

**10.** In order to support a virtual server, which two steps should you complete?

   **A.** Assign an IP address for each virtual server to a single network adapter in Control Panel ➤ Network.

   **B.** Assign a home directory to each IP address through the Directories tab in WWW Service Properties.

**C.** Assign multiple IP addresses for each virtual server in the General tab of WWW Service Properties.

**Answer:** A and B

## Chapter 13 Answers

**1.** What two tasks configure an NT machine as a DHCP Relay Agent?

**A.** Install the TCP/IP protocol. Enable IP Routing.

**B.** Install the DHCP Relay Service. Configure the TCP/IP properties with the IP address of a DHCP server.

**C.** Install the DHCP Relay Service. Configure the IP address of a DHCP server in the DHCP Manager.

**D.** Enable IP Routing. Create an LMHOSTS file.

**Answer:** B

**2.** Which protocols is NT 4.0 capable of routing? Choose all that apply.

**A.** IPX

**B.** NetBEUI

**C.** TCP/IP

**D.** NetBIOS

**Answer:** A and C

**3.** If you have a combination of dynamic NT routers using RIP and static NT routers, what will you have to do so all routers can see all network routes?

**A.** Do nothing. The routers will automatically share information.

**B.** Manually add the static routes to the dynamic routers and manually add the routes from the dynamic routers to the static routers.

**C.** Install the RIP protocol on the dynamic routers.

**Answer:** B

# Chapter 14 Answers

1. Which WAN connections are supported by RAS? Choose all that apply.

   **A.** PSTN

   **B.** ISDN

   **C.** X.25

   **D.** PPTP

   **E.** V.32

   > **Answer:** A, B, C and D

2. Which LAN protocols are supported by RAS? Choose all that apply.

   **A.** AFP

   **B.** TCP/IP

   **C.** NetBEUI

   **D.** DLC

   **E.** IPX

   > **Answer:** B, C and E

3. Which utility can be used to find available COM ports in NT Server?

   **A.** Control Panel ➤ Modems (detect available COM ports option)

   **B.** NT Diagnostics

   **C.** Dr. Watson for NT diagnostics

   **D.** Control Panel ➤ Network (detect available COM ports option)

   > **Answer:** B

4. Which LAN protocol requires the least amount of configuration for use with RAS?

   **A.** AFP

   **B.** TCP/IP

   **C.** NetBEUI

   **D.** DLC

   **E.** IPX

    **Answer:** C

**5.** Which of the following protocols supports RAS dial-out and RAS dial-in capabilities?

   **A.** SLIP

   **B.** PPP

   **C.** NetBEUI

   **D.** DLC

   **E.** IPX

    **Answer:** B

**6.** Which RAS callback option provides the greatest level of security?

   **A.** Set By Caller

   **B.** Set by RAS Server

   **C.** Preset To

   **D.** Callback and Confirm RAS password

    **Answer:** C

**7.** Which RAS encryption option also has an additional option to encrypt data?

   **A.** Require encrypted authentication

   **B.** Require C2 encrypted authentication

   **C.** Require C2/E2 encrypted authentication

   **D.** Require Microsoft encrypted authentication

    **Answer:** D

8. Where in NT Server do you specify which users have dialin permission to the RAS server?

   **A.** User Manager for Domains

   **B.** Control Panel ≻ Network ≻ Services ≻ RAS ≻ Properties

   **C.** Administrative Tools ≻ Remote Access Admin

   **D.** Control Panel ≻ Remote Access Admin

   **Answer:** C

## Chapter 15 Answers

1. What needs to be done in order to enable disk counters in Performance Monitor?

   **A.** Enable disk counters through Tools in Disk Administrator.

   **B.** Enable disk counters through Tools in Performance Monitor.

   **C.** Run the DISKMON command.

   **D.** Run the DISKPERF command.

   **Answer:** D

2. Which utilities can be used to display your CPU's current utilization? Choose all that apply.

   **A.** Performance Monitor

   **B.** Network Monitor

   **C.** Task Manager

   **D.** Windows NT Diagnostics

   **Answer:** A and C

3. Which of the following views is not available through Performance Monitor?

   **A.** Chart

   **B.** Report

**C.** Log

**D.** Graph

**Answer:** D

4. Which view through Performance Monitor would you choose if you wanted to create a baseline for future reference?

**A.** Chart

**B.** Report

**C.** Log

**D.** Graph

**Answer:** C

5. Which Server Optimization method is recommended if your server supports under 10 users?

**A.** Minimize Memory Used

**B.** Balance

**C.** Maximize Throughput for File Sharing

**D.** Manage Throughput for Network Applications

**Answer:** A

6. Which Server Optimization method is recommended if your server supports distributed applications such as SQL server?

**A.** Minimize Memory Used

**B.** Balance

**C.** Maximize Throughput for File Sharing

**D.** Manage Throughput for Network Applications

**Answer:** D

## Chapter 16 Answers

1. Which of the following can be tracked with Network Monitor in NT Server? Choose all that apply.

   **A.** Any packet sent over the local network

   **B.** Any packet sent over the network, even packets across a router

   **C.** Packets sent to or from the server

   **D.** Broadcast packets

   **Answer:** C and D

2. If you want to use a fully functional Network Monitor, which additional package should you purchase?

   **A.** SQL

   **B.** SMS

   **C.** Network Monitor v2.0

   **D.** Network Monitor v3.0

   **Answer:** B

3. Assuming that NT Server has been installed to C: in the WINNT directory, what is the default directory that captured data is saved in by default through Network Monitor?

   **A.** C:\WINNT\SYSTEM32\NETMON\CAPTURES

   **B.** C:\WINNT\NETMON\CAPTURES

   **C.** C:\WINNT\SYSTEM32\REPL\NETMON\CAPTURES

   **D.** C:\NETMON\CAPTURES

   **Answer:** A

4. Which properties can be filtered through the Network Monitor filter process? Choose all that apply.

   **A.** Hex strings

   **B.** Protocols

**C.** Computer address

**D.** Protocol properties

**Answer:** B, C and D

5. Where would you set a password that could only be used to view previously saved network captures with Network Monitor?

**A.** Network Monitor through Administrative Tools

**B.** Network Monitor through Control Panel

**C.** Monitoring Agent through Administrative Tools

**D.** Monitoring Agent through Control Panel

**Answer:** D

# Chapter 17 Answers

1. You have a system and boot partition on drive `C:`. You want to protect them with disk fault tolerance. Which options of RAID can you use through NT Server software? Choose all that apply.

**A.** RAID 1

**B.** RAID 2

**C.** RAID 3

**D.** RAID 4

**E.** RAID 5

**Answer:** A

2. Your primary drive in a mirrored set has just failed. The drive contains the boot partition. What is the best way to recover from the failure?

**A.** Replace the failed hardware, use the NT startup disk you created prior to failure, regenerate the mirror set.

**B.** Replace the failed hardware, use the NT emergency repair disk, regenerate the mirror set.

**C.** Replace the failed hardware and boot to the Last Known Good option and then regenerate the failed set.

**D.** Replace the failed hardware and restore your system through your tape backup.

**Answer:** A

3. One of your drives fails in your stripe set with parity. What do you do?

**A.** Replace the failed hardware, use the NT startup disk you created prior to failure, regenerate the stripe set.

**B.** Replace the failed hardware, use the NT emergency repair disk, regenerate the stripe set.

**C.** Replace the failed hardware and use Disk Administrator to regenerate the stripe set.

**D.** Replace the failed hardware and restore your system through your tape backup.

**Answer:** C

4. Two of your drives fail in your stripe set with parity. What do you do?

**A.** Replace the failed hardware, use the NT startup disk you created prior to failure, regenerate the stripe set.

**B.** Replace the failed hardware, use the NT emergency repair disk, regenerate the stripe set.

**C.** Replace the failed hardware and use Disk Administrator to regenerate the stripe set.

**D.** Replace the failed hardware and restore your system through your tape backup.

**Answer:** D

5. Which RAID levels are supported through NT Server software? Choose all that apply.

**A.** RAID 1

**B.** RAID 2

**C.** RAID 3

**D.** RAID 4

**E.** RAID 5

**Answer:** A and E

# Chapter 18 Answers

1. If you were dual-booting to DOS and DOS would not load, which boot file would you check first?

   **A.** NTLDR

   **B.** BOOT.INI

   **C.** BOOTSECT.DOS

   **D.** NTDETECT.COM

   **Answer:** C

2. Which file is used to specify the location of the boot partition during NT system startup?

   **A.** NTLDR

   **B.** BOOT.INI

   **C.** BOOTSECT.DOS

   **D.** NTDETECT.COM

   **Answer:** B

3. You just added a new driver to NT and now your computer won't reboot successfully. What should be your first course of action?

   **A.** Use the ERD.

   **B.** Restore from tape backup.

   **C.** Use the Last Known Good configuration.

   **D.** Do a cold boot on your computer so NTDETECT can attempt to fix the problem.

   **Answer:** D

4. Which Registry subtree contains information regarding the computer's configuration and hardware settings?

   **A.** HKEY_CURRENT_USER

   **B.** HKEY_USERS

   **C.** HKEY_CURRENT_CONFIG

**D.** HKEY_CLASSES_ROOT

**E.** HKEY_LOCAL_MACHINE

**Answer:** C

5. Your NT Server keeps crashing. You have called Microsoft for help and they tell you to send them a Memory Dump. How do you create this file?

**A.** Configure the recovery option to write debugging information to a file through Startup/Shutdown Properties in Control Panel ➤ System.

**B.** Through NT diagnostics, configure Create a crash debug file under the Memory tab.

**C.** Use the Event Viewer to view the Memory Dump automatically.

**D.** Use Dr. Watson for NT to create the Memory Dump file.

**Answer:** A

6. Which utility do you use to create an emergency repair disk?

**A.** ERD

**B.** REPAIRDSK

**C.** Windows NT Diagnostics

**D.** RDISK

**Answer:** D

7. Which of the following statements is true of the ERD?

**A.** The ERD is bootable.

**B.** You can copy needed files from the ERD to a hard drive.

**C.** To use the ERD, you must first boot to the NT setup disks.

**D.** To restore from the ERD, use the RDISK utility.

**Answer:** C

Glossary

APPENDIX

B

**Access Control Entries (ACE)** Each Access Control List (ACL) has an associated ACE which lists the permissions that have been granted or denied to the users and groups listed in the ACL. See *Access Control List*.

**Access Control List (ACL)** Lists of security identifiers contained by objects that allow only certain processes—those identified in the list as having the appropriate permission—to activate the services of that object. See *Object, Security Identifier, Permissions*.

**Access Tokens** Objects containing the security identifier of a running process. A process started by another process inherits the starting process's access token. The access token is checked against each object's ACL to determine whether or not appropriate permissions are granted to perform any requested service. See *Access Control List, Access Control Entries, permissions, object, Security Identifier, Process*.

**Account Lockout** Used to specify how many invalid logon attempts should be tolerated before a user account is locked out. Account lockout is set through User Manager for Domains. See *Security, User Manager for Domains*.

**Account Policies** Account policies are used to determine password and logon requirements. Account policies are set through User Manager for Domains. See *User Manager for Domains*.

**Accounts** Containers for security identifiers, passwords, permissions, group associations, and preferences for each user of a system. The User Manager for Domains utility is used to administer accounts. See *Security Identifier, Preferences, Permissions, Passwords, Groups*.

**ACE** See *Access Control Entries*.

**ACL** See *Access Control List*.

**Adapter** Any hardware device that allows communications to occur through physically dissimilar systems. This term usually refers to peripheral cards that are permanently mounted inside computers and provide an interface from the computer's bus to another media such as a hard disk or a network. See *Network Interface Card, SCSI*.

**Address Resolution Protocol (ARP)** An Internet protocol for resolving an IP address into a Physical layer address (such as an Ethernet media access controller address). See *Physical layer, Internet Protocol.*

**Administrative Tools** A program group on NT domain controllers that contains utilities such as User Manager for Domains, Server Manager, Disk Administrator, Performance Monitor, and Network Monitor. See *User Manager for Domains, Server Manager, Disk Administrator, Performance Monitor, Network Monitor.*

**ADMINISTRATOR Account** A special account in Windows NT that has the ultimate set of security permissions and can assign any permission to any user or group. The ADMINISTRATOR account is used to correct security problems. See *Permissions.*

**Administrators** Users who are part of the ADMINISTRATORS group. This group has the ultimate set of security permissions. See *Administrator Account, Permissions, Groups.*

**Advanced Projects Agency Network (ARPANET)** Predecessor to the Internet that was developed by the Department of Defense in the late 1960's.

**AppleTalk** The built-in (to firmware) suite of network protocols used by Macintosh computers. Windows NT Server uses AppleTalk to service Macintosh clients by simulating an Apple server. See *Macintosh, Network Protocol.*

**Applications** Large software packages that perform a specific function, such as word processing, Web browsing, or database management. Applications typically consist of more than one program. See *Programs.*

**Application Layer** The layer of the OSI model that interfaces with User mode programs called applications by providing high-level network services based upon lower-level network layers. Network file systems like named pipes are an example of Application-layer software. See *Named Pipes, OSI Model, Application.*

**ARP** See *Address Resolution Protocol.*

**ARPANET** See *Advanced Research Projects Agency Network.*

**Asymmetrical Multiprocessing** A multiple processor architecture in which certain processors are designated to run certain threads or in which scheduling is not done on a fair-share basis. Asymmetrical multiprocessing is easier to implement than symmetrical multiprocessing, but does not scale well as processors are added. See *Microprocessor, Symmetrical Multiprocessing.*

**Asynchronous Transfer Mode (ATM)** A wide area transport protocol that runs at many different speeds and supports real-time, guaranteed packet delivery in hardware, as well as lower-quality levels of service on a bandwidth-available basis. ATM will eventually replace all other wide area protocols, as most worldwide PTSN providers have declared their support for the international standard. See *Public Switched Telephone Network, Wide Area Network.*

**ATM** See *Asynchronous Transfer Mode.*

**Audit Policy** Audit policy determines which user events you wish to track for security reasons. Audit policy can track the success or failure of specified security events; it is set in the User Manager for Domains. See *Security, User Manager for Domains.*

**Back Up** The process of writing all the data contained in online mass storage devices to offline mass storage devices for the purpose of safe keeping. Backups are usually performed from hard disk drives to tape drives. Also referred to as archiving. See *Hard Disk Drive.*

**Backup Browser** A computer on a Microsoft network that maintains a list of computers and services available on the network. The Master Browser supplies this list. The backup browser distributes the Browsing service load to a workgroup or domain. See *Master Browser.*

**Backup Domain Controllers** Servers that contain accurate replications of the security and user databases; these servers can authenticate workstations in the absence of a primary domain controller (PDC). See *Primary Domain Controller.*

**Baseline** A snapshot record of your computer's current performance statistics that can be used for analysis and planning purposes.

**Basic Input/Output System (BIOS)** A set of routines in firmware that provides the most basic software interface drivers for hardware attached to the computer. The BIOS contains the bootstrap routine. See *Boot, Driver, Firmware*.

**Bindery** A NetWare structure that contains user accounts and permissions. It is similar to the Security Accounts Manager in Windows NT. See *Security Accounts Manager*.

**Binding** The process of linking network services to network service providers. The binding facility allows users to define exactly how network services operate in order to optimize the performance of the system. By default, Windows enables all possible bindings. The Network control panel is used to change bindings. See *Network Layer, Data Link Layer*.

**BIOS** See *Basic Input/Output System*.

**Bit** A binary digit. A numeral having only two possible values, 0 or 1. Computers represent these two values as high (voltage present) or low (no voltage present) state on a control line. Bits are accumulated in sets of certain sizes to represent higher values. See *Byte*.

**Boot** The process of loading a computer's operating system. Booting usually occurs in multiple phases, each successively more complex until the entire operating system and all its services are running. Also called bootstrap. The computer's BIOS must contain the first level of booting. See *Basic Input/ Output System*.

**Boot Partition** The boot partition is the partition that contains the system files. The system files are located in C:\WINNT by default. See *Partition, System Partition*.

**BOOTP** See *Bootstrap Protocol*.

**Bootstrap Protocol (BOOTP)** Predecessor to the DHCP protocol. BOOTP was used to assign IP addresses to diskless workstations. See *Dynamic Host Configuration Protocol*.

**Bottlenecks** Components operating at their peak capacity that restrict the flow of information through a system. Used singularly, the term indicates the single most restrictive component in a system.

**Bridge** A device that connects two networks of the same Data Link protocol by forwarding those packets destined for computers on the other side of the bridge. See *Router, Data Link Layer.*

**Browser** A computer on a Microsoft network that maintains a list of computers and services available on the network.

**Browsing** The process of requesting the list of computers and services on a network from a browser.

**Caching** A speed optimization technique that keeps a copy of the most recently used data in a fast, high-cost, low-capacity storage device rather than in the device upon which the actual data resides. Caching assumes that recently used data is likely to be used again. Fetching data from the cache is faster than fetching data from the slower, larger storage device. Most caching algorithms also copy next-most-likely to be used data and perform write caching to further increase speed gains. See *Write-Back Caching, Write-Through Caching.*

**CD-ROM** See *Compact Disk-Read Only Memory.*

**Central Processing Unit (CPU)** The central processing unit of a computer. In microcomputers such as IBM PC compatible machines, the CPU is the microprocessor. See *Microprocessor.*

**Client** A computer on a network that subscribes to the services provided by a server. See *Server.*

**Client Services for NetWare (CSNW)** A service provided with Windows NT that connects an NT client to NetWare file servers. See *NetWare, Client Services for NetWare.*

**Client/Server** A network architecture that dedicates certain computers called servers to act as service providers to computers called clients, which users operate to perform work. Servers can be dedicated to providing one or more network services such as file storage, shared printing, communications, e-mail service, and Web response. See *Share, Peer.*

**Client/Server Applications** Applications that split large applications into two components: computer-intensive processes that run on application servers and user interfaces that run on clients. Client/server applications communicate over the network through interprocess communication mechanisms. See *Client, Server, Interprocess Communications.*

**Code** Synonymous with software but used when the software is the object of discussion, rather than the utility it provides. See *Software*.

**COM Port** Communications port. A serial hardware interface conforming to the RS-232 standard for low-speed serial communications. See *Modem, Serial*.

**Compact Disk-Read Only Memory (CD-ROM)** A media for storing extremely large software packages on optical read-only discs. CD-ROM is an adaptation of the CD medium used for distributing digitized music. CD-ROM discs can hold up to 650MB of information and cost very little to produce in mass quantity. See *Hard Disk Drive*.

**Components** Interchangeable elements of a complex software or hardware system. See *Module*.

**Compression** A space optimization scheme that reduces the size (length) of a data set by exploiting the fact that most useful data contains a great deal of redundancy. Compression reduces redundancy by creating symbols smaller than the data they represent and an index that defines the value of the symbols for each compressed set of data.

**Computer** A device capable of performing automatic calculations based upon lists of instructions called programs. The computer feeds the results of these calculations (output) to peripheral devices that can represent them in useful ways, such as graphics on a screen or ink on paper. See *Microprocessor*.

**Computer Name** A 1-15 character NetBIOS name used to uniquely identify a computer on the network. See *Network Basic Input/Output System*.

**Control Panel** A software utility that controls the function of specific operating system services by allowing users to change default settings for the service to match their preferences. The Registry contains the Control Panel settings on a system and/or per-user basis. See *Registry, Account*.

**Cooperative Multitasking** A multitasking scheme in which each process must voluntarily return time to a central scheduling route. If any single process fails to return to the central scheduler, the computer will lock up. Both Windows and the Macintosh operating system use this scheme. See *Preemptive Multitasking, Windows for Workgroups 3.11*.

**CPU** See *Microprocessor*.

**CSNW** See *Client Services for NetWare*.

**Data Link Control (DLC)** An obsolete network transport protocol that allows PCs to connects to older IBM mainframes and HP printers. See *TCP/IP*.

**Data Link Layer** In the OSI model, the layer that provides the digital interconnection of network devices and the software that directly operates these devices, such as network interface adapters. See *Physical Layer, Network Layer, OSI Model*.

**Database** A related set of data organized by type and purpose. The term also can include the application software that manipulates the data. The Windows NT Registry (a database itself) contains a number of utility databases such as user account and security information. See *Registry*.

**DDE** See *Dynamic Data Exchange*.

**Default Shares** Resources shared by default when Windows NT is installed. See *Share, Resource*.

**Desktop** A directory that the background of the Windows Explorer shell represents. By default the desktop contains objects that contain the local storage devices and available network shares. Also a key operating part of the Windows GUI. See *Explorer, Shell*.

**DHCP** See *Dynamic Host Configuration Protocol*.

**Dial-Up Connections** Data Link-layer digital connections made via modems over regular telephone lines. The term *dial-up* refers to temporary digital connections, as opposed to leased telephone lines, which provide permanent connections. See *Data Link Layer, Public Switched Telephone Network, Modem*.

**Directories** In a file system directories are containers that store files or other directories. Mass storage devices have a root directory that contains all other directories, thus creating a hierarchy of directories sometimes referred to as a *directory tree*. See *File, File System*.

**Directory Replication** The process of copying a directory structure from an import computer to an export computer(s). Anytime changes are made to the export computer, the import computer(s) is automatically updated with the changes.

**Disk Administrator** Graphical utility used to manage disks.

**Disk Duplexing** Disk duplexing is similar to disk mirroring, but in addition to the features of disk mirroring, also uses two separate controllers for better performance and reliability. See *Disk Mirroring*.

**Disk Mirroring** The process of keeping an exact duplicate of data on two different partitions located on different physical drives. Used for fault tolerance. See *Disk Duplexing*.

**Disk Striping** Data that is stored across partitions of identical size on different drives. Also referred to as RAID 0. See *Redundant Array of Inexpensive Disks*.

**Disk Striping with Parity** Disk striping with parity distributed across the stripe set for fault tolerance features. Also referred to as RAID 5. See *Stripe Set, Redundant Array of Inexpensive Disks*.

**DLC** See *Data Link Control*.

**DNS** See *Domain Name Service*.

**Domain** In Microsoft networks, a domain is an arrangement of client and server computers referenced by a specific name that share a single security permissions database. On the Internet, a domain is a named collection of hosts and subdomains, registered with a unique name by the InterNIC. See *Workgroup, InterNIC*.

**Domain Controllers** Servers that authenticate workstation network logon requests by comparing a username and password against account information stored in the user accounts database. A user cannot access a domain without authentication from a domain controller. See *Primary Domain Controller, Backup Domain Controller, Domain*.

**Domain Name** The textual identifier of a specific Internet Host. Domain names are in the form of `server.organization.type` (`www.microsoft.com`) and are resolved to Internet addresses by Domain Name Servers. See *Domain Name Server*.

**Domain Name Server** An Internet host dedicated to the function of translating fully qualified domain names into IP addresses. See *Domain Name*.

**Domain Name Service (DNS)** The TCP/IP network service that translates textual Internet network addresses into numerical Internet network addresses. See *TCP/IP, Internet.*

**Drive** See *Hard Disk Drive.*

**Drive Letters** Single letters assigned as abbreviations to the mass storage volumes available to a computer. See *Volumes.*

**Driver** A program that provides a software interface to a hardware device. Drivers are written for the specific device they control, but they present a common software interface to the computer's operating system, allowing all devices (of a similar type) to be controlled as if they were the same. See *Data Link Layer, Operating System.*

**Dynamic Data Exchange (DDE)** A method of interprocess communication within the Microsoft Windows operating systems.

**Dynamic Host Configuration Protocol (DHCP)** DHCP is a method of automatically assigning IP addresses to client computers on a network.

**Electronic Mail (e-Mail)** A type of client/server application that provides a routed, stored-message service between any two user e-mail accounts. E-mail accounts are not the same as user accounts, but a one-to-one relationship usually exists between them. Because all modern computers can attach to the Internet, users can send e-mail over the Internet to any location that has telephone or wireless digital service. See *Internet.*

**Emergency Repair Disk** A disk containing the critical system files (such as portions of the Registry, the `autoexec.bat` file, and the `config.sys` file) necessary to recover your NT machine in some cases.

**Encryption** The process of obscuring information by modifying it according to a mathematical function known only to the intended recipient. Encryption secures information being transmitted over nonsecure or untrusted media. See *Security.*

**Enterprise Network** A complex network consisting of multiple servers and multiple domains over a large geographic area.

**Environment Variables** Variables, such as the search path, that contain information available to programs and batch files about the current operating system environment.

**ERD** See *Emergency Repair Disk*.

**Ethernet** The most popular Data Link-layer standard for local area networking. Ethernet implements the carrier sense multiple access with collision detection (CSMA/CD) method of arbitrating multiple computer access to the same network. This standard supports the use of Ethernet over any type of media including wireless broadcast. Standard Ethernet operates as 10 megabits per second. Fast Ethernet operates at 100 megabits per second. See *Data Link Layer*.

**Exchange** Microsoft's messaging application. Exchange implements Microsoft's mail application programming interface (MAPI) as well as other messaging protocols such as POP, SNMP, and faxing to provide a flexible message composition and reception service. See *Electronic Mail, Fax Modem*.

**Explorer** The default shell for Windows 95 and Windows NT 4.0. Explorer implements the more flexible desktop objects paradigm rather than the Program Manager paradigm used in earlier versions of Windows. See Desktop.

**FAT** See *File Allocation Table*.

**Fault Tolerance** Any method that prevents system failure by tolerating single faults, usually through hardware redundancy.

**Fax Modems** Special modems that include hardware to allow the transmission and reception of facsimiles. See *Modem, Exchange*.

**FDDI** See *Fiber Distributed Data Interface*.

**Fiber Distributed Data Interface (FDDI)** A Data Link layer that implements two counter-rotating token rings at 100 megabits per second. FDDI was a popular standard for interconnecting campus and metropolitan area networks because it allows distant digital connections at high speed, but ATM is replacing FDDI in many sites. See *Asynchronous Transfer Mode, Data Link Layer*.

**File Allocation Table (FAT)** The file system used by MS-DOS and available to other operating systems such as Windows (all versions), OS/2, and the Macintosh. FAT has become something of a mass storage compatibility standard because of its simplicity and wide availability. FAT has few fault tolerance features and can become corrupted through normal use over time. See *File System*.

**File Attributes** Bits stored along with the name and location of a file in a directory entry that show the status of a file, such as archived, hidden, read-only, etc. Different operating systems use different file attributes to implement such services as sharing, compression, and security.

**File System** A software component that manages the storage of files on a mass storage device by providing services that can create, read, write, and delete files. File systems impose an ordered database of files on the mass storage device, called volumes, that use hierarchies of directories to organize files. See *Mass Storage Device, Files, Database, Volumes, Directories.*

**File Transfer Protocol (FTP)** A simple Internet protocol that transfers complete files from an FTP server to a client running the FTP client. FTP provides a simple no-overhead method of transferring files between computers but cannot perform browsing functions. You must know the URL of the FTP server to which you wish to attach. See *Internet, Uniform Resource Locator.*

**Files** A set of data stored on a mass storage device identified by a directory entry containing a name, file attributes, and the physical location of the file in the volume. See *Volume, Mass Storage Device, Directory, File Attributes.*

**Firmware** Software stored permanently in nonvolatile memory and built into a computer to provide its BIOS and a bootstrap routine. Simple computers may have their entire operating system built into firmware. See *BIOS, Boot, Software.*

**Format** The process of preparing a mass storage device for use with a file system. There are actually two levels of formatting. Low-level formatting writes a structure of sectors and tracks to the disk with bits used by the mass storage controller hardware. The controller hardware requires this format, and it is independent of the file system. High-level formatting creates file system structures such as an allocation table and a root directory in a partition, thus creating a volume. See *Mass Storage Device, Volume.*

**Frame** A data structure that network hardware devices use to transmit data between computers. Frames consist of the addresses of the sending and receiving computers, size information, and a check sum. Frames are envelopes around packets of data that allow the packets to be addressed to specific computers on a shared media network. See *Ethernet, FDDI, Token Ring.*

**FTP** See *File Transfer Protocol.*

**Gateway** A computer that serves as a router, a format translator, or a security filter for an entire network.

**Gateway Services for NetWare (GSNW)** An NT Server service that is used to connect NT Servers and NT clients to NetWare resources via the gateway software. See *Gateway, NetWare, Client Services for NetWare*.

**GDI** See *Graphical Device Interface*.

**Global Group** A special group that only exists on NT Server domain controllers. A global group can only contain members from within its domain. See *Local Group*.

**Gopher** Serves text and links to other Gopher sites. Gopher pre-dates HTTP by about a year, but has been made obsolete by the richer format provided by HTTP. See *Hypertext Transfer Protocol*.

**Graphical Device Interface (GDI)** The programming interface and graphical services provided to Win32 for programs to interact with graphical devices such as the screen and printer. See *Programming Interface, Win32*.

**Graphical User Interface (GUI)** A computer shell program that represents mass storage devices, directories, and files as graphical objects on a screen. A cursor driven by a pointing device such as a mouse manipulates the objects. See *Shell, Explorer*.

**Group Identifiers** Security identifiers that contain the set of permissions given to a group. When a user account is part of a group, the group identifier is appended to that user's security identifier, thus granting the individual user all the permissions assigned to that group. See *Security Identifier, Accounts, Permissions*.

**Groups** Security entities to which users can be assigned membership for the purpose of applying the broad set of group permissions to the user. By managing permissions for groups and assigning users to groups, rather than assigning permissions to users, security administrators can keep coherent control of very large security environments. See *Permissions, Accounts, Security, Local Group, Global Group*.

**GSNW** See *Gateway Services for NetWare*.

**GUI** See *Graphical User Interface*.

**HAL** See *Hardware Abstraction Layer*.

**Hard Disk** See *Hard Disk Drives*.

**Hard Disk Drives** Mass storage devices that read and write digital information magnetically on discs that spin under moving heads. Hard disk drives are precisely aligned and cannot normally be removed. Hard disk drives are an inexpensive way to store gigabytes of computer data permanently. Hard disk drives also store the installed software of a computer. See *Mass Storage Device*.

**Hardware Abstraction Layer (HAL)** A Windows NT service that provides basic input/output services such as timers, interrupts, and multiprocessor management for computer hardware. The HAL is a device driver for the motherboard circuitry that allows different families of computers to be treated the same by the Windows NT operating system. See *Driver, Service, Interrupt Request*.

**Hardware Compatibility List (HCL)** The listing of all hardware devices supported by Windows NT. Hardware on the HCL has been tested and verified as being compatible with NT. You can view the current HCL at `http://microsoft.com/ntserver/hcl`.

**Hardware Profiles** Used to manage portable computers which have different configurations based on their location.

**HCL** See *Hardware Compatibility List*.

**High Performance File System (HPFS)** The file system native to OS/2 that performs many of the same functions of NTFS when run under OS/2. See *File System, New Technology File System*.

**Home Directory** A directory used to store users' personal files and programs.

**Home Page** The default page returned by an HTTP server when a URL containing no specific document is requested. See *Hypertext Transfer Protocol, Uniform Resource Locator*.

**Host** An Internet Server. Hosts are constantly connected to the Internet. See *Internet*.

**HPFS** See *High Performance File System*.

**HTML** See *Hypertext Markup Language.*

**HTTP** See *Hypertext Transfer Protocol.*

**Hyperlink** A link embedded in text or graphics that has a Web address embedded in it. By clicking the link, you jump to another Web address. You can identify a hyperlink because it is a different color from the rest of the Web page. See *World Wide Web.*

**Hypertext Markup Language (HTML)** A textual data format that identifies such sections of a document as headers, lists, hypertext links, etc. HTML is the data format used on the World Wide Web for the publication of Web pages. See *Hypertext Transfer Protocol, World Wide Web.*

**Hypertext Transfer Protocol (HTTP)** Hypertext transfer protocol is an Internet protocol that transfers HTML documents over the Internet and responds to context changes that happen when a user clicks on a hypertext link. See *Hypertext Markup Language, World Wide Web.*

**Icon** A graphical representation of a resource (in a graphical user interface) that usually takes the form of a small (32 × 32) bitmap. See *Graphical User Interface.*

**IDE** A simple mass storage device interconnection bus that operates at 5Mbps and can handle no more than two attached devices. IDE devices are similar to but less expensive than SCSI devices. See *Small Computer Systems Interface, Mass Storage Device.*

**IIS** See *Internet Information Server.*

**Industry Standard Architecture (ISA)** The design standard for 16-bit Intel compatible motherboards and peripheral buses. The 32/64-bit PCI bus standard is replacing the ISA standard. Adapters and interface cards must conform to the bus standard(s) used by the motherboard in order to be used with a computer.

**Integrated Services Digital Network (ISDN)** A direct, digital dial-up PSTN Data Link-layer connection that operates at 64KB per channel over regular twisted pair cable between a subscriber site and a PSTN central office. ISDN provides twice the data rate of the fastest modems per channel. Up to 24 channels can be multiplexed over two twisted pairs. See *Public Switched Telephone Network, Data Link Layer, Modem.*

**Intel Architecture** A family of microprocessors descended from the Intel 8086, itself descended from the first microprocessor, the Intel 4004. The Intel architecture is the dominant microprocessor family. It was used in the original IBM PC microcomputer adopted by the business market and later adapted for home use.

**Interactive User** A user who physically logs on to the computer where the user account resides is considered interactive, as opposed to a user who logs in over the network. See *Network User*.

**Internet** A voluntarily interconnected global network of computers based upon the TCP/IP protocol suite. TCP/IP was originally developed by the U.S. Department of Defense's Advanced Research Projects Agency to facilitate the interconnection of military networks and was provided free to universities. The obvious utility of worldwide digital network connectivity and the availability of free complex networking software developed at universities doing military research attracted other universities, research institutions, private organizations, businesses, and finally the individual home user. The Internet is now available to all current commercial computing platforms. See *FTP, Telnet, World Wide Web, TCP/IP*.

**Internet Explorer** A World Wide Web browser produced by Microsoft and included free with Windows 95 and Windows NT 4.0. See *World Wide Web, Internet*.

**Internet Information Server (IIS)** Serves Internet higher level protocols like HTTP and FTP to clients using Web browsers. See *Hypertext Transfer Protocol, File Transfer Protocol, and World Wide Web*.

**Internet Protocol (IP)** The Network layer protocol upon which the Internet is based. IP provides a simple connectionless packet exchange. Other protocols such as UDP or TCP use IP to perform their connection-oriented or guaranteed delivery services. See *TCP/IP, Internet*.

**Internet Service Provider (ISP)** A company that provides dial-up connections to the Internet. See *Internet*.

**Internetwork Packet eXchange (IPX)** The Network and Transport layer protocol developed by Novell for its NetWare product. IPX is a routable, connection-oriented protocol similar to TCP/IP but much easier to manage and with lower communication overhead. See *IP, NetWare, NWLink*.

**InterNIC** The agency that is responsible for assigning IP addresses. See *Internet Protocol, IP Address.*

**Interprocess Communications (IPC)** A generic term describing any manner of client/server communication protocol, specifically those operating in the application layer. Interprocess communications mechanisms provide a method for the client and server to trade information. See *Named Pipes, Remote Procedure Call, NetBIOS, Mailslots, NetDDE, Local Procedure Call.*

**Interrupt Request (IRQ)** A hardware signal from a peripheral device to the microcomputer indicating that it has I/O traffic to send. If the microprocessor is not running a more important service, it will interrupt its current activity and handle the interrupt request. IBM PCs have 16 levels of interrupt request lines. Under Windows NT each device must have a unique interrupt request line. See *Microprocessor, Driver, Peripheral.*

**Intranet** A privately owned network based on the TCP/IP protocol suite. See *Transmission Control Protocol/Internet Protocol.*

**IP** See *Internet Protocol.*

**IP Address** A 4-byte number that uniquely identifies a computer on an IP internetwork. InterNIC assigns the first bytes of Internet IP addresses and administers them in hierarchies. Huge organizations like the government or top-level ISPs have class A addresses, large organizations and most ISPs have class B addresses, and small companies have class C addresses. In a class A address, InterNIC assigns the first byte, and the owning organization assigns the remaining three bytes. In a class B address, InterNIC or the higher level ISP assigns the first two bytes, and the organization assigns the remaining two bytes. In a class C address, InterNIC or the higher level ISP assigns the first three bytes , and the organization assigns the remaining byte. Organizations not attached to the Internet are free to assign IP addresses as they please. See *IP, Internet, InterNIC.*

**IPC** See *Interprocess Communications.*

**IPX** See *Internetwork Packet eXchange.*

**IRQ** See *Interrupt Request.*

**ISA** See *Industry Standard Architecture.*

**ISDN** See *Integrated Services Digital Network.*

**ISP** See *Internet Service Provider*.

**Kernel** The core process of a preemptive operating system, consisting of a multitasking scheduler and the basic security services. Depending upon the operating system, other services such as virtual memory drivers may be built into the Kernel. The Kernel is responsible for managing the scheduling of threads and processes. See *Operating System*, *Drivers*.

**LAN** See Local Area Network.

**LAN Manager** The Microsoft brand of a network product jointly developed by IBM and Microsoft that provided an early client/server environment. LAN Manager/Server was eclipsed by NetWare, but was the genesis of many important protocols and IPC mechanisms used today, such as NetBIOS, named pipes, and NetBEUI. Portions of this product exist today in OS/2 Warp Server. See *OS/2, Interprocess Communications*.

**LAN Server** The IBM brand of a network product jointly developed by IBM and Microsoft. See *LAN Manager*.

**Local Area Network (LAN)** A network of computers operating on the same high-speed, shared media network Data Link layer. The size of a local area network is defined by the limitations of high speed shared media networks to generally less than 1 kilometer in overall span. Some LAN backbone Data Link-layer protocols such as FDDI can create larger LANs called metropolitan or medium area networks (MANs). See *Wide Area Network, Data Link Layer*.

**Local Group** A group that exists in an NT computer's local accounts database. Local groups can reside on NT Workstations or NT Servers and can contain users or global groups. See *Global Group*.

**Local Printer** A local printer is a printer that uses a physical port and that has not been shared. If a printer is defined as local, the only users who can use the printer are the local users of the computer that the printer is attached to. See *Printer, Printing Device, Network Printer*.

**Local Procedure Call (LPC)** A mechanism that loops remote procedure calls without the presence of a network so that the client and server portion of an application can reside on the same machine. Local procedure calls look like remote procedure calls (RPCs) to the client and server sides of a distributed application. See *Remote Procedure Call*.

**Local Security** Security that governs a local or interactive user. Local security can be set through NTFS partitions. See *Security, Interactive User, New Technology File System, Network Security*.

**LocalTalk** A Data Link-layer standard for local area networking used by Macintosh computers. LocalTalk is available on all Macintosh computers. The drawback of LocalTalk is that is only transmits at 230.4 kilobits per second (as opposed to Ethernet which can transmit at 10 megabits per second). See *Data Link Layer, Macintosh*.

**Logging** The process of recording information about activities and errors in the operating system.

**Logical Port** Printers can be attached to a network through a logical port. A logical port uses a direct connection to gain access to the network. This is done by installing a network card on the printer. The advantages to using logical ports are that they are much faster than physical ports and that you are not limited to the cabling limitations imposed by parallel and serial cable distances allowed when connecting a printer to a PC's parallel or serial ports. See *Printer, Printing Device*.

**Logoff** The process of closing an open session with a server. See *Logon*.

**Logon** The process of opening a network session by providing a valid authentication consisting of a user account name and a password to a domain controller. After logon, network resources are available to the user according to the user's assigned permissions. See *Domain Controller, Logoff*.

**Logon Script** Command files that automate the logon process by performing utility functions such as attaching to additional server resources or automatically running different programs based upon the user account that established the logon. See *Logon*.

**Long Filename (LFN)** A filename longer than the eight characters plus three-character extension allowed by MS-DOS. In Windows NT and Windows 95, long filenames may be up to 255 characters.

**LPC** See *Local Procedure Call*.

**Macintosh** A brand of computer manufactured by Apple Computers, Inc. Macintosh is the only successful line of computers neither based upon the original IBM PC nor running the UNIX operating system. Windows NT Server supports Apple computers despite their use of proprietary network protocols.

**MacOS** The operating system that runs on an Apple Macintosh computer. See *Macintosh*.

**Mailslots** A connectionless messaging IPC mechanism that Windows NT uses for browse request and logon authentication. See *Interprocess Communications*.

**Mandatory User Profile** A profile created by an administrator and saved with a special extension (`.man`) so that the user cannot modify the profile in any way. Mandatory user profiles can be assigned to a single user or a group of users. See *User Profile*.

**Mass Storage Device** Any device capable of storing many megabytes of information permanently, but especially those capable of random access to any portion of the information, such as hard disk drives and CD-ROM drives. See *SCSI, IDE, Hard Disk Drive, CD-ROM Drive*.

**Master Browser** A network computer that keeps a list of computers and services available on the network and distributes the list to other browsers. The Master Browser may also promote potential browsers to be browsers. See *Browser, Browsing, Potential Browser, Backup Browser*.

**Member Server** An NT server that has been installed as a non-domain controller. This allows the server to operate as a file, print and application server without the overhead of accounts administration.

**Memory** Any device capable of storing information. This term is usually used to indicate volatile random access semiconductor memory (RAM) capable of high-speed access to any portion of the memory space, but incapable of storing information without power. See *Random Access Memory, Mass Storage Device*.

**Microprocessor** An integrated semiconductor circuit designed to automatically perform lists of logical and arithmetic operations. Modern microprocessors independently manage memory pools and support multiple instruction lists called threads. Microprocessors are also capable of responding to interrupt requests from peripherals and include onboard support for complex floating point arithmetic. Microprocessors must have instructions when they are first powered on. These instructions are contained in nonvolatile firmware called a BIOS. See *BIOS, Operating System*.

**Microsoft Disk Operating System (MS-DOS)** A 16-bit operating system designed for the 8086 chip that was used in the original IBM PC. MS-DOS is a simple program loader and file system that turns over complete control of the computer to the running program and provides very little service beyond file system support and that provided by the BIOS.

**Migration Tool for NetWare** A utility used to migrate NetWare users, groups, file structures, and security to an NT domain. See *NetWare*.

**Modem** Modulator/demodulator. A Data Link layer device used to create an analog signal suitable for transmission over telephone lines from a digital data stream. Modern modems also include a command set for negotiating connections and data rates with remote modems and for setting their default behavior. The fastest modems run at about 33Kbps. See *Data Link Layer*.

**Module** A software component of a modular operating system that provides a certain defined service. Modules can be installed or removed depending upon the service requirements of the software running on the computer. Modules allow operating systems and applications to be customized to fit the needs of the user.

**MPR** See *MultiProtocol Router*.

**MS-DOS** See *Microsoft Disk Operating System*.

**Multilink** A capability of RAS to combine multiple data streams into one network connection for the purpose of using more than one modem or ISDN channel in a single connection. This feature is new to Windows NT 4.0. See *Remote Access Service*.

**Multiprocessing** Using two or more processors simultaneously to perform a computing task. Depending upon the operating system, processing may be done asymmetrically, wherein certain processors are assigned certain threads independent of the load they create, or symmetrically, wherein threads are dynamically assigned to processors according to an equitable scheduling scheme. The term usually describes a multiprocessing capacity built into the computer at a hardware level in that the computer itself supports more than one processor. However, *multiprocessing* can also be applied to network computing applications achieved through interprocess communication mechanisms. Client/server applications are, in fact, examples of multiprocessing. See *Asymmetrical Multiprocessing, Symmetrical Multiprocessing, Interprocess Communications*.

**MultiProtocol Router (MPR)** Services included with NT Server that allow you to route traffic between IPX and TCP/IP subnets. MPR also allows you to facilitate DHCP requests and forward BOOTP relay agents. See *Internetwork Packet Exchange, Transmission Control Protocol/Internet Protocol, Dynamic Host Configuration Protocol, Bootstrap Protocol.*

**Multitasking** The capacity of an operating system to switch rapidly among threads of execution. Multitasking divides processor time among threads as if each thread ran on its own slower processor. Multitasking operating systems allow two or more applications to run at the same time and can provide a greater degree of service to applications than single-tasking operating systems like MS-DOS. See *Multiprocessing, Multithreading.*

**Named Pipes** An interprocess communication mechanism implemented as a file system service, allowing programs to be modified to run on it without using a proprietary application programming interface. Named pipes were developed to support more robust client/server communications than those allowed by the simpler NetBIOS. See *OS/2, File Systems, Interprocess Communications.*

**NDIS** See *Network Driver Interface Specification.*

**NDS** See *NetWare Directory Services.*

**NetBEUI** See *NetBIOS Extended User Interface.*

**NetBIOS** See *Network Basic Input/Output System.*

**NetBIOS Extended User Interface (NetBEUI)** A simple Network layer transport protocol developed to support NetBIOS installations. NetBEUI is not routable, and so it is not appropriate for larger networks. NetBEUI is the fastest transport protocol available for Windows NT.

**NetBIOS Gateway** A service provided by RAS that allows NetBIOS requests to be forwarded independent of transport protocol. For example, NetBIOS requests from a remote computer connected via NetBEUI can be sent over the network via NWLink. See *Network Basic Input/Output System, NWLink, NetBIOS over TCP/IP, NetBEUI.*

**NetBIOS over TCP/IP (NetBT)** A network service that implements the NetBIOS IPC over the TCP/IP protocol stack. See *NetBIOS, Interprocess Communications, TCP/IP.*

**NetBT** See *NetBIOS over TCP/IP.*

**NetDDE**  See *Network Dynamic Data Exchange.*

**NetWare**  A popular network operating system developed by Novell in the early 1980s. NetWare is a cooperative, multitasking, highly optimized, dedicated-server network operating system that has client support for most major operating systems. Recent versions of NetWare include graphical client tools for management from client stations. At one time, NetWare accounted for more than 70 percent of the network operating system market. See *Windows NT, Client Services for NetWare, Gateway Services for NetWare, NWLink.*

**NetWare Directory Services (NDS)**  In NetWare a distributed hierarchy of network services such as servers, shared volumes, and printers. NetWare implements NDS as a directory structure having elaborate security and administration mechanisms. The CSNW provided in Windows NT 4.0 supports the NDS tree. See *NetWare, Client Services for NetWare, Gateway Services for NetWare.*

**NetWare Link (NWLink)**  A Windows NT transport protocol that implements Novell's IPX. NWLink is useful as a general purpose transport for Windows NT and for connecting to NetWare file servers through CSNW. See *Internetwork Packet eXchange, Client Services for NetWare, Gateway Services for NetWare.*

**NetWare NetBIOS Link (NWNBLink)**  NetBIOS implemented over NWLink. See *NetBIOS, NWLink, NetBT.*

**Network**  A group of computers connected via some digital medium for the purpose of exchanging information. Networks can be based upon many types of media, such as twisted pair telephone-style cable, optical fiber, coaxial cable, radio, or infrared light. Certain computers are usually configured as service providers called *servers*. Computers that perform user tasks directly and that utilize the services of servers are called *clients*. See *Client/Server, Server, Network Operating System.*

**Network Basic Input/Output System (NetBIOS)**  A client/server interprocess communication service developed by IBM in the early 1980s. NetBIOS presents a relatively primitive mechanism for communication in client server/applications, but its widespread acceptance and availability across most operating systems makes it a logical choice for simple network applications. Many of the network IPC mechanisms in Windows NT are implemented over NetBIOS. See *Interprocess Communication, Client/Server.*

**Network Client Administrator** A utility within the Administrative Tools group that can be used to make installation startup disks, make installation disk sets, copy client-based administration tools, and view remoteboot information.

**Network Driver Interface Specification (NDIS)** A Microsoft specification to which network adapter drivers must conform in order to work with Microsoft network operating systems. NDIS provides a many-to-many binding between network adapter drivers and transport protocols. See *Transport Protocol*.

**Network Dynamic Data Exchange (NetDDE)** An interprocess communication mechanism developed by Microsoft to support the distribution of DDE applications over a network. See *Interprocess Communication, DDE*.

**Network Interface Card (NIC)** A Physical layer adapter device that allows a computer to connect to and communicate over a local area network. See *Ethernet, Token Ring*, Adapter.

**Network Layer** The layer of the OSI model that creates a communication path between two computers via routed packets. Transport protocols implement both the Network layer and the Transport layer of the OSI stack. IP is a Network layer service. See *Internet Protocol, Transport Protocol, Open Systems Interconnect Model*.

**Network Monitor** A utility used to capture and display network traffic.

**Network Operating System** A computer operating system specifically designed to optimize a computer's ability to respond to service requests. Servers run network operating systems. Windows NT Server and NetWare are both network operating systems. See *Windows NT, Server, NetWare*.

**Network Printer** A network printer can use physical or logical ports. By defining a printer as a network printer, you make the printer available to local and network users. See *Printer, Printing Device, Local Printer*.

**Network Security** Security that governs a network. See *Security, Network User, Local Security*.

**Network User** A user who logs on to the network using the SAM from a remote domain controller. See *Interactive User*.

**New Technology File System (NTFS)** A secure, transaction-oriented file system developed for Windows NT that incorporates the Windows NT security model for assigning permissions and shares. NTFS is optimized for hard drives larger than 500MB and requires too much overhead to be used on hard disk drives smaller than 50MB.

**Nonbrowser** A computer on a network that will not maintain a list of other computers and services on the network. See *Browser, Browsing.*

**NT Directory Services** The synchronized SAM database that exists between the PDC and the BDCs within a domain. Directory Services also controls the trust relationships that exist between domains. See *Security Accounts Manager, Primary Domain Controller, Backup Domain Controller, Trust Relationship.*

**NTFS** See *New Technology File System.*

**NWLink** See *NetWare Link, Internetwork Packet eXchange.*

**NWNBLink** See *NetWare NetBIOS Link.*

**Object** A software service provider that encapsulates both the algorithm and the data structures necessary to provide a service. Usually, objects can inherit data and functionality from their parent objects, thus allowing complex services to be constructed from simpler objects. The term *object oriented* implies a tight relationship between algorithms and data structures. See *Module.*

**Object Counters** Containers built into each service object in Windows NT that store a count of the number of times an object performs its service or to what degree. You can use performance monitors to access object counters and measure how the different objects in Windows NT are operating. See *Object.*

**Open Graphics Language (OpenGL)** A standard interface for the presentation of two- and three-dimensional visual data.

**Open Systems Interconnect Model (OSI Model)** A model for network component interoperability developed by the International Standards Organization to promote cross-vendor compatibility of hardware and software network systems. The OSI model splits the process of networking into seven distinct services. Each layer uses the services of the layer below to provide its service to the layer above. See *Physical Layer, Data Link Layer, Network Layer, Transport Layer, Session Layer, Presentation Layer, Application Layer.*

**OpenGL** See *Open Graphics Language.*

**Operating System** A collection of services that form a foundation upon which applications run. Operating systems may be simple I/O service providers with a command shell, such as MS-DOS, or they may be sophisticated, preemptive, multitasking, multiprocessing applications platforms like Windows NT. See *Network Operating System, Preemptive Multitasking, Kernel.*

**Operating System 2 (OS/2)** A 16-bit (and later, 32-bit) operating system developed jointly by Microsoft and IBM as a successor to MS-DOS. Microsoft bowed out of the 32-bit development effort and produced its own product, Windows NT, as a competitor to OS/2. OS/2 is now a preemptive, multitasking 32-bit operating system with strong support for networking and the ability to run MS-DOS and Win16 applications, but IBM has been unable to entice a large number of developers to produce software that runs native under OS/2. See *Operating System, Preemptive Multitasking.*

**Optimization** Any effort to reduce the workload on a hardware component by eliminating, obviating, or reducing the amount of work required of the hardware component through any means. For instance, file caching is an optimization that reduces the workload of a hard disk drive.

**OS/2** See *Operating System 2.*

**OSI Model** See *Open Systems Interconnect Model.*

**Owner** Used in conjunction with NTFS volumes. All NTFS files and directories have an associated owner who is able to control access and grant permissions to other users. See *New Technology File System.*

**Page File** See *Swap File.*

**Partition** A section of a hard disk that can contain an independent file system volume. Partitions can be used to keep multiple operating systems and file systems on the same hard disk. See *Volume, Hard Disk Drive.*

**Password** A secret code used to validate the identity of a user of a secure system. Passwords are used in tandem with account names to log on to most computer systems.

**PC** See *Personal Computer.*

**PCI** See *Peripheral Connection Interface.*

**PDC** See *Primary Domain Controller.*

**Peer** A networked computer that both shares resources with other computers and accesses the shared resources of other computers. A nondedicated server. See *Server, Client*.

**Performance Monitor** A utility provided with NT that provides graphical statistics that can be used to measure performance on your computer.

**Peripheral** An input/output device attached to a computer. Peripherals can be printers, hard disk drives, monitors, and so on.

**Peripheral Connection Interface (PCI)** A high speed 32/64-bit bus interface developed by Intel and widely accepted as the successor to the 16-bit ISA interface. PCI devices support I/O throughput about 40 times faster than the ISA bus.

**Permissions** Security constructs used to regulate access to resources by user name or group affiliation. Permissions can be assigned by administrators to allow any level of access, such as read only, read/write, delete, etc., by controlling the ability of users to initiate object services. Security is implemented by checking the user's security identifier against each object's access control list. See *Security Identifier, Access Control List*.

**Personal Computer (PC)** A microcomputer used by one person at a time (not a multiuser computer). PCs are generally clients or peers in a networked environment. High-speed PCs are called workstations. Networks of PCs are called local area networks. The term PC is often used to refer to computers compatible with the IBM PC.

**Physical Layer** The cables, connectors, and connection ports of a network. The passive physical components required to create a network. See *OSI Model*.

**Physical Port** Printers can be connected directly to a computer through a serial (COM) or parallel (LPT) port. If a printer is connected in this manner, it is using a physical port. See *Printer, Print Device*.

**Point-to-Point Protocol (PPP)** A Network-layer transport that performs over point-to-point network connections such as serial or modem lines. PPP can negotiate any transport protocol used by both systems involved in the link and can automatically assign IP, DNS, and gateway addresses when used with TCP/IP. See *Internet Protocol, Domain Name Service, Gateway*.

**Point-to-Point Tunneling Protocol (PPTP)** Protocol used to connect to corporate networks through the Internet or an ISP. See *Internet, Internet Service Provider*.

**Policies** General controls that enhance the security of an operating environment. In Windows NT, policies affect restrictions on password use and rights assignment and determine which events will be recorded in the Security log.

**Potential Browser** A computer on a network that may maintain a list of other computers and services on the network if requested to do so by a Master Browser. See *Browser, Master Browser*.

**PowerPC** A microprocessor family developed by IBM to compete with the Intel family of microprocessors. The PowerPC is a RISC-architecture microprocessor with many advanced features that emulate other microprocessors. PowerPCs are currently used in a line of IBM computers and in the Apple Power Macintosh. Windows NT is available for the PowerPC.

**PPP** See *Point-to-Point Protocol*.

**PPTP** See *Point-to-Point Tunneling Protocol*.

**Preemptive Multitasking** A multitasking implementation in which an interrupt routine in the Kernel manages the scheduling of processor time among running threads. The threads themselves do not need to support multitasking in any way because the microprocessor will preempt the thread with an interrupt, save its state, update all thread priorities according to its scheduling algorithm, and pass control to the highest priority thread awaiting execution. Because of the preemptive nature of the implementation, a thread that crashes will not affect the operation of other executing threads. See *Kernel, Thread, Operating System, Process*.

**Preferences** Characteristics of user accounts, such as password, profile location, home directory and logon script.

**Presentation Layer** The layer of the OSI model that converts and translates (if necessary) information between the Session and Application layers. See *OSI Model*.

**Primary Domain Controller (PDC)** The domain server that contains the master copy of the security, computer, and user accounts databases and that can authenticate workstations. The PDC can replicate its databases to one or more backup domain controllers. The PDC is usually also the Master Browser for the domain. See *Backup Domain Controller, Domain, Master Browser*.

**Print Device**  A print device is the actual physical printer or hardware device you will print to. See *Printer*.

**Print Driver**  Each printing device has it's own command set. The print driver is the specific software that understands your print device. Each print device has an associated print driver. See *Print Device*.

**Print Processor**  Once a print job has been sent to the spooler, the print processor looks at the print job and determines whether or not the job needs further processing. The processing (also called rendering) is used to format the print job so that it can print correctly at the print device. See *Print Spooler*.

**Print Server**  Print servers are the computers on which the printers have been defined. When you send a job to a network printer, you are actually sending it to the print server first. See *Printer, Print Device*.

**Print Spooler (Print Queue)**  The print spooler is a directory or folder on the Print Server that actually stores the print jobs until they can be printed. It's very important that your Print Server and Print Spooler have enough hard disk space to hold all of the print jobs that could be pending at any given time. See *Print Server*.

**Printer**  In NT terminology, a printer is the software interface between the physical printer (see print device) and the operating system. You can create printers through the Printers folder. See *Print Device*.

**Printing Pool**  Printing pools are created when you have more than one printing device associated with a single printer. Printing pools can be used when you have printers that all use the same print driver that are in the same location. By using printing pools, you are then able to send your print job to the first available printer. See *Printer, Print Device*.

**Priority**  A level of execution importance assigned to a thread. In combination with other factors, the priority level determines how often that thread will get computer time according to a scheduling algorithm. See *Preemptive Multitasking*.

**Process**  A running program containing one or more threads. A process encapsulates the protected memory and environment for its threads.

**Processor**  A circuit designed to automatically perform lists of logical and arithmetic operations. Unlike microprocessors, processors may be designed from discrete components rather than be a monolithic integrated circuit. See *Microprocessor*.

**Program** A list of processor instructions designed to perform a certain function. A running program is called a process. A package of one or more programs and attendant data designed to meet a certain application is called software. See *Software, Application, Process, Microprocessor.*

**Programming Interfaces** Interprocess communications mechanisms that provide certain high-level services to running processes. Programming interfaces may provide network communication, graphical presentation, or any other type of software service. See *Interprocess Communication.*

**Protocol** An established rule of communication adhered to by the parties operating under it. Protocols provide a context in which to interpret communicated information. Computer protocols are rules used by communicating devices and software services to format data in a way that all participants understand. See *Transport Protocol.*

**PSTN** See *Public Switched Telephone Network.*

**Public Switched Telephone Network (PSTN)** A global network of interconnected digital and analog communication links originally designed to support voice communication between any two points in the world, but quickly adapted to handle digital data traffic when the computer revolution occurred. In addition to its traditional voice support role, the PSTN now functions as the Physical layer of the Internet by providing dial-up and leased lines for the interconnections. See *Internet, Modem, Physical Layer.*

**RAID** See *Redundant Array of Inexpensive Disks.*

**RAID Controllers** Hard disk drive controllers that implement RAID in hardware. See *Redundant Array of Inexpensive Disks.*

**RAM** See *Random Access Memory.*

**Random Access Memory (RAM)** Integrated circuits that store digital bits in massive arrays of logical gates or capacitors. RAM is the primary memory store for modern computers, storing all running software processes and contextual data. See *Microprocessor.*

**RARP** See *Reverse Address Resolution Protocol.*

**RAS** See *Remote Access Service.*

**Real-Time Application**  A process that must respond to external events at least as fast as those events can occur. Real-time threads must run at very high priorities to ensure their ability to respond in real time. See *Process*.

**Redirector**  A software service that redirects user file I/O requests over the network. Novell implements the Workstation service and Client services for NetWare as redirectors. Redirectors allow servers to be used as mass storage devices that appear local to the user. See *Client Services for NetWare, File System*.

**Reduced Instruction Set Computer (RISC)**  A microprocessor technology that implements fewer and more primitive instructions than typical microprocessors and can therefore be implemented quickly with the most modern semiconductor technology and speeds. Programs written for RISC microprocessors require more instructions (longer programs) to perform the same task as a normal microprocessor but are capable of a greater degree of optimization and therefore usually run faster. See *Microprocessor*.

**Redundant Array of Inexpensive Disks (RAID)**  A group of hard disk drives, coordinated by a special controller, that appears as one physical disk to a computer but stores its data across all the disks to take advantage of the speed and/or fault tolerance afforded by using more than one disk. RAID disk storage has several levels, including 0 (striping), 1 (mirroring), and 5 (striping with parity).  RAID systems are typically used for very large storage volumes or to provide fault-tolerance features such as hot swapping of failed disks or automatically backing up data onto replacement disks.

**Registry**  A database of settings required and maintained by Windows NT and its components. The Registry contains all of the configuration information used by the computer. It is stored as a hierarchical structure and is made up of keys, hives, and value entries. You can use the Registry Editor (REGEDT32 command) to change these settings.

**Remote Access Service (RAS)**  A service that allows network connections to be established over PSTN lines with modems. The computer initiating the connection is called the RAS client; the answering computer is called the RAS host. See *Modem, Public Switched Telephone Network*.

**Remote Procedure Calls (RPC)**  A network interprocess communication mechanism that allows an application to be distributed among many computers on the same network. See *Local Procedure Call, Interprocess Communications*.

**Remoteboot** The remoteboot service is used to start diskless workstations over the network.

**Requests for Comments (RFCs)** The set of standards defining the Internet protocols as determined by the Internet Engineering Task Force and available in the public domain on the Internet. RFCs define the functions and services provided by each of the many Internet protocols. Compliance with the RFCs guarantees cross-vendor compatibility. See *Internet*.

**Resource** Any useful service, such as a shared network directory or a printer. See *Share*.

**Reverse Address Resolution Protocol (RARP)** The TCP/IP protocol which allows a computer that has a Physical-layer address (such as an Ethernet address), but does not have an IP address to request a numeric IP address from another computer on the network. See *TCP/IP*.

**RFC** See *Request For Comments*.

**RIP** See *Routing Information Protocol*.

**RISC** See *Reduced Instruction Set Computer*.

**Roaming User Profile** A user profile that is stored and configured to be downloaded from a server. The purpose of roaming user profiles is that they allow a user to access their profile from any location on the network. See *User Profile*.

**Router** A Network layer device that moves packets between networks. Routers provide internetwork connectivity. See *Network Layer*.

**Routing Information Protocol (RIP)** A protocol within the TCP/IP protocol suite that allows routers to exchange routing information with other routers. See *Transmission Control Protocol/Internet Protocol*.

**RPC** See *Remote Procedure Calls*.

**SAM** See *Security Accounts Manager*.

**Scheduling** The process of determining which threads should be executed according to their priority and other factors. See *Preemptive Multitasking*.

**SCSI** See *Small Computer Systems Interface*.

**Search Engine** Web sites dedicated to responding to requests for specific information, searching massive locally stored databases of Web pages, and responding with the URLs of pages that fit the search phrase. See *World Wide Web, Universal Resource Locator.*

**Security** The Measures taken to secure a system against accidental or intentional loss, usually in the form of accountability procedures and use restriction. See *Security Identifiers, Security Accounts Manager.*

**Security Accounts Manager (SAM)** The module of the Windows NT executive that authenticates a username and password against a database of accounts, generating an access token that includes the user's permissions. See *Security, Security Identifier, Access Token.*

**Security Identifiers (SID)** Unique codes that identify a specific user or group to the Windows NT security system. Security identifiers contain a complete set of permissions for that user or group.

**Serial** A method of communication that transfers data across a medium one bit at a time, usually adding stop, start and check bits to ensure quality transfer. See *COM Port, Modem.*

**Serial Line Internet Protocol (SLIP)** An implementation of the IP protocol over serial lines. SLIP has been obviated by PPP. See *Point-to-Point Protocol, Internet Protocol.*

**Server** A computer dedicated to servicing requests for resources from other computers on a network. Servers typically run network operating systems such as Windows NT Server or NetWare. See *Windows NT, NetWare, Client/Server.*

**Server Manager** Utility in the Administrative Tools group used to manage domains and computers.

**Service** A process dedicated to implementing a specific function for another process. Most Windows NT components are services used by User-level applications.

**Services for Macintosh** A service available through NT Server that allows Macintosh users to take advantage of NT file and print services. See *Macintosh.*

**Session Layer** The layer of the OSI model dedicated to maintaining a bidirectional communication connection between two computers. The Session layer uses the services of the Transport layer to provide this service. See *OSI Model, Transport Layer.*

**Share**  A resource (e.g., directory, printer) shared by a server or a peer on a network. See *Resource, Server, Peer*.

**Shell**  The user interface of an operating system; the shell launches applications and manages file systems.

**SID**  See *Security Identifier*.

**Simple Mail Transfer Protocol (SMTP)**  An Internet protocol for transferring mail between Internet Hosts. SMTP is often used to upload mail directly from the client to an Intermediate host, but can only be used to receive mail by computers constantly connected to the Internet. See *Internet*.

**Simple Network Management Protocol (SNMP)**  An Internet protocol that manages network hardware such as routers, switches, servers, and clients from a single client on the network. See *Internet Protocol*.

**Site**  A related collection of HTML documents at the same Internet address, usually oriented toward some specific information or purpose. See *Hypertext Markup Language, Internet*.

**SLIP**  See *Serial Line Internet Protocol*.

**Small Computer Systems Interface (SCSI)**  A high-speed, parallel-bus interface that connects hard disk drives, CD-ROM drives, tape drives, and many other peripherals to a computer. SCSI is the mass storage connection standard among all computers except IBM compatibles, which use SCSI or IDE.

**SMTP**  See *Simple Mail Transfer Protocol*.

**SNMP**  See *Simple Network Management Protocol*.

**Software**  A suite of programs sold as a unit and dedicated to a specific application. See Program, Application, Process.

**Spooler**  A service that buffers output to a low-speed device such as a printer so the software outputting to the device is not tied up waiting for it.

**Stripe Set**  A single volume created across multiple hard disk drives and accessed in parallel for the purpose of optimizing disk access time. NTFS can create stripe sets. See *NTFS, Volume, File System*.

**Subdirectory**  A directory contained in another directory. See *Directory*.

**Subnet Mask** A number mathematically applied to Internet protocol addresses to determine which IP addresses are a part of the same subnetwork as the computer applying the subnet mask.

**Surf** To browse the Web randomly looking for interesting information. See *World Wide Web.*

**Swap File** The virtual memory file on a hard disk containing the memory pages that have been moved out to disk to increase available RAM. See *Virtual Memory.*

**Symmetrical Multiprocessing** A multiprocessing methodology wherein processes are assigned to processors on a fair share basis. This balances the processing load among processors and ensures that no processor will become a bottleneck. Symmetrical Multiprocessing is more difficult to implement than Asymmetrical multiprocessing as certain hardware functions such as interrupt handling must be shared between processors. See *Asymmetrical Multiprocessing, Multiprocessing.*

**System Partition** The system partition is the active partition on an Intel based computer that contains the hardware specific files used to load the NT operating system. See *Partition, Boot Partition.*

**System Policy** A policy used to control what a user can do and the users environment. System policies can be applied to a specific user, group, a computer, or all users. System policies work by overwriting current settings in the Registry with the system policy settings. System policies are created through the System Policy Editor. See *Registry, System Policy Editor.*

**System Policy Editor** A utility found within the Administrative Tools group used to create system policies. See *System Policies.*

**Task Manager** An application that manually views and closes running processes. Task Manager can also be used to view CPU and memory statistics. Press Ctrl+Alt+Del to launch the Task Manager.

**TCP** See *Transmission Control Protocol.*

**TCP/IP** See *Transmission Control Protocol/Internet Protocol.*

**TDI** See *Transport Driver Interface.*

**Telnet** A terminal application that allows a user to log into a multiuser UNIX computer from any computer connected to the Internet. See *Internet*.

**Thread** A list of instructions running in a computer to perform a certain task. Each thread runs in the context of a process, which embodies the protected memory space and the environment of the threads. Multithreaded processes can perform more than one task at the same time. See *Process, Preemptive Multitasking, Program*.

**Throughput** The measure of information flow through a system in a specific time frame, usually one second. For instance, 28.8Kbps is the throughput of a modem: 28.8 kilobits per second can be transmitted.

**Token Ring** The second most popular Data Link-layer standard for local area networking. Token Ring implements the token passing method of arbitrating multiple-computer access to the same network. Token Ring operates at either 4 or 16Mbps. FDDI is similar to Token Ring and operates at 100Mbps. See *Data Link Layer*.

**Transmission Control Protocol (TCP)** A Transport-layer protocol that implements guaranteed packet delivery using the Internet Protocol (IP). See *TCP/IP, Internet Protocol*.

**Transmission Control Protocol/Internet Protocol (TCP/IP)** A suite of Internet protocols upon which the global Internet is based. TCP/IP is a general term that can refer either to the TCP and IP protocols used together or to the complete set of Internet protocols. TCP/IP is the default protocol for Windows NT.

**Transport Driver Interface (TDI)** A specification to which all Windows NT transport protocols must be written in order to be used by higher-level services such as programming interfaces, file systems, and interprocess communications mechanisms. See *Transport Protocol*.

**Transport Layer** The OSI model layer responsible for the guaranteed serial delivery of packets between two computers over an internetwork. TCP is the Transport-layer protocol for the TCP/IP transport protocol.

**Transport Protocol** A service that delivers discreet packets of information between any two computers in a network. Higher level connection-oriented services are built upon transport protocols. See *TCP/IP, NWLink, NetBEUI, Transport Layer, IP, TCP, Internet*.

**Trust Relationship** An administrative link that joins two or more domains. With a trust relationship users can access resources in another domain if they have rights, even if they do not have a user account in the resource domain.

**UDP** See *User Datagram Protocol.*

**UNC** See *Universal Naming Convention.*

**Uniform Resource Locator (URL)** An Internet standard naming convention for identifying resources available via various TCP/IP application protocols. For example, `http://www.microsoft.com` is the URL for Microsoft's World Wide Web server site, while `ftp://gateway.dec.com` is a popular FTP site. A URL allows easy hypertext references to a particular resource from within a document or mail message. See *HTTP, World Wide Web.*

**Universal Naming Convention (UNC)** A multivendor, multiplatform convention for identifying shared resources on a network.

**UNIX** A multitasking, kernel-based operating system developed at AT&T in the early 1970s and provided (originally) free to universities as a research operating system. Because of its availability and ability to scale down to microprocessor-based computers, UNIX became the standard operating system of the Internet and its attendant network protocols and is the closest approximation to a universal operating system that exists. Most computers can run some variant of the UNIX operating system. See *Multitasking, Internet.*

**User Datagram Protocol (UDP)** A non-guaranteed network packet protocol implemented on IP that is far faster than TCP because of its lack of flow-control overhead. UDP can be implemented as a reliable transport when some higher-level protocol (such as NetBIOS) exists to make sure that required data will eventually be retransmitted in local area environments. At the Transport layer of the OSI model, UDP is connectionless service and TCP is connection-oriented service. See *Transmission Control Protocol.*

**User Manager for Domains** A Windows NT application that administers user accounts, groups, and security policies at the domain level.

**User Profile** Used to save each user's desktop configuration. See *Roaming Profile, Mandatory Profile.*

**User Rights Policies** Used to determine what rights users and groups have when trying to accomplish network tasks. User Rights Policies are set through User Manager for Domains. See *User Manager for Domains.*

**Username** A user's account name in a logon-authenticated system. See *Security*.

**VDM** See *Virtual DOS Machine*.

**Virtual DOS Machine (VDM)** The DOS environment created by Windows NT for the execution of DOS and Win16 applications. See *MS-DOS, Win16*.

**Virtual Memory** A kernel service that stores memory pages not currently in use on a mass storage device to free up the memory occupied for other uses. Virtual memory hides the memory swapping process from applications and higher level services. See *Swap File, Kernel*.

**Volume** A collection of data indexed by directories containing files and referred to by a drive letter. Volumes are normally contained in a single partition, but volume sets and stripe sets extend a single volume across multiple partitions.

**WAN** See *Wide Area Network*.

**Web Browser** An application that makes HTTP requests and formats the resultant HTML documents for the users. The preeminent Internet Client, most Web browsers understand all standard Internet protocols. See *Hypertext Transfer Protocol, Hypertext Markup Language, Internet*.

**Web Page** Any HTML document on an HTTP server. See *Hypertext Transfer Protocol, Hypertext Markup Language, Internet*.

**Wide Area Network (WAN)** A geographically dispersed network of networks, connected by routers and communication links. The Internet is the largest WAN. See *Internet, Local Area Network*.

**Win16** The set of application services provided by the 16-bit versions of Microsoft Windows: Windows 3.1 and Windows for Workgroups 3.11.

**Win32** The set of application services provided by the 32-bit versions of Microsoft Windows: Windows 95 and Windows NT.

**Windows 3.11 for Workgroups** The current 16-bit version of Windows for less-powerful, Intel-based personal computers; this system includes peer networking services.

**Windows 95** The current 32-bit version of Microsoft Windows for medium-range, Intel-based personal computers; this system includes peer networking services, Internet support, and strong support for older DOS applications and peripherals.

**Windows Internet Name Service (WINS)** A network service for Microsoft networks that provides Windows computers with Internet numbers for specified NetBIOS names, facilitating browsing and intercommunication over TCP/IP networks.

**Windows NT** The current 32-bit version of Microsoft Windows for powerful Intel, Alpha, PowerPC, or MIPS-based computers; the system includes peer networking services, server networking services, Internet client and server services, and a broad range of utilities.

**Windows Sockets** An interprocess communications protocol that delivers connection-oriented data streams used by Internet software and software ported from UNIX environments. See *Interprocess Communications*.

**WINS** See *Windows Internet Name Service*.

**Workgroup** In Microsoft networks, a collection of related computers, such as a department, that don't require the uniform security and coordination of a domain. Workgroups are characterized by decentralized management as opposed to the centralized management that domains use. See *Domain*.

**Workstation** A powerful personal computer, usually running a preemptive, multitasking operating system like UNIX or Windows NT.

**World Wide Web (WWW)** A collection of Internet servers providing hypertext formatted documents for Internet clients running Web browsers. The World Wide Web provided the first easy-to-use graphical interface for the Internet and is largely responsible for the Internet's explosive growth.

**Write-Back Caching** A caching optimization wherein data written to the slow store is cached until the cache is full or until a subsequent write operation overwrites the cached data. Write-back caching can significantly reduce the write operations to a slow store because many write operations are subsequently obviated by new information. Data in the write-back cache is also available for subsequent reads. If something happens to prevent the cache from writing data to the slow store, the cache data will be lost. See *Caching*, *Write-Through Caching*.

**Write-Through Caching** A caching optimization wherein data written to a slow store is kept in a cache for subsequent re-reading. Unlike write-back caching, write-through caching immediately writes the data to the slow store and is therefore less optimal but more secure.

**WWW** See *World Wide Web*.

**X.25** A Standard that defines packet switching networks.

# Index

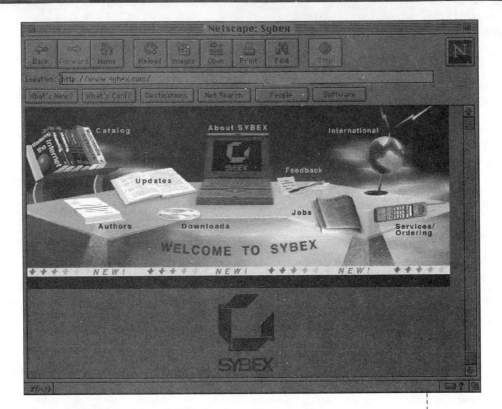